SOURCES FOR MODERN BRITISH HISTORY

General Editors: John Ramsden, Kathleen Burk, John Turner

THE DESTRUCTION
OF
LORD ROSEBERY

THE DESTRUCTION OF LORD ROSEBERY

From the Diary of Sir Edward Hamilton, 1894–1895

Edited with an introductory essay by

DAVID BROOKS

British Library Cataloguing in Publication Data

Hamilton, Edward Walter
    The Destruction of Lord Rosebery
    1. Great Britain—Politics and government—1894–1895
    I. Title   II. Brooks, David Richard
    DA 565   941.081

ISBN 0 9508900 1 4

NE/110/1280/-900/2/041286/500

PUBLISHED BY THE HISTORIANS' PRESS,
9 DAISY ROAD, LONDON E18 1EA.

Produced by Alan Sutton Publishing Limited
30 Brunswick Road, Gloucester GL1 1JJ
Printed in Great Britain

CONTENTS

ACKNOWLEDGEMENTS

The Hamilton Papers, from which the following extracts appear, are deposited in the British Library, and I am grateful to the staff of the Manuscripts Room for their assistance, and to Mr J.C. Moberly for permitting their publication. I am grateful also to the Harcourt family for allowing me to quote from certain of their papers now deposited at the Bodleian Library, Oxford, and to the staff of that and other libraries of whose facilities I have fortunately been able to make use.

Without the enterprise and support of my colleagues of the University of London, Dr Kathleen Burk, Dr John Ramsden, and Dr John Turner, the directors of the Historians' Press, this book would not have appeared. In the work of preparation my greatest single debt has been to my mother, Mrs Margaret Brooks, who has painstakingly typed out so much of the manuscript and offered useful suggestions in the process. I am happy also to have been able to turn to my wife, Gill, for encouragement and advice.

The Historians' Press gratefully acknowledges the assistance of The Twenty-Seven Foundation in supporting the series of which this volume forms a part.

PREFACE

The 1890s constitute a dark age in modern British historiography. Their political conflicts and tergiversations—epitomised first by the election of the most radical government of the century, and then by the formation of the most long-lasting of those coalitions which England is deemed not to love—have had few recent interpreters; though contemporaries were not disposed to treat their significance so lightly. Politically the character of the decade was determined not only by the events of 1886 and their legacy but also by the long period of often painful adjustment to changing economic conditions which marked the final quarter of the nineteenth century. The period of Rosebery's premiership illustrates particularly well the balance of political forces at this time; and it provides also an object lesson in the workings of the British constitution in those conditions of strain usually associated with the existence of a minority government. With a new leader in early 1894, the Liberals faced both considerable dangers and considerable opportunities. The following year and a half was to demonstrate with what degree of success they faced up to them. The Rosebery Government is credited with a number of legacies, but it is natural that two in particular should come to mind. First, it contributed substantially, by the 1894 budget, to the transformation of English landownership which was a major social feature of the late nineteenth and early twentieth centuries. Second, it was responsible for the heaviest electoral reverse suffered by the Liberals in all their days as a party of government.

The diary of Sir Edward Walter Hamilton is a fertile source for the political history of late nineteenth century Britain. Its value, as far as the 1880s are concerned, has already been made clear by the edition produced by D.W.R. Bahlman, which covers the period of the second Gladstone administration.[1] Thanks to this two-volume work, we have become familiar with the personality of the diarist, and we have been provided with a detailed political narrative of five rather turbulent years. Hamilton's close relationship with Glastone, whom he served as private secretary, gives his diary a particular interest and point of vantage.

The nature of the present edition is somewhat different, for it seeks to complement Hamilton's record of events with a more extensive political analysis. But part of the intention is the same: to use the language of the diarist to bring alive the political world of the mid-1890s. Once again it is Hamilton's close association with the Prime Minister of the day which gives his account a particular relevance, and indeed poignancy; for Rosebery was a former schoolfellow and life-long friend whose career he followed with alternating enthusiasm and anxiety.

Edward Walter Hamilton was born in 1847, and was educated, like Rosebery, at Eton and Christ Church, Oxford. His father, the Bishop of Salisbury, had been a close friend of Gladstone's since their own days at Eton, and it was Gladstone who in 1870 appointed the young Hamilton to his first position, as a clerk at the Treasury. During Gladstone's second administration of 1880–5, Hamilton served as his private secretary. In 1885 he was appointed Principal Clerk of the Finance Division, and in 1892 Assistant Financial Secretary. Hamilton's final position was that of Permanent Financial Secretary, which he held from 1902 to 1907, a year before his death. Although increasingly afflicted by ill-health from 1889 onwards, in the form of a vascular disease affecting his legs, Hamilton contrived to lead a highly active social life. A life-long bachelor, he delighted in the company of his many friends and acquaintances. Music was his particular passion and hobby.

As a well-connected man, a friend of the Gladstones, and a prominent civil servant, Hamilton was at the centre of the world of public affairs. He possessed in addition other advantages and qualities which make his diary an illuminating political document. Clearly he was well-liked and trusted, and was thus favoured with confidences by politicians of many different points of view. One of the most attractive features of his diary is its fair-mindedness. There is in his writing little of the asperity or sense of frustration which characterises the work of other political diarists, such as Croker or Beatrice Webb. To some extent this makes his diary less humourous, but it also enables him to provide a more rounded view of the leading personalities with whom he was in regular contact. Hamilton is particularly rewarding and perceptive when writing about Rosebery. He had long taken an interest in his Eton contemporary's developing career, and he was touchingly excited when Rosebery attained the summit of his political ambition in early 1894. At the same time he was alive to the flaws and idiosyncracies of character which helped to undermine Rosebery's ability to make a success of his premiership, and as his diary shows he did his best to try to remedy them. For his part Rosebery, reserved and isolated, both politically and personally, seems to have found it easier to unburden himself to Hamilton than to anybody else.

As is well-known, Rosebery's appointment and record as Prime Minister were to contribute to an estrangement between himself and Harcourt which, while not as fatal as that between Asquith and Lloyd George in later years, was to trouble the Liberal party at least until the end of the 1890s. Liberals at the time took sides, as historians have tended to do subsequently. Hamilton is one of the few commentators who has managed to hold the balance reasonably even as between the two men. He was a friend and counsellor to Rosebery, but at the same time he had considerable affection for Harcourt; and he was aware how far both men suffered from the impression they made on other people, most especially on their colleagues. In his account of the years 1894 and 1895, Hamilton perhaps comes down hardest on leading Liberals like Asquith and John Morley, who, he felt, had first supported Rosebery and then abandoned him.

As a public servant, Hamilton had a duty to keep his own political principles and prejudices in the background; but they become clear enough in the pages of his diary. He was of Whiggish outlook and temperament; he believed in fiscal orthodoxy and political moderation; and he still managed to think of the Liberal party, which had for so long been dominated by his hero, Gladstone, as the natural repository of such virtues. Hamilton distrusted the Unionists' economic sectionalism; he suspected Salisbury of a want of political judgement, and Chamberlain of dangerously radical and unorthodox tendencies. Rather naively he hoped that Rosebery would prove a barrier against similar tendencies within the Liberal party. Like any good Whig, Hamilton was sensitive to the movement of public opinion; but, along with most politicians, he underestimated the degree of swing towards the Unionists during the first half of 1895.

Hamilton's manner, in his diary, is however relatively self-effacing. Undoubtedly he had a political role—as the confidant of a Prime Minister, and a not infrequent channel of communication between him and his colleagues—but it is not one he cares to emphasise too much. Hamilton's advice may have helped to decide Rosebery in favour of resignation in June 1895; at other times he was, as he admits, not very successful in influencing the Prime Minister, as when he attempted to persuade him to try to mend his fences with Harcourt. It is interesting also that Hamilton does not mention the occasion when he made an error of calculation, noted by Lewis Harcourt, in the preparation of the budget of 1894.

This edition of the diary concentrates, as has been indicated, on its political narrative. Much of the material relating to Hamilton's very full social life, his detailed record of dinner parties and week-ends away from London, has been omitted. At the same time, not all non-political references have been excluded. Hamilton's diary contains a wealth of incidental commentary on the world of his day; and some of this has been included, both to do justice to Hamilton's breadth of observation, and to provide a flavour of the times and some illustration of the ways in which his world was changing. As can be seen, Hamilton took a more than passing interest in developments in sport, fashion, and society. His comments, even on such mundane matters, are often rewarding; and his remarks on the weather serve as a reminder of the extremes of climate—so they seemed by British standards—which were not without their effect on the politics of 1894 and 1895. Throughout the diary one is confronted with Hamilton's strong sense of history. As a civil servant he was fascinated by the elaborate workings of the British constitution, and by the historical precedents on which it was based. He is usually careful to place the events which he describes in an historical perspective, and his diary records the passing of the great men of his age with obituary references of elegance and perception. In frequent conversations with his retired patron, Gladstone,

Hamilton shows himsellf anxious to capture as many as possible of the Grand Old Man's reminiscences, and to Boswellise his observations and recollections for the benefit of posterity.

Hamilton as a writer is so clear and conscientious that his diary requires little in the way of detailed annotation and exegesis. However most of the lesser-known political personalities have been identified in some way, and additional biographical information has been provided in the footnotes respecting leading members of the Rosebery administration. The text of the diary has been coupled with an extended historical introduction, dealing in depth with the period with which the extracts are concerned. The political history of the 1890s is, as has been noted, a somewhat shadowy one. Its *dramatis personae* are perhaps well enough known.[2] Less well appreciated however are the themes and developments which give the struggle to survive of the last Liberal Government of the century its particular significance. The economy, the 1894 budget, and the movement of public opinion which culminated in the 1895 general election, are essential elements in the often complex domestic history of an administration whose eventual fate was not such a foregone conclusion as has sometimes been supposed.

PREFACE NOTES

1   Bahlman, D.W.R., *The Diary of Sir Edward Walter Hamilton 1880–5* 2 vols. (1972).
2   See particularly in the pages of:
    Rhodes James, R., *Rosebery: a biography of Archibald Philip, fifth Earl of Rosebery* (1963);
    Stansy, P., *Ambitions and strategies: the struggle for the leadership of the Liberal Party in the 1890s* (1964).

INTRODUCTION

Chapter One : The Formation of the Government

On 3 March 1894 the Queen accepted Gladstone's resignation as Prime Minister and invited Rosebery to form a government. It was a fateful decision in Liberal party history, and one that was to help to keep Liberalism divided and out of power for over ten years. In many ways the choice of Rosebery as Prime Minister was an extraordinary one. He had had less experience of office than almost any other member of his Cabinet. He was unreliable in that he too often showed an unpredictable disposition to retire to his tent away from the political fray; and on his party's return to power in 1892 it had only been with the greatest difficulty that he had been prevailed upon once again to become Foreign Secretary. On certain key aspects of Liberal policy he appeared to be seriously out of line with many of his colleagues. He seemed to favour mending rather than ending the House of Lords, and he was regarded as an apostle of imperial expansion. Also he was evidently deeply sceptical about Home Rule, as had been made clear in his famous speech in the House of Lords in September 1893. Finally he was a peer of the realm, belonging to a Party in which indignation against the upper chamber had reached a new level following its treatment of the Government's legislative programme in the Parliamentary session of 1893-94.

Rosebery had been a member of the House of Lords since early manhood, and had not had to make his way politically by fighting elections or speaking in the House of Commons. Prior to 1894 he had not found this a particular disadvantage. As a wealthy landed magnate of the Scottish Lowlands, he had acted as Gladstone's aristocratic sponsor in his contest for the 'pocket' county seat of Midlothian in 1879-80, and, while still in his early thirties, he had been rewarded with junior office in Gladstone's second administration. At critical moments subsequently he had come to Gladstone's aid. He had first entered the Cabinet at the time of the disaster at Khartoum in early 1885, and a year later he had accepted office in Gladstone's Home Rule ministry, receiving the post of Foreign Secretary by way of consideration. During the subsequent period in opposition Rosebery's political capital had further accumulated; he had become chairman of the newly-formed L.C.C. in 1889 and therewith the doyen of London Liberalism. His return to ministerial office in 1892 finally confirmed him as his party's next likely leader. He impressed himself, both on his colleagues by his ability to get his own way over Uganda and Egypt, and on the country by his successful arbitration in the coal strike of late 1893.

As a contender for the premiership, Rosebery's strength lay in his general acceptability. He had few enemies in the Liberal Party in early 1894. No one knew much about his real opinions, and most therefore saw in him what they wanted to see. Rosebery's somewhat cultivated air of mystery was indeed one of his political assets. The peers in the Cabinet naturally supported his claims to the premiership as one of themselves; but so too did younger Ministers like Asquith and Acland, who, besides not being averse to seeing the Liberal leadership miss a generation, hoped that Rosebery would favour new ideas and release the party somewhat from the Gladstonian straitjacket. Many Liberal backbenchers, it was known, also favoured a Rosebery premiership. Radicals generally were said not to dislike the notion of a peer prime minister at their head on the grounds that it would force him to go out of his way to be hostile to the House of Lords. These kind of generalised expectations, founded on the prospect of Rosebery as Prime Minister, were well-illustrated in the columns of the *Daily Chronicle*, which launched a determined campaign in his favour towards the end of February 1894. 'There is', it declared, 'a belief in his star, and his honesty of opinion, and there is a hope that on social questions he will satisfy aspirations which have only found a timid embodiment in the policy of the last eighteen months'.[1]

Rosebery, it was hoped, would also prove effective as an electoral asset. He was young and charismatic, an elegant speaker with a gift for rounding a phrase or pointing an epigram. His imperialism and belief in a strong foreign policy would, it was thought, reassure the middle classes, while his advocacy of social reform would appeal to the working classes. According to the *Daily Chronicle* he had already helped to restore his party's position in the 'mining districts which are the Liberal stronghold in the North, and where the settlement of the coal strike has given the Foreign Secretary a following among thousands of working men who are every year becoming more detached from average party politics'.[2] Much more than Gladstone, Rosebery was popular in London, though Dilke thought this had a lot to do with the 'music-hall' element's liking for his racing proclivities.[3] Finally Rosebery's name was judged to be an especially potent electoral influence in Scotland, a consideration of some importance for a Government in which a fair proportion of Cabinet Ministers, in addition to the Chief Whip, sat for constituencies north of the border.

When the Queen therefore invited Rosebery to form a government, she did so in some confidence, passing over not only Harcourt, the Liberals' senior Parliamentarian, but also Kimberley, the Liberal leader in the House of Lords, whose ministerial experience went back to the time of the Aberdeen coalition. Her confidence was not misplaced. Rosebery had long been a favourite of hers, and once he had been given this, the latest seal of royal approval, it rapidly became clear that there was neither sufficient opposition to the idea of his succession nor sufficient enthusiasm for any alternative candidate to prevent him from becoming Prime Minister.

Harcourt was Rosebery's only serious rival, and the only man who could have mounted a major challenge to the appointment of a peer premier. For various reasons no such challenge was to be forthcoming. Harcourt's political position was not quite as strong at the beginning of 1894 as it had been earlier or was to be again subsequently. In the Liberal cabinet of 1892–94 he had become somewhat isolated. His close political associates of former days, Hartington, Chamberlain, and Sir Henry James, had long since gone over to the Liberal Unionists; and Harcourt's brusque ways had not endeared him to many of his latter-day ministerial colleagues, who had often felt the sharp edge of his tongue in criticism of their departmental spending requirements. In particular Harcourt had since 1892 fallen out with John Morley, with whom he had on the whole worked constructively in opposition. There was nothing very surprising in this development. The two men, as the leading Liberals in the House of Commons after Gladstone, were in a sense meant to be rivals, and they were also temperamentally poles apart. In addition Harcourt had in 1893 incensed Morley by his intemperate criticisms of the Home Rule Bill, while Morley had further come to resent what he regarded as Harcourt's opportunism on the eight hours question. Some significance has been attached, especially by Lewis Harcourt, to the breach between the two men, as it ended an unwritten understanding between them, known as the Malwood compact, to oppose the appointment of a Liberal peer as Prime Minister. However it is erroneous to view Morley's role as crucial in deciding the succession. Certainly he was an honoured figure in his Party, with some claim to being regarded as its moral conscience after Gladstone's departure; and he was important also as a symbol of Liberal-Irish understanding. But amongst his colleagues he lacked authority, for he had too often made threats of resignation which he did not mean to carry out. Just how much Rosebery felt indebted to Morley, or valued his services, is shown by the fact that he denied him promotion throughout the fifteen and a half months of his premiership.

Harcourt was not at this time strong enough in the country or in the House of Commons to balance his weakened position in the Cabinet. He was a boisterous public speaker, who had campaigned hard for his party during its years in opposition. But he had not made a major impact at a general election since 1885, nor had he managed to develop in the East

Midlands the secure regional base which Chamberlain had built up for himself in the West Midlands. His claims to speak for popular Liberalism as a whole were further dented by the attitude of the London Liberal press, which came out strongly for Rosebery in February and March 1894. In the House of Commons, Harcourt had suffered from being too long in Gladstone's shadow. He had had little chance to display in office his undoubted Parliamentary prowess, and he had not had charge of a major government measure since he had steered the Prevention of Crime (Ireland) Bill into law in 1882. As Chancellor of the Exchequer he had not as yet achieved very much. His 1893 budget had raised the standard rate of income tax, but had not complied with any of the Radicals' main demands, such as the introduction of payment of M.P.s. The Irish section of the governing majority remained suspicious of Harcourt, whom they viewed as even less sympathetic to their cause than Rosebery.

In any case Harcourt was not the man to try to stop the formation of a new government merely because of frustrated ambition. Unlike Rosebery, or even Gladstone, a guiding principle of his political life was party loyalty. Harcourt had laboured hard, and in the end successfully, in 1892 and 1893 to keep the Cabinet together over Uganda and Egypt, and he had done his best in early 1894 to dissuade Gladstone from resignation. Once Gladstone's departure became inevitable, Harcourt's main concern was to limit the damage. He was anxious that a Liberal government should be able to carry on, even in the absence of the Grand Old Man. Otherwise he feared that Salisbury would be sent for by the Queen and a general election held on the issue of naval rearmament in which the Liberals would be heavily defeated. Harcourt did not like the idea of a peer Prime Minister, and he had complained forcefully when Gladstone appointed five peers to the Cabinet in 1892. But he had no particular animosity against Rosebery personally. Indeed the two men had hitherto got on well enough together in office, and shared a common scepticism about Home Rule. Nor did Harcourt possess an overriding ambition on his own account, though his son confessed to have a 'double dose' for him. The leadership of the House of Commons, which he obtained in 1894, and the prospect of carrying into effect the most important budget in nearly half a century, in any case offered Harcourt enticing fields to conquer. In a sense he may almost have preferred his position of second-in-command, because it enabled him to continue to exercise his favourite role of thorn in the flesh, and indeed to remain a kind of opposition figure even when in government. Though Rosebery subsequently chose to view their relationship otherwise, he in fact owed Harcourt a great deal during his fifteen and a half month premiership. In the House of Commons it was Harcourt's resource and leadership that to a considerable extent served to maintain the Government in office. Privately Harcourt was often difficult and obstreperous as a colleague, but hardly more so than during previous administrations. Publicly he remained loyal to his chief, to a more noticeable extent indeed than one or two other Ministers like Asquith.

Only one man could probably have prevented Rosebery from becoming Prime Minister in March 1894; and that man was Rosebery himself. Hesitation and self-doubt had so often afflicted him at crucial moments of his career, that it would have been by no means surprising for him to have refused the Queen's commission to form a government. Intellectually at least he could make out a good case for refusal. His great hero, the Younger Pitt, had declined the offer of the premiership when it had first been made to him, and had emerged all the stronger as the indispensable man after others had been tried and found wanting. Rosebery later professed to regret that he had not himself used this tactic with regard to Harcourt in 1894. Outwardly he had long maintained that Harcourt ought to be given the chance to form a government, on the grounds that he would endeavour to make his own administration a success and anyone else's a failure. In the event neither of these considerations caused Rosebery to reject the premiership when it was actually offered to him. It was only natural for him to accept the opportunity of a lifetime once it was placed in his hands; but still there was a sense in which Rosebery in 1894 became Prime Minister against his own better judgement. As on other occasions, saying he would ne'er consent, he consented. An underlying lack of conviction was to mar his political career, and was all too soon in his premiership to be exploited by his enemies.

On balance it was a misfortune for Liberalism that Rosebery rather than Harcourt became Prime Minister in 1894. Harcourt had evident faults certainly, but unlike Rosebery's they were mainly on the surface, and they were also offset by formidable political talents. Twenty-five years in the House of Commons had given Harcourt considerable Parliamentary experience as well as a thorough knowledge of the Liberal party. He was an effective public speaker, able to match the ablest orators on the Unionist side in terms of verbal pugilism; and he possessed a lawyer's ability to master a complicated and contentious subject. It is unlikely that under his leadership the Liberals would have got into such embarrassments in late 1894 over the constitutional question of the House of Lords. Harcourt's personal idiosyncracies and faults of temper, which colleagues at times found so wearing, would probably, as even Rosebery admitted, have been better-controlled if he had been placed in a position of supreme responsibility; and in addition Harcourt possessed in his son, Lewis, a devoted and capable political aide whose own personality, subtle, discreet and diplomatic, ideally complemented his father's.

As matters turned out of course it was Rosebery who achieved the supreme prize, becoming Prime Minister over the head of a leading

Parliamentary figure twenty years his senior, under whom he had himself first served his ministerial apprenticeship as an Under-Secretary of State at the Home Office a dozen years earlier. It would have been more than human for Harcourt not to have felt the slight to some degree. As it was, he acquiesced loyally in the appointment not only of a Prime Minister, but also of a Foreign Secretary, in the House of Lords, stipulating only that he should be consulted on matters of patronage and kept informed on developments in foreign policy. It is not clear how far Rosebery agreed to these conditions, and they were subsequently productive of much disagreement. On the whole, during his months as Prime Minister, it was Rosebery who was more obsessed by Harcourt rather than the other way round. Rosebery was uneasily aware how smooth had been his path to the top, and he may have wondered in his heart of hearts how far he deserved it. A highly sensitive man, he may have projected his sensitiveness onto others, and have been the more inclined to view Harcourt's habitual vehemence and argumentativeness in Cabinet as evidence of political recalcitrance and disloyalty.

Rosebery formally kissed hands as Prime Minister on 5 March 1894. He made few significant adjustments in the Cabinet which he had inherited from Gladstone, and which in any case contained a good store of political and administrative expertise. Kimberley moved up to take Rosebery's place as Foreign Secretary. Along with Ripon, the Colonial Secretary, he was one of the most experienced men in British public life; for both had held junior office in the 1850s and had first entered the Cabinet in the 1860s. Fowler replaced Kimberley as Indian Secretary. As well as being one of the few men in the Liberal cabinet who could get on well with the Queen, he was a member of a front bench rich in debating talent, which included not ony Harcourt but also Asquith and Campbell-Bannerman, the latter arguably the most popular senior figure on either side of the House of Commons. Acland and Asquith represented the younger talents in the Cabinet, and the latter in particular was to advance his reputation during 1894 and 1895. As well as being regarded as a skilful debater and as an energetic administrator, Asquith was emerging as the Liberal party's leading propagandist in the country. He appeared almost as regularly as Rosebery on public platforms at this time, and much more than his chief he proved himself adept not only at fastening upon the divisions and uncertainties within the ranks of the Opposition but also at evoking the spirit of a Liberalism of the future compounded of a desire, as he put it, for 'equality of opportunity to share in the social heritage that has been built up and bequeathed by the labours of unnumbered generations'.[4] Rosebery made few real alterations in the Cabinet's working arrangements. He started out with the intention of holding weekly Cabinet meetings, by way of contrast with the recent slipshod methods of the Gladstonian regime;

but like most good resolutions this one soon came to be honoured more in the breach than the observance. Rosebery did however take the decision to remove the chamberpot from the room in which Cabinets were normally held on account of the associations with the years 1880–85 'of Childers and Granville constantly pumpshipping in a cupboard in the corner'.[5]

Rosebery added only one new name to his cabinet. This was Tweedmouth, who as Edward Marjoribanks had been lately Government Chief Whip, and who, having inherited a peerage, now moved up to become Lord Privy Seal. Marjoribanks's skills as a political fixer were missed in the House of Commons. His wealth was still at the disposal of the Liberal party, as emerged later in the year in the affair of the Tweedmouth cheques. Rosebery could have taken the opportunity to remodel his Cabinet more substantially in March 1894 and to enhance his own authority into the bargain. Two or three Ministers were acknowledged liabilities. Trevelyan was considered a particular embarrassment, likely to make a mess of anything he turned his hand to. Shaw Lefevre's reputation, at least in Parliamentary terms, was not much better. Mundella was under a cloud because of his association with a bankrupt company which his department, the Board of Trade, was supposed to be investigating. Waiting in the wings were three Under Secretaries, Grey, Buxton, and Hibbert, who were considered especially deserving of promotion. Yet Rosebery made no move. He retained Trevelyan and Shaw Lefevre in the Cabinet, and he agonised for several weeks before requesting Mundella's resignation and transferring his duties to another Cabinet Minister. Of course promotions involved bye-elections and a possible loss of seats if the Unionists were able to mount a strong enough challenge. But a newly formed government could probably afford to take such a risk. Later in the year the Liberals were gratuitously to make a gift of the seats of Forfar and Brigg to the Unionists by appointing their Liberal M.P.s to lucrative positions outside Parliament on the judicial bench.

All incoming Prime Ministers arouse expectations. Few however have disappointed them so swiftly as Rosebery. Up to 1894 he had been regarded in particular as a man of general parts and promise. He had earned good marks as Foreign Secretary, and as an apparently effective political boss and manager of men. His performance as Prime Minister was to diminish his reputation in these two respects. Prior to 1894 also, Rosebery had developed and fostered other attributes which went to make up a distinct political personality. He had come to be distinguished as an elegant orator, a man of mystery, a notably popular statesman, who could command respect and support on all sides of the political spectrum. In the early months of his premiership all these faculties began to play him false. Rosebery's ability to round a phrase or point an epigram betrayed him into verbal indiscretions; his quality of mysteriousness too often expressed itself to his colleagues as secretiveness and isolation; his gift of popularity was called in question by electoral setbacks for the Liberals in areas where he was supposed to hold particular sway; his capacity to be all things to all men came to seem consequent on a lack of conviction about anything. An old man in a hurry, it was said, had been succeeded by a young man apparently in no hurry at all. Hamilton put his finger on Rosebery's chief weakness as a domestic politician when he spoke of a want of discipline that had resulted from his friend never having had to serve in the ranks. Rosebery had inherited his peerage and his seat in the House of Lords at the age of twenty. He had missed the traditional apprenticeship on the hustings and in the House of Commons; he had not been trained in the hardest school to defend a contentious and complicated case, and to guard his words while so doing; and a vital element in British democratic statecraft was thereby denied to him.

Rosebery first badly dented his reputation by a series of speeches which he made early in his premiership. This was ironic, as few Prime Ministers have worked harder to establish themselves on the public platform. Most of Gladstone's many Midlothian orations, it will be remembered, were delivered when he was in opposition. In an endeavour to break out of his confinement in the House of Lords, Rosebery determined to carve out for himself the role of leading Liberal propagandist in the country. In the course of his short premiership he delivered some dozen major platform speeches, and visited most of the larger cities of Britain. His first notorious utterance however was made in the House of Lords a week after he became Prime Minister when, replying to Salisbury in the debate on the Address, he declared that "before Irish Home Rule is conceded by the Imperial Parliament England, as the predominant member of the partnership of the three kingdoms, will have to be convinced of its justice and equity".[6]

The phrase 'predominant partner' was to haunt Rosebery for the remainder of his premiership. In the short term it helped to cause his Government grave embarrassment by contributing to its defeat on Labouchere's amendment to the Address, though, as will be explained below, there were additional reasons for this particular misadventure. Salisbury later thought that the Prime Minister would have been better advised to have stuck to the phrase rather than to have equivocated about it. In a sense Rosebery's problems properly began when he sought to explain away his choice of words in a major speech at Edinburgh on 17 March 1894. He meant no more, he declared, than that the Liberals had to win additional seats in England, and in Scotland too for that matter. A hostile House of Lords could, he trusted, be overborne, as after the 1868 and 1880 general elections, by a Liberal majority of over one hundred in the House of Commons; and he calculated that this state of affairs could be brought about if the Unionist advantage in England were reduced from 69 seats, as in 1892, to 45. After all the furore that had been aroused, this seemed a rather tame explanation; and Chamberlain, in his own speech at Edinburgh a few days later, made great fun of the inference that England could be said to have been converted to Home Rule once the English majority against Home Rule had fallen to forty-five.[7]

The Edinburgh speech marked a turning-point in Rosebery's political fortunes. Hitherto he had appeared a safe enough man, in happy possession of the political middle ground. After Edinburgh he began to seem, even more than Gladstone in his later years, at the mercy of the Irish and of the Radical wing of his own party. As Chamberlain trenchantly put it, 'Mr Gladstone was one of whom it was sometimes said that his earnestness ran away with his judgement, but Rosebery...allows his judgement to be run away with by the earnestness of other people'.[8] The Prime Minister made two other unguarded statements in his Edinburgh speech which were to trouble him in the months to come and which added to his appearance of lacking conviction and an ability to provide a firm lead. Anxious to make the question of the House of Lords in some sense his own special concern, Rosebery, perhaps unwisely, committed himself at Edinburgh to the principle of maintaining an effective bicameral legislature. Otherwise he offered no indication as to how he proposed to deal with a constitutional problem which particularly exercised Liberal opinion at this time, in the wake of the destruction or dislocation by the House of Lords of so much of the previous year's legislative programme. With regard to the upper chamber, it was, he seemed to suggest, for popular forces to take the initiative. In a phrase which was construed by his detractors as an abdication of ministerial responsibility and as an invitation to revolutionary agitation, he informed his Edinburgh audience that the question of the House of Lords, "if it is to be dealt with by the present Government . . . can only be dealt" with with the backing and on the summons of a great and popular feeling"; and he added, "we await your guidance and your direction, and when we have it we shall be prepared to take what measures you may inspire". Rosebery also referred at Edinburgh to the matter of Scottish Church disestablishment, and here again he incurred some censure for proposing to tamper with an ancient institution for reasons which he admitted to be purely partisan. "Every manse", he declared, in a phrase which was also to be much used against him in the following year, "or nearly every manse, of the Established Church in Scotland is an agency for the Tory party, and...the continuance of the Establishment and of the Liberal party side by side in Scotland are coming to be inconsistent."[9]

Insofar as Rosebery possessed any discernible political strategy in his early months as Prime Minister, it was perhaps best expressed by his attempt to put out feelers to the Liberal Unionists. This may have been the consideration in his mind when he made his 'predominant partner' remark at the start of the Parliamentary session. It was certainly a major element in three platform speeches which he delivered, at the City Liberal Club in April and at Manchester and Birmingham in May 1894. Here, using a variety of arguments, he more or less appealed to the Liberal Unionist rank and file – the leadership he apparently deemed by now beyond hope of redemption – to consider returning to the party which still possessed the authentic title-deeds of British Liberalism. He spoke of the Liberal party's newly demonstrated devotion to the interests of the empire, and he defended Irish Home Rule as being based on that "principle of nationality" that itself formed "the secret which pervades our entire empire". He reminded his listeners of the Liberal Government's success in ruling Ireland without coercion, of the Conservatives' failure during their time in office to pass an Irish local government measure, and of the extent to which Liberal Unionist objections to the Home Rule Bill of 1886 had been met by the Bill of 1893. Finally he insisted that Home Rule was not the real cause of the division in the Liberal fold. The split, he believed, dated from the Third Reform Act of 1884, which ushered in democracy with all its implications. It was the duty of all men of progressive bent to rally to the one true Liberal party.[10]

It cannot be claimed that this appeal was very effective. In the circumstances it was not very realistic to try to deal with the Liberal Unionists independently of their leadership; and by concentrating so much of his speech at Birmingham at the end of May on attacking Chamberlain for apostasy from Liberalism, Rosebery rather laid himself open to the charge of acting in a manner somewhat unbecoming for a Prime Minister. The charge of inconsistency with past opinions was one that Chamberlain found it easy to answer by referring to some of Rosebery's speeches of late 1885, made just prior to Gladstone's public concession to Home Rule.[11] In any case the speeches delivered by Rosebery since he had become Prime Minister often seemed in contradiction with each other. Either Home Rule was important or it was not; and Rosebery appeared to say one thing at the City Liberal Club and another at Manchester. Even if it was his view that Home Rule should not be accorded too much significance, what guarantee was there that he could get his supporters to agree? He had made his 'predominant partner' remark in the House of Lords only to withdraw it, under pressure of party opinion, a few days later at Edinburgh. Also the argument that the split within Liberalism dated from 1884 rather than 1886 was a dangerous one to use as it implied that Liberals were divided by other matters of substance apart from the form of Irish government. By 1894 the time of Liberal reunion had probably long passed. More than anything else perhaps the Rosebery Government demonstrated how permanent had become the split of 1886, enduring even after Home Rule itself had ceased to be in the forefront of political debate.

Rosebery's speeches of the spring of 1894 proved disappointing, indeed counter-productive, in another respect. They failed to give a lead to public opinion or any indication of the direction in which he proposed to take the Liberal party. To some extent Rosebery's problem was one of style. Unlike his predecessor, as a speaker he did not easily dominate his audiences or excite their passions. "When he is face to face with a great audience", commented one newpaper, "Mr Gladstone is all life and movement, and his least emotion finds visible expression in the play of his features." In Rosebery's case, however, "a somewhat mournful cadence of tone or a deepened solemnity of visage is the customary prelude to one of his quaint conceits".[12] Rosebery was perhaps too fond of referring *ad misericordiam* to the difficulties of being a peer premier; and, as has been seen, he had a knack of supplying his opponents with useful phrases. Every time he appeared on a public platform Rosebery raised expectations that he would provide a clear indication of his Government's policy and legislative priorities and of his own concept of Liberalism. In major speeches at Edinburgh, Manchester and Birmingham, he fell short of doing any of these things. Instead it was Chamberlain who took the opportunity, in speeches at Birmingham and Bradford, to give a clearer definition to Liberal Unionist policies and to argue the case for his party as a credible vehicle of social reform. Responding in part to Rosebery's accusation that the Liberal Unionist secession had stemmed from opposition to the democratic implications of the Third Reform Act, Chamberlain held up his own 'unauthorised programme' of 1885 as representative of the kind of practical and progressive reform that could be achieved by the Government of 1886–92; and he went on to outline a number of social reforms which were to loom large in his speeches up to the 1895 general election and which were in effect to add up to a new unauthorised programme: housing loans, old age pensions, and employers' liability.[13] Compared to Chamberlain, Rosebery sounded much less incisive on the public platform; and he was denied the opportunity of speaking at length on the great subject of the budget, which so dominated the 1894 session, by his serious reservations about his own Government's financial policy. By mid-1894 the Prime Minister whose youth, charm, and freshness of purpose, it had been hoped a few months earlier, was to have captured the imagination of the country, was in some danger of becoming politically isolated and irrelevant.

CHAPTER 1 NOTES

1 *Daily Chronicle* 27 February 1894.
2 ibid. 28 February 1894.
3 Dilke, C.W., 'Lord Rosebery's administration', *North American Review* May 1894.
4 Speech at Huddersfield, *The Times* 5 April 1894.
5 Harcourt Mss.405, 9 March 1894.
6 4 *Hansard* XXII 25–33 (12 March 1894).
7 *The Times* 19 and 23March 1894; Add. Mss.48669 3 June 1896.
8 Speech at Edinburgh, *The Times* 23 March 1894.
9 *The Times* 19 March 1894.
10 *The Times* 25 April, 3 and 24 May 1894.
11 Speech at Bradford, *The Times* 4 June 1894.
12 *Manchester Guardian* 3 May 1894.
13 *The Times* 4 May and 4 June 1894.

Chapter Two: The 1894 Session and the Budget

A year later, in early 1895, the collapse of the Government's popularity in the country was matched by its continuing resilience in the House of Commons. In the early spring of 1894 the opposite seemed to be the case. During its first month of office the Rosebery Government experienced several Parliamentary upsets, and for a time seemed close to collapse in the House of Commons. To the two-vote defeat on Labouchere's amendment in mid-March were added some fumbling performances in early April over the setting up of a Scottish grand committee.

It would be unfair to blame Rosebery entirely for his Government's initially poor Parliamentary showing. No doubt he had helped, by his ill-advised remarks in the upper house, to provoke defeat on Labouchere's amendment on the first day of the session. But there were also other factors at work. Morale was shaky and nerves were strained on the Liberal benches. A session of almost unprecedented length had just closed, on 5 March. Its labours had been heavy but had in the end only resulted in the passage into law of the Parish Councils Bill. Two other major measures, the Home Rule Bill and the Employers' Liability Bill, had both been lost in the House of Lords. Ministers had uttered various, generalised threats against the upper chamber. Gladstone had spoken in this sense in his final speech in the House of Commons as Prime Minister on 2 March. Harcourt had done the same in his address to the National Liberal Federation at Portsmouth in mid-February, and he was to do so again in his speech to the Party meeting at the Foreign Office prior to the opening of the new session. After expectations had been thus aroused, Liberals were rewarded with a Speech from the Throne that made no mention of the issue of the House of Lords at all. It was not surprising that discontented backbenchers should move their own amendment hostile to the upper chamber and that they should be joined in this by the great majority of Irish Nationalist members, uneasy at Rosebery's 'predominant partner' expression and at the omission of all mention of Home Rule from the Queen's speech.[1] Considerable uncertainty surrounded Irish intentions at this time. The nine Parnellite M.P.s, under Redmond's leadership, took the opportunity of Gladstone's resignation to withdraw their support from the Government. As a result Ministers were made even more dependent for a majority on their alliance with the Anti-Parnellites, but these in turn were divided between the factions led by Dillon and Healy; also they were short of money and thus inclined to be lax in their attendance at Westminster. This laxness was partly responsible for the Government's low majorities in the early weeks of the new session.

The new Government, it seemed, had little sense of direction or of legislative priorities. Eleven bills were promised in the Queen's speech. Clearly most of them were included only for show, in order to keep as many as possible of the variegated interests that comprised the Liberal Party up to the mark. Thus mention was made of several items drawn from the Newcastle programme: registration and franchise reform, liquor control, London rates equalisation, and Welsh and Scottish Church disestablishment. Relief for Irish evicted tenants was also included, in order to sustain Ireland's commitment to the Government in the absence of Home Rule. All these proposed measures contained highly controversial material, and only one or two of them could expect to come even anywhere near to passing into law in the course of a single session. The work of drafting the promised bills had as yet hardly begun, and proposed legislation on registration and evicted tenants was not laid before the House until the middle of April. Consequently much time was lost at the beginning of the session which, had it been better employed, might have made the Parliamentary year seem less legislatively barren (apart from the great budget) by the time it ended.

There was also a problem of Parliamentary leadership. The situation was virtually unprecedented. A Prime Minister in the House of Lords was dependent for the day-to-day functioning of the Government in the House of Commons on the co-operation of a man twenty years his senior whose hopes of the premiership he had defeated. It was as though Randolph Churchill in 1886 had been twenty years older than Salisbury and had besides occupied the second place in his party for a long time previously. Harcourt's leadership of the House of Commons was to be crucial to the Government's future; and, for all his displays of temperament, he proved a loyal and hard-working lieutenant. It was Harcourt's Parliamentary resource that enabled the Government to escape the predicament caused by Labouchere's amendment by the expedient of negativing its own Address. Real problems arose in the House of Commons only when Harcourt was absent. This was the case in early April 1894 when the Government got into a mess over Scottish devolution. Trevelyan, the Scottish Secretary, proposed to establish a Parliamentary grand committee to consider purely Scottish legislation. This was not part of the Government's stated programme and was rather a distraction from it. Unionists attacked the proposal as favouring M.P.s from Scotland (many of whom were English anyway) with privileges denied to those from other areas of the United Kingdom. Many Liberals felt the idea did not go far enough; one, Dalziel, put down a motion in favour of Scottish Home Rule and this was carried by ten votes in a virtually full House of Commons. M.P.s were treated to the spectacle of the unhandy Trevelyan supporting a motion quite at variance with the one he had proposed the previous day. Two days later the Government managed to adjourn the debate, but with a noticeably reduced majority. The problem was again one of uncertain leadership. Harcourt had suffered a family bereavement, and leadership in the House of Commons was assumed by John Morley. This was despite an understanding that Campbell-Bannerman should be Harcourt's deputy, arrived at after John Morley, in some pique at his lack of promotion, had declared that he would refuse to speak on any non-Irish matters.[2]

In contrast to the unsatisfactory state of affairs at Westminster, bye-elections at this time seemed to bring a more encouraging message from the country. Seven were held in late March and early April in a kind of miniature general election caused partly by Rosebery's appointments to minor office. Liberal majorities were seriously reduced in Montgomeryshire, Leith Burghs, and Mid-Lanarkshire, in the latter instance due to the intervention of a labour candidate who polled 1,200 votes. On the other hand the Liberals retained Berwickshire and Wisbech which they had thought might be lost. Asquith visited Berwickshire and spoke with apparent success in support of his wife's relative, H.J. Tennant. Wisbech was typical of many English seats which the Liberals had carried in 1892; it was a mainly rural constituency containing also an industrial element, in this case railwaymen, and success here seemed to show that the Government had benefited from its efforts to pass parish councils and employers liability legislation. At Hawick the Liberals secured an increased majority; and they also cut heavily into the Unionist majority at Romford, at this time a well-populated county constituency, where first-time voters in expanding industrial suburbs like Stratford and Beckton appear to have opted for the Liberals.[3] The Unionists claimed that they had won some five hundred votes on aggregate in these seven contests. On the other hand, and this was probably more significant, no seat was lost by the Government, which seemed to be holding on to its support. Only Rosebery may have had cause to be disconcerted. The large reduction in the Liberal poll at Leith came just after Rosebery had made a major speech in neighbouring Edinburgh. It was the first of many electoral rebuffs for him.

In mid-April the Government regained the initiative in the House of Commons. On 9 April Harcourt, in a quiet speech, moved to take Tuesdays and Friday mornings for Government business, and secured a majority of 24. The Government had been thought to be in some danger on this vote; but a threatened backbench revolt, of the kind that had occurred a month earlier, failed to materialise. Partly this was because Harcourt managed to postpone for a few days any announcement regarding Uganda, which was thought likely to provoke protests from the Radicals. The promise of determined efforts at domestic reform, to replace the sense of drift of previous weeks, also played its part. On 13 April the Registration Bill was introduced; a top-heavy measure, which in the end failed to become law partly because it attempted too much, it pleased Liberals by proposing to reduce residence requirements, remove disqualifications, and abolish plural voting. Monday 16 April saw the introduction of the budget: the measure which above all set its stamp on the session of 1894, and which enabled the Government to recover its position and to survive into the following year.

Harcourt's budget was the most significant domestic reform of the 1890s. Revision of the death duties was a long-deferred Liberal objective. Gladstone had intended to tackle the subject in 1881, and might have done so if the crisis in Ireland had not supervened. In 1894 Gladstone's successors acted on his intentions—and went beyond them. The budget of this year was the point at which the Liberals first broke decisively with the Gladstonian legacy, at least in the all-important field of finance. It is important to bear this in mind as so much has been made of the novelty of the so-called new Liberalism of a decade and a half later. Naval rearmament had provoked Gladstone's resignation early in 1894, and in making financial provision to meet it the new government departed further from the canons of Gladstonian orthodoxy. Two of the principles of Gladstone's 1853 budget—that income tax should embrace as many social classes as possible, and that agriculture should be given special consideration—were now abandoned; and Harcourt appeared to relinquish the old Gladstonian imperative of combatting increased public spending. "You have before you", he declared, "a future of ever-increasing expenditure—demands not only for the Army and Navy but for every kind of social reform".[4]

The 1894 budget was a dexterous piece of Liberal politics. It effected a substantial redistribution of taxation in favour of the less well-off, and particularly in favour of the lower middle classes, the 'black-coated classes', the 'struggling professional men and the struggling tradesmen', whose disillusionment with Unionist finance, it was thought, had helped to bring a Liberal government to power in 1892. The budget also served Liberal purposes in other ways. It struck hard at landowners and at the drink interest, two of the main bogeys of Radicalism. And in making new provision for naval expenditure, it did away with the machinery of the Naval Defence Act of 1889, which Liberals had found objectionable partly because it seemed to involve the House of Lords in financial matters that were properly the concern of the Commons.

In a subtler, even conservative, sense, the budget also served the interests of Liberalism. The years of Liberal Government in the 1890s were also years of economic recession: the last deep trough in that period of generally lower prices and lower profits categorised by some economic historians as the 'great depression' of c.1873–1896. Elements in both main political parties blamed the other, so far as they could, for this state of affairs. For Liberals part of the value of Harcourt's budget was that it demonstrated that economically things were not as bad as they seemed. As Harcourt admitted in his opening budget speech, the previous year, 1893, had been a particularly fraught one for the world economy. India, Australia, and the United states—some of Britain's main trading partners—had all experienced major currency or financial difficulties; and Britain herself had had labour troubles and a severe drought on top of continuing agricultural depression. Yet in spite of all this the country's basic prosperity held up well. Government revenue, as realised in income tax and levies on consumption, remained buoyant, and it was this that gave Harcourt the scope to introduce a great reforming budget and not simply one that raised taxes all round. There was no call, Harcourt took pleasure in emphasising, for the kind of protectionist and inflationary experiments desired by some Conservatives. Harcourt also made the most of statistics that showed how real wealth had increased during the free trade era. Though the burden of taxation had practically doubled in the previous fifty years, the value of property and profits assessed to income tax had almost trebled and the value of British exports had increased nearly fourfold. It was this expanding national revenue which had made possible expensive social reforms like free education.[5]

Harcourt's name is rightly coupled with the 1894 budget. It brought him immortality, and, somewhat belatedly, a reputation for radicalism, the lack of which helped to prevent him becoming Prime Minister earlier in the year. The budget gave expression to some of Harcourt's principal ideas and aspirations: it attacked landed privilege, encouraged temperance, and did away with some of Goschen's expedients, in particular the Naval Defence Act of 1889. It was Harcourt's ability and commitment which, more than anyone's, carried the measure through the Cabinet and the House of Commons. No Chancellor of the Exchequer had scored such a distinct political success since Gladstone's heyday in that office. But of course Harcourt's was not the only influence on the budget. Various elements had had a hand in fashioning it before it even reached the House of Commons, among them Harcourt's colleagues in Cabinet and on the backbenches, his professional advisers, and, not least, his son. It is necessary to examine each of the influences in turn.

Radical members of Parliament demanded early in 1894 a major shift in financial policy. There were several pressures at work. Reform of the death duties had long been promised by Liberal governments, beginning with Gladstone in 1853. It had been attempted in 1871, 1881, and 1885; and it now seemed high time to redeem the pledge. Also many Liberals felt that they owed their seats to the promises of large-scale fiscal reform made by their party in 1892, and to the attacks then made on Goschen's shifty and regressive financial expedients. There seemed a strong case for fiscal redistribution where 60% of national taxation was raised from indirect sources, and where the bulk of income-tax payers were people on small contingent incomes. Finally the increasingly hostile attitude adopted by the House of Lords made it all the more desirable to outflank that assemby by some great democratic stroke. "For many years", it was said, "budgets have been more or less rich men's budgets—it is time we should have a poor man's budget".

The Radical demands were spelt out in a memorial to the Chancellor of the Exchequer of 12 January 1894. Signed by 94 backbenchers, it is an ambitious document, which provides a useful summary of the attitudes of advanced Liberalism at that time. The Radicals proposed to effect a drastic redistribution of taxation in three ways. The death duties should be consolidated and graduated; the income tax should also be graduated for the first time in order to remove "the unfairness by which incomes derived from accumulated property pay no more than incomes dependent upon personal exertions"; finally grants-in-aid, which had increased from £1.4 millions in 1889 to £7.2 millions in 1893, and which were seen as a device of Goschen's to relieve the rural ratepayer out of national taxation, should be abolished. As their statement made plain, the Radicals expected a good deal from the proposals:

> If these reforms or even a considerable portion of them were adopted, it would be possible to announce a free breakfast table, by abolishing the remaining duties on tea, cocoa, coffee, and dried fruits, to provide funds for making the Government a model employer as regards both hours and wages, to carry into effect payment of members of Parliament and of election expenses, to extend national education, and to improve the position of the aged and deserving poor.[6]

Labouchere added his own cynical gloss. The Radical programme, he declared, would, if adopted, not only give the Chancellor "millions to play with" but would also considerably strengthen his claims to the succession. Payment of M.P.s, Labouchere thought, would be a particularly useful bribe for the average Liberal backbencher. "The lot in this Parliament seem mainly paupers, and they think more of this solatium, & returning officers' expenses being thrown on the rates, than their country's future." Harcourt would have none of this, and informed a Radical deputation that the estimates were already too high to allow for any further expenditure. His attitude can hardly have helped him in the ensuing 'contest' for the succession.[7]

As eventually implemented, Harcourt's budget was to have little in common with this Radical blueprint. Only in respect of the death duties was there much common ground. Otherwise the budget proposals fell well short of the formulations of advanced Liberalism. In fact the strongest impulse behind the 1894 budget came not from the Liberal party but from the pressure of financial circumstances. Economic depression had held back the rise in government revenue; and the demands of increased naval spending required an extra levy of £3,126,000.[8] Among the important personal influences on the budget, Harcourt was necessarily to the fore; but he owed a great deal to the labours of certain other key individuals. Fowler, Hibbert, and Rigby, amongst ministers, proved particularly helpful when the measure came before Parliament. Before that time Harcourt was most of all indebted to two men: his son, Lewis, and Alfred Milner, the Chairman of the Board of Inland Revenue.

Lewis Harcourt was probably a more significant Radical influence on the budget than were the Liberal backbenchers. It seems to have been his idea to raise the basic rate of income tax (not a popular proceeding) and at the same time to extend relief, by means of abatements and exemption, to income-tax payers at the lower end of the scale. This was done, and was to prove one of the notable features of the budget; though Lewis Harcourt would have preferred a larger increase and a larger amount of relief. The Chancellor's son however failed to get his way in two other respects. He pressed, unsuccessfully, for the introduction of sur-tax, or graduation at the higher levels of income tax. And, equally unsuccessfully, he opposed any increase in the beer and spirit duties, considering that indirect taxation was already heavy enough. His father was determined to strike a blow for temperance, but Lewis Harcourt probably had a more developed electoral sense. "It is true", he wrote, "that the consumer never feels or pays the increased duty, but he thinks he does all the same, and the cry of 'taxing the poor man's beer' is a very effective one on the platform."[9]

Few politicians have been luckier in their offspring. Lewis Harcourt proved invaluable to his father as a personal secretary and as a shrewd and loyal counsellor. His diary provides some illuminating vignettes of the work of budget-making in the spring of 1894. On one occasion he stayed up all night in order to fathom out "a most incomprehensible calculation" in Gladstone's 1853 budget, which neither his father nor Milner had been able to understand. 1853 was seen as a landmark in nineteenth century financial history, and as an essential point of reference. Lewis Harcourt proudly recorded his eventual success at 6 o'clock in the morning. On another occasion he had the better of an argument with Hamilton, the Assistant Financial Secretary. As the extracts from his diary make clear, Hamilton played an important role in preparing the budget, though he probably contributed few of its original ideas. According to Lewis Harcourt's account of the incident in question, Hamilton

> accused me of supplying . . . tables of Revenue & Expenditure and of the National Debt which were inaccurate and which had never passed through his, E. Hamilton's, hands . . . Ultimately I was able to produce the original of the tables, one in E. Hamilton's own handwriting, the other in that of Boyle, his subordinate clerk in the Treasury. E.H. then became most apologetic and promised *inter alia* to pay a fine of £1 to me and the other Private Secys. for his blunder.

Perhaps not surprisingly, Hamilton does not mention this somewhat humiliating episode in his diary. Lewis Harcourt saw himself as a necessary counterweight to the influence of the permanent officials. He got on well enough with both Milner and Hamilton, but seems to have regarded them as the "sentinels of the Landlord and Capitalist classes".[10]

Milner's role in the elaboration of the budget is a shadowy one, but it was of undoubted importance. Rosebery and Harcourt concurred in saying that the measure could hardly have been possible without his assistance; and, like Hamilton, Milner was in 1894 to receive a K.C.B. for his pains. Milner had a more radical cast of mind than Hamilton, and his predilection for 'thorough' was to make him famous in a wider field than that of inland revenue. He sympathised with the Liberal desire for a bold budget, and at first treated the idea of a sur-tax with some enthusiasm. On the other hand Milner was beholden to the interests of his department, the Board of Inland Revenue, a body jealous of its responsibilities. When Harcourt endeavoured to shorten the Death Duties Bill in collusion with Sir Henry Jenkyns, the Parliamentary draftsman, he was faced with a virtual rebellion by the senior officials of the Board, who regarded the work of drafting as their prerogative. It may well have been the influence of his colleagues of the Inland Revenue that determined Milner to change his mind about the introduction of sur-tax, perhaps on the grounds that administering it would have made the department even more unpopular. As Lewis Harcourt recorded it on 10 March 1894:

> Milner sent us last night an extremely able memo. of his against the sur-tax I have proposed. He admits that it is perfectly sound in theory and easily worked in practice but argues against it on the ground that it would make the Income Tax so odious in its levy that it might have to be swept away. I don't believe a word of all this but it has produced its effect on [the Chancellor of the Exchequer] . . . Milner may have saved him financially but I am sure he has ruined him politically.[11]

The Cabinet were at first rather more nervous about the budget than were the permanent officials. They feared that any increase in the beer and spirit duties would cause the defection of Scottish and Irish M.P.s who were vital to the continuance of their majority; and they were worried also by the proposed new graduation of the Inhabited House Duty. Harcourt abandoned the latter proposal at the end of March, partly in deference to his colleagues, and partly because overall revenue seemed buoyant enough to do without it. Harcourt also conceded a modification in the scale of graduation of death duties, as a gesture to Rosebery, who had contested the issue in Cabinet.[12]

Rosebery in fact had the greatest reservations about the budget. On 4 April 1894 he sent Harcourt a memorandum severely critical of certain of its implications. In particular he was concerned about the possible alienation of wealth and vested interest. "Property", he declared, "is an enormous and insidious force; it influences innumerable employees and dependants; it subscribes the election funds; its mere panic is a power." There was something in this; but Rosebery went on to claim that the graduation of death duties and the wider exemptions for less well-off income tax payers would lead to an increased hostility between the upper and lower classes. At the same time he implied that the budget did not give enough real benefits to the masses. Rosebery could have backed up his objections with more detailed argument. As it was, his memorandum lacked substance, and Harcourt took great pleasure in demolishing it when he replied the same day. Harcourt argued: that the gratitude of income tax payers earning less than £500 *per annum*, who formed, he claimed, nine-tenths of the constituencies, was well worth obtaining; that the masses were hardly likely to be won over by continuing Liberal complaisance towards the fiscal privileges of the wealthy; and that the real cleavage between the classes had come about through household suffrage. No government, Harcourt maintained, was likely to lack election funds as long as it could reward its wealthier sympathisers with honours and titles. As to Rosebery's fear of higher taxation causing commercial panic and a shortage of capital, Harcourt pointed out that panic had already occurred earlier in the decade, due to the over-abundance and idleness of capital, and its consequent squandering in unsound speculative ventures in South America.

This exchange marked a crisis in the relationship of Rosebery and Harcourt. Hitherto they had remained on fairly friendly terms, even through the events leading to Gladstone's resignation and the reconstruction of the Government. After April they were hardly to be on speaking terms for six months. Rosebery's biographer put the blame on Harcourt and on the tone he adopted in his reply to the Prime Minister's memorandum. No doubt Rosebery felt some of the inferences keenly.

Harcourt enjoyed rhetorical flourishes, but he could probably have spared his allusions to "young men who will go away sorrowful because they have great possessions" and to the availability of election funds from "rich men who are already peers or those who desire to become peers". However this was Harcourt's style, and Rosebery had known him long enough to be prepared for it. Had Rosebery served in the House of Commons, he might have learned better how to cope with the debating manner which Harcourt tended to employ even outside the walls of Parliament. It is certainly unwarranted to describe, as Rhodes James does, Harcourt's letter of 4 April as "outrageous". It was flamboyant and a trifle pompous—Harcourt not omitting to remind Rosebery that he was old enough to remember Gladstone's efforts at reforming the death duties in 1853—but its actual arguments were reasonable enough. And indeed on the matter of the scale of graduation, about which Rosebery felt strongly, Harcourt came some way towards meeting the wishes of the Prime Minister.[13]

Rosebery made two main errors in this particular affair. In the first place he should never have taken up the budgetary issue at all. He knew Harcourt's temper and his taste for controversy. He knew also that his best chance of making his Government work, in difficult enough circumstances, was to allow Harcourt a free hand in the financial sphere which he considered peculiarly his own. That was no more than he himself had claimed as Foreign Secretary, when Gladstone had been Prime Minister. In the second place, having taken the issue up, Rosebery should have pursued it wholeheartedly. He ought to have accepted Harcourt's offer to put the points in dispute before the Cabinet, and to have allowed the whole matter to be thrashed out there. By not doing so, Rosebery appeared to be running away from a fight. Harcourt had grounds enough for resentment. He had been beaten to the premiership in the previous month by a much younger man who was deemed to be both a vote-winner and a social reformer. Since becoming Prime Minister, however, Rosebery had embarrassed his colleagues by verbal indiscretions, and had conspicuously failed to influence a bye-election by his one major platform speech. To cap it all, he had expressed a view of the budget which, Harcourt thought, would have been considered "extreme in its Toryism by Lord Eldon". After this particular episode, Harcourt never had the same respect for Rosebery again. It is evident that he allowed Rosebery to realise this, and the relationship between the two men was to be permanently damaged.

Harcourt at least soon had other things to think about. On Monday 16 April 1894 he introduced in the House of Commons his third, and certainly his most famous, budget. The occasion brought him a distinct Parliamentary success. He was particularly praised for the lucidity of exposition with which he treated a highly complex subject; and it is perhaps convenient at this juncture to look at the budget as a whole and to summarise what main changes it proposed to effect.

The budget was designed to provide for the largest peacetime estimates in British history. They amounted to £102,720,000, and had been exceeded only in 1813 and 1814. They surpassed even those of the famous "£100 million budget" of 1885, the year of Penjdeh and the death of Gordon, which had helped to destroy Gladstone's second government. In 1894 the provision for both the Army and the Navy, £18 millions and £17 millions respectively, was the biggest asked of Parliament in time of peace. The £3,126,000 increase in the naval estimates represented the crucial item in a potential deficit of £4,624,000.[14]

Harcourt proposed to meet this figure, partly by increased taxation, and partly by what his opponents regarded as a piece of sharp practice. This was the removal of the procedure set up by the Imperial and Naval Defence Acts of 1889, by which the large-scale naval rearmament programme of that year was to be paid for in successive stages over several years. Harcourt had opposed the whole idea at the time as a dubiously constitutional mortgaging of the finances of the future, and he was glad to have the excuse of getting rid of it in 1894. The annual charges due under the Imperial and Naval Defence Acts were now all paid off at one go by raiding the New Sinking Fund, which had been set up by Northcote in the 1870s. At the same time the first dividend on Disraeli's Suez Canal shares purchase of 1876 became due, and Harcourt gratefully appropriated the proceeds. In this way the deficit on the year was reduced by as much as £2,123,000 before any fresh taxation had to be imposed. Unionists tried to make some capital out of Harcourt's utilisation of two legacies of the Disraeli era. In fact Harcourt was breaking new ground for a Liberal Chancellor. His recourse to borrowing, or at least of his suspension of his predecessor's debt repayment programme, at a time of depression, marked a departure from the strict tenets of Gladstonian financial orthodoxy, and showed Harcourt to be a more resourceful and open-minded Chancellor than had been anticipated.

Of the new taxation that was to be raised in 1894-95, estimated at some £2,710,000, over half—£1,400,000—was to come from the increased duties on beer and spirits. This point requires stressing. As a temperance advocate, Harcourt was keen to add to the levies on alcohol, but he took some political risk in increasing the taxes on consumption in a budget that was supposed to shift the burden of taxation from indirect to direct taxation. The revised death duties, for which the 1894 budget is famous, were only expected to bring in £1,000,000 in their first year. Thereafter their yield was expected to rise to £3,500,000. The reforms effected by Harcourt had a long-term significance, and they endeavoured to apply to the death duties the principles of consolidation, equalisation, and graduation.

The death duties in 1894 resembled a patchwork quilt, put together by the efforts of various Treasury ministers over the previous two hundred years. As Harcourt explained, in his lucid budget statement, they fell into two main categories. The Probate, Account, and Estate Duties, which originated in 1694, 1881, and 1889 respectively, were levied on the whole *corpus* of property passing at death, prior to its distribution. The Legacy and Succession Duties on the other hand, which dated from 1795 and 1853, were only levied on such property after its division and distribution, and the amount to be paid varied in accordance with the relationship of the heir to the deceased. Harcourt proposed to consolidate these various charges. The Legacy and Succession Duties were to be kept separate for administrative reasons, but the other three duties were to be brought together in a new combined Estate duty. This would accompish a longstanding Liberal objective. It would enable land, or realty, to be taxed on the same basis as personalty (or, indeed, as leasehold property, which counted for this purpose as personalty): that is, on its true capital value. Hitherto land, or at least freehold and settled land, had escaped the main burden of death duties on the grounds that it already bore sufficient charges in the form of local rates. Land had remained exempt from the Probate, Account and Legacy Duties. In 1853 it was made liable to Gladstone's new Succession Duty; but this was a more lenient version of the death duties on personalty, for it taxed land not on its true capital vaue but on its value to the successor, calculated in terms of his life interest and the land's annual rental. Goschen added a further element in 1889 in the form of his own new Estate Duty, which taxed all property worth over £10,000 on its net annual vaue, not exceeding 24 years purchase.

Harcourt's scheme of 1894 was designed to end the discrimination between realty and personalty. Henceforth land passing at death was to pay on its true capital worth, and it was to be valued as such, just like jewels or pictures, by professional experts. In addition both realty and personalty would be taxed on a graduated scale, beginning at 1% for estates worth between £100 and £500, and rising to 8% for estates worth over £1,000,000. These were two radical features of what Harcourt considered a great programme of democratic finance. A third, which was thought likely to prove the most popular aspect of the budget, concerned the income tax, the standard rate of which was now increased by 1d to 8d in the pound. This made possible a more generous system of allowances for the lower range of income-tax payers, categorised, in the political parlance of the time, as "the class just above the working class, and which was just beginning to wear a black coat". According to one newspaper, this 'class' consisted of "higher-paid workmen, clerks, struggling professional men, the smaller shopkeepers, manufacturers and agriculturalists". At all events, it formed a key section of the electorate. Harcourt's budget increased the allowance on incomes of under £400 p.a. from £120 to £180, and established a new allowance of £100 for incomes of between £400 and £500 p.a. It also favoured the interests of small farmers and householders by allowing a deduction of 10% on land and 15% on houses, to cover repairs and outgoings, under Schedue A.[15]

The 1894 budget was at first generally well-received. Among Unionist newspapers, only the *Morning Post* proved highly critical from the start, discerning the progressive thrust beneath its financial complexities. At the outset, indeed, it was more Radical complaints that were voiced. The Budget, it was said, did not go far enough in shifting the burden from the poor to the rich, from indirect to direct taxation. It should have graduated the income tax on the higher as well as the lower scales, and introduced sur-tax; it should have distinguished between earned and unearned income; it should have taxed the rich man's wine and not the poor man's beer. With the money thus made available, it could have lessened taxation on tea and sugar, and thus moved towards the old Radical objective of a 'free breakfast table'; it could even perhaps have provided funds for old age pensions.[16]

Gradually the budget's full implications came to be understood and condemned by the Unionists. They attacked it as a demagogic and electioneering device, designed to set class against class. They branded it as socialistic, partly because Harcourt saw fit to make sweeping claims for the fiscal rights of the State, based on his study of feudal tenures. But above all the Unionists regarded the budget as an act of spoliation towards landed property. Realty, they claimed, already bore a heavy and increasing rates burden. Now it was to be faced every generation with a substantial levy on its capital value; and this levy would only be paid with difficulty, for land, unlike personalty, could not easily be realised in terms of ready money, especially at a time when agriculture was in such a state of depression. To some Unionists the budget seemed a first step towards land nationalisation. Its more immediate consequences seemed likely to be the closing down of certain great houses, the sale of some old properties to *nouveaux riches* purchasers, and the parcelling out of others to their respective tenants. The latter eventuality, at least, was welcomed by Radicals as of a piece with their general schemes of land redistribution which had already found a limited form of expression in the Parish Councils Act of early 1894.

The Unionists however were faced with a dilemma in trying to oppose the budget. They admitted the need for increased naval expenditure; on the other hand they were loth to make their cause unpopular by opposing the new scheme of income-tax allowances or by proposing fresh methods of taxation as an alternative to death duties. Unionist leaders in particular were worried by the implications of taking office after defeating the Government on its financial proposals. They would, it was said, have to increase the duty on tea and other necessities, or even bring in a 10d income tax. Nevertheless the Unionist rank and file were not prepared to let the case against the budget go by default. Feeling ran high on the backbenches, especially among the 'country' element, outraged at what it saw as Harcourt's ruinous intentions towards the landed interest, and also among the many representatives of brewing and distilling concerns. Under this pressure the Unionist leadership took the unprecedented step of opposing the budget on its second reading. There was a good chance of defeating the Government. Nominally it still possessed a majority of thirty-seven, but this would be halved if, as expected, the Parnellites voted with the Opposition. Also other Liberal votes were known to be uncertain. The Liberal brewers and distillers were doubtful, as were the two 'labour' representatives, Hardie and Saunders, who had taken up an independent attitude towards the Government. Finally the Anti-Parnellites were uneasy about the increased duty on spirits, though Harcourt had done his best to mollify them by conceding that it should be in force for one year only.

The Liberals survived the challenge on the second reading in a debate culminating on 10 May. On the actual vote, Hardie supported, and Saunders opposed, the Government; three Liberal representatives of the drink interest abstained; others, such as Hoare and the Whitbreads, obeyed the Party whip. The Government had a majority of fourteen. The honours of the occasion went to Harcourt, who made one of the most effective debating speeches of his career. Believing attack to be the best form of defence, he assailed two of the chief bugbears of Liberalism, the landlords and the drink interest. The latter, he declared, could well afford to pay higher taxation out of the profits being made thanks to an increasingly monopolistic structure and the cheapness of raw materials. As for the former, rural landlords had been grossly favoured by the previous Government's policy of grants-in-aid, while urban landlords were enjoying unprecedented profits on property development and speculation. Harcourt also made the most of divisions between Conservatives and Liberal Unionists on the subject of graduation, and he challenged the Opposition to declare what its alternative fiscal programme would be. Balfour was in no position to do this. His own arguments, which spoke of death duties as being somehow arbitrary because the moment of a man's death could not be predicted, seemed feeble and specious in comparison.[17]

Victory on the second reading marked a crucial stage for the Government in the passing of the budget. There remained however a long period of guerilla warfare in the House of Commons which was to last into mid-summer. The committee stage of the Finance Bill began on 23 May after the Whitsun recess. On 31 May Harcourt moved successfully to take the whole time of the House for Government business until the end of the session. The committee stage lasted until the 2 July, and the third reading was taken on 17 July. Finally, at the very end of July, the House of Lords let through the budget, without a vote, but not without a degree of vexation and foreboding.

Before that time was reached, the Government had some bad scares in the House of Commons. The first was on 24 May when Bowles, a Conservative backbencher, described by Hamilton as "an extremely sharp little Parliamentary ferret", drew attention to the fact that the proposed alteration in the Succession Duty had not been covered by the preceding budget resolutions. His discovery caused consternation. Harcourt and Milner thought that Bowles was being coached by a disaffected official in the Board of Inland Revenue. His point of order threatened to make necessary the withdrawal of the whole budget. However, luckily for Ministers, the Speaker ruled that it would merely require the House to go again into Committee of Ways and Means in order to pass the additional resolution. The Government had another scare on 7 June, when the question arose of taxing property passing from husband to wife or *vice versa*. Again this was felt to involve the future of the budget, as a considerable amount of revenue was at stake. Some Liberal backbenchers were felt to be weak on the issue; but in the event the Government got home with a majority of forty, partly, is it seems, because Milner wrote to Balfour and Goschen warning them of the effects on revenue generally if the principle of not taxing property passing to spouses were maintained.[18] Finally, at the end of June, the budget got past the last of its sharp corners, when the clauses increasing the beer and spirit duties were approved.

Generally, after the second reading, the Opposition were content to play for time and to try to score points off the Government rather than to defeat the measure outright. Most of the acrimony and ill-feeling about the budget was to be found on the Unionist backbenches, especially among the agricultural and brewing interests. The Unionist leaders in the House of Commons were more detached and circumspect. They made the most in debate of the budget's complexities, and of the fact that the Government was forced constantly to clarify and amend its own measure during the report stage in July. No effort was made to closure debate; but Ministers were aware of the threat posed by prolonged discussion to their Parliamentary timetable, and this was the main reason why the Opposition was able to obtain a significant modification of the budget during the committee stage. On 13 June 1894 Hicks Beach, a once and future Unionist Chancellor of the Exchequer, lunched with Harcourt and won his agreement to limit the valuation of agricultural land to a maximum of twenty-five years purchase. This was a major concession to the rural landowner; though it offered no comfort to the urban landlord on whom the Radicals had also set their sights. In return the Unionists undertook to support the proposed new scales of income-tax relief on Schedule A.[19] Such a working arrangement had also been made earlier in the year during the debates on the Parish Councils Bill. Both compromises were a tribute to another of Harcourt's Parliamentary talents: his ability to maintain usually good working relations with his Unionist opposite numbers across the floor of the House of Commons.

The successful passage of the budget certainly owed much to Harcourt. He was a master of the art of browbeating an opponent or of squaring an uncertain supporter. His gruff, partisan speeches, excoriating landlords and brewers, enthused his own side and made his budget appear resolutely Radical. On the other hand Harcourt was not always master of the Finance Bill's finer details; he was at times open to the accusation of not even fully understanding his own budget. Also he relied heavily on his team of advisers, chiefly comprising the leading Treasury civil servants and the two Law Officers, which met regularly during the course of the session in order to hammer out verbal clarifications and amendments. Chaired by Harcourt, their proceedings often took on a rowdy and argumentative character which put Lewis Harcourt in mind of a bear-pit; "I have", he wrote, "laid in a supply of buns which I mean to poke in to these consultations at the end of an umbrella".[20] In terms of Parliamentary debate, Harcourt was helped by two ministerial colleagues, both men well-versed in questions of rates and taxation: Fowler, the Secretary of State for India, and Buxton, the Under-Secretary of State for the Colonies. Most of all, in the House of Commons, Harcourt depended on the expertise and forensic skills of the Attorney-General and the Solicitor-General, respectively Sir John Rigby and Sir Robert Reid. Even they could sometimes fail to provide the right advice, as in the case of the controversial clause of the budget which proposed to tax the colonial properties of men normally resident in the United Kingdom. Colonial governments protested in the name of 'no taxation without representation'; Unionists ominously recalled the lessons of the American War of Independence; Harcourt made an unwise comment about the colonies not having contributed to the cost of their own naval defence; finally he was forced to climb down and allow an abatement on his proposed taxation of property held by British residents in the self-governing colonies wherever a similar charge was locally imposed.

"It is the uncertainty of your position which saves you, remarked Arthur Balfour to Lewis Harcourt. "The narrower your majority becomes, the more insolent you grow".[21] Fear of a dissolution is indeed the key to the politics of 1894; it imposed discipline on the Liberals and their allies, and restraint on the Conservatives and Liberal Unionists. Neither side was confident of doing particularly well in a general election held at that time. The Liberals had detected no obvious trend in their favour in the bye-elections held in the spring; whilst their Anti-Parnellites allies were in serious financial straits as a result of diminishing contributions from the United States, a consequence it would seem mainly of economic depression in that country and a disillusionment with the state of Irish politics since 1890. Impecuniousness made the majority of Nationalist M.P.s anxious to avoid a general election, and faithful in their attendance at Westminster during the period of the budget debates, in order to prevent the defeat of the Government. Help from Liberal Party funds seems to have paid for their travelling expenses. The Unionists, on the other hand, regretted the temporary supplanting of Home Rule as the leading question of the day; it was after all the issue on which they most expected to win. In any case they laboured under particular difficulties with regard to the budget. They could hardly object to the purposes of naval defence for which the extra money was being raised; and they were embarrassed at the thought of suggesting alternative methods of finding the necessary revenue. Also they were troubled by cross-currents within their own ranks. Chamberlain, who had been a tower of strength in the Home Rule debates of the previous year, remained noticeably quiet on the Opposition benches during much of 1894. He had supposedly been in favour of higher progressive taxation since the days of the 'unauthorised programme', and his organ, the *Birmingham Daily Post*, came out for equalisation of the duties on realty and personalty in April 1894.[22] The problems of the Opposition were pointedly revealed in a debate on the principle of graduation, as applied to the death duties, on 4 June 1894. Many Unionists preferred to abstain rather than to oppose a principle of apparent equity that had already been partially admitted in Goschen's budgets. Accordingly the Government was able to carry the day on graduation by a majority of 104.

In the country, the budget never became a burning topic of controversy. Too few leading politicians had an interest in making it so. On the Liberal side, matters were complicated by the ill-feeling between Rosebery and Harcourt. The Prime Minister continued his round of speeches in major provincial centres, but he could not bring himself to make more than passing reference to the budget. In so doing, he denied himself the opportunity to offer a positive theme to his audiences. It could not be said that his speeches at Manchester, early in May, and at Birmingham, towards the end of the same month, added greatly to his reputation. At Manchester, Rosebery was expected to provide a clear indication of his Government's legislative priorities, but he contented himself with platitudes and generalities. At Birmingham, he filled his speech mainly with citations from Chamberlain's oratorical efforts of more Radical days. No doubt, this was part of Rosebery's strategy of weaning away Unionists of Liberal background from their present leadership. But it was a disappointing and undignified performance for a Prime Minister; and it gave Chamberlain every excuse, when he spoke a few days later at Bradford, to ignore the budget in his turn, and to lay his own charges of inconsistency against Rosebery. Harcourt, for his part, scorned to take part in partisan, platform oratory, so long as his bugbear, Rosebery, seemed bent on doing so. His only real foray outside Parliament, during the period of the budget debates, was to the London Chamber of Commerce, where he delivered himself in mid-June of a characteristic panegyric on the workings of the existing economic system, even in time of depression, full of Panglossian observations on the fall in prices, the increase in savings, and the steadiness of wages.[23]

Only John Morley, amongst leading Liberals, made much of the budget in his public speeches during 1894. At Newcastle in late May, and at Rotherham in late June, he presented the new financial arrangements as a great democratic advances, a reform which, if taken in conjunction with the Parish Councils Act, put 1894 on a par with momentous years of Liberal achievement like 1869 and 1870. Following Gladstone's retirement, Morley had good claim to be regarded as the conscience of Liberalism. He even regretted that the taxes on alcohol had not been increased further, in the interests of temperance. And, like Harcourt in the House of Commons, he was determined to make the most on the public platform of the Unionists' unprincipled alliance with the Parnellites in their attempt to defeat the budget on the second reading. As he declaimed in a populist oration at Newcastle:

> They voted in favour of the landlord of a great London estate receiving enormous increment of the annual value of his property. They voted . . . against protecting small savings of men like you and me . . . The great lights of the Church of England Temperance Society, I believe, were seen marching unabashed to protect whisky and beer. Radical Unionists, who had for years been clamouring for graduation of the fiscal burdens, went trooping with brows of brass into the lobby against the graduation of the death duties.[24]

On the Unionist side, Salisbury set judicious tone with regard to the budget in his public speeches. There were points to be made against it certainly. At St James's Hall, in early June, he referred to the Government's mean-mindedness in taxing widows. And at Trowbridge he dilated on ministerial insensitivity towrds the problems of agriculture, and promised that a Unionist administration would relieve the burden of local rates in the countryside. But generally Salisbury's line was to dismiss the budget politically as largely an irrelevance. The real point at issue between the parties remained Home Rule. Tax reform, like almost everything else in the Newcastle programme, was a smokescreen. The Separatist majority of 1892 had been "filched and swindled out of the country by contrivances of this kind". Salisbury's line was followed, for the most part, by the other Unionist leaders in their public speeches. Only Devonshire strayed from the path of caution when he attacked the budget, at Buxton, as a threat to employment and wages which would oblige landowners like himself to retrench on their contributions to charity and close down their country homes. His speech was an isolated occurrence, but it supplied a sample of the dangers lurking for the Unionists in the budget issue, and a foretaste of the cruder efforts of Conservtive oratory in 1909.[25]

It is difficult to assess the response of public opinion towards the budget. Liberal M.P.s, returning from their constituencies after the Whitsun recess, were said to be pleased at its reception. Lewis Harcourt was confident that the abatements under Schedule A, and for men earning less than £500 p.a., would prove popular. In any case his barber assured him that many of his customers were particularly pleased at the relief afforded to small incomes.[26] On the other hand very few bye-elections, which might have supplied some indication of popular feeling, were held at this time. Only two contests were fought during the months of spring and summer when the budget was before Parliament, and both were complicated by local factors. It was in fact remarkable that more seats did not become vacant, considering the rigours of life in a Parliament that had been in more or less continuous session since early 1893.

The first of these bye-elections, held at South Hackney in early May, proved something of a shock for the Liberals. A Liberal majority of 1,244 at the general election was now reduced to one of 192. To some extent the budget disappointed Londoners. It did not increase their share of the Probate Duty grant to which many of them had thought themselves entitled since Goschen had set up the system of grants-in-aid for localities in 1889. It also threatened to delay the introduction of promised legislation for the equalisation of rates between London's boroughs. A significant defection was that of the local trades council, which urged voters to abstain rather than vote for the Liberals, who were said to be no longer the friends of the working classes. The result was another slap in the face for Rosebery, who was supposed to be as popular in London as he was in Scotland. The bye-elections held in the summer were also influenced, in a more direct way, by the intervention of Labour. At Attercliffe, in early July, local feeling against the nomination of an employer as the Liberal standard-bearer led to the running of a separate Labour candidate who managed to poll over one thousand votes. As he seemed to take votes from Liberals and Conservatives in roughly equal proportions however, the large Liberal majority was not greatly reduced. At the end of August a double bye-election was held to fill the two vacant seats in the two-member constituency of Leicester. Here again the nomination of a local Liberal employer provoked the intervention of a Labour candidate, who garnered well over four thousand votes and nearly delivered the second seat into the hands of the Unionists.[27]

Still, a general election held in the late summer or early autumn of 1894 need not have proved too disadvantageous for the Liberals. There were some who urged the Government to take the plunge and dissolve, if the House of Lords did not in the meantime provide the excuse by rejecting the budget.[28] Certainly circumstances would have been much more favourable than they were to be in the following year. The Government had some substantial achievements to its credit thanks to the passage of the Parish Councils Act and the 1894 budget. Chamberlain's admission that the year 1894 had been more productive than any, from the point of view of Liberal legislation, since 1870 was gleefully quoted on Liberal platforms. The Government could claim the need for a renewed mandate to enable it to deal in its own way with questions like employers' liability, on which it had felt obliged to withdraw its legislative proposals earlier in the year after they had been substantially amended in the House of Lords. To be sure, parts of the Liberal programme, such as Home Rule, were not popular; but then neither was the presumed Unionist alternative of coercion. Under a Home Rule government, which was yet unable to bring about Home Rule, Ireland at least remained quiet; and the Liberals made much at this time of the lowest Irish crime figures in nearly two decades. The Unionists in 1894 had nothing very positive to put before the electorate; and the mood of the country, while not particularly radical, was not noticeably conservative. A year later it was all to be very different. Following Rosebery's unavailing campaign against the House of Lords and the protraction of economic depression through one of the worst winters of the century, the Unionists could claim a new *raison d'être*, as the party of practical social and economic improvement as opposed to revolutionary experiment. With the benefit of hindsight one can say confidently that the Liberals would have avoided the electoral debacle of 1895 had they chosen to dissolve in 1894; but the dissolution of Parliament by a Government as yet undefeated in either House would have been an unusual proceeding, and probably one more at variance with accepted constitutional practice than the reputedly Radical administration of 1892-95 was capable of. A general election, called voluntarily by the Liberals in mid-1894, might well have cost them some seats, but, as Balfour privately admitted, would probably not have given the Unionists much of an advantage in a new Parliament.[29] And if the House of Lords had forced a dissolution by rejecting the budget, it is likely that Liberal prospects would have been markedly improved.

It was by no means clear what the House of Lords could or could not do with a money bill. Precedent, as in so many areas of the British constitution, remained obscure. In a resolution of 1671, the House of

Commons had laid claim to special privileges in the field of finance. A money bill, it was asserted, could not originate, or be amended, in the House of Lords, though one could be rejected there. Their Lordships had never explicitly accepted this proposition, and the whole issue had surfaced again in the dispute over the repeal of the Paper Duties in 1860–61. On that occasion the House of Commons had reaffirmed by resolution its standpoint of 1671, and the House of Lords had seemed implicitly to concur when it finally accepted the repeal of the Paper Duties, not as a separate measure, as in 1860, but as part of the budget of 1861. However there were many who claimed that the House of Lords had never surrendered its right to amend, let alone to reject a budget. Salisbury took this line when the 1894 budget had its first reading in the Lords on 19 July. More surprisingly Gladstone himself had conceded the same theoretical rights to the House of Lords in 1860, though he maintained that it had failed to keep them up in practice; and his authority was of course gleefully quoted by Unionist peers in 1894 who were anxious to pit the greatest name in Liberal finance against his less worthy successors.

To Salisbury the House of Lords was a necessary element in a popular constitution. In his view it represented national interests in a more permanent sense than could a House of Commons at the mercy of fluctuating party majorities. This had been his position in 1893 when he had dared the Government to go to the country on the rejection of its Home Rule Bill. There were however compelling reasons why the same kind of challenge could not be mounted in 1894. Rejection of a measure designed to increase taxation on landed property would open their Lordships to the imputation of interested motives, and would undermine their claim to be regarded as the Areopagus of the nation. Salisbury was a canny leader of Conservatism in an increasingly democratic age. He sensed that pubic opinion was a fickle element that tended to more away from the party in power. The decline in Liberal popularity had begun in the bye-elections of mid–1893, but by mid–1894 it appeared to have halted temporarily. The success of the budget had enabled the Government to regain some of the initiative. It must be given the chance to lose it again.

Circumstances in 1894 were different from those which provoked a conflict between the two Houses of Pariament over the budget in 1909. In the latter year more vested interests were arrayed against the Government's financial proposals. Many right-wing Liberals were known to be uneasy, and the City was more openly hostile, on the grounds that the budget might impair confidence and increase the already high level of interest rates. In 1894 on the other hand commercial and financial interests were largely unaffected, and interest rates were at an all-time low. Feeling against the People's Budget was allowed to develop a momentum of its own in the course of 1909, so that its rejection by the House of Lords came almost to be taken for granted; but in 1894 Salisbury had discouraged any such campaign, and only Devonshire among leading Unionists had betrayed his personal feelings on the public platform. In 1909 many Unionists believed that the whole future of the House of Lords was bound up with the rejection of the budget; otherwise governments would be able to bypass the upper chamber by tacking all manner of controversial items onto the annual Finance Bill. Most important of all the Unionists in 1909 were supplied with an alternative fiscal strategy in the shape of tariff reform. There was no possibility, as there was in 1894, of their defeating the Government and then facing the embarrassing task of suggesting different methods of raising the necessary revenue for the year.

The budget of 1894 was therefore allowed to go through all its stages in the House of Lords without a division. Unionist peers however growled angrily at its provisions. Devonshire once again deployed the arguments he had used at Buxton, that the new death duties would diminish the amount of capital and employment available on the land. Rutland and Argyll warned against allowing the powers of the House of Lords in matters of finance to fall into desuetude. For the Government only the Lord Chancellor, Herschell, spoke at length in the budget's defence. Rosebery was conspicuous by his silence. Salisbury allowed himself the luxury of a Parthian shot on the third reading. He denied Government claims to have borrowed the idea of graduation from Unionist Chancellors of the Exchequer; Northcote and Goschen, he declared, had graduated only at the lower end, and not at the higher end of the scale. Along with other Unionists, he lamented the departure from Gladstonian financial principles, such as the budgeting for the likely expenditure of a specific year. As before, Salisbury kept clear of arguments about the best methods of raising revenue. His main contention was that ministers no longer had any real authority to govern. The budget's second reading in the House of Commons, he pointed out, had only been carried by 14 votes; and with that penchant for psephological minutiae, to which both he and Gladstone were prone, Salisbury went on to assert that the Government's mandate was based on no more than a plurality of 150 votes scattered amongst its eight most marginal constituencies. "150 householders and lodgers", he averred, were "not better than 150 peers".[30]

Perhaps fittingly, it was Harcourt who had the last word for the time being on the budget controversy. Liberal M.P.s arranged a banquet for him at the start of August to celebrate his budget's triumphant passage. Here Harcourt chose to make a lengthy and sarcastic reply to the observations recently made in the House of Lords. His speech is worth quoting at some length, both as an example of Harcourt's trenchantly partisan style, and as an indication of the spirit in which a general election would have been fought had the House of Lords forced a dissolution on the budget. Dealing first with Salisbury, Harcourt asked:

> After all his analyses, and when he has reduced the constitutional rights of the House of Commons to what he calls '150 householders and lodgers', will he dare to say that the majority in the House of Commons on the Finance Bill did not represent the national opinion and the national will? Why, as he says he had the moral right in the House of Lords, did he not reject the Bill? . . . Because he knew very well that the nation would have made very short work with his legal rights and his moral rights if he had ventured to do anything of the kind. Well, I venture to say that this mumbling of the game he dare not bite is not dignified—I was almost going to call it contemptible.

Harcourt then turned his attention to Devonshire, and mocked his apparent belief in landowners as the special patrons of mankind.

> Of their grace and bounty they are willing to dispense a largesse to their inferiors, but to tax them upon the footing of the rest of mankind is an invasion of their privileges and of their monopoly, and to treat them as ordinary industrial millionaires is nothing short of an outrage. He says that if the payment of death duties on equal terms with other properties reduces for a short time the landowner's income he will have to retrench, but, like the rich brewer, he takes care to assure us that it is not he who is going to suffer at all. He will take care to shift the burden on other shoulders, and that of those who, he also assures us, are persons who are the least capable of bearing it . . . Poor human nature, from whose frailties apparently even the most exalted personages are not exempt. No, if these great people are to pay it is not they who are to suffer; it is the local charities and the unfortunate labourers. The retrenchment is, as he says, to be that which least affects himself. What a high-minded notion of retrenchment! What a patriotic conception of contribution to the defences of the Empire! . . . I want to know how far this doctrine is to be carried. Why will you not exempt, we will say, people of this exalted character from the duty on champagne? Why not exempt them from the income tax and the house tax? They would then have a larger surplus for their charities and their labourers. When this is put forward—and, mind you, this is what they are going to put forward—I will ask you whether, when the landlords in the heyday of their prosperity had great wealth, in the heyday of the time when wheat was 100s. per quarter, the labourers were in a better case. Do not we all know that today, even in the midst of agricultural depression, and know

it with satisfaction, the wages of the labourer are double what they were in the much-regretted days of the old war.[31]

The successful passing of the budget did not quite complete the work of the 1894 session of Parliament. Back in March, the Queen's Speech had included twelve proposed items of legislation. The budget had not been expected to engross quite so much time, and the Government had hoped to carry at least one major bill through all its stages in the House of Commons. The Period of Qualification and Elections Bill had originally occupied pride of place. Designed further to democratise the workings of the country's electroal machinery, and to move nearer to the implementation of the principle of 'one man one vote', it seemed an obvious Liberal measure, certain to please the Radicals and to unite the Party over and above any considerations of regional sectionalism. Unfortunately at the same time it contained many pitfalls. The coming of democracy, it was starting to be realised, posed as many problems for Liberalism as opportunities.

The Government had first to decide on its overall strategy. Was it intended to accomplish at least some degree of reform, and to persuade the House of Lords to accept some improvement in the machinery of electoral registration? In this case any bill should be kept as compact and confined as possible. Or was it intended rather to invite rejection of any measure by the House of Lords in order the swell the indictment against them? In that case any bill should be made as comprehensive and wide-ranging as possible. Most Ministers were not optimistic about a confrontation with the Lords over a further instalment of democracy. It therefore made sense to expose as little surface as possible in any such bill to attack. Lewis Harcourt, who made it his business to advise a Cabinet committee on the subject, advocated the restriction of legislation to questions of residence and perhaps registration. It was desirable to avoid "opening the door to every question connected with the franchise . . . including the question of female franchise". As one memorandum, circulated to the Cabinet, put it,

> While the reduction of the term of residence was universally agreed to by the Government supporters, and would have been supported by a considerable number of the Opposition, there was a great division of opinion among Government supporters as to the provisions respecting the machinery for registration.
>
> Those provisions involved endless opportunities of discussion and obstruction, as the details of the registration law are very numerous and very intricate, and the proposals in the Bill undoubtedly attacked the interests of various persons, particularly the registration agents and the revising barristers.

I therefore suggest that the proposal for the reduction of the term of residence should be put in a separate Bill from the provisions for amending the registration machinery, though perhaps it might be desirable to add a single clause providing for two registrations instead of one in every year.[32]

The extension of democracy was after all bound up with sectional interests and expectations. Liberals were broadly committed to the principle of 'one man one vote', but many of them were worried by the implications of female sufrage. The Government was under some pressure, particularly from representatives of labour interests, to provide for the payment of election expenses out of general taxation. This would enable more men without private means to stand for Parliament; but the Government decided against the change on the grounds that it would lead to a proliferation of candidates, of the kind which had often in the past proved harmful to Liberal interests, and which could only be avoided, it was thought, by provision for a second ballot, which was itself considered to be impractical in English conditions.[33]

The Government's Bill, introduced on 13 April 1894, had the worst of both worlds. It tried to do both too much and too little. It proposed to reduce the period of residential qualification from twelve months to three months, to end the requirement for personal payment of rates, and to provide for the registration of the electorate twice rather than once every year. At the same time it proposed to take all elections on the same day and to abolish plural voting. Radicals objected that the new machinery would still not ensure that enough new voters obtained the franchise. Unionists demanded to know why certain anomalies in the electoral system were being tackled while others were ignored. Why, for instance, was no attempt being made to reduce the over-representation of Ireland at Westminster, although the case for it had been conceded by the terms of the second Home Rule Bill? Why were provisions for state payment of election expenses, and for the extensions of the lodger franchise, which had figured in the Government's legislative proposals of 1893, not included in those of 1894? Was it not because an enlargement of the lodger vote was thought likely to benefit the Unionists, enfranchising, as it would, the sons of the middle classes still living at home? The Government's latest Bill was attacked as a blatant piece of gerrymandering. In addition it was likely to prove expensive, the cost of improved registration machinery being estimated at between £300,000 and £500,000.[34] Not surprisingly, after the Period of Qualification and Elections Bill had passed its second reading on 4 May 1894 by the not very substantial majority of sixteen, it was not proceeded with, and was subsequently withdrawn.

Even though the budget took until the middle of July to pass the House of Commons, the Government was still determined to press on with a portion of its legislative programme. On 18 July Harcourt announced the timetable for the remainder of the session. It was hoped that Parliament would be able to rise before the end of August, but in the meantime the Government would press forward its proposed legislation concerning evicted tenants in Ireland, equalisation of rates in London, and local government in Scotland. Facilities would also be allowed to a private member's bill dealing with the eight hours day for miners. Unionists protested against the further prolongation of the session. Chamberlain, in an unguarded phrase which subsequently did good service on Liberal platforms, declared that Parliament in 1894 had already accomplished "as much legislative work as any Parliament which has sat for 20 years".[35]

The Evicted Tenants (Ireland) Arbitration Bill was the most significant of the proposed items of legislation, and represented the necessary payment of a debt to the Government's Nationalist allies for their unstinting support during a Parliamentary session mainly given over to measures of English relevance. Liberals hoped it would not prove too controversial. All parties, it was assumed, had an interest in removing a source of social irritation, and a threat to stable property relations and law and order in Ireland. And the previous Conservative administration had already taken a step towards the rehabilitation of the evicted tenant by section 13 of the Land Act of 1891, which had provided financial incentives for a landlord to reinstate a former tenant, with a view to allowing him to purchase his holding.

Morley's proposed measure of 1894 aimed to make the process of reinstatement compulsory rather than voluntary where necessary. A three-man Board of Arbitration was to be set up to which dispossessed tenants might appeal. If the Board saw fit, it could order the reinstatement of an evicted tenant to any holding which remained in the direct possession of the landlord. The pill would be sugared for the landlord by the payment of up to two years arrears of rent. Half would be provided by public money. The rest would be made up by the tenant or by his friends in the Irish Parliamentary Party, who were supposed to have set aside the notorious Paris Funds for this very purpose. The public money in question would mainly be provided for out of the Irish Church Temporalities Fund, a useful nest egg which had become available for general secular purposes following the disestablishment and disendowment of the Church of Ireland in 1869. Morley was at pains to emphasise that his Bill involved no major departure from precedent. The principle of using public money to pay off arrears of rent had appeared in the Arrears Act of 1882. That of applying compulsion on the landlord had figured in the freedom of sale provisions of the Land Act of 1881.[36]

Unionists found much to object to in these proposals. They held that Morley had underestimated the cost to public funds, which they put at least at £250,000 instead of £100,000. They looked askance at the creation of yet another Irish land court, to add to those already set up by legislation of 1851 and 1881. In particular they were opposed to any further reduction in the rights of the beleaguered Irish landlord. The right not to take back a tenant who had been evicted was one of the few remaining to an Irish landowner; now it was proposed to take even this away from him. In a country where, through land purchase legislation, the state was as guarantor increasingly stepping into the shoes of the departing landlord, it made no sense to reward and to rehabilitate men who had defied the law and defaulted on their debts and obligations.

Above all the Unionists were influenced by a more purely political consideration. Most of the men whom the Bill was designed to benefit were tenants who had been evicted at the time of the Plan of Campaign in the late 1880s. Numbering some 1,350, they were mainly confined to the seventeen estates which had been investigated by the Mathew Commission in the days of Gladstone's fourth administration. It was understood that there were thousands more evicted tenants, about whom less was known, who might possibly claim a remedy as having lost their holdings in various circumstances since 1879. But, quite apart from this, Unionists objected to singling out for public favour men who had engaged in an organised political agitation and conspiracy against the law of contract and the law of the land. They blamed the leaders of the Plan of Campaign, Dillon and O'Brien, for sabotaging the Unionists' own scheme of conciliation as contained in section 13 of the Land Act of 1891. It was clear that no lasting agrarian settlement was possible in Ireland with these men. No reciprocal gesture had come from the Nationalist side, no undertaking that in return for evicted tenants legislation further agrarian disturbance would be discouraged. Instead the Nationalists could be expected to use any measure which passed into law as a means to extract further concessions. Morley's Bill proposed to reinstate evicted tenants only to holdings which were in their landlord's possession, and which had not been let out to any new tenants. But what would be the position of new tenants, in the midst of a hostile community, once it was realised that they were the only obstacle to the return of evicted men to their former holdings?

For their part, Dillon and O'Brien were not in the position to offer an olive branch. As leaders of the Anti-Parnellite wing of the Irish Parliamentary Party, they were forced to look over their shoulders at the Parnellite minority, whose attitude to the Government and all its works was far more critical. In particular the Parnellites, led by Redmond, attacked the Bill for failing compulsorily to dispossess those new tenants—planters or grabbers, as they were called, often of an Ulster Protestant origin—who had been brought in to replace evicted ones. In these circumstances, with agreement so far away, and with debate on the

Bill likely to be prolonged, the Government was obliged to guillotine its remaining stages as from 31 July 1894. This in turn made it inevitable that it would fail in the House of Lords when it reached that body. On 14 August the Evicted Tenants Bill was roundly defeated there by 249 votes to 30.

The 1894 session did not end without some legislative accomplishment, quite apart from the successful passage of Harcourt's budget. The Government was able to carry into law two, albeit secondary, measures of the Newcastle programme, concerning Scottish local government and the equalisation of rates in London. It was less successful however in making progress with the Miners' Eight Hours Bill. In principle this enjoyed considerable support in both main parties, particularly among M.P.s who represented industrial constituencies, and its second reading had been carried by the large majority of eighty-seven in the spring. But in August its passage was thwarted by the carrying of a local option amendment, which would have allowed coalfields like Northumberland and Durham, that had already negotiated an even shorter working day, not to abide by the Bills' provisions. The amendment was supported by, among others, Gladstone, who represented what was in part a mining constituency, and who wrote an open letter on the subject to the South Wales M.P., D.A. Thomas. It was not acceptable to the Bill's backbench authors, and the whole measure was accordingly abandoned.[37]

Of the two successful efforts at legislation, the Scottish Local Government Act represented an attempt to bring the northern kingdom into line with the provisions that were to be applied south of the border by the Parish Councils Act, passed earlier in the year. The measure was attended with some controversy as it proposed to give Scotland's parish councils greater powers, in respect of finance and police, than those enjoyed by their English equivalents. Its successful passage was greeted as a minor triumph by the Government supporters, not least because the Scottish Secretary, Trevelyan, was regarded as tactless and unhandy, and likely to make a mess of carrying it through the House of Commons. The Equalisation of Rates Act was potentially even more controversial, for it proposed to subsidise the poorer districts of London, which found it difficult to provide adequate services without imposing a heavy rates burden on their inhabitants, at the expense of the richer. In the debates on the Bill, before it was carried into law, Unionists complained bitterly about its unfairness and anomalies. Population was made the yardstick in determining how poor a district was. This made Islington, a large and comparatively well-managed borough, entitled to receive substantial subsidies which were denied to poorer but less populous districts such as Bow and St George's-in-the-East. The Bill had also, it was pointed out, been based on the assumption that in London all the rich lived in one area and all the poor lived in another. Whereas in fact both West End and East End each contained a mix of social classes, the main difference beng that whilst in the West End the large class of tradespeople and the less well-off generally paid their rates directly, in parts of the East End, such as Bethnal Green, tenants usually compounded for their rates as part of their rent. In the latter case therefore, landlords could be expected to raise the rents on their property in line with the amount of rates abated.[38]

Thus with some justification the whole measure could be desribed by its opponents as one to relieve the landlords of the East End at the expense of the tenants of the West End. On the other hand the Unionists did not care to push their opposition to the Bill to the limit. Equalisation of rates, whatever it might mean in practice, was a popular idea in principle; and the Unionists had admitted as much by redistributing the Indoor Pauper Grant in 1888. Many Unionist M.P.s also represented areas that expected to benefit from the legislation of 1894. Finally the House of Commons was emptying fast in August 1894, as Members headed for the grouse moors and elsewhere, many of them no doubt voting with their feet against eighteen months of almost uninterrupted legislative activity. Accordingly the Bill reached the House of Lords, where it received a grudging assent. Salisbury observed that it did but rough justice, but expressed the hope that its anomalies might force a reconsideration of the general problem of rates and rating throughout the entire country.[39] Shrewdly perhaps he calculated that, like the 1894 budget, the Equalisation of Rates Act would not redound to the Liberal Government's advantage in the long run.

CHAPTER 2 NOTES

1 75 of the 149 who voted for Labouchere's amendment were Irish M.P.s, and the rest were backbench Liberals.
2 Harcourt Mss.407, 7 April 1894.
3 *The Times* 23, 26 and 27 March 1894.
4 4 *Hansard* XXIV 884–901 (10 May 1894).
5 ibid.; Memo. Harcourt Mss.65.
6 Williams, W.M.J., 'A poor man's budget', *Fortnightly Review* March 1894. Memo. 12 January 1894, Harcourt Mss.122.
7 Harcourt Mss.399, 14 January 1894; Labouchere to Lewis Harcourt, 8 January and 8 February 1894, Harcourt Mss.426.
8 Memo. Harcourt Mss.65.
9 Harcourt Mss.398, 1 January 1894.
10 Harcourt Mss.406, 16, 24 and 25 March and 5 April 1894.

11 Harcourt Mss.401, 405 and 406, 16 February, 5 and 10 March, 6 April 1894.
12 Harcourt Mss.406 and 407, 29–31 March, 4 April.
13 Rhodes James, *op. cit.* p.372.
   Gardiner, A.G., *The Life of Sir William Harcourt*, II (1923) pp.283–87.
14 Memo. Harcourt Mss.65.
15 *Hansard* XII 469–509 (16 April 1894).
   Birmingham Daily Post 23 April 1894.
16 *Daily Chronicle* 17 April 1894.
   Daily News 23 April 1894.
17 4 *Hansard* XXVI 884–901 (10 May 1894)
18 Harcourt Mss.408 and 409, 23 May and 7 June 1894.
19 Harcourt Mss.409, 12 June 1894.
20 Harcourt Mss.408, 30 May 1894.
21 Harcourt Mss.408, 31 May 1894.
22 *Birmingham Daily Post* 23 April 1894.
23 *The Times* 3 and 24 May, 4 and 14 June 1894.
24 *The Times* 22 May and 28 June 1894.
25 *The Times* 4 May, 9 and 11 June 1894.
26 Harcourt Mss.408, 21 May 1894.
27 J. Stuart to Harcourt, 20 April 1894. Harcourt Mss.122.
   The Times, 4 and 7 May, 6 July, 30 August 1894.
28 Massingham, H.W., 'Why not dissolve?', *Contemporary Review* June 1894.
29 Harcourt Mss.408, 23 May 1894.
30 4 *Hansard* XXVII 1222–9 (30 July 1894).
31 *The Times* 2 August 1894.
32 Memo. 16 March 1894. Harcourt Mss.122.
33 Harcourt Mss.406, 29 March 1894.
34 4 *Hansard* XXIV 378–407 (4 May 1894).
35 4 *Hansard* XXVII 399–409 (19 July 1894).
36 4 *Hansard* XIII 865–77 (19 April 1894), XXVIII 424–35ff. (19 July 1894).
37 *The Times* 10 August 1894; 4 *Hansard* XXIII 1329ff. (25 April 1894).
38 4 *Hansard* XXVII 813ff. (24 July 1894).
39 4 *Hansard* XXVIII 1161–3 (16 August 1894).

Chapter Three: The 'Campaign' Against the House of Lords

The month of September 1894 opened a new phase in political activity. In a relatively short time this was to see a definitive decline in the fortunes of the Government. The focus was no longer on the struggle for fiscal reform which had dominated the debates of spring and summer. With the close of the Parliamentary session on 25 August, the Government had lost its chance of having a dissolution in the least unfavourable conditions. Political attention was now to be concentrated on plans for the forthcoming session due to begin in early 1895. It was evident that the mood of the country was becoming more conservative, for reasons both specific and diffuse. Partly this was in reaction to over a year and a half of almost continuous Parliamentary activity and legislative endeavour. In only one month, October 1893, had Parliament not been in session since February 1893. Partly also it marked a disappointment at the failure of the economy to recover sufficiently from the trough of depression in 1893. The spring of 1894 had seen a flurry of optimism in commercial circles, but expectations had not been realised. No economic revival had as yet occurred in the United States to encourage industrial prospects, and agricultural prices were more depressed than they had ever been. Unionist speakers had already begun to make a theme of the continuing economic recession, and to suggest that the Government was in some measure responsible for the widespread distress, for having devoted its energies to constitutional tinkerings rather than to practical schemes of economic and social improvement. Typical of this line of attack was Chamberlain's address to an audience of working men at Heywood in Lancashire in late November. As he put it:

we are suffering in this country, and you in Lancashire are suffering perhaps as much as anywhere else, from a depression in trade which has been more prolonged and more severe than any that we have known in recent times. I am not going to say that it is due to one cause more than another . . . But I will say this—that the Government have done nothing to relieve it; and I will say also that a period of unrest, whether in foreign affairs or home affairs, is fatal to that confidence without which you cannot have the promotion of great commercial enterprises or great commercial prosperity. Therefore, I believe, in the interests of the country at large, it is desirable that this period of unrest should come to an end.[1]

Unionists made much of what they saw as the increasingly radical and destructive tendencies of the Rosebery administration. Two cases in point in particular seemed to confirm their diagnosis. In early September 1894 a meeting of the Trades Union Congress passed a number of resolutions of a politically advanced nature calling among other things for the banning of free labour associations and a change in the method of empanelling jurymen. Attention was especially drawn to a resolution proposing "to nationalise the land and the whole of the means of production, distribution and exchange", which passed by 219 votes to 61.[2] A similar motion had been carried in the previous year, but not by nearly so large a majority. Of course none of this had anything to do with the Government directly; but the Unionists chose to treat the collectivist resolution as evidence of the turbulent forces at work in society which the present administration was more likely to defer to than to resist. The menace of socialism became a key theme of Unionist rhetoric at this time.[3] The other case in point was provided by the issue which was above all to dominate the autumn recess. This arose from Rosebery's attempt to work up the question of the House of Lords, the most misguided and mismanaged action of his premiership.

The Unionists had already sensed that the issue of the House of Lords might prove advantageous for them. During September Chamberlain, ever the most energetic of politicians, delivered major speeches at Liverpool and Leeds. Much of his material was familiar, and in line with speeches he had made earlier in the year. He attacked the Irish Nationalists as the main obstacle to British domestic legislation, and mentioned subjects of concern—old age pensions, hours of shopkeepers, restriction of alien immigration—in the field of social reform, which the Unionists could be expected to take up and pursue. He spoke of the bankruptcy of the Liberal programme, based as it was on the competing claims of various minority interest groups, who were united only in the design of "doing something disagreeable to somebody"; and he warned that the Government would try to cover its difficulties by getting up a plausible cause of quarrel with the House of Lords. One significant social reform had already in 1894 been sacrificed to the Liberals' need for a partisan cry against the upper chamber. The Employers' Liability Bill, which, in Chamberlain's view, the House of Lords had amended in order to widen its scope, had for that very reason been discarded the previous February.[4]

The Liberals were by the autumn of 1894 under accumulated pressures to make some kind of move against the House of Lords. The early months of the year had been marked by talk of conflict with the upper chamber. Gladstone had made it the theme of his valedictory speech as Prime

Minister, and early in Rosebery's premiership Liberal backbenchers had defeated their own Government on an amendment to the Address which called for the abolition of the House of Lords' veto. Rosebery had felt the need to make some response. In his first major speech outside Parliament as Prime Minister, at Edinburgh in March 1894, he had told his audience that the problem of the House of Lords could "only be dealt with with the backing, and on the summons, and on the inspiration of a great popular feeling", and he had added, "we await your guidance and your direction". Unionists accused him of not knowing his own mind and of making a feeble attempt to stir up revolution. In June 1894 a conference of the National Liberal Federation at Leeds gave Rosebery a kind of answer when it voted to take away the power of the House of Lords to veto any measure which the House of Commons should pass twice in a single session.[5]

The Liberals' problem lay in how to come to grips with the powers of the House of Lords. No change in the constitution was possible without legislation, and the Lords were hardly likely to pass any bill that proposed to curtail their authority. In any case the timing was wrong for any campaign against the upper chamber. The House of Lords had done nothing to make itself unpopular during the 1894 session. The only piece of legislation it had rejected had been the Irish Evicted Tenants Bill, and this was certainly not a measure about which British public opinion felt strongly. A demonstration against the House of Lords in Hyde Park in late August 1894 drew only 1,500 people, far fewer than had turned out earlier in the year to protest against the mutilation of the Employers' Liability Bill. In his first main speech on the subject, Rosebery rather forlornly argued that it was better to tackle the question of the House of Lords at a time when popular passions were not aroused. Balfour compared him to a dentist who proposed to remove a man's teeth because they were healthy.[6]

The Liberals were in a serious predicament with regard to the House of Lords. They could neither ignore the issue, nor apparently could they do anything very effective about it. Their best strategy was to keep up a sense of resentment against the institution, without showing their hands too clearly as to how they proposed to alter the country's constitutional arrangements. Obviously the House of Lords, as a non-elected body, was always liable to be overawed by a striking display of popular feeling. Asquith was a particularly adept exponent of this strategy. His speeches of the autumn of 1894 consolidated his reputation as the Government's ablest apologist, and gave him an authority in constitutional matters that was to remain with him through the critical years of his own premiership.[7]

Rosebery could not be content with this 'wait and see' attitude. He was under considerable pressure to assert himself by late 1894, and to make his own distinct contribution to the debate. His public speeches earlier in the year had not been a success, and, while the budget was before Parliament, he had seemed almost to surrender the leadership of the Liberal Party to Harcourt. The issue of the House of Lords offered him the chance once again to grasp the initiative, and to exercise the lead that was his by right. It was after all a subject which he could claim to know something about. He had spent the whole of his adult political life in the House of Lords, and he had on a couple of occasion there initiated debates on resolutions calling for its reform.[8] Rosebery was however the wrong man to lead an agitation in late 1894. As subsequent events were to show, he was out of sympathy with the bulk of his party as to the need for an effective second chamber. He was not an expert on constitutional questions, and he was unable or unwilling to take advice from his leading colleagues in the Commons.

It would have made much better sense for Rosebery to have campaigned instead on a policy of social reform. Somewhat unjustifiably, he was regarded as an expert on social questions, and this had been one contributing factor in his rise to the premiership. So far Rosebery's only really effective speech as Prime Minister had been on social policy. At St James's Hall, London, in late March 1894, he had defended in considerable detail the Liberal Government's record in industrial and economic matters. Limitation of hours, he claimed, had been brought about on the railways and in several government departments; parish councils would bring about land reform, and, hopefully, a remedy for unemployment; employers' liability, equalisation of rates, and taxation of ground values were future boons to be looked for.[9] In fact Rosebery, in his Whiggish way, was less interested in social policy than was supposed. Still, thanks to his service on the London County Council, he was at least as conversant with it as he was with the constitutional problems surrounding the House of Lords. Also, practical measures, in the economic and social sphere, were what public opinion in late 1894 was generally supposed to desire, as opposed to further constitutional wranglings over Home Rule or the House of Lords. Had Rosebery made social policy his platform, he might have been able to exploit emergent differences and divisions in the Unionist camp. Chamberlain had responded to what he believed to be the developing national mood by elaborating a new 'unauthorised programme'. At Birmingham in mid-October he had called for legislation in support of old age pensions, temperance, employers' liability, industrial arbitration, and the restriction of alien immigration. The only proposal which he outlined in any detail was one, based on the analogy of the Irish Land Purchase Acts, that the state should lend money to the urban artisan to enable him to buy his own home.[10] Chamberlain's programme drew not very favourable comment in the Conservative press. In private Salisbury deprecated it as a premature move that might confuse the electorate. It was soon evident that Chamberlain's initiative had caused embarassment and disarray in the Unionist camp; but amongst leading Ministers only Asquith was enterprising enough to point out the obvious moral, that only the Liberals could be regarded as the credible party of social reform.[11]

For Rosebery the issue of the House of Lords was to remain his chosen *champ de bataille*. In his much-heralded speech at Bradford in late October 1894, he unveiled what purported to be his master plan for dealing with the constitutional controversy. He began by describing himself as "a second chamber man in principle", but went on to define the existing state of affairs as an invitation to revolution. It was, he declared, "the greatest issue that has been put in this country since your fathers resisted the tyranny of Charles I and James II". Liberals must be prepared for a tough struggle in the manner of Cromwell's Ironsides. Their principal object must be to get the country clearly on their side, and they could best obtain their mandate by first bringing the House of Commons into play. Rosebery proposed to introduce a resolution asserting the legislative supremacy of the House of Commons, rather on the lines, so he supposed, of previous resolutions, such as that of 1678, which had claimed special privileges for the lower House in respect of finance or of disputed election returns. As he explained his *modus operandi*:

It will be the duty of the Government to move the House of Commons to pass such a resolution, and, if they do pass it, remember that never before in the history of Parliament has such a resolution, at the instance and on the responsibility of the Government, been passed in the House of Commons against the House of Lords. What will it represent? The joint demand of the executive Government of the day and of the House of Commons for the revision of the Constitution, and in that way the question will enter in itself on a new phase. That resolution will stand for ever upon the journals of the House. No Government, however bold, however cynical, that may eventually succeed ours, will be bold enough or cynical enough to propose its reversal. Not all the perfumes of Araby itself will wash that resolution out of the books of the House.[12]

Rosebery did not specify the terms of his proposed resolution. The Bradford speech supplied an instructive sample of his political style and of its attendant weaknesses. Rosebery's secretiveness, isolation, and lack of self-confidence had precluded him from seeking the advice of his cabinet colleagues before launching his initiative on the House of Lords. Lacking experience of the House of Commons, he was not well-placed to suggest new methods of Parliamentary procedure. He made too much of the precedents of 1678 and 1860, which had not in themselves settled anything. Like so many of his speeches that at Bradford lacked substance. As always he relied too much on elegant phrases, veiled allusions, and a general air of mystery. Lewis Harcourt thought the ideas contained in the Bradford address "thin and meaningless". "I don't", he declared, "see how we are to get the issue joined over a resolution of which the Lords may or may not take notice. It would have been a different matter if we had passed a declaratory Bill which they would have had to accept or reject."[13]

Only after the Bradford speech did the Cabinet have the chance to discuss the policy it contained. It soon became clear how little Rosebery had thought through the implications of what he had proposed. He had no form of words to hand in which his resolution might be expressed. Nor had he considered the fact that any debate in the House of Commons on the powers of the House of Lords would open up also the question of its composition and of its very existence. At Bradford Rosebery had declared himself to be a two chamber man in point of principle, and he was surprised to find out subsequently how many of his colleagues took the view that a single chamber legislature would be preferable. Also Rosebery had paid no heed to the problems of the Parliamentary timetable. He seemed to think that his proposed resolution could be postponed to as late a period of the session as possible, whereas Harcourt considered that it would be impossible to proceed with other business whilst this great matter was waiting in the wings, and that the Opposition would be able to force the Government to bring it on earlier and then dissolve. Finally Rosebery had promised the Queen that no resolution would be introduced without her consent, although it was not clear whether this was constitutionally necessary.[14]

Rosebery's proposals presented the Unionists with an inviting target. They made the most of his hints that a movement of popular feeling, almost revolutionary in scope, might be required in order to alter the constitution. They warned of the dangers of entrusting the management of the empire to a single chamber, in which the balance of power might well be held by the representatives of "the south and west of Ireland...men animated by a patriotism which they, at all events, believe in, but which is not our patriotism". Unionist speakers once again accused the Government of diverting the country's attention from more useful and practical concerns. The men in power, declared Balfour, "have inevitably deferred the boon of social legislation and social reform". "Every workman who has received uncompensated injuries . . . has been sacrificed to the desire of the Government to accumulate a case against the House of Lords". The Newcastle programme had proved a failure, and it was found necessary now "to provide party wire-pullers with a cry".[15] Unionists drew attention to the vagueness and unreality of the Prime Minister's proposals.

At Glasgow in mid-November, Rosebery attempted to give further definition to his ideas on the House of Lords, and succeeded only in making his problems worse. Unwisely he acknowledged the existence of divisions in his Government. As to its future legislative programme, he indicated his preference for dealing with temperance on the lines of the local option proposals associated with a Liberal backbencher, McLagan. At the time this was interpreted as a reflection on Harcourt, who was still identified with the alternative method of local veto. As to the House of Lords, Rosebery admitted that "many of the most eminent members of the Liberal party, and many who are not eminent, are in favour of a single Chamber". His own predilection was for a bicameral legislature, and he went on to argue the case for this in a lengthy passage which reviewed the constitutional arrangements of most of the world's representative assemblies. Finally Rosebery put forward his own latest solution for averting future conflict between the House of Lords and the House of Commons. There should, in his view, be a joint conference of both branches of the legislature in the event of any serious dispute, which would meet to resolve the differences between them.[16]

At the next Cabinet, a few days later, the Prime Minister was severely taken to task for committing his Government to his scheme for a Parliamentary conference in which Unionist commoners and peers together would enjoy a permanent majority. For almost the first time Ministers gave their attention to the possible terms of Rosebery's proposed House of Commons resolution. It soon became clear that the majority of them leaned to a single omnicompetent chamber in theory, and in practice to Bright's old proposal of a limitation to one year of the House of Lords' power of rejection. Herschell, the Lord Chancellor, was detailed to try his hand at drafting a resolution on these lines.[17] In the meantime Asquith was due to speak at Birmingham, where he would be under pressure to provide some indication of the Government's latest thinking. This task he discharged with his usual adroitness, skating, it was said, over very thin ice. Believing in attack as the best form of defence, Asquith made the most of hints contained in recent speeches by Chamberlain and Salisbury that a reform of the House of Lords, as opposed to the sort of emasculation envisaged by most Liberals, was desirable as a means of making it at the same time stronger and more representative. "You can see already", he declared, "that a new second chamber is on the stocks . . . All this ancient structure, in support of which so much rhetorical ink is being spilt—this ancient structure, with its Norman porch, and Plantagenet and Tudor buttresses,—is going to pass into the hands of the speculative builder". As for the existing House of Lords, it was a grotesque parody of a second chamber. Its part-time legislators had hurried back from their grouse moors to vote down Home Rule in September 1893, but six years earlier they had endorsed, in the Coercion Act of 1887, "perhaps the most serious and the most formidable inroad upon our ancient constitutional principles which had ever been made". Finally Asquith hit on a formula which, in default of the promised

Parliamentary resolution, supplied a degree of coherence to ministerial thinking. As he defined it,

> The question which is going to be submitted first of all to the House of Commons, and then to the judgement of the electors of the country, is this—Whether or not, where the two Chambers differ—the representative and the non-representative Chambers—the presumption is not, and ought not to be acknowledged to be, on the side of those who are elected by and responsible to the people; and whether, subject at any rate and at the outset to reasonable precautions for consultation and reconsideration, the predominance of the popular House, which is the national and legitimate organ of the national will, ought not to be asserted for all time to come.

At the same time Asquith's Birmingham speech revealed further pitfalls and opened up fresh causes of controversy. Asquith acknowledged the existence of differences within the Liberal party as to the future of the House of Lords; and in stating his own considered preference for a single chamber he seemed to speak of his Prime Minister in less than respectful terms. Furthermore he qualified his support for the unicameral principle with a proviso:

> I think it is a mistake to assume that all those who are in favour of a single chamber are necessarily in favour of that chamber possessing an unchecked power, without referring to the people, by a casual majority, to pass into law measures which may be contrary to the settled determination of the nation. There are means, there are safeguards, there are precautions which might well be taken, even if there were only one chamber, to prevent the possibility of such a contingency as that.[18]

This raised further questions about ministerial intentions. What "safeguards" might they have in mind? Were they considering referenda; or shorter Parliaments? Arnold Morley had referred to the possibility of the latter at a speech at Nottingham.[19] Rosebery however had talked facetiously about annual Parliaments when he visited Glasgow. Finally Asquith, in discussing the Government's general legislative programme, used a phrase that was to rebound against him in the months ahead. Attempting to pass legislation, like Welsh disestablishment, in the face of the opposition of the House of Lords, would, he said, be like trying to "plough the sands of the seashore". This amounted almost to a confession that the Government was no longer in control of its destiny and was proposing to waste the time of Parliament in the forthcoming session. The phrase 'ploughing the sands' was to do yeoman service in Unionist speeches in the period up to and including the 1895 general election.

By the end of November 1894 the Cabinet had achieved a degree of coherence in its policy. This involved Rosebery's virtual submission to his colleagues' point of view. At a meeting on 21 November, he had suggested a resolution in which the House of Commons was to declare that it would not have its decisions revised by an hereditary and unrepresentative second chamber. Harcourt objected, as he said that this would leave the door open to revision by a reformed, non-hereditary or representative upper chamber—the very design which Salisbury and Chamberlain were supposed to have in mind. At the next Cabinet meeting, on 26 November 1894, Rosebery appeared finally to acquiesce in the solution favoured by the majority of his colleagues. This was the "Bright scheme", or what Harcourt called the "one bite plan", whereby it was proposed to limit the House of Lords' power of rejection to one year, and of amendment to one submission to the House of Commons.[20] Unreformed the House of Lords would remain, as a non-representative, enfeebled, and essentially superfluous element in the constitution. Rosebery followed this line at Devonport in mid-December, in the most spirited of his three campaign speeches of late 1894. Most of his speech was taken up with a defence of the Government's administrative and legislative record, with an emphasis on parish councils and the reduction of the hours of work in government departments. As to the House of Lords, he indicated that he was now thinking in terms solely of the removal of its absolute veto. "I say confidently enough", he declared somewhat disingenuously,

> that no such act of insanity as our proposing reform of the House of Lords has ever occurred to us...Though I say you will not expect me tonight to state precisely what our plan of operations may be, I will tell you this much, and it will be sufficient for your purpose. We are determined, if the power be given us by the country, so to limit and circumscribe the powers of mischief and mutilation possessed by the House of Lords that we shall have little or nothing to dread from that power in the future.[21]

By this stage, however, much of the potential momentum in the campaign against the House of Lords had been lost; and the whole question was beginning to take its toll on the Government. Unionists fastened on the disunion and uncertainty which had been revealed in the Liberal ranks. Were Ministers, it was asked, 'enders', 'menders', or even 'benders' of the House of Lords? Attention was drawn to the contradictory pronouncements of various members of the Government as to the kind of legislature they envisaged. Rosebery, initially at least, had expressed himself in favour of two effective chambers; those of his colleagues who had spoken had for the most part sounded like single chamber partisans; Asquith however had qualified his own adherence to the single chamber principle; Bryce's new-found unicameralism contradicted his previous academic writings on the constitution; Harcourt had remained conspicuous by his silence throughout. This confusion of tongues was grist to the mill of Unionist propaganda. Balfour, in an address at Nottingham, spoke of a "spectacle discreditable . . . to English statesmanship, of a Cabinet which has started a revolution on a course on which it is not agreed itself, which it cannot control, which it cannot manage, which it scarely even desires either to control or to manage".[22]

Within the ranks of the political establishment, probably only the Queen took the threat of constitutional revolution very seriously. She was greatly exercised by the Bradford speech, and wrote to Rosebery to protest at what she regarded as his provocative use of language, and in particular his references to revolution and Cromwell's Ironsides. Rosebery defended himself in his reply: he had deliberately spoken out at a time of quiet rather than of popular excitement; he expressed himself in favour of a second chamber; before "a tumultuous audience of 5,000 people" it was necessary to use "broad popular language" and impossible to argue points "in the style appropriate to a drawing-room or a library"; in any case *The Times* had described his speech as feeble. Unconvinced the Queen sounded out Unionist leaders as to the desirability of an early dissolution of Parliament, which she would take it upon herself to bring about. Salisbury considered the idea: some in his party, he admitted, thought that a general election "would be better for them now than later, when a lengthened agitation against the House of Lords has banished the Irish question from men's minds". But both he and his leading colleagues enjoined caution, especially once it became clear that Rosebery's campaign was not going to rouse the country. A premature dissolution, argued Sir Henry James, would divert popular attention to "considerations affecting the treatment of the Ministry". Ten days after Rosebery's Bradford speech, Salisbury's view of the agitation against the House of Lords was that "at present opinion is so sluggish on the whole question that people would be startled by the direct intervention of the Crown; and a force and significance might be given to the movement which, as far as we can judge, it is very far from possessing now".[23]

The question of the House of Lords was in fact to play a significant part in the downfall of the last Liberal ministry of the century. It is possible to locate almost the precise moment at which public opinion turned decisively against the Rosebery Government. In the early autumn of 1894 the omens still seemed relatively favourable. A bye-election in mid-October at Birkenhead, at which perhaps significantly the Liberal candidate had virtually discarded Home Rule from his programme, saw the Unionist majority reduced from 604 to 106. Hardly more than a month later the picture appeared very different. In late November, at Forfar, the Rosebery Government suffered its first actual bye-election loss, when a Liberal majority of 866 was turned into a Unionist majority of 288. Three weeks later, at Brigg, the Liberals lost a second seat, their majority of 427 giving way to a Unionist majority of 77.

Several factors help to explain the Liberal reverses of late 1894. The victors at Forfar and Brigg, and indeed the Liberal candidate who did so well at Birkenhead, were all local men, while their opponents had more than a hint of the carpet-bagger about them. Home Rule remained an issue, particularly at Brigg, where the anti-Catholic prejudices of Lincolnshire nonconformists were played on by what one Liberal M.P. referred to as "hoards of paid canvassers from Ireland". However, of much greater importance, in such essentially rural constituencies as Forfar and Brigg, was the failure of the Liberal programme for the countryside. The Liberal Government had come to power in 1892 partly on the strength of its promises to provide a new deal for the agricultural labourer. It had passed a much-vaunted piece of legislation establishing parish councils; and Rosebery still felt able to speak at Devonport of "the new upheaval and awakening into life that this Bill by one magic touch has called into being right through the rural districts of England and Wales". Circumstances in late 1894 made a mockery of these claims. The countryside remained sunk in prolonged agricultural depression. Labourers' wages, which usually declined as the winter months approached, were under further pressure from the fall in agricultural prices which had continued during 1894. The first elections to the new councils, which took place in late 1894, revealed the limitations of the legislation all too well. Parish councils had received insufficient powers, particularly as far as spending money was concerned, and village politics often continued to be dominated by the squire. Clearly the rural millennium was not yet at hand.

The Unionists considered that the mishandling of Rosebery's campaign against the House of Lords had also helped to swing the country against the Liberals. Sir Henry James, who had remained on good terms with the Harcourts despite the split of 1886, informed them in late December of his own side's latest electoral calculations. According to James, the Unionists, who had counted on an overall majority of no more than 20 or 25 three months earlier, were now, folllowing reports from the borough constituencies, confident of obtaining one of 70 or 80. "He says", wrote Lewis Harcourt, "that the budget was very popular and the Government distinctly stronger, but that since R. began his speaking tour our organisation has gone to pieces all over the country—partly from disgust at R.'s shilly-shally attitude." Nowhere was the erosion of Rosebery's position more marked than in Scotland, where large-scale Unionist gains were predicted. James also stressed how far moderate opinion had been antagonised by the agitation against the House of Lords, mixed up as it was in many men's minds with the socialistic implications of the T.U.C.'s Norwich programme.[24]

So far from building up a head of steam against the upper chamber, the Government had witnessed a sharp decline in its own electoral popularity. The premise on which Ministers' arguments had been based, that the lower chamber was the legitimate organ of the national will, no longer appeared to have much validity, at least as far as the existing House of Commons was concerned. There was a number of reasons for this apart from those mentioned above. The House of Lords, as has been seen, had done little to make itself unpopular since the Liberals had returned to power in 1892. The rejection of Home Rule and the Evicted Tenants Bill cut little ice with the majority of British voters; and it is significant that Liberal orators, when trying to work up indignation against the House of Lords in late 1894, were obliged to go back to 1884 and even to 1831.[25] The House of Commons, on the other hand, was not in the best possible odour at this time. It was criticised, both for the obstruction and time-wasting which had characterised its proceedings for some years past, and for the machinery which it had developed to deal with these problems; the 'guillotine', it was claimed, would enable dangerously radical proposals such as those contained in the Norwich programme to be forced by a tiny majority through the House of Commons. Also there was more than a usual whiff of corruption in the air. One or two M.P.s, notably the elusive Jabez Balfour, were still under investigation as a result of the company failures which had followed on from the Baring crisis of 1890; while the affair of the Tweedmouth cheques, in which Irish M.P.s were supposed to have been bribed by the Liberal Chief Whip to continue in attendance at Westminster, supplied a topic of political gossip through the winter of 1894–95. All in all, it was not a good moment for the House of Commons to put forward claims to be the sole, legislative body. Added to this, public opinion generally was apathetic, and exhausted by the prolonged Parliamentary activity and legislative wranglings of the previous two years. Radicals, who might have been inspired by a straightforward attack on the pretensions of the House of Lords, were dismayed and confused by Rosebery's *obiter dicta* about the desirability of a second chamber; and some of them feared that an untimely general election, held ostensibly on the issue of the House of Lords, might, if it resulted in a Unionist victory, succeed only in reinforcing the position of the upper chamber.[26]

"The battle with the House of Lords", wrote Lewis Harcourt, "has been declared at the wrong time and in the wrong way; the party is thoroughly demoralised and disheartened and disorganised."[27] It is difficult to dispute this verdict. Rosebery had done the Liberal party a grave disservice by the manner in which he had raised the whole question. He had failed to consult his Cabinet colleagues adequately, and to agree on a plan of campaign; though it is fair to say that most Ministers were not much clearer in their own minds as to the best course to pursue. (Harcourt refused to address any public meetings during the autumn because, as he said, he did not know what to say.)[28] In his Bradford and Glasgow speeches, Rosebery failed to provide an effective lead, and he made suggestions about policy that proved embarrassing to his colleagues. Labouchere, hardly an objective critic, nonetheless had a point when he referred to Rosebery's "Jekyll and Hyde mode of speaking", and his apparent belief that he could express opinions publicly as a private person and not as Prime Minister.[29] By tentatively airing solutions of his own, Rosebery exposed the divisions and uncertainty in ministerial ranks far more than the rest of the variegated Newcastle programme had done. The Liberals had not been clear in their own minds before 1893 about the nature of the second Home Rule bill, but they had not revealed their doubts in public, and in consequence they had returned to power in 1892. Rosebery should have confined himself in late 1894, as his leading colleagues like Asquith and Campbell-Bannerman concentrated on doing in their autumn speeches, to denunciations of the House of Lords as a one-party institution and as a source of constitutional instability and danger.[30] Once he started speculating what could be done about it, Rosebery soon revealed the poverty of ministerial thinking.

Rosebery limited his Government's credibility and freedom of man-oeuvre also in other ways. By promising to introduce a resolution in the House of Commons before the next dissolution of Parliament, he denied himself the option of calling an early general election. By making so much of the obstructive role of the Houe of Lords, he seemed to infer that no worthwhile legislation would be passed so long as the present Liberal Government remained in office. (Though it is fair to say that Asquith also made this admission, in a fatal phrase.) By at first stating his own predilection in favour of an effective second chamber, Rosebery denied his fellow Liberals the opportunity of taking advantage of Salisbury's avowedly patrician sentiments on the subject. Salisbury's arrogance and candour had at times done good service for Liberalism in the past; his remarks about tariffs, and comparing parish councils to circuses, had helped to lose his party votes in the 1892 general election. But it was difficult to take Salisbury to task for the views contained in his Edinburgh speech of October 1894, in which he had hinted at the need for a reformed and strengthened upper chamber, when the Liberal Prime Minister seemed to have much the same opinions. Asquith, who tried to do so in his speech at Birmingham three weeks later, incurred thereby the suspicion of disloyalty to his chief. Finally, by abandoning his second chamber views in his Devonport speech in mid-December, Rosebery seemed to show that he was a man of straw, incapable of standing up to the extremists in his party like Labouchere. Something similar, it was recalled, had happened earlier in his premiership, when he had been forced to explain away his 'predominant partner' remarks in a subsequent speech at Edinburgh. By the end of 1894, moderate opinion was rapidly becoming disillusioned with Rosebery. The lordly Whig seemed to have become clay in the hands of the Radicals; and the constitution could no longer be considered safe in his hands.

By the beginning of 1895, the Government had clearly lost its way. It had run out of ideas as to what to do about the House of Lords. Ministers no longer desired to speak on the subject in the country. Rosebery belatedly suggested the appointment of a Cabinet committee to consider the question; but Harcourt objected, saying that it would only find new areas of disagreement, and that the time to have done this had been before the Bradford speech. In his public pronouncements, Rosebery was now much more guarded in his references to the House of Lords. Addressing the National Liberal Federation at Cardiff in mid-January, in what was to prove the last of his speeches as Prime Minister in a major provincial centre, he argued that the successful carrying of his promised Parliamentary Resolution would entail an immediate general election, and that it was necessary to put a business programme through the House of Commons first. Most of his speech he devoted to the question of Welsh disestablishment. "You may ask", he declared, "how we can hope to pass all these measures before the dissolution of Parliament. Well, the fate of the Government is in your hands. It is for you to give us the propelling power which will enable the Liberal Government to pass the Liberal measures".[31] Of course it was true that the House of Lords had rarely risked confrontation with the House of Commons over proposals that had clear popular support. Circumstances however were somewhat different in 1895 from those of 1861 or 1869. The Parliament elected in 1892 seemed unlikely to survive much longer; and the Liberals could only hope that they would be able to put one or two vote-winning measures through Parliament which the House of Lords would have second thoughts about rejecting in what promised to be an election year. In private, Rosebery was hardly confident of success; and he was said to be ready to "chuck up the sponge" after another bye-election setback, at Evesham in mid-January. Evesham was in fact a Unionist seat; but the Liberals had been successful in reducing the majorities against them in the two bye-elections held in Unionist seats since Rosebery had become Prime Minister; and they had hopes of making progress in this mainly rural constituency after the death of the popular local member. But Evesham was within Chamberlain's sphere of influence; the needleworkers of the constituency were said to be attracted by his Birmingham programme, whilst the market-gardeners were said to feel let down by the Liberal Government's failure to give them security of tenure. In the event, the Unionist candidate doubled his majority, which increased from 580 votes to 1,175; and, after Forfar and Brigg, the Liberals were made to feel even more that the national tide had turned against them.[32]

In so far as the Government had a policy as regards the House of Lords when Parliament reconvened at the beginning of February, it was to seek to postpone the issue as long as possible. Asquith, who, almost alone of Ministers, was apparently still willing to discuss the matter on the public platform, indicated in a speech at Hull in late January that a long-term evolutionary transformation was to be looked for. As he pointed out, much had already changed since 1783, when the House of Lords had last brought about a change of government.[33] A clue to Rosebery's latest thinking was provided by an article, written by his protégé, Fletcher Moulton, the M.P. for South Hackney, which appeared in the February number of the *Contemporary Review*. According to this article, the contents of which attracted considerable press comment at the end of January, it would be unwise to hold an early general election on the issue of the House of Lords. The debacle of 1886 served as a warning of the dangers of rushing the electorate. A premature dissolution would mix up the question of the House of Lords in the voters' minds with the socialistic implications of the Norwich programme, and it might lead to the return of a Conservative government pledged to entrench even further the powers of the upper chamber. The hand of Rosebery seemed especially evident in certain of the article's arguments. Abolition of the House of Lords' veto, it was said, would be more radical than abolition of the House of Lords altogether. The whole issue could be postponed until it could usefully be settled within the context of a general scheme of devolution to the constituent parts of the United Kingdom, or what was known to many Liberals as Home Rule All Round.[34]

Accordingly, no mention was made in the Queen's Speech of February 1895 about any move against the House of Lords, and the Government exerted itself to prevent discussion of the subject during the remaining months of its life. One reason for the Cabinet's decision to resign in June 1895, rather than to struggle on or to dissolve Parliament, was to avoid having to present a definite policy on the House of Lords either in the House of Commons or in the country. However the issue could not be escaped altogether. It overshadowed the fortunes of the Rosebery administration during the rest of its short lease on life, and in mid-February it contributed to a Cabinet crisis that came close to breaking up the Government prematurely.

Rosebery had taken very much to heart the failure of his autumn initiative on the House of Lords. He had set out to remedy the impression, created by his speeches in the previous spring, that he was a weak Prime Minister, with no clear ideas of his own, and very much at the mercy of the radical elements in his party. Instead, his autumn speeches had served merely to reinforce this impression. Rosebery was aware that he had further damaged his authority with the country, the Liberal party, and the Cabinet. His Glasgow speech had been rewarded a few days later by his Government's first loss of a seat at a bye-election, and this in nearby Forfar, in his own native Scotland. In early 1895, Rosebery did not even feel confident enough to face a party meeting on the eve of the reassembly of Parliament. Worst of all perhaps, even those men, like Asquith and Acland, whom he had regarded as his allies in the Cabinet, began to distance themselves from him. Rosebery's sense of isolation was partly a matter of personality. As Hamilton pointed out, he could not unbend sufficiently, and often gave an impression of aloofness to his colleagues. But in early 1895 this was compounded by bitter political disappointment, and by continuing frustration at his imprisonment in the "gilded dungeon" of the House of Lords, where he felt more keenly than ever his inability to influence events in the political world at large.

Matters came to a head after a debate in the House of Commons on 15 and 18 February 1895 on a motion of Joseph Chamberlain, which called for the judgement of Parliament to be taken on the recently proposed "grave constitutional changes" rather than on measures which had no chance of passing into law. This was the third of three practical votes of censure, moved by the Opposition in the form of amendments to the Queen's Speech, which will be described in greater detail below. It represented an attempt to make capital out of the Government's reluctance to press home its attack on the House of Lords, and its recourse to the barren and undignified expedient of 'ploughing the sands'. For the Government Asquith, Campbell-Bannerman and Harcourt spoke in the debate, and not without considerable effect. But they had to listen to a recapitulation of the whole bungled, and by now tacitly abandoned, campaign against the House of Lords. Wounding criticism came not only from the Unionists, but also from the two Liberal mavericks, Labouchere and Dilke. Labouchere considered that a dissolution of Parliament would be preferable to the present humiliating position. Dilke, in a powerfully-argued speech, contended that the Government was forfeiting the support of the "advanced Radical element in the constituencies". "What had deadened the agitation", he declared, "what had taken the whole life out of the movement against the House of Lords, was the great discrepancies and variations of language on the part of the Government and the doubt as to whether they were in earnest". And he concluded with the warning that "the Government were going forward to disaster under the command of those whose ambiguous language he had described, and if Radicals were to prepare themselves for this battle, "the Prime Minister's trumpet would have to give forth a much more certain sound".[35]

Although his Government survived this particular vote of censure by a majority of 14, Rosebery took these strictures as a reflection on his leadership. He was angry also that, amongst Ministers, only Campbell-Bannerman had associated himself with his Prime Minister in the debate. At a Cabinet meeting on 19 February, Rosebery read out a four page memorandum complaining that he had been insufficiently supported in the House of Commons and intimating his intention to resign. Ministers reacted with dismay and, in private, a good deal of anger. After all, as a consequence of Rosebery's ill-considered venture against the House of Lords, they had found themselves having to defend an essentially meaningless policy in the House of Commons. In Cabinet, Harcourt endeavoured to be conciliatory, arguing that the Front Bench had been wise to ignore Dilke's recriminations. Spencer warned that Rosebery risked finding himself in the same position as Casimir-Périer, the French President who had recently resigned because he had been abused by the Socialists and insufficiently supported by his Ministers in the Chamber of Deputies: people would only say that he had deserted his post in the hour of danger. This last argument seemed to make some impression on Rosebery.[36]

It is not clear how far Rosebery was in earnest. The Harcourts took him seriously enough to consider at least the possibility of a Harcourt premiership. They were no longer very enthusiastic at the prospect, being all too well aware of the difficulties of the present position. Harcourt thought of making Fowler Chancellor of the Exchequer, and of replacing him at the India Office by one of the younger men, Grey or Buxton. The problem was that none of their seats could be considered safe, and would be at risk in the ensuing bye-elections. Also other prominent figures in the party, like Labouchere, could be expected to claim promotion. Lewis Harcourt preferred Rosebery to stay on and take responsibility for the expected electoral smash. Failing that he thought his father might become Prime Minister and retain the Chancellorship of the Exchequer. Otherwise he favoured the return of Glastone to the premiership as the move most likely to strike the imagination of the electorate and to secure a majority against the House of Lords. Asquith, at all events, was insistent that the Liberal Government should continue in some form. To resign would be to hand over the initiative and the power of dissolution to the Unionists at the most critical juncture; besides Ministers could hardly admit that they could dispense with Gladstone's services in 1894 but not with Rosebery's in 1895.[37]

It is intriguing to consider what might have been the implications of a change of Prime Minister in February 1895. Probably, without the incubus of Rosebery's preoccupation with the House of Lords, the Cabinet might not have given up so readily in June 1895. The Government itself might have survived the session and lasted into 1896. It is unlikely that it could have avoided a major discomfiture at the polls. But, with the gradual return of prosperity in late 1895, the margin of defeat might not have been so great; and this in turn might have affected the balance of power as between Conservatives and Liberal Unionists in the succeeding Coalition Government.

All this is speculation; the contingency was not realised. "Rosebery", wrote Lewis Harcourt on 20 February, "is behaving like a spoilt child and needs slapping. He will probably have a sleepless night and if he does not commit suicide (which I think possible) I believe he will take back tomorrow all he said today". At the Cabinet on 21 February, Rosebery did indeed take back his intention to resign. The day before, he and Harcourt had met to thrash out their differences. The accounts by the two men naturally diverge. Rosebery accused Harcourt of not keeping him properly informed, and in particular of misleading him as to his intention to resign the previous summer. Harcourt, as usual when the fate of the Government hung in the balance, went out of his way to be conciliatory; but he in turn complained of Rosebery's failure to communicate with his colleagues. Nothing was settled; but the discussion seemed to clear the air somewhat between the two men, and they became less obsessed with each other for the remainder of the Government's existence.[38]

The whole episode did nothing to enhance Rosebery's authority over the Cabinet. Once again he had taken a certain position, and then backed away from it. He had behaved in much the same way about his first Cabinet office, and over his appointment as Foreign Secretary in 1892. During the final months of his premiership Rosebery continued to exercise some sway over foreign affairs, but his influence on domestic policy was virtually gone. His political effectiveness was further diminished by a breakdown in health which commenced in late February 1895, the chief characteristic of which was insomnia. Partly this was a product of the influenza that was rife in the winter of 1894–95, partly also, it seems likely, of a nervous relapse which was itself a consequence of the agitated Cabinet proceedings of mid-February. Rosebery remained out of action for most of March; and in a further effort to repair his health he went on two yachting excursions, totalling three weeks in all, during May and June. He hardly spoke in the country during his last months as Prime Minister. When he did so, to the National Liberal Club in early May, he caused great embarrassment by losing the thread of his speech and having to sit down in the middle of it.

Reginald Brett, who was almost unique in being on good terms with both Rosebery and Lewis Harcourt, has bequeathed a perceptive and affecting portrait of Rosebery in this tragic phase of his career:

His rapid and early growth into manhood, with the aloofness entailed by it, and that necessary element of what is called 'pose' in everyone who is a man at that age when others are boys, fitted him for oligarchic rule, but not to be Chief of a Democracy. He is curiously inexperienced in the subtler forms of happiness which come from giving more than one gets. He has been satiated with the sweets of life; and the long process has left him longing for affection, uiniversal approval, omnipotent authority . . . I tell him that he dried up the fount by becoming a man too soon. Pascal said that the happiest life – the life he would choose – begins with love and ends with ambition.

R. has reversed the order. He has – while in the prime of life – everything that men toil for; wealth, power, position, everything. Yet he is a lonely sleepless man . . . I suppose the Prime Minister cannot in these days have a mistress. Certainly he requires an intimate friend.[39]

CHAPTER 3 NOTES

1   *The Times* 23 Nov. 1894.
2   *The Times* 7 Sept. 1894.
3   As in Devonshire's speech at Barnstaple, *The Times* 27 Nov. 1894.
4   *The Times* 6, 7 & 26 Sept. 1894.
5   *The Times* 21 June 1894.
6   Speech at Newcastle, *The Times* 14 Nov. 1894.
7   For instance at Leven, *The Times* 23 Oct. 1894.
8   3 *Hansard* CCLXXXIX 937–58 (20 June 1884), CCCXXIII 1548–76 (19 Mar. 1888).
9   *The Times* 22 Mar. 1894.
10   *The Times* 12 Oct. 1894.
11   Garvin, J.L., & Amery, J., *The life of Joseph Chamberlain* (1935) II pp. 616–17; Marsh, P., *The Discipline of Popular Government: Lord Salisbury's domestic statecraft 1881–1902* (1978) p. 236; *The Times* 22 Nov. 1894.
12   *The Times* 29 Oct. 1894.
13   Harcourt Mss. 411, 29 Oct. 1894.
14   Harcourt Mss. 411–12, 31 Oct., 5 & 9 Nov. 1894.
15   Speech at Newcastle, *The Times* 14 Nov. 1894.
16   *The Times* 15 Nov. 1894.
17   Harcourt Mss. 412, 21 Nov. 1894.
18   *The Times* 22 Nov. 1894.
19   *The Times* 15 Nov. 1894.
20   Harcourt Mss. 412 21 & 26 Nov. 1894.

21 *The Times* 12 Dec. 1894.
22 *The Times* 6 Dec. 1894.
23 Buckle, G. E. (ed.), *The letters of Queen Victoria, third series: a selection from Her Majesty's correspondence and journal between the years 1886–1901* (1931) II, pp. 429–49.
24 Harcourt Mss. 413, 28 Dec. 1894.
25 For instance Acland at Rotherham, *Daily Chronicle* 14 Nov. 1894, and Fowler at Wolverhampton, *The Times* 6 Dec. 1894.
26 Atherley-Jones, L.A., 'Lord Rosebery's enterprise against the House of Lords', *Nineteenth Century* Dec. 1894; Wallace, R., 'Single chamber "democrats"', *Nineteenth Century* Feb. 1895.
27 Harcourt Mss. 415, 19 Feb. 1895.
28 Harcourt Mss. 412, 26 Nov. 1894.
29 4 *Hansard* XXX 877–87 (15 Feb. 1895).
30 For instance Campbell-Bennerman at Stirling and Dunfermline, *The Times* 2 7 Oct. & 7 Dec. 1894, and Asquith at Leven and Birmingham, *The Times* 23 Oct. & 22 Nov. 1894.
31 *The Times* 19 Jan. 1895.
32 *The Times* 4 Jan. 1895; Harcourt Mss. 414, 24 and 29 Jan. 1895.
33 *The Times* 23 Jan. 1895.
34 Fletcher Moulton, J., 'The Lords: a plea for deliberation', *Contemporary Review* Feb. 1895.
35 4 *Hansard* XXX 877–87 (15 Feb. 1895), 1001–08 (18 Feb. 1895).
36 Harcourt Mss. 415, 19 Feb. 1895.
37 Harcourt Mss. 415, 19 Feb. 1895.
38 Harcourt Mss. 415, 20–21 Feb. 1895.
39 Brett, M. V., *Journals and letters of Reginald, Viscount Esher* (1934) I, pp. 186–7.

Chapter Four: The 1895 Session and the Fall of the Government

The 1894 Parliamentary Session had been dominated by the budget, and the ensuing recess by the question of the House of Lords. In so far as there was an underlying theme to political debate during the first half of 1895 it was furnished by the state of the economy. Britain showed few signs of recovering from depression. This was not really the Government's fault. The world economy was in the doldrums in the mid-1890s, in consequence of the feverish expansion of overseas investment a few years previously. This had caused over-production, a fall in prices, and a round of commercial failures and debt repudiations, which had impaired business confidence generally. The United States, which was already a key element in the world economy, was troubled by bitter labour disputes and by continuing controversy over the future of the currency. Britain, as the world's premier free-trading country, could not escape the consequences of this international state of affairs; and an added edge was given to her own difficulties by the exceptionally severe winter of 1894–95. In particular the long, hard frost of early 1895 focussed attention on the problems of the unemployed, whose numbers had remained high throughout the Liberal's period in power. Trades union statistics suggest that at least 8% of the skilled labour force were out of work at the beginning of 1895. Keir Hardie put the overall total at over one million.[1]

The Unionists determined to make the state of the economy their main point of attack at the opening of the new Parliamentary session. It suited their main line of argument, that the Liberals, by expending so much effort trying to effect drastic constitutional changes such as Home Rule and the reform of the House of Lords, had shaken business confidence generally, and neglected useful measures of economic and social regeneration which the circumstances of the times required. The Unionists also intended to exploit the Liberals' failure to do anything for agriculture, despite the promises made at the time of the 1892 general election and in the Queen's Speech of 1893; and they hoped also to detach certain dissatisfied labour representatives, such as Hardie and Saunders, from the ranks of the Government's supporters. All in all the Liberals were unlikely to offer any more rewarding target than their economic record, for the Queen's Speech of February 1895 would make no mention of either Home Rule or the reform of the House of Lords.

In one sense it is surprising that the Government survived for as long as it did, until the middle of 1895. Its position at the start of the year seemed anything but secure. Its majority had sunk below twenty, and was likely to be further eroded by bye-elections; also its composite nature made it seem less than reliable, especially as far as the Irish, and certain Radical and Labour Members were concerned. On the other hand the Government possessed considerable debating talent, as the early encounters of the session were to show. Men like Harcourt, Asquith and Campbell-Bannerman, the latter two in the country as well as in Parliament, exerted themselves to expose the weaknesses of the Opposition case, and to demonstrate how Unionist talk of palliatives masked a most ill-defined social programme and serious divisions over fiscal and economic policy. Above all the Government majority possessed the courage of despair. Apart from one or two mavericks like Dilke and Labouchere, who thought that clinging to office was unwise and undignified, Liberal backbenchers were anxious to postpone a general election which they feared might sweep many of them away. The same held true of their Anti-Parnellite allies, who were short of money and conscious of the Parnellite challenge in their constituences. Ministers, some of whom professed to favour an early dissolution, were surprised to find how disciplined and loyal their small and heterogeneous majority had become.

The Queen's Speech, which was presented to Parliament on 5 February 1895, contained eleven proposed items of legislation, and repeated some of the main demands of the Newcastle programme. Mention was made of Welsh disestablishment, the reform of the liquor laws, and the abolition of plural voting. On the other hand no place was found for payment of M.P.s or an eight hours bill, though the Government hoped to retain the allegiance of the labour interest by further factory legislation. Another significant omission was Irish Home Rule. This had caused a serious scene at a Cabinet meeting in late January, when Rosebery and Harcourt had refused to place Home Rule unqualifiedly in the forefront of the Government programme, and John Morley had threatened to resign after accusing his colleagues of deserting the cause. In the end a form of words was founds to the effect that Home Rule, in a sense "satisfactory to the Irish people and the Irish representatives", remained the Liberals' "primary policy", subject only to "necessary safeguards for the unity of the Empire". This was inserted by Harcourt into his speech following the Address, and seemed to satisfy the Anti-Parnellite M.P.s for the time being.[2]

The Government's programme reflected two main considerations. In the first place it was designed to appeal to as wide a spectrum of the Government's supporters as possible. To some extent indeed the Unionists were justified in accusing Ministers of cynical log-rolling, and of wasting the time of Parliament by making a parade of measures which had no chance of passing. There was disestablishment for the Welsh Liberals, and a new Irish land bill for the Nationalists; the interests of labour were to be gratified by improved factory legislation, and there was also the promise of a crofters' measure for the Scottish highland M.P.s The order of priority for these proposals was unclear. Ministers had given differing indications in their various speeches in the country. Rosebery had stressed Welsh disestablishment at Glasgow and Cardiff; in the first speech he had seemed to speak disparagingly of Harcourt's temperance proposals, and in the second he had omitted to mention Morley's Irish land bill. Harcourt, in a rare and, for him, mediocre speech at Derby in January 1895, had naturally given pride of place to local option. Similarly Morley, speaking at much the same time at Newcastle, had re-emphasised his commitment to Irish Home Rule.[3] In the second place however, the Government may actually have counted on being able to pass some of its proposed measures into law. Morley calculated that the Unionists would find it difficult to obstruct the passage of his Irish land bill; both Irish landlords and Ulster Protestant tenantry had an interest in replacing the 1881 Land Act with legislation with fewer rough edges. It would be hard also, it was thought, for them to oppose a new factory bill in what promised to be an election year.

The real threat to the Government during 1895 seemed likely to come not on the Newcastle programme nor on foreign policy but on its handling of finance and the economy. There were three main points of controversy and danger. One of the them had already put the Government's future in jeopardy in the months prior to the reopening of Parliament. This was the vexed question of naval reamament, which overshadowed the Liberals' three years in office, and which had brought to an end Gladstone's ministerial career as it now threatened to do that of this successors. The 1880s and 1890s witnessed major developments in naval technology and put Britain under pressure to match progress and construction in other countries. The Admiralty's demands for an additional £3 millions on the naval estimates in late 1893 had precipitated Glastone's resignation a few months later. In late 1894 a further demand for £2 millions threatened a new Cabinet crisis. Harcourt initially declared that he would not be a party to such a transaction; then as usual his sense of loyalty to his colleagues and the Government got the better of him. By dint of ruthless paring of the army and civil service estimates, and by a piece of budgetary sharp practice in the form of pledging part of the following year's supplementary estimates (a proceeding which Harcourt thought quite immoral but which was enjoined upon him by his son), enough money was made available to satisfy the Admirals without recourse to fresh taxation. The political price to be paid was that Harcourt was denied the opportunity of making popular tax reductions in his 1895 budget, and of providing a sop for

Radicals and Labour by the introduction of payment of M.P.s. In the short run the budgetary cheeseparing nearly brought about Morley's resignation (yet again) as Chief Secretary for Ireland when his seed potato grant was cut. In the long run it helped to seal the fate of the Government, by giving rise to the shortage of cordite which was the occasion of the fatal Parliamentary division at the end of June 1895.[4]

The Government's life was endangered early in 1895 by two other economic questions. One concerned Indian finance, a serious matter as it threatened to set British and imperial interests at odds with one another. The Indian economy had been progressively affected for some years past by the depreciation of its silver standard of currency, the rupee. In consequence it suffered from a grave imbalance of trade with gold-standard countries like Britain. The Liberal Government attempted to right the situation by actions not very conformable with its free trade principles: it closed the Indian mints to the coinage of silver in 1893, and in 1894 it imposed customs duties on the import into India of cotton textiles. The result was an outcry in Lancashire, which depended heavily on the Indian market; and for a time it seemed possible that the Government might be brought down by the defection of Liberal M.P.s with seats in that county. The other major economic question concerned British agriculture, the state of which had become more depressed than ever during 1894. The Government had little to show for itself on this front after two and a half years in power beyond the appointment of a second royal commission to investigate the subject. One or two Ministers wished to anticipate the comission's findings by including bold measures for agriculture in the Queen's Speech. Shaw Lefevre proposed a programme of capital investment based on state loans to landlords, and he was backed up in this by Rosebery who considered it a humiliation that the Government had no firm proposals to put before Parliament. Harcourt however shied at the financial risks involved, and he was supported by the three landowning peers, Kimberley, Spencer and Ripon, who declared that they had lost all the money they had invested in agricultural improvements in the preceding fifteen years. In the end the only proposal made in the Queen's Speech which had reference to the problems of the countryside was one to facilitate the construction of light railways.[5]

Ministers anticipated trouble from Parliament on economic questions during 1895, but they also feared a sudden downfall on one of the subjects of scandal which periodically troubled the Rosebery administration. Two matters in particular threatened it at the start of the 1895 Parliamentary session. One concerned the so-called Tweedmouth cheques, whereby the former Liberal Chief Whip was supposed to have offered financial incentives to Irish M.P.s to encourage them to remain in attendance at Westminster. Harcourt observed that only Gladstone could lie successfully through a debate on a business of this kind. The other concerned a judge in the Bankruptcy Court, Vaughan Williams, whom the Lord Chancellor, Herschell, had recently returned to circuit duties. Vaughan Williams had been examining the affairs of the 'bubble companies' that had collapsed in the wake of the Baring crisis of 1890. He had already been responsible for the resignation of one minister, Mundella, and it was rumoured that he was now being moved in order to protect someone even more significant, perhaps Rosebery or one of his Rothschild relations. Ministers were even more apprehensive on this score than on that of the Tweedmouth cheques. But the Opposition did not press home the attack on either matter, and Herschell got away with a personal explanation in the House of Lords, which in the view of some sailed very close to the wind.[6] The Government still remained vulnerable to imputations of impropriety and of protecting its own. Its appointment of Sir Hercules Robinson as High Commissioner to South Africa was criticised because of his banking and commercial connections. More seriously Ministers were reproached with failing to procure the extradition of Jabez Balfour from Argentina. Balfour had been a director of the Liberator Building Society which had crashed in 1892. Even more to the point he was a Liberal M.P., and reflections were cast on the Government's slowness to act in his case. Chamberlain did not allow the matter to be forgotten in his speeches at the time of the general election.

As expected the Unionists concentrated their main effort in early 1895 on economic questions. They moved three practical votes of censure on the Government in the form of amendments to the Queen's Speech, of which the first referred specifically to the depression and the third also involved discussion of economic and social issues. In addition they challenged the Government on the subject of the Indian cotton duties. All in all the Parliamentary proceedings of February 1895 represented the most extended confrontation between the main parties over economic policy during the decade.

The Opposition launched their first major attack on the depressed state of trade and agriculture. It could well have made use of an amendment put forward by Keir Hardie on unemployment which promised to cause the Government severe embarrassment. But several Unionists baulked at too close an association with the Socialist from West Ham, and instead a more composite amendment was preferred. This stood in the name of Jeffreys, the Tory M.P. for Basingstoke, and drew attention to the absence of any reference in the Queen's Speech to "the disastrous condition of the agricultural interest and the prolonged depression of the textile and other industries, and the consequent increase in the number of the unemployed". Harcourt contemptuously dubbed it the "Hampshire-cum-West Ham amendment", designed as it was to catch as wide a variety of fishes as possible. Still it was dangerous enough ground for the Government. The link between rural depopulation and urban unemployment was well-understood; and in a wide-ranging debate lasting several days many Liberal M.P.s made clear their feelings that more could have been done, for instance by loans and afforestation schemes, to keep labour remuneratively employed on the land. On the other hand Liberals found a common theme in their opposition to landlordism, which they blamed for many of the troubles of the countryside, and in their support for the 1894 budget which had, so they claimed, relieved the small farmer at the expense of the large landowner. Unionist prescriptions were more varied, and this was a source of weakness for them. Some favoured bimetallism; some favoured protection; and some, notably Goschen, who unwisely announced that he expected to be the next Chancellor of the Exchequer, advocated an extended system of grants-in-aid for the relief of rates.[7]

The Government had seemed in trouble at the start of the debate when Harcourt was suddenly taken ill with influenza and was unable to come to the House, and when, in the opinion of his son, John Morley bungled the opportunity of postponing consideration of the amendment till the following day. On 8 February Harcourt returned from his sick-bed to the House of Commons and delivered one of his wittiest, and most effective, fighting speeches. He was particularly severe on Goschen, making fun of his pretensions to office, and demanding to know how he proposed to pay for extended grants-in-aid if not by increased taxation. Harcourt defended his Government's policy, or lack of it, on orthodox Liberal lines: it was rank socialism to suggest that the Government was responsible for maintaining full industrial capacity annd employment, and in any case the bulk of the country's by now predominantly urban population had benefitted from low agricultural prices. He also had another card up his sleeve: the promise of a select committee to inquire into the causes of unemployment. This proved sufficient to pull disaffected London Liberals back from the brink of voting for the Tory amendment, and the Government survived the debate with a majority of twelve.[8]

The next practical vote of censure was moved by a different section of the Opposition. On 11 February the Parnellite leader, Redmond, introduced an amendment to the Queen's Speech calling for the immediate dissolution of Parliament and the submission of the question of Irish Home Rule to the electorate. Redmond's own speech complained of the progressive betrayal of Ireland by the Liberals which, he declared, had begun with the "sandwiching policy" inherent in the Newcastle programme of 1891. The Unionists had no difficulty in voting for the amendment as they too desired a general election on the subject of Home Rule. Equally the Liberals and Anti-Parnellites, who feared for their seats, had no difficulty in voting against it. The Government at first appeared to be in greater danger in another Irish debate which took place on 13 and 14 February. This was on an amendment also moved by a Parnellite M.P., Clancy, which called for reconsideration of the sentences of men imprisoned for dynamite offences a decade previously. The subject was an emotive one in Ireland, where it was argued that men who in some cases had been convicted only of possessing explosives should not have been sentenced under the full rigours of the 1848 Treason Felony Act to penal servitude for life. For once Anti-Parnellites and Parnellites seemed certain to vote together, and many Liberals, including normally safe men like Illingworth, were also inclined to defect. If, as seemed likely, the Unionists abstained, the Government would face the possibility of defeat. Harcourt however set his face against any concession and insisted on treating the question as one of confidence; and in this he was supported by Asquith and John Morley who like him calculated that defeat on such an issue would be the most honourable of endings for the Government. At this point the nerve of the dissenting Liberal backbenchers failed them. Their fear of a dissolution was greater than that of most Ministers, and they meekly trooped through the Government lobby to defeat the amendment by a crushing majority.[9]

The third and final practical vote of censure on the Address was moved by Chamberlain on 15 February. It regretted that so much of the time of Parliament should be taken up with measures which, by Ministers' own admission, had no chance of passing into law, when much graver constitutional changes had been announced on which the judgement of Parliament should be taken without delay. This reference to the abortive campaign against the House of Lords proved, as has been seen, embarrassing for the Government; but Ministers were able to deal rather more confidently with Chamberlain's allegations about wasting the time of Parliament by a policy of "filling the cup". Asquith, in a most effective speech, demonstrated that this particular phrase was Chamberlain's own, having been used by him first in his days as a Radical opponent of the House of Lords. As to wasting the time of Parliament, Asquith challenged Chamberlain to state his intentions as regards Welsh disestablishment, of which he had long been a declared supporter, and which had now been given priority in the Queen's Speech. Campbell-Bannerman took issue with another of Chamberlain's arguments, that it was time to occupy the time of Parliament usefully with measures of social reform. Where, Campbell-Bannerman asked, was the Unionist social programme? Unionist leaders had been studiously vague on the subject, with the exception of Chamberlain, whose Birmingham programme had drawn no enthusiastic response from his Conservative partners. Finally Harcourt made the most of the contradictory and self-defeating character of the Opposition amendments. The Unionists had supported successive

motions, the first of which urged the Government to devote its attention to
the economy, the second to dissolve without delay, and the third to devote
its attention to the House of Lords. These motions had nothing in common
except their opportunism. They were all part of an attempt to defeat the
Government by cobbling together an unreal majority, combining, as
Harcourt said, the "true blue flag" with "the faded yellow of Birmingham,
a little touch of green from Waterford, and a little spot of red from West
Ham".[10]

The Opposition made one last major effort to topple the Government,
on a question of economic policy. On 21 February Sir Henry James moved
the adjournment of the House on the subject of the Indian cotton duties.
Lancashire M.P.s, both Liberal and Unionist, were extremely unhappy at
the imposition of taxation on the export of British goods to India at a time
when the textile industry was so depressed. It seemed likely that the
Government would be defeated. But at the last moment many Unionists
had second thoughts, realising that they might be placed in office on a
'perish India' policy with the responsibility of finding alternative sources of
revenue. Another good ministerial speech, this time by Fowler, the
Secretary of State for India, added to the Unionist disarray. He
emphasised the dangers of alienating Indian opinion and of weakening the
bonds of empire by setting too much store by the sectional interests of
Lancashire. The outcome of the debate was a Government triumph.
Chamberlain was said to have locked himself in the lavatory in order to
avoid having to vote, and the amendment was defeated by a majority of
195.[11]

There were a number of reasons for the Government's success in the
Parliamentary set-piece battles of February 1895. Ministerial leadership
was one. Harcourt, ably assisted by Asquith, Fowler and Campbell-
Bannerman, led the Government side in the House of Commons with skill
and determination. Realising that an administration resting on such a
narrow majority could not afford to show weakness, Harcourt set his face
against any expedient concessions, and his attitude was vindicated by the
Government's triumph in the debates on Ireland and India. How much
depended on Harcourt was shown by what happened when he was absent
from the House of Commons. On 19 February the Unionists put down a
quasi-protectionist motion against the importation of foreign, prison-made
goods. In command on the Government side were John Morley and Bryce;
and mindful perhaps of the interest shown by the T.U.C. in the subject at
Norwich the previous September, they weakly conceded a committee of
inquiry, although the Liberal Chief Whip was convinced that the motion
could be defeated.[12] Harcourt on the other hand understood that weak
governments cannot afford to be seen to give in to pressure. He knew that

the Labour members, like any other section of the Government majority, could be bullied by the threat of dissolution; and he proved this again on 28 February when he successfully moved to take more of the time of the House of Government business without making any concession on the eight hours question or payment of M.P.s. On 8 March also the Liberal backbenchers again ran away from the possibility of defeating the Government, even though a substantial issue of principle, arising from Britain's failure to put down slavery in Zanzibar, was involved.[13]

The Government was also helped by the fact that the Opposition did not know its own mind. At times its leaders seemed uncertain how far they should go in attempting to turn out the Ministry. The relationship of Liberal Unionists and Conservatives was still somewhat uneasy. The latter enjoyed Harcourt's chaffing of Goschen; whilst Goschen in turn caused offence by voting in favour of the Indian cotton duties. Most important of all the Unionists were, in terms of domestic policy, in considerable disarray. They had no coherent programme to lay before Parliament or the country on the economic and social questions of the day. Some were protectionists, some were free-traders; some were bimetallists, some were monometallists; some favoured social reform, some were opposed to it. Indeed, in so far as economic and social questions were concerned, the Unionists were prey to the faddism and sectionalism which they too readily in other matters attributed to their opponents.

The history of the next few months however was to demonstrate that though the Government could for the time being hold its own in Parliament it could not thereby recoup its popularity in the country. The results of local and bye-elections continued to paint a depressing picture. For a moment, in mid-February, the tide had seemed to turn for the Liberals when they actually gained a seat at a bye-election at Colchester. The circumstances however were unusual. The Tory M.P. resigned unexpectedly, partly, it would seem, because he was tempted by the offer of a baronetcy if he changed sides; and the ensuing contest was won by the Liberal, who was also a rich and munificent local employer.[14] A much more significant test of the Government's popularity came in early March with the triennial elections to the London County Council. Though the parties contesting London were called Moderates and Progressives, they were broadly identifiable with Unionists and Liberals, and national politicians accepted this fact by campaigning in London in early 1895 as never before. The London County Council elections of March 1892, when the Progressives had gained fourteen seats, had served as a curtain-raiser to the general election later in the year. Those of March 1895 were widely expected to do the same.

In the event the L.C.C. elections constituted a severe setback for the Progressives, and illustrated the difficulties of Liberalism in the country at

large. The Progressives lost their huge, fifty-seat majority, and came back
with fifty-nine seats in all, equal in number to the Moderates. A reversal on
such a scale had hardly been anticipated. In late 1894 political indications
had seemed to point the other way, when the Moderates' majority had been
drastically reduced in the London School Board elections. In terms of
educational policy the Moderates were perceived as the party of the Church
of England, of denominationalism and religious dogmatism. In other
respects however it was the Progressives who appeared to be the more
sectarian. By March 1895 they had, rightly or wrongly acquired a reputation
for putting narrow party interests before those of London as a whole. They
were accused of favouring inner London over the suburbs, and of neglecting
to undertake major improvements, such as an approach to the newly-
opened Tower Bridge, which might have helped to reduce unemployment,
in order to pursue a quarrel with the House of Lords over betterment and
unearned increment. The Progressives also suffered from their association
with the militant Nonconformist conscience which, in the person of the
formidable Mrs Ormiston Chant, had instigated the ill-advised prosecution
of the Empire Theatre. Finally it was argued that in paying above-average
wages to Council employees the Progressives were maintaining a privileged
class of workmen and political henchmen at the ratepayers' expense. This
was not something likely to appeal either to non-union labour or to the large
class of shopkeepers and artisans who already felt threatened by the
extension of municipal enterprises and by the kind of collectivism fore-
shadowed by the Norwich programme.

Like many local elections, those in London were heavily influenced by the
perennial issue of local taxation. The crucial fact here was that the level of
rates had increased by 3¼d, or 30%, since the Progressives had returned
with an increased majority in 1892. Unionist speakers made the most of a
remark of Sidney Webb's that he could see no limit to the possible extension
of municipal taxation. Chamberlain, on one of his campaigning visits to
London, argued that higher rates would aggravate the housing problem by
increasing the price of rented accommodation. The Progressives also
suffered from disappointment at the Liberal Government's failure to do
more for London. The only relevant piece of legislation passed, the
Equalisation of Rates Act of 1894, had proved a very blunt instrument, and
had failed to reapportion local taxation adequately in favour of the poorer
districts. The resulting dissatisfaction may help to explain why the
Progressives lost East End seats like St George's-in-the-East and Mile End.
Increased unemployment, especially amongst casual labour, during the
severe winter of 1894-95 may also have been a factor. John Burns'
explanation of the Progressives' defeat, that the six weeks hard frost had led
to a corruption of lower class morale by soup kitchens and the distribution of
bread and beer, was doubtless exaggerated but not entirely devoid of truth.[15]

Against this background the future of the Liberal Government appeared bleak at the end of the first quarter of 1895. Only two developments seemed capable of reviving its prospects. One was that some aspect of its programme should catch light and capture the imagination of the country; and in the existing circumstances this did not seem very likely. The other was that the Opposition should be disabled by a split between Conservatives and Liberal Unionists. This remained a more distinct possibility, and one which lent increased significance to the problem of finding a new Speaker of the House of Commons which preoccupied leading politicans in March and early April 1895.

At the end of February Arthur Peel intimated his intention to resign as Speaker as soon as possible. The news was unwelcome to the leaders of both main parties, as it posed the problem of replacing him in a dying Parliament. Traditionally the Speaker belonged to the majority, and was often a recent member of the Government of the day. But the existing majority, small enough anyway, seemed likely to be overturned before the new Speaker should have time to establish his position as a worthy occupant of the Chair and thereby to ensure his automatic re-election. The Government was placed in a particular dilemma. On the one hand it seemed humiliating to accept a Conservative as the new Speaker; indeed it amounted almost to an admission that the Liberals expected to lose the general election. On the other hand the Government could hardly, it was thought, afford to lose one of the voting members of its all too slender majority to the impartiality of the Chair.

Most Ministers were anxious that the new Speaker should not be one of themselves. Their reasons for this throw considerable light on the predicament of the Rosebery administration. One Minister, Campbell-Bannerman, the Secretary of State for War, would, it was acknowledged, make an ideal Speaker. He was acceptable to both sides of the House, and moreover he desired the position having been first promised and then denied the responsibility of deputy-leader in the House of Commons as a result of John Morley's temperamental tergiversations. But it was generally felt in the Cabinet that Campbell-Bannerman could not be spared. Morley, who was fretting to leave his Irish office, and who had been so jealous at Fowler's promotion a year previously, would undoubtedly claim the vacant Secretaryship of State. But the prospect of Morley, the archetypal Little Englander, at the War Office and having to deal with the cantankerous Duke of Cambridge, was not one to be contemplated by the majority of his colleagues. In addition any ministerial reshuffle, and the promotion of new men into the Cabinet, would mean bye-elections in possibly unsafe seats. In its fragile condition the Government preferred to leave existing appointments just as they were.

The man favoured for the Speakership by Harcourt and the bulk of the Cabinet was Courtney. He was not a Liberal, but a Liberal Unionist, albeit one of markedly independent views, who had acquired considerable experience in chairing House of Commons committees. To Harcourt there was obvious advantage in thus reducing by one vote the Opposition's strength in the House of Commons. On the other hand Courtney's election was by no means straightforward. The Conservatives, who had not provided a Speaker for sixty years, felt that it was time that one of their own occupied the Chair. Certain Radicals were very hostile to Courtney; Labouchere declared that he for one could not stand his "smug God Almightyism".[16] Even so Courtney could still have been chosen if the Liberal Unionists had backed him solidly. Here Chamberlain's attitude was to prove crucial.

The question of the Speakership dovetailed with a particular crisis in the Unionist alliance. As a Liberal M.P. and, from 1884, as Speaker, Peel had sat for Warwick and Leamington. By proposing to resign his Parliamentary seat at the same time as the Speakership, he now sparked off a potentially damaging quarrel in the Unionist ranks which seriously threatened the compact of 1886. Chamberlain claimed the representation in the constituency for the Liberal Unionists, and with Balfour's concurrence he put forward the Speaker's son, George Peel, as the official Opposition candidate. The local Conservative party however was up in arms. It had its own preferred candidate, Sir Montague Nelson, who had come within 400 votes of winning the seat ten years earlier in the days before the Liberal split. Nelson had not stood against the Speaker, whose private sympathies were believed to be Liberal Unionist, in 1886 and 1892, but it was felt that he had established a reversionary claim to the constituency. The local Conservatives also greatly disliked the idea of a private deal being struck by Chamberlain and Balfour over their heads; it savoured of the kind of electoral wire-pulling which Conservatives usually liked to identify with the Liberal Party. Akers-Douglas, the Conservative whip, warned Balfour that:

> what our people most resent is the caucus, and further that it is not the leaders or even the middle class voters which are difficult to manage but the working men . . . the feeling against Peel is chiefly that he is Chamberlain's and your nominee—that no local man or association was even nominally consulted before he was announced as candidate.[17]

The dispute had wider implications beyond the constituency boundaries of Warwick and Leamington. It helped to bring into the open a lurking Conservative discontent with Chamberlain's ambiguous position in politics. The most obvious expression was given to this in letters to *The*

Times and in articles in the London Conservative press; one notable piece, supposedly written by a Tory M.P., in the *New Review* compared Chamberlain and Randolph Churchill as dangerous and untrustworthy demagogues. Chamberlain, it was held, had damaged the interests of Conservatism over the past year by his efforts to sit on the fence. He had voted in favour of the principle of graduated taxation in the debates on the 1894 budget, and much worse, he had supported the Welsh Church Disestablishment Bill on its second reading in the spring of 1895. One Conservative M.P., Howorth, in a letter to *The Times*, considered the electoral compact of 1886:

> a big price to pay for an alliance which is only to be kept up in order to continue flogging a dead horse like Home Rule, and which is meanwhile to be used to secure the return of candidates out of sympathy with Tory policy. It will be an intolerable thing if candidates pledged to destroy the Welsh Church and in favour of so-called unsectarian education on holding aloof like Gallio from the discussion of these burning issues should be returned by the votes of men to whom matters like these are of supreme moment.[18]

What was the Unionist alliance now for? This was the large question posed by the apparently local dispute at Warwick and Leamington at a time when Home Rule seemed ruled out of court for the foreseeable future by the failure of the 1893 Bill, the continuing split in the Irish party, and the Liberal Government's refusal to dissolve on the issue. In changing circumstances Chamberlain no longer seemed to have so much to offer to his Conservative allies. Electorally he was an uncertain asset; some Conservatives thought him worth no more than six seats, and believed that their own party could win some of his West Midlands strongholds. One Tory ex-Cabinet Minister blamed his Stepney speech of February 1895 for the Moderates' single unsatisfactory poll in the L.C.C. elections. Chamberlain's 'unauthorised' Birmingham programme of October 1894 had caused the Conservative leadership some embarrassment. Even his famous combattiveness in debate had proved counter-productive. On more than one occasion, it was said, the Government would have been defeated "but for his desire to have the demagogue's reward".[19]

Balfour however, and most leading Conservatives, wanted to preserve the Unionist alliance. They wanted to have Chamberlain on their side, and they reckoned that Liberal Unionism was still a factor in swaying moderate opinion. They still hoped to fight the next general election, at least in part, on anti-Irish sentiment and Home Rule, on which issues Chamberlain's oratory and influence would be most effective. In a speech at the end of April, Balfour was careful to describe Home Rule as not dead but "sick unto death".[20] There was also no doubt a concern as to what Chamberlain might do if he was provoked; he was the rogue elephant of British politics, and anyone stood a chance of getting hurt if he went on the rampage. Accordingly efforts were made by the Conservative hierarchy to accommodate his interests in Warwick and Leamington: Nelson, the local Conservative nominee, was prevailed upon to withdraw. On the other hand Chamberlain had to make concessions too. He had to acquiesce in the withdrawal of his own nominee, George Peel, from the contest at Warwick and Leamington, and his replacement by a new, compromise, albeit Liberal Unionist candidate, Alfred Lyttleton. He had to acquiesce also in a Conservative candidate for the constituency of Hythe, which too had been in dispute between the two Unionist parties. Finally it is probable that Chamberlain was influenced by local considerations at Warwick and Leamington to humour his Conservative allies in the House of Commons by supporting a Conservative, Ridley, for the Speakership, in preference to the Liberal Unionist, Courtney.

Thus ended, without too much ado, an episode which had at one time threatened to have much more serious consequences for British party politics. It might have split the Unionist forces at Warwick and Leamington and handed the seat over to the Liberals at the ensuing bye-election, thus giving the Government a much-needed fillip. Indeed at one stage it was claimed that disgruntled local Conservatives would sooner vote for a Home Ruler rather than for George Peel.[21] The quarrel might have spread further, and set Conservative against Liberal Unionist throughout the West Midlands. It might even have provoked Chamberlain's retirement from public life. He was depressed in early 1895 by the failure of his private business ventures in the West Indies and by the difficulty of bringing the Conservatives round to his precise way of thinking on social reform. As the most thin-skinned individual in British politics, apart from Rosebery and John Morley, he took very much to heart the criticism made of him in sections of the Conservative press. What the Warwick and Leamington affair did do was to make virtually inevitable the formation of a coalition government when the Liberals fell from power in mid-1895. Chamberlain could not remain any longer in the political wilderness.

Otherwise the affair's repercussions at Westminster were few. Once Chamberlain had disavowed Courtney's candidacy, the contest for the Speakership took place on normal party lines. On 10 April 1895 the Government carried its own nominee, Gully, by eleven votes, in what was to prove its last clear Parliamentary success. In a sense its triumph was somewhat unreal, as the fate of the Government was not here at stake. Still it was by no means inevitable. Once Courtney had withdrawn, Harcourt had been prepared to accept the Conservative candidate, Ridley, *faute de mieux*. Pressure from colleagues, and from backbench Liberals who had no desire to see the Government go cap in hand to the Opposition for a Speaker, made him drop his prejudices against Gully, a Liberal lawyer favoured by the Lord Chancellor but whom Harcourt had at first thought too little-known. Even so a number of Liberals retained serious doubts about Gully's lack of Parliamentary experience (he had been in the House of Commons for nine years but rarely participated in its debates) and perhaps also about his dubious family associations as mentioned by Hamilton. In the end the issue was only settled after a confrontation between Balfour and Harcourt across the floor of the House. Balfour made the mistake of attacking Gully's qualifications for the Chair. By doing so he united Liberals in loyalty to their party's candidate, and Harcourt scored his last debating success of the 1892-95 Parliament in a speech in which he accused the Unionists of blocking the election of the best-qualified man available, Courtney.

The Speakership contest had no discernible effect on public opinion in the country. Bye-elections held at this time continued to register a decline in ministerial fortunes. The first, at Bristol East in late March, was a straight fight between a Liberal and an Independent Labour candidate, which the Liberal was lucky to win by 132 votes. More significant in the immediate context were two bye-elections in late April, in the City of Oxford and Mid-Norfolk. At Oxford the Conservative candidate had been expected to do badly as the University was still on vacation and many sympathetic dons were absent. In the event he increased his majority over that of 1892 by nearly 500 votes. Lewis Harcourt thought the result due in large measure to the question of disestablishment. Still more striking was the outcome in Mid-Norfolk. The constituency was a predominantly rural one, in which the agricultural labourers formed the largest single class; and their continuing Radical sympathies, it was thought, had been attested in recent elections to the local parish councils. On this occasion however they abandoned the Liberal cause in considerable numbers and elected a Liberal Unionist on the largest poll since 1885. Probably two main influences were at work. Home Rule was still a factor to be reckoned with in English bye-elections at this time. In Mid-Norfolk, as earlier in Brigg and Evesham, the Irish Unionist Alliance was able to concentrate its canvassers and resources on one contest at a time, and to play upon the anti-Catholic susceptibilities of Nonconformist electors. That the Goverment had been placed on the defensive was shown by a speech delivered by a junior Minister, Buxton, in Mid-Norfolk, in which he had recourse to the old appeal to self-interest, arguing that Home Rule would benefit British workers by keeping Irishmen in Ireland where they would not compete in the British labour market. The other crucial factor was the agricultural depression. Norfolk, along with Suffolk and Cambridgeshire, was one of the three English counties most given over to arable farming, which had suffered with particular severity from the collapse in grain prices. It was also a part of the country where the Liberals had in 1891-92 made their most extravagant promises to the rural electorate. The record low wheat prices of 1894 and the resulting reduction of agricultural labourers' wages from 12s to 9s a week made a mockery of previous rhetoric. The Government was revealed as not having a policy for agriculture, and the subject was ignored altogether in a speech delivered in Norfolk at this time by the local Liberal magnate, Lord Kimberley. One other point requires to be stressed. Despite their acrimonious relations at Warwick and Leamington, in the bye-election campaigns in both Oxford and Mid-Norfolk Conservatives and Liberal Unionists cooperated wholeheartedly and with conspicuous success.[22]

There was little in the Government's legislative programme to remedy its standing in the country. Not that there was any lack of proposed measures; arguably indeed this was part of its problem. The Queen's Speech had contained eleven suggested items of legislation. There was something in it to appeal to most segments of the governing majority, but nothing to stir the imagination of the country. Priority was understood to be attached to Welsh disestablishment and Irish land reform, while Harcourt was known to be personally committed to promoting the fortunes of his Local Option Bill. None of these three proposed measures could be described as popular in Britain as a whole.

The item which loomed largest in the Parliamentary debates of 1895 was the Welsh Church Disestablishment Bill. 1895 was supposed to be the year of Wales, legislatively speaking, just as 1893 had been given over to Ireland, and 1894 to England and to a lesser extent to Scotland. Harcourt had promised as much in the House of Commons at the end of the 1894 session. Rosebery had gone out of his way, in his speeches at Glasgow and Cardiff, to put Welsh disestablishment in the forefront of the Government programme. Perhaps he still felt a sense of obligation to young Welsh M.P.s like Lloyd George who were known to have supported his succession to the premiership in early 1894. No doubt also he hoped to embarrass the Liberal Unionists, some of whom like Chamberlain had committed themselves to the principle of disestablishment in their more radical days.

The significance of the Welsh disestablishment issue in the mid-1890s should not be underestimated. To most politicians it was far more than a provincial concern; it touched on matters involving the national life of the United Kingdom as a whole. The debates on the subject in 1895 aroused strong passions and were characterised by a high standard of Parliamentary speaking. They also illustrated the extent to which political and social conditions had changed since a question of disestablishment was last discussed at length in 1869.

Asquith introduced the Welsh Church Disestablishment Bill in the House of Commons on 25 February 1895. Substantially it was on the same lines as the bill which had made a brief appearance in the preceding year. It proposed to terminate the existing Anglican establishment in Wales as from 1 January 1897. Welsh bishops were no longer to be summoned to Convocation or the House of Lords, Welsh ecclesiastical corporations were to be dissolved, and the ecclesiastical courts in Wales were to lose their coercive jurisdiction. The Welsh clergy however would be allowed to constitute for themselves a representative body to administer their own affairs and any property that remained in their hands.[23]

The crux of the Bill lay in its provisions for disendowment. Asquith proposed to draw a line at the year 1703, the date of the foundation of Queen Ann's Bounty and also a convenient starting-point for the main expansion of Nonconformity in Wales. Grants made to the Church in Wales since that date would be treated as the rightful property of the Anglican denomination. Grants made before that date would be regarded as belonging to the Welsh community as a whole, and would accordingly be made over to largely secular purposes. This sequestered property, estimated at some £150,000 in value, would be divided up between central and local authorities. Diocesan and capitular possessions would be handed over to a board of commissioners nominated by the state. Glebes and burial grounds would be transferred to the parish councils; whilst the largest division of Church property, comprising tithes and tithe rent-charges, would be placed at the disposal of the county councils, with the qualification that it should be applied to useful social purposes such as the provision of labourers' dwellings and allotments, libraries, museums, cottage hospitals, and trained nurses for the sick poor.

These proposals touched on a sensitive nerve. For most Unionists they smacked of confiscation and collectivism. If the property of the Church in Wales was not safe, what British citizen could regard his individual possession as his own? The fixing of 1703 as the date before which all endownments made would be liable to appropriation appeared arbitrary and unfair. The handing over of ecclesiastical property to local authorities seemed in the nature of a bribe to local ratepayers. The Welsh Disestablishment Bill in fact marked a stage in the process whereby the Unionists were to lay claim, as they were to do so successfully in the 1895 general election, to a large part of the Liberal heritage of the previous sixty years, a heritage bound up with the ideas of liberty, legal equality and respect for the rights of property. The whole measure, they claimed, was conceived in a spirit of narrow sectarianism and inequality. The Church in Wales was to be treated much more harshly than the Church of Ireland had been in 1869. There was to be no compensation for curates, churchyards were to be handed over to the parish councils, and no incentive was provided, as it had been in 1869, to commute and compound vested interests for the benefit of a new Church body. Nor was it proposed to disendow the Nonconformist institutions at the same time as the Anglican establishment in Wales. Nonconformist bodies would continue to enjoy, under an act of 1844, an unlimited tenure of any endowment they had held for twenty-five years, a privilege which contrasted sharply with the proposal to take away all the endowments which had been made to the Established Church in Wales before 1703.[24]

The Welsh Disestablishment Bill also fitted in with the accusations of anti-English prejudice which the Unionists were able to use with considerable effect against the Government in the 1895 general election. Wales had been legally a part of England too long for its institutions to be easily separated from the structure of English life. Even the exact boundary between Wales and England was in dispute. Monmouthshire had been annexed to England by Henry VIII, but it was also part of the diocese of Llandaff, and for the purposes of its bill the Government chose to define Wales in terms of its diocesan boundaries. It was accused of trying to lay its hands on additional endowments, and of surrendering portions of England wherever, as in parts of Shropshire and Herefordshire, parishes belonged to a Welsh diocese. Attempts to define the exact line of cultural demarcation between Wales and England made the House of Commons sound at times like a branch of an Austro-Hungarian legislature. Where, Unionists asked, was the whole process of pandering to local majorities to end? The Government's case for disestablishment rested on the fact that 31 out of 34 Welsh M.P.s were in favour of it. Arguably the difference in actual votes was much less than the difference in representation suggested. But in any case was the same principle shortly to be applied to those parts of England where Nonconformity was strong, such as the North, East Anglia, or the West Country?

The Unionists also made use of another argument that had not been much in evidence in 1869. The present age, they declared, was one that was increasingly secularist in tone, and they appealed to the Nonconformists not to weaken, by their policies of disestablishment and disendowment, the barriers against the growth of religious indifference. Much use was made of statistics by both sides in the debates. The Nonconformists could maintain that they had a greater number of active adherents than the Established Church, but they still could not claim to constitute a majority of the people of Wales. Already the bulk of the population was to be found in the counties of Monmouthshire and Glamorgan, in the growing urban and industrial communities where formal religious observance was in decline, but where, it was claimed by Anglican apologists, the Established Church was beginning to make some progress. Certainly Anglicanism had been reviving markedly in Wales since the middle of the century, and it possessed also the advantage of a parochial organisation and a resident ministry; but all this, it was said, would change in the event of disestablishment and disendowment. The Liberals countered with the assertion that disestablishment would give the Churh new life by setting it free from the trammels of the state. The terms of the debate were interesting, even ironic. More and more the Anglicans, with an eye to reclaiming the increasingly heathen population of South Wales, were posing as the Church of the poor, a title that Gladstone had awarded a few years earlier to the Nonconformist congregations. It was another example of the reversal of values that seemed somehow characteristic of the closing decade of the nineteenth century. The disestablishment issues also emphasised the divergent interests of town and country. The handing over of tithes to the county councils promised to benefit rural Wales, proportionally to population, much more than the town and cities. Subsidies to local taxation were likely to breed in Wales the same kind of regional jealousies as they had already done in London by the so-called Equalisation of Rates Act of 1894. Urban Wales had in fact little to gain from disestablishment, and this may help to explain the Liberal losses in Welsh towns and cities in the 1895 general election.

The Parliamentary struggle for Welsh disestablishment took up a considerable amount of time between February and June 1895. The Government managed to carry the Bill's second reading by a majority of forty-four at the beginning of April. Two Liberal Unionists, including Chamberlain, voted with the Government, and sixteen other Liberal Unionists were absent unpaired. On the committee stage however, which began in early May, progress was slow, and by the fourth week of June the House of Commons had only been able to deal with 6 of the Bill's 31 clauses. Clearly the measure was not going to pass without some recourse to the 'guillotine', and in that event the House of Lords would have the excuse to treat it as it had done the similarly-closured Irish Evicted Tenants Bill in 1894. In any case Salisbury intimated that the upper house would not pass a bill of such revolutionary implications, whose key provisions were by the middle of 1895 only being carried in committee by a handful of votes. The Welsh Disestablishment Bill had in fact become symbolic of that policy of 'ploughing the sands' which the Unionists imputed so successfully to the Government in the course of 1895. It was in vain for Asquith, who had first supplied the Opposition with the fatal phrase, to argue as he did at Nottingham in early April, in his last major public speech as Home Secretary, that great Liberal reforms had always required a sometimes lengthy period of incubation. Welsh disestablishment in 1895 seemed irrelevant to the United Kingdom's real needs. Indeed, in so far as it was relevant at all, as Salisbury pointed out in his Bradford speech at the end of May, it was as a threat to property and thus to business confidence and the return of prosperity.[25]

Only one kind of measure could probably have done much to retrieve the Government's declining popularity at this stage. A large stroke of financial policy might have enabled it to appeal to a wider range of opinion than could any of its more sectional proposals for legislation. Labouchere wrote to Lewis Harcourt that "if some fine democratic bribe could appear in the budget, and the Cabinet get a fall *before* the bribe is paid, and a general election follows, we might have a chance of winning".[26] As usual Labouchere was over-cynical and too clever by half. But it was true that the 1894 budget had been popular with the crucial class of voters whose income-tax allowances had been extended. And for a time it seemed possible that a similar tax-remitting operation could be effected in 1895. Revenue remained buoyant despite the continuing depression in several economic sectors, the death duties introduced in the preceding year were bringing in an increasing sum, and the beginnings of a revival of trade with the United States in early 1895 boosted the returns on the stamp duties. What really limited the Chancellor of the Exchequer's freedom of man-oeuvre was the £2 millions increase in naval expenditure agreed on by the Cabinet during the winter, which came on top of the extra £4 millions authorised in the previous year at the expense of Gladstone's resignation. There was to be no leeway in 1895 for extending relief to income tax payers, or for introducing the free breakfast table or payment of M.P.s. In this sense the fate of the Liberal Government of the 1890s was determined much more by the forces of militarism than of imperialism.

There might still however have been some scope for a reforming Chancellor. One piece of financial business that was overdue was a reform of the Bank Charter Act of 1844, and specifically an alteration of the strict £14 millions limit which applied to the issue of banknotes as against securities. Gladstone had toyed with the idea during his first ministry. So had Goschen when he was Chancellor of the Exchequer, and he had been reprimanded by Harcourt for not proceeding further with the idea. In 1895 Harcourt himself had the chance to take the matter up. At a time of low prices generally he could have pleased the producing classes by proposing to inject a degree of inflation into the economy. He could also have obtained further revenue by encouraging more of the remaining country banks to surrender their independent right of note issue. By the terms of the Act of 1844 the Government was entitled to a considerable share of the proceeds when any local bank relinquished its note-issuing privileges to the Bank of England, and Harcourt could have improved his financial position by renewing the incentives formerly offered to such banks to abandon this part of their business.[27] Such a reform would have been in line with the Rosebery Government's not unreasonable claim to represent sound administrative principles, a claim usually obscured by the controversy surrounding the legislative proposals of the Newcastle programme. It was however more than Harcourt desired to take up. His interests were not pre-eminently financial. He had put a great deal of work into the 1894 budget, but in 1895 his main concern was to forward the prospects of his Local Option Bill. And as to the level of prices, he was content to make a virtue of the fact that they were low, and to fight the next general election in part on the rising living standards of the working classes.

The budget that was introduced on 2 May 1895 was therefore necessarily a somewhat dull affair. The only remission of taxation was of the 6d on a gallon of spirits which had been imposed in 1894. This was required in order to keep the Anti-Parnellites loyal to the Government in the absence of any measure of Home Rule. Its effect however was to give the budget a sectional and lop-sided character. 6d on a barrel of beer had also been imposed at the same time as the duty on spirits, but this was not being treated in the same way as the disloyal Irishman's whiskey. Not only did the budget do nothing for agriculture in its time of greatest depression, but it proposed to extend taxation on the beverage which was brewed from home-grown barley. The Government was taxing both the drink and the employment of the English urban and rural labourer. Ireland was still favoured with imperial grants for railway-building and the relief of distress, but nothing was offered to the depressed areas of England.[28] The budget therefore contributed to the overall disenchantment with Liberal policies that was to find expression at the polls in July 1895.

Bye-elections held during the spring made the Government's tenure of power more precarious. Only one such contest resulted in a swing to the Liberals. This was at East Leeds at the end of April, where the Liberal candidate, Leuty, increased his party's majority from 827 to 1,131 on a reduced poll. Leuty was a former mayor of Leeds, who had proved not only to be firm on questions of law and order, but who had also done much for the people of his city in terms of housing and unemployment provision.[29] Leuty's success, given the Liberals' overall circumstances at the time, was exceptional, and demonstrated the advantages of having a strong local candidate. Another bye-election, held at the same time in Ireland, revealed new dangers for the Government in an increasing restlessness amongst their Irish allies. The Anti-Parnellite M.P., Sweetman, applied for the Chiltern Hundreds in protest against the Government's failure to do more for Ireland, and fought the ensuing bye-election in Wicklow as the candidate of the Parnellite party. He just failed to win; less than one hundred votes separated the three main candidates, for the Unionists also mounted a strong challenge in the East Wicklow constituency, which was one of the few rural areas in the south of Ireland where Protestantism had any numerical strength.[30]

Bye-elections held during May 1895 revealed a relentless trend against the Government. In West Dorset and West Edinburgh the Unionists increased their majorities; and they also won Warwick and Leamington by a sizeable margin. This was the constituency which had not been contested since 1885, where the Liberals hoped to profit from internal Unionist dissensions. The Government's worst setback was at Walworth, where it lost yet another seat following the death of the Liberal and labour representative, Saunders. The contest was notable perhaps for the intervention of a so-called Social Democratic candidate, Lansbury, who attacked the Government for failing to impose higher taxes on alcohol which would have enabled it to fulfil its promises with regard to the introduction of payment of M.P.s and of election expenses. Lansbury's tally of 347 votes however could not account for the Conservative's 571 vote margin of victory over the Liberal. This was explained partly by Conservative promises of extended financial grants for church schools, which, as the issue of Home Rule was no longer to the fore, made a particular impression on electors of Irish descent in the constituency. The result augured badly for the Liberals, as Walworth was a seat which had been won by the Progressives in the L.C.C. elections in March.[31]

The Government's growing demoralisation was reflected in a virtual cessation of ministerial speaking in the country. Even Asquith abandoned his appearances on the public platform after a speech at Nottingham in early April in which he had tried to argue that even a Parliamentary session devoted to a Welsh Disestablishment Bill which failed to pass would not in the long run be wasted. Rosebery and Harcourt addressed the National Liberal Club in early May, but the occasion was mainly memorable for the Prime Minister's breakdown in the middle of his speech. Otherwise the only rhetorical effort made by a minister at this time outside the walls or Parliament was John Morley's speech at Newcastle at the end of May, in which he bravely defended the Local Option Bill and argued, as against Salisbury's interpretation, that the economic depression had begun in 1890 and not during the Liberals' period in office.[32]

By contrast Unionist speeches became more frequent as the Opposition gained in confidence. The remarks to which Morley took exception were made by Salisbury in a major address at Bradford towards the end of May. Salisbury spent some time defending the House of Lords. He argued that it was the House of Commons that was responsible for the existing legislative log-jam, as the Government was trying to pass too many controversial bills with too narrow a majority; and he warned that the concentration of authority in the hands of a single chamber would of necessity expose the country to the inconvenience of more frequent general elections. But the main thrust of his speech was on economic and social concerns. It was time, he declared, to seek out remedies for unemployment and for the other consequences of the depression, which the Liberals had helped to foist on the country by their policies, so unsettling for business confidence, of undermining property rights and setting class against class. Salisbury's analysis of economic circumstances was forceful if tendentious:

"What I want to say is that is it is largely due to the action of statesmen in this country that money left this country and went to Brazil, Argentina, and other parts of the world, with the result that there was a general breakdown and bankruptcies in all these interesting communities and that distress and fear which has settled upon the whole of the business community in recent years."[33]

It was notable that Salisbury's speech made hardly any reference to Home Rule. To a considerable extent this was true also of the speeches of two other senior Unionist politicians who stepped back into the limelight at this time. Goschen broke his long silence on provincial platforms with two appearances in April at Devonport and Plymouth, where he argued that the House of Lords was more than ever necessary as an antidote to the factionalism and incoherence of the House of Commons. More significant still was Chamberlain's rehabilitation as a major Unionist figure after a period of lessened political effectiveness in consequence of his embroilment at Warwick and Leamington and his questionable performance in the early part of the Parliamentary session. As usual Chamberlain could not resist referring to Ireland. In his speech at Birmingham at the end of May he once again attacked the 1893 Home Rule Bill's proposal to subsidise Ireland with English money at a time of depression and to leave the Irish with their troublesome representation at Westminster. But in general Chamberlain's speeches at this time showed a reinforced awareness that the Unionists could no longer live by the issue of Home Rule alone. Thus he taunted the Liberals with sacrificing their principles, as for instance with regard to the building of the Uganda railway, in order to cling on to office. The Unionists on the other hand, he maintained, offered coherent policies in respect of social reform and imperial development; it was in a speech to the Birmingham Jewellers Association in the spring of 1895 that Chamberlain first compared the empire to an improvable landed estate. The Unionist alliance, according to Chamberlain, represented the libertarian spirit of the old Liberalism against the restrictive and destructive spirit of the new. He even made a virtue of the difficulties at Warwick and Leamington, as showing that the Unionists were not under the tyranny of the caucus as were their opponents.[34]

The Government's legislative programme certainly wore an air of unreality by the late spring of 1895. The Welsh Disestablishment Bill was dragging its weary way through committee; by the time of the Government's fall discussion had only reached the sixth of thirty-one clauses.

As for the Irish Land Bill, the second string in the Government programme, it had not yet entered its committee stage. Despite their existing commitments, Ministers continued to bring forward new legislative proposals; some of them, like the Plural Voting Bill, which was introduced on 30 April, opened up major areas of controversy. It was no wonder that Unionists such as Goschen could accuse the Government of having a programme only of "first nights", and of wasting the time of Parliament by "pounding away on bills which are intended to be sops and bribes, red herrings, will-o'-the-wisps". According to Chamberlain, "the problem which the Government have set themselves to solve is how to get a majority by hook or by crook from the byeways or the highways . . . and then to use the majority for some purpose in which the majority is not at all interested".[35] Certainly the 1895 session had the odour of a dying Parliament about it. But in fairness to the Liberals, it should be pointed out that they refrained from taking the whole time of the House for Government business, and thus found their programme necessarily delayed by private member legislation, and by the demands of supply which were eventually to occasion their downfall. The Unionists, in a new Parliament and with a massive majority, hardly made a better job of managing House of Commons business in the following year.

What the Liberal programme required in 1895 was some measure concerned with practical social improvement, which would not involve protracted debate on the controversial subjects of religion, the constitution and the rights of property. Surprisingly, it may seem, there were Liberals who considered that the Local Option or Intoxicating Liquor Traffic Bill fell into this category. Foremost amongst these was Harcourt, who seemed during the first half of 1895 to regard temperance reform as the last main object of his political life. Harcourt considered local option to be a thoroughly practical proposition. All classes, he felt, had an interest in reducing alcoholism, and the poverty and crime that went with it. He himself had been converted to the need for legislation in the early 1880s when as Home Secretary he had confronted the social depravity and deprivation which the problem of drink engendered. Important Unionist figures such as Chamberlain were committed to some kind of temperance reform; so was the Church of England. The middle classes could surely be expected to support a measure which proposed to restrict the number of public houses, and thereby to increase the residential property values, in the areas in which they lived. And what could be objectionable in the principle of allowing a local referendum to decide a question of such obvious local concern? Harcourt realised that his Local Veto Bill of 1893 had appeared too arbitrary in making it possible for public houses to be outlawed altogether in any given area. His 1895 proposals were evidently more moderate, for they constituted a licensing as well as a local option bill, whereby the size of any local majority against public houses would determine the number by which they would be reduced.

Nonetheless the Local Option Bill was open to grave objections that were to haunt the Liberal party for months after its introduction in the House of Commons in early April 1895. For one thing it did not even serve to unite Liberal opinion on the subject. Gladstone, in one of those communications 'from beyond the grave' which characterised his years of supposed political retirement, had sown dissension by an open letter in the autumn of 1894 in which he had endorsed Chamberlain's plan of taking the whole brewing industry into public ownership. This, the so-called Gothenburg scheme, after the example practised in Sweden, seemed a viable if arbitrary answer to the problem of increasing monopoly that was frequently made a charge against the drink interest in the United Kingdom. Harcourt's Local Option Bill, on the other hand, which seemed straightforward enough, contained several conundrums and complications. If the electorate in a given area were to vote that one quarter of its pubs were to close, who was to decide which ones were to be singled out? And if, after the prescribed three year period, the electorate were to vote in an opposite sense, how were the condemned hostelries to be brought back to life again? The whole procedure was calculated to disturb property rights and business confidence. It was at variance with the libertarian traditions of Liberalism, and undermined its claim that the social and economic progress of the previous sixty years had been due to the acceptance of laissez-faire. Above all the Local Option Bill made two invidious distinctions. It excluded Ireland from its provisions, and it excluded also hotels and restaurants. Therefore it discriminated both against people living in Britain and against the working classes who could not afford such favoured facilities. Even though the Local Option Bill never reached its second reading, the Unionists would not allow these aspects of it to be forgotten, and they served as potent propaganda against the Liberals in the 1895 general election.[36]

Temperance reform was always too partisan and controversial a subject to be proceeded with easily. The Liberal Government had also some supposedly uncontentious items of legislation up its sleeve. The Conciliation Bill was introduced as a sop to public opinion which, alarmed by what it considered to be a growing recourse to strike action, was demanding some form of industrial arbitration. It, too, failed to reach its second reading, as did the Light Railways Bill, which had been inserted into the Queen's Speech as a provision of possible benefit to the depressed agricultural sector. This merely proposed to try to cheapen the cost of the litigation associated with construction by transferring the responsibility for vetting new light railway lines from Parliament to the local authorities. There was no offer of any subsidy from the state to help with actual construction, and the Government's proposals appeared once again to discriminate against England by failing to give her the same advantages that had been enjoyed by Ireland since the legislation of 1889. In the middle of May Ministers seemed to acknowledge their programme's lack of appeal to the agricultural constituencies when they decided to give general support to the Land Tenure Bill, moved by a Liberal backbencher, Lambert, the M.P. for South Molton. This proposed to bring English land tenure more into line with Irish conditions by abolishing restrictive agreements and the landlord's right of distress for non-payment of rent and by providing compensation for disturbance.[37] As it turned out, the only substantial measure brought forward in the 1895 session which was to be carried successfully into law was the Factories and Workshops Bill. This tightened up the existing rules relating to overcrowding, overtime and the care of machinery. It enacted more stringent provisions for dangerous trades, such as those associated with lead and chemicals; and it extended the existing factory legislation to cover the whole area of industry, thus bringing in laundries, bakehouses and tenement factories. Such a piece of legislation could not safely be opposed. It went rapidly through all its stages in the House of Commons, and eventually became law in early July, after the change of Government but before the dissolution. Both Liberals and Unionists claimed credit for it at the general election.[38]

Before that time the Government had run into trouble with one final aspect of its multifarious programme. One of the sections of its majority which claimed some consideration were the representatives of the crofters of the Scottish Highlands. A croft was defined as an individual arable holding, with additional rights of pasturage held in common with others. In 1886 following considerable disturbances in the Highlands, legislation had been passed to remedy the crofters' grievances by giving them security of tenure, fair rent, and the ability to extend their holdings. By 1895, after years of agricultural depression, it was felt that further reform was due, and the Government's Bill of that year proposed both to extend the operation of the 1886 Act beyond the original six crofting counties and to allow leaseholders paying less than £30 rent a year, instead of £15 as formerly, to claim compensation from their richer neighbours in the form of enlarged holdings. To the Unionists this seemed once again a case of the Liberals tackling a genuine problem in the wrong way. 'Honourable Gentlemen opposite', declared Balfour, 'have always preferred the simpler and easier, and, above all, the cheaper course of not spending a sixpence out of the imperial funds, but of carving out from the prosperity of one class any advantage, real or supposed, which they intended to give to another class'. To the crofters' own M.P.s on the other hand the new proposals did not go nearly far enough, for they did nothing for the numerous class of landless cottars who scratched a living from fishing or from increasingly eroded rights of common pasturage. One Liberal backbencher, MacGregor, felt so strongly about what he considered to be the Government's lack of commitment to the crofters' cause that he resigned his seat in Parliament. At the ensuing bye election, in Invernesshire, the cards were heavily stacked against the Liberals. Their official candiate was imposed on the constituency by a Lowland wire puller, and his disestablishmentarian views apparently went down badly with 'Wee Free' voters who yet recalled that the secession of the Free Church in 1843 had taken place in protest against all interference with religious property. The Unionist candidate played on the economic grievances of the region. He stressed the lack of the light railway facilities that had been provided in Ireland, and he promised that he would support the extension of the Ashbourne Land Purchase Act to the Scottish Highlands. The result was the last and the worst humiliation which the Rosebery Government suffered at a bye election, with a Liberal majority of 329 being turned into a Unionist majority of 650.[39]

The end of the Government came, as is well known, after defeat by seven votes in the House of Commons, on a motion to reduce the Secretary of State for War's salary by £100 on account of allegations of a shortage of cordite and small arms ammunition. The fatal division was on 21 June. Apart from the shock of the Invernesshire bye-election, the Government had already suffered two Parliamentary embarrassments in the preceding few days. The first concerned the provision of £500 in the estimates to enable a statue of Oliver Cromwell to be built in the precincts of the Palace of Westminster. The idea was favoured by Liberal M.P.s from the eastern counties, but was strongly opposed by Irish Nationalists who recalled all the Protector's deeds in their country. Unionists enjoyed themselves pointing out that Cromwell had supported union with Ireland and reform of the House of Lords, and that he had sent a Parliament that had sat too long about its business. In the end the Government ran away and withdrew the proposed allocation. The second embarrassment was potentially more serious, for it concerned the future of the leading legislative item of the session, the Welsh Disestablishment Bill. On 20 June the Government came within seven votes of defeat on Thomas's amendment, which proposed to hand over tithes to the Welsh Commissioners rather than to the county councils. It has been argued that it was this event that determined Ministers to resign a couple of days later. Thomas's amendment to clause six threatened the future of the Welsh Disestablishment Bill by arousing financial jealousies between the various parts of Wales, and further trouble was to be expected on clause nine which dealt with the uses to which the newly secularised church property should be put. On the other hand the Government had survived debates on the bill by small majorities before, for instance on Macdona's amendment of 20 May which had struck at the root of the Welsh Disestablishment Bill by proposing to limit disendowment to property conferred by Act of Parliament.[40]

Defeat on the reduction of the War Secretary's salary need not have involved the resignation of the Government. Of its former majority only two M.P.s, Colonel Nolan (Parnellite) and Dilke (Liberal), actually voted against it. The real problem for the Government was that a good number of its supporters did not vote at all. No less than six Ministers (John Morley, Asquith, Shaw Lefevre, Robertson, Buxton, and Hibbert) were absent unpaired. Another Liberal M.P., Sir Theodore Fry, was detained unpaired on the continent, while an Anti Parnellite seat was temporarily vacant owing to the bankruptcy of William O'Brien. The real failure had been on the part of the whips, as it had been at the time of Labouchere's amendment to the Address in 1894, on an issue which did not seem to threaten the Government's existence directly; and, as on that pevious occasion, it should have been possible to reverse the vote subsequently in the House of Commons. This seems to have been the Government's initial intention—a strong summons was issued for its supporters to be present on the following Monday—but in the circumstances of mid-1895 this was easier said than done. The adverse vote could, hopefully, be overturned on the report stage of the estimates, but this would not be reached till some time later. Meanwhile the Government woud have to subsist with a Secretary of State who had been officially censured by the House of Commons, and whose strong inclination in the circumstances was himself to resign; but whose resignation, if it occurred, would plunge the Government into the difficulties that had been avoided at the time of the Speakership contest earlier in the year. The Government could resolve the problem immdiately by provoking a vote of confidence. But, taking account of enforced absences and the desire of one or two Radicals, like Dilke and Labouchere, to put the Government out of its misery, there was no guarantee that Ministers would win such a vote; it might look worse in the country to be defeated in a full dress debate than on a relatively minor matter. The courage that was necessary to carry on was lacking at a time when the Government's majority seemed in any case to be rapidly diminishing towards vanishing point; and in the circumstances it appeared more advisable to slip quietly out of office.

The Government had the option also of dissolving Parliament instead of resigning. This course was in fact favoured by Asquith and a majority of the cabinet, but it came up against the rare combination of Rosebery and Harcourt, who for different reasons now welcomed the opportunity to lay down their seals. Rosebery had had enough of the responsibility without power which had done so much to undermine his health earlier in the year. Harcourt was worried by the implications of calling a general election. If the Liberal Government were to go to the country it would have to do so on a definite programme, and this would mean among other things specifying its intentions regarding the House of Lords. The Government had so far managed to avoid bringing on the Parliamentary resolution promised by Rosebery in his campaign speeches of the previous autumn, but since then postponed on the grounds that it would cause embarrassing divisions in the Liberal ranks. The Chief Whip also argued against a snap dissolution as the party organisation was not yet ready for it, whereas putting the Conservatives into office would at least give the Liberals a breathing space. And there was always the chance that Salisbury would refuse to form an administration in the circumstances, thus allowing the Liberals to carry on for the time being in a position to disregard minor adverse votes in the House of Commons.

Liberal backbenchers may also have favoured resignation rather than dissolution. This is suggested by a letter written at the time to Lewis Harcourt by the ever scheming Labouchere. Of course it is necessary to treat Labby's communications warily; he is the most tendentious of sources. But his remarks on this occasion are worth quoting at length as they provide a realistic if cynical appraisal of the political situation as it appeared just prior to the fatal vote of 21 June. Labouchere's opinion was that 'M.P.s will vote anything to put off an election for years, but, when it comes to months, it is another matter'.

There are bills, Welsh and Irish, that no one cares for except the Welsh and Irish. In the mean while, the elections are declaring themselves against the 'filling of the cup'. Our majority is now 7 all told. With O'Driscoll in Australia, Fry with a broken arm in Italy, and Jacob Bright in bed, it is 4, if the Opposition has the sense not to pair them. This means that the division depends upon whipping. On the Welsh Bill, there are about 8 Liberal Unionists who refuse to vote, so it is difficult to be beaten on it. The only chance is on the 9th clause. But is the Party to be tied to remaining in until the majority of one has disappeared? If so, really steps ought to be taken to reduce it to nothing, and Ellis should be told to operate on these lines. Morton M.P., who is the sharpest of the London Members, tells me we shall do far worse in London on next year's Registration than on this. In the country, the longer we 'fill up', the worse it will be for us. I believe that almost any M.P. on our side would be glad if a Dissolution were announced. But would it not be possible to arrange a defeat, and then for the Government to resign, leaving it to the Unionists to come in and to go to the country with their programme, whatever it may be? We have practically none. The Lords will not 'fight'. Liquor will lose us votes. Home Rule is dead. By the Welsh Church we certainly do not gain votes in England, and Scotland seems to be going against us. I never yet hard of any Government that it can gain by going on with a falling majority until it has disappeared, and it is—as it seems to me—the very worst of tactics. If I were the Unionists, and I really wanted a Dissolution, I should buy half a dozen of our Irish. They would stop away—missing trains, or being ill—any night for £50 per head. But I take it that the Unionists are not all really in earnest, and I think that the waiting game will be more advantageous to them. It certainly is not to us.[41]

It is highly unlikely that Ministers deliberately courted defeat on the cordite vote, which was probably due much more to carelessness on an issue on which they did not believe themselves to be particularly at risk.[42] But certain Ministers, perhaps encouraged by Balfour's complacent attitude a week earlier towards the Government's taking more of the time of the House for its own business, may have allowed themselves to believe, either that the Unionists would refuse to take office, or that at least they would not call an immediate general election. If so, they miscalculated badly. Arguably a Liberal dissolution of Parliament would have had its drawbacks, but, as it turned out, simple resignation probably had more. Up to this time Ministers had been able to some extent to present the Opposition as a house divided against itself, composed of two distinct elements that would not be able to come together in government. The formation of the third Salisbury administration, an apparently successful coalition of Conservatives and Liberal Unionists, rather put paid to this illusion. The new Government was able to lay claim to the political middle ground, and to put itself forward as representing the best in both the Liberal and the Conservative traditions. As to accusations of its not having a policy, it soon disabused critics of that notion by making its immediate policy one of dissolving Parliament. The Liberals had surrendered the initiative by resigning office on grounds that were not really appreciated in the country, and their action helped to ensure that the ensuing general election was fought more on the record of the late Government than on any Liberal programme for the future. In addition the Liberal Government was to be criticised effectively, especially by Chamberlain in his campaign speeches, for having run away from its responsibilities at the last. Any idea that some Radicals may have had of obstructing discussion of the estimates during July, and thus delaying a dissolution of Parliament until later in the summer, soon evaporated. Once the change of government had occurred, it was evident that public opinion favoured having a general election to clarify the situation, and no M.P. was likely to risk unpopularity and the loss of his seat by trying to hinder the democratic process. Necessary financial business was quickly disposed of, and the new Government provided with funds, so that it was possible to dissolve Parliament just two weeks after Salisbury had assumed office.

Had the Liberal Government chosen to challenge or ignore the vote of 21 June 1895, it might well have lasted the session and survived into 1896. Probably the result of the general election, when it came, would not have been greatly different, unless some new difficulty had arisen between Conservatives and Liberal Unionists in the meantime. The Government would have benefitted somewhat from the revival of trade that was under way in the manufacturing, though not in the agricultural, districts by the second half of 1895, and Harcourt's oft repeated argument that there was nothing inherently wrong with the free trade system would have carried greater conviction. By electing to resign in June 1895, the Liberal Government arguably chose the worst of the three options available to it. Going out of office on an issue of military peparedness could do it no good in the country, and the Liberals forfeited thereby part of the entitlement which they could have claimed by virtue of their extensive programme of naval rearmament to be regarded as reliable custodians of national security. Campbell Bannerman also compounded the offence by attempting to shift responsibility for the ammunition shortage, in dubiously constitutional fashion, onto his professional advisers—neither a very plausible nor dignified line of argument at a time when he had just admitted the need for a major reorganisation of War Office administration by announcing the enforced retirement of the Commander in Chief, the Duke of Cambridge.[43]

It was in a sense appropriate that the cordite defeat should have closed the history of the century's last Liberal Government. Both the Gladstone and Rosebery administrations, like other European regimes in the 1890s, had been dogged by the spiralling costs of military expenditure. The price paid for adapting the country's armed forces to the rapid transformations in military technology proved a heavy one for the Liberals in power between 1892 and 1895. Naval rearmament brought about Gladstone's resignation in early 1894, and prevented the Liberals from implementing financial policies in these years which might have bolstered their failing popularity. The necessity of re-equipping the Army with ammunition based on cordite instead of black powder caused the final defeat of the Government in June 1895, for Ministers had tried to skimp on the required additional expenditure in order to pay for their enlarged naval programme. The burden of military deficits was not to disappear with a change of administration. Reviving trade and the increasing yield of Harcourt's death duties enabled the Unionists to get by for a number of years; but after the South African War they were faced with the whole problem in a far more aggravated form, and it was not the least of the circumstances which contribued to their own political debacle a decade after the events of 1895.

CHAPTER 4 NOTES

1. *The Times*, 18 Dec. 1894. *British Labour Statistics: historical abstract, 1881–1968* (1970) p. 305.
2. 4 *Hansard* XXX 75–82 (5 Feb. 1895). Harcourt Mss. 414, 25 Jan. 5 Feb. 1895.
3. *The Times*, 24 Jan. 1895.
4. Harcourt Mss. 413, 1 & 10–11 Jan. 1895.
5. Harcourt Mss. 414, 29 Jan. 1895.
6. Harcourt Mss. 414, 31 Jan. & 12 Feb. 1895; 416, 12 Mar. 1895.
7. 4 *Hansard* XXX 164ff. (6–8 Feb. 1895).
8. 4 *Hansard* XXX 372–87 (8 Feb. 195). Harcourt Mss. 414, 6 Feb. 1895.
9. Harcourt Mss. 415, 13 Feb. 1895.
10. 4 *Hansard* XXX 847ff. (15 & 18 Feb. 195).
11. 4 *Hansard* XXX 1285ff. (21 Feb. 1895); Harcourt Mss. 415 21 Feb. 1895.
12. 4 *Hansard* XXX 1135–79 (19 Feb. 1895).
13. 4 *Hansard* XXXI 664–83 (8 Mar. 1895).
14. *The Times* 20 Feb. 1895.
15. *The Times* 7, 13 & 23 Feb., 1, 4 & 5 Mar. 1895; *Saturday Review* 2 Mar. 1895. Apparently Progressive candidates like Sidney Webb, who increased his already substantial majority in Deptford, did markedly better than Lib Labs. like Burns, whose majority in Battersea was cut by 1200 votes.
16. Labouchere to Lewis Harcourt, 20 Mar. 1895. Harcourt Mss. 426.
17. Akers Douglas to Balfour 22 Apr. 1895. Add. Mss. 49772.
18. 'Two demagogues: a parallel and a moral', *New Review* Mar. 1895; *The Times* 18 Mar. 1895.
19. Burroughs, A., 'The contest', *New Review* Aug. 1895; *Saturday Review* 16 Mar. 1895.
20. Speech at Covent Garden Theatre *The Times* 27 Apr. 1895.
21. Chilston, Viscount, *Chief Whip: the political life and times of Aretas Akers Douglas, Viscount Chilston* (1961) ch. xiv.
22. *The Times* 12, 19, 22 & 25 Apr. 1895; Harcourt Mss. 418 21 Apr. 1895.
23. 4 *Hansard* XXII 1455–84 (26 Apr. 1894); XXX 1487ff. (25 Feb. 1895).
24. 4 *Hansard* XXXII 49ff (25 Mar.—1 Apr. 1895). Bell, P.M.H., *Disestablishment in Ireland and Wales* (1969) ch.7 passim. Morgan, K.O., *Wales in British politics 1868–1922* (1970).
25. *The Times* 4 Apr. & 23 May 1895.
26. Labouchere to Lewis Harcourt, 3 Mar. 1895. Harcourt Mss. 426.
27. *Saturday Review* 22 Mar. 1895.

28. 4 *Hansard* XXIII 293–319 (2 May 1895).
29. The Times 29–30 Apr. 1895.
30. *The Times* 8 & 29 Apr. 1895.
31. *The Times* 8, 9, 15, 16, 24, 31 May 1895.
32. *The Times* 4 Apr., 9 & 30 May 1895.
33. *The Times* 23 May 1895.
34. *The Times* 23 & 29 May 1895, 18 & 20 Apr. 1895.
35. *The Times* 18 Apr. & 29 May 1895.
36. 4 *Hansard* XXXII 1161–84 (8 Apr. 1895).
37. 4 *Hansard* XXXIII 1245ff. (15 May 1895).
38. 4 *Hansard* XXXI 168ff. (1 Mar. 1895).
39. *The Times* 31 May, 7, 17 & 20 June 195.
40. 4 *Hansard* XXXIII 1666–7 (20 May 1895); XXXIV 1598ff. (20 June 1895). Labouchere to Lewis Harcourt, 19 Jan. & 16 June 1895. Harcourt Mss. 426.
42. It has been argued that the actual vote was the result of an ambush worked by the Liberal Unionists in a thin House of Commons. Chamberlain was said to have whipped in his own supporters unbeknown even to the Conservatives, and, along with the military members who had a specialised interest in the subject, to have obtained a snap majority over the unsuspecting Government. (*Vide* Chilston, Visc., *Chief Whip: the political life times of Aretas Akers Douglas* (1961), p. 273). Chamberlain certainly had an interest in cutting short the debates on the Welsh Disestablishment Bill, which threatened some embarrassment for the Liberal Unionists.
43. 4 *Hansard* XXXV 100–06 (2 July 1895).

Chapter Five: The General Election of 1895

Parliament was finally dissolved on 8 July 1895. Campaigning had more or less begun with the fall of the Liberal Government a fortnight earlier; and the first actual pollings in a contest that, as usual in the pre-1918 period, extended over two or three weeks, were held on Saturday 13 July. Before that date, the large number of unopposed returns had provided an indication of the likely outcome and of the extent of Liberal demoralisation. In England alone the Liberals failed to challenge the Unionists in 129 seats in 1895, as compared to only 23 in 1892 and 1 in 1885. The Unionists on the other hand left only 22 Liberal seats in England uncontested.

'The main topic the electorate have had before them', claimed Balfour towards the end of the campaign, 'has been the merits and demerits of the action of the late Government'.[1] By resigning and allowing Salisbury to put together a coalition ministry, the Liberals had in effect made their own record in office the main issue of the election. Given the economic circumstances of the period 1892–95, it was not the easiest of records to defend. The Unionists were now able to put to particularly good use the arguments they had been rehearsing for a year and more, to the effect that the country's unresolved social and economic problems were the result of Liberal misgovernment. By raising contentious and unnecessary constitutional issues, it was said, the Liberals had perforce neglected pressing and practical subjects of legislation. By their quasi-revolutionary proposals, and by policies which threatened the rights of property and tended to set class against class, they had undermined business confidence and hampered economic recovery. Unionist rhetoric contained, usually not too explicitly, the promise of better times to come. Its keynote was perhaps provided by a speech made by Salisbury in the House of Lords just prior to the dissolution, in which he spoke of 'problems full of difficulty, but also full of the promise of the reward which attends the restoration of prosperity and the decrease of suffering among the poorer classes of the population'. Everybody, declared Salisbury, 'confesses the lamentable condition into which the great industry of agriculture has fallen'. He did not profess to have a panacea for it. But he thought that, along with other economic and social concerns, it was 'worthy of the most careful study'. And more specifically he talked of measures to relieve agricultural taxation, revise the operation of the Poor Law, and 'increase the generality of possession by working men of their own dwellings'.[2]

This was in fact Salisbury's only effective contribution to the campaign, for as a peer he was still considered as debarred from direct intervention at the hustings. For the Unionists the main burden of speechmaking was borne by two contrasting and complementary personalities, Balfour and Chamberlain. For Balfour the 1895 campaign represented probably the high point of his career as a democratic statesman. He was never to be so successful again, certainly not in the elections held after he had become party leader. His speeches in 1895 however were models of elegant and reasoned eloquence. Campaigning extensively in the North of England and the Scottish Lowlands, he on the whole avoided making specific promises, and concentrated instead on exposing the record of the late Liberal administration. Again and again he emphasised his theme, that the newly formed coalition was a truly national Government, whereas the Liberals had shown themselves by their policies to be divisive and at variance with popular traditions. Thus the late Government had moved to attack the House of Lords, an institution which, in Balfour's view, served to defend popular rights because it prevented hurried and drastic constitutional change without specific reference to the people. In pursuit of its quarrel the late Government had thrown away the chance of passing an Employers' Liability Bill, a measure which, in the meantime, would have saved many lives. Such narrowly partisan considerations similarly lay behind its efforts to disestablish the Welsh, and by implication also, the Scottish Churches, although that would involve the sequestration of endowments which enabled the poor in every parish to receive 'the religion of their fore-fathers'. Balfour laboured to demolish the Liberals' case even where it appeared most favourable to them, for instance with regard to the level of crime in Ireland. He rarely overstated the case for his own side. For example he admitted that the Local Option Bill had not figured very largely in the late Government's programme, but at the same time he adroitly insisted that temperance reform could be advanced in other ways than by threatening the liberty of the individual and drawing an invidious distinction between rich and poor.[3]

Chamberlain's style of campaigning was different but equally effective. Naturally combative and abrasive, his indictment of the late Government was even more wide-sweeping than Balfour's. He virtually accused it of corruption because of its slowness in extraditing Jabez Balfour. Whereas Balfour preached the need for national unity, Chamberlain played upon the divisions in the community, and he was not averse to setting 'class against class' in the manner so often deprecated by Salisbury when he was criticising what he perceived to be the spirit of latter-day Liberalism. Chamberlain appealed to non-unionists against those who belonged to trades unions, and to the interests of those who had votes against those who did not. He attacked the Liberals' temperance proposals for subordinating the rights of Englishmen to the interests of 'a small minority that could not take care of itself'. At times indeed Chamberlain seemed almost to have fallen back on Bright's old doctrine of the 'residuum'. He accused the late Government of having clung to power so long by dint of wire pulling and pandering to minorities. As he put it, 'this country has been governed during the last three years by a faction of disloyal Irishmen, of intolerant Welshmen, and of extreme teetotallers'. Chamberlain made the most of what he saw as the Liberals' favouritism towards Ireland. The recent 1895 budget, he pointed out, had lifted taxation on Irish whiskey while leaving it on English beer; the Local Option Bill, which so assaulted Englishmen's liberties, was not to be extended to Ireland; the late Government's proposals for franchise reform made no effort to tackle the scandal of Irish over-representation at Westminster. In particular Chamberlain strove to keep the provisions of the 1893 Home Rule Bill in the forefront of the electorate's mind. As he recalled, it had proposed to give an untrustworthy Ireland autonomy at a cost of £2 million a year to the British taxpayer whilst leaving virtually untouched the curse of continued Irish representation at Westminster.

More than Balfour, Chamberlain concentrated attention on social and economic questions. He disputed the late Government's claim to have carried into law at least two significant pieces of legislation in the shape of the Parish Councils and Factory and Workshops Acts, arguing that these were essentially bipartisan measures that owed their success to Unionist cooperation and forbearance. As to employers' liability, Chamberlain continued his running debate with Asquith, insisting that his own scheme of compulsory universal insurance was superior to the Liberal Bill. Most effectively of all he attacked the late Government's failure to do anything about the twin evils of depression and unemployment. Speaking in agricultural districts, Chamberlain made the most of Harcourt's frequent panegyrics on the benefits of low prices, which had brought near ruin to the British arable farmer. Before urban audiences he drew attention to the Liberals' neglect in taking no adequate measures to safeguard employment. They had failed to prevent unfair competition in the shape of imported prison-made goods; and, though they had set up a committee to investigate distress, it had 'sat through the frost and sat through the heat' without leading to anything, at a time when Ministers had managed to find an additional £80,000 in relief for Ireland. Chamberlain outlined a range of policies which he promised that a Unionist government would apply to the country's social and economic predicament, and he included in them a few particular ideas of his own. He spoke of help for the British farmer in the shape of reduced railway rates, relief of taxation, compensation for tenants' improvements, and the extension to Britain of the Irish Land Purchase Acts. Urban employment would be safeguarded by checks on alien immigration and on the importation of foreign prison-made goods. Social reforms would be available in the shape of old age pensions and measures to enable artisans to buy their own dwellings. Economic prosperity, he promised, would revive, thanks not only to the restoration of confidence which would accompany the return to office of a Unionist administration, but also to a more energetic programme of imperial development which would provide additional markets for Britain's goods in her colonial possessions.[4]

The Liberal leadership offered little effective competition to Balfour and Chamberlain. One historian has blamed this on the fact that the three prominent Liberals, Rosebery, Harcourt and Morley, campaigned mainly on separate policies, respectively the House of Lords, temperance and Home Rule.[5] It would be truer to say that they campaigned on hardly any clear policies at all. Rosebery delivered two speeches before the formal dissolution of Parliament on 8 July 1895 debarred him from further intervention in the elections.[6] He argued the need for the Liberal party to abandon ambitious programmes, like that associated with Newcastle, and to concentrate on one major issue at a time, beginning with that of the House of Lords. But he gave no indication of how he proposed to deal with the problem of the upper chamber. Indeed he had virtually disqualified himself from proposing any radical initiatives in the matter by his last action as Prime Minister when he had raised to the peerage two men of dubious reputation whose only merit was to have contributed substantially to Liberal Party funds. Neither this, nor the granting of a baronetcy to the former Conservative M.P. whose desertion had cost his party a bye-election at Colchester earlier in the year, was allowed to be forgotten by the Unionists, and Rosebery was still finding it necessary to defend the transaction in public a year later. Of Rosebery's colleagues, neither Harcourt nor John Morley had anything new to say. So far from concentrating on the issue of temperance, Harcourt spent most of his time in his Derby constituency defending the overall record of the late Government, and in the end it was probably Morley who delivered the more spirited speeches in favour of local option. Amongst leading Liberals only Asquith and Campbell-Bannerman campaigned with anything like effective vigour, and managed to carry the battle into the enemy's camp. Asquith's speeches in particular pointed to the likely divisions between Conservatives and Liberal Unionists in office, and to the vagueness of the new Government's intentions. "The last glimpse they had of the Prime Minister", he declared, referring to Salisbury's closing address in the House of Lords, "was that of a statesman in a brown study, wrapt in profound meditation over problems he could not solve". An electorate that looked to social reform could not in honesty expect it from an insincere and makeshift coalition, whose

> policy which is, in appearance, radical or socialist . . . is so contrived and manipulated as to conciliate, and, if necessary, to purchase, the support of all those monopolies and interests of which the Tory party is today, just as much as it has ever been at any time in its history, the guardian, the champion, the friend.[7]

Asquith and Campbell-Bannerman were both rewarded for their efforts by increased majorities, against the prevailing tide. Asquith in fact succeeded in doubling the size of his majority in East Fife, and may thereby have been lulled into a false sense of security for when he next faced a severe electoral test there in 1918.

The first contests, held on 13 July 1895, revealed an immediate trend. The Unionists gained 8 seats, as against only one seat gained by the Liberals. The sensation of the day, indeed the biggest sensation of the whole campaign, was Harcourt's defeat at Derby, a defeat moreover registered by a substantial turnover of votes which changed a Liberal majority of 1,843 into a Unionist majority of 1,122. Most Liberals at the time blamed local option, which was certainly a factor. Harcourt himself chose to attribute it to economic depression, which was probably more important. The true explanation is probably best summed up in a remark made by Harcourt to his colleagues just prior to the dissolution. "I shall have no manifesto", he said. "I shall simply say to my constituents 'I have been your member for fifteen years and I hope to be so again'."[8] In the circumstances of 1895 this was no longer sufficient. Increasingly Harcourt was perceived as a figure from the past, who went on too much about the Liberal record of the previous sixty years and the abolition of slavery and the corn laws. Nor could he get very far talking to his urban constituents about parish councils and death duties after the hard time many of them had been through during the winter of 1894–95. Even his somewhat bombastic claim—"I should like to know if there was ever a more extensive or useful reform than the Railway Servants Act [of 1893]"—did him little good in Derby, for by limiting the hours of labour it interfered with the piecework rates earned by many railwaymen.[9] Harcourt seemed to have nothing to offer for the future, and, apart from dilating on the evils of drink as a prime cause of crime and poverty, he failed to offer an adequate defence and explanation of his local option proposals. He had come to take his position in Derby too much for granted; he had rarely visited the constituency of late, and only once during the period of the Rosebery administration. In 1895 however he was faced, in this two-member seat, not only by an opponent who, as a former secretary of the Royal

Commission on the Aged Poor, was associated with social reform, but also by a strong local candidate, a philanthropist and churchman who, wisely perhaps, campaigned less on the disendowment of the publicans than on the disendowment of the Church in Wales.[10]

The Derby result was a microcosm of the whole election. Coming on the first day of polling, the defeat of so senior a Liberal set the pattern for what was to follow and spread alarm and despondency in the Opposition ranks. The ensuing week saw the widespread rejection of Liberalism throughout urban Britain. On the second day of polling the party lost 16 seats, on the third day 15 seats, and on the fourth day 9 seats. The Liberals surrendered many of their former strongholds in the large provincial cities. They lost all three seats in Bradford, and two each in Manchester and Glasgow. In the latter city, they now returned M.P.s for only two constituencies, as compared with seven in 1885. Overall the Liberals did less well in the larger cities in 1895 than they had done in 1886, partly, it seems, owing to the defection of the Irish vote at a time when the issue of Home Rule was in abeyance and that of religious education more to the fore. The defeat of John Morley at Newcastle-upon-Tyne was attributed partly to such Irish desertion, coupled with the continued hostility of labour interests towards him because of his opposition to the principle of a statutory eight-hour day.[11] Liberal losses were also heavy in the medium-sized boroughs and county towns of England; and for once even normally Liberal Wales was not proof against the tide. The Unionists gained six seats in Wales in 1895, mostly in urban areas where the Welsh Church was said to be reviving and which could expect few financial advantages from disestablishment. Apart from Harcourt and John Morley, other former Ministers, Hibbert, Shaw-Lefevre and Arnold Morley, went down to defeat. Amongst it all, there were a few crumbs of comfort for the Liberals. The dockyard constituencies remained loyal to them, thanks no doubt to the late Government's programme of naval expansion and to its endorsement of a minimum wage for Admiralty dock employees. And in some places the Liberals even managed to gain seats, especially, it was said, where candidates of a progressive bent were standing, as at West Nottingham and Ipswich.[12]

The dimensions of the Liberal debacle were especially evident in London. In 1892 the Liberals had made some promising gains in the metropolis; but these were more than reversed in 1895, and the party ended up with 8 seats out of 62, even fewer than in 1886. Disillusionment with the record of the late Government, at a time of economic hardship, was a principal factor. The main piece of Liberal legislation respecting London, the Equalisation of Rates Act, had proved disappointing and unfair. Designed to redistribute the burden of rates in favour of the more populous areas, it was said to have in practice subsidised the landlords of the heavily-populated East End at the expense of tenants living in other parts of London. Where Radical-controlled vestries, such as Newington, Bermondsey, Southwark, and St George's-in-the-East, had received rate-aid, they had tended to spend it rather than use it to reduce the level of local taxation. Like the Progressive-controlled L.C.C., the Liberal Government was associated with higher taxes and the imposition of additional legislative burdens upon manufacturers; and it was thus made an easy scapegoat for economic depression. The Liberals were accused of having done nothing for London, while having given so much attention to the Celtic fringe. The long and unfruitful labours of the select committee on distress from want of employment were held up to particular derision. In these circumstances London Liberals could hardly campaign with much confidence in 1895, while the Unionists blithely appropriated much of their former social programme, adding to it popular elements of their own such as the restriction of alien immigration. Many well-off Unionist candidates were also said to have strengthened their position locally by philanthropic activities and the provision of soup kitchens during the hard winter of 1894–95.[13]

Apart from disappointing their own supporters in London, the Liberals had aroused many apprehensions and antagonised some powerful interests. This was revealed in the pages of the *Daily Chronicle* towards the end of July after it had asked unsuccessful Liberal candidates in London to reflect on the causes of defeat. Local option had clearly excited considerable opposition, and was said to have been a principal factor in causing Keir Hardie's defeat at West Ham. Many shopkeepers appear to have been worried not only by rising rates but also by the late Government's tendency to favour the interests of organised labour in its arbitration in trade disputes. Religious education was also an important issue. Acland's policy, as education Minister, of putting pressure on voluntary and church schools, had helped to cost his party Catholic as well as Anglican support. Now that Home Rule had been relegated, Catholics had more to look for from the Conservatives, in the shape of additional rate-aid for church schools, and this was cited as a cause of Liberal defeat in constituencies such as Bermondsey, Limehouse and St George's-in-the-East.[14]

Another geographical entity which swung decisively against the Liberals was Lancashire. On previous occasions it had also reflected the national mood in somewhat exaggerated form; in 1880 it had swung markedly towards the Liberals, and in 1885 it had led the urban reaction against them. In 1895 the Liberals lost 15 seats in Lancashire, though they also managed to gain 2 against the prevailing trend. Two factors in particular were cited in explanation. One was the Indian cotton duties, by which the late Government was held to aggravate the general distress of the

Lancashire textile industry. Significantly, where the Liberals managed to win seats, it was at the expense of Conservatives who had voted in favour of taxing Lancashire's exports to India. The other factor, once again, was that of religious education. Lancashire had an especially high number of Church of England schools, and Balfour had made a particular issue of Acland's and the late Government's tightening up of building regulations and adding to the local expense of running such establishments, in his speeches at Manchester and Birkenhead at the start of the election campaign. Catholic interests were similarly affected. The remonstrations of Cardinal Vaughan, the former bishop of Salford, on behalf of increased rate-aid for church schools, were thought to have cost the Liberals seats such as Liverpool Exchange and North Salford.[15]

Nationally the first week of polling was mainly taken up with the contests in the cities and boroughs. The second week was dominated by the results from the counties. Some Liberals cherished a hope that as in 1885 the rural constituencies would reverse the trend established against them in urban Britain. They were soon disabused of this notion. On 18 July the county results began in earnest with the loss of five Liberal seats. Four more went down on the following day, and the climax was reached on 20 July when the Unionists wrested control of eleven English county constituencies. The process of attrition continued into the last week of July, with the loss of county seats also north of the border. Many of the Liberal defeats were in semi-industrial divisions of Yorkshire and Lancashire; but the Liberals also lost heavily in a broad band of agricultural constituencies across the centre of England, from Suffolk in the east, through Cambridgeshire, Bedfordshire, Northamptonshire, Oxon and Gloucestershire, to Wiltshire and Somerset. The county divisions of the south-east of England had long been solidly Unionist. Now their perimeter was appreciably extended. Interestingly, and in contrast to 1886, the Liberals lost no county seat in Norfolk, and only one in Devon and Cornwall combined. Their worst showing was in Cambridgeshire, where they lost control of all three county divisions. There was a certain poetic irony in this, for it was in Cambridge, in a notorious speech delivered in September 1891, that John Morley had seemed to suggest that the return to power of a Liberal government would make the fields of an agriculturally depressed England once again 'wave with golden corn'.[16]

According to Harcourt, in one of the defensive speeches with which he desperately tried to stave off defeat at Derby, "a Tory government did not make trade good or bad any more than they made the weather good or bad".[17] Evidently a considerable body of opinion, not least in the countryside, did not agree with him. The Liberal defeats in 1895 in rural England reflected the accumulated misfortunes of British agriculture, beginning with the growth of American competition after 1873, and culminating in the singularly unfavourable conditions of the mid-1890s. The Liberals' years in power were ones, for Britain at least, of exceptional agricultural disaster. International competition had rarely been greater, thanks to abundant harvests in the United States in 1891 and 1892, and in Europe in 1892 and 1893, along with a sevenfold increase in Argentine cereal exports between 1890 and 1894. In Britain, on the other hand, the harvest had been burnt up by an abnormally dry summer in 1893 and ruined by an abnormally wet one in the following year. Not surprisingly, wheat prices had fallen in the autumn of 1894 to a record low of 17s 6d a quarter, and this at a time when some men could remember certain years before the repeal of the Corn Laws when they had stood at over 100s. The weather once again promised to blight agricultural prospects in 1895. The prolonged hard frost of the early months of the year had delayed the work of preparing the soil, and the prolonged drought of the spring and early summer (which did so much for W.G. Grace) threatened a repetition of the conditions of 1893. Even more than usual, the agricultural classes were frustrated in July 1895, and they took out their frustrations on the departing Government as they had done in virtually every general election since 1874.

The weather however was not the only cause of Liberal unpopularity in wide areas of the countryside in 1895. The late Government had come to power in 1892 on a tide of expectations, swelled by rhetoric of which Morley's Cambridge speech was only one example among many. Parish councils in particular had been presented as a panacea for the problems of rural England. They would, it had been asserted, make it possible for the agricultural labourer to acquire land of his own, end the Church of England's virtual monopoly of village education, and bring a new spirit to the administration of the Poor Law. By "the quickening of a new life in the villages", they would, it had been hoped, halt the drift of the able-bodied rural population towards the towns, where it so often swelled the numbers of unemployed; and by helping to "create a public opinion in the English village" they would bring to an end the age-old domination of parson and squire.[18] The reality proved somewhat different. The first elections for the newly-created councils were held at the end of 1894, and by mid-1895 it had become apparent how inadequate were their powers and how disproportionate had been the expectations founded on them. The election of Poor Law guardians now appeared to be no substitute for the provision of old age pensions, which was increasingly desired by the labouring population in the countryside. The Unionists in 1895 had more to offer the rural electorate. They promised positive measures to promote agricultural recovery, such as the relief of taxation and reduced railway rates. Many Unionist candidates, though not amongst the leadership, recommended a return to protective tariffs in their manifestoes, and many also gave pledges on old age pensions. Chamberlain referred pointedly to his recent service on the Royal Commission on the Aged Poor. In addition the Unionists made the most of the fact that many of the late Government's policies had tended to be prejudicial to the interests of British agriculture. The 1894 budget had added to the burdens on land, and forced many landowners to retrench by reducing investment and employment on their estates. The Parish Councils Act had further increased the rate burden in the countryside. The Local Option Bill threatened one of the outlets for home-grown barley, while the 1895 budget had favoured the products of Irish agriculture at the expense of British by lowering the excise duty on whiskey and leaving it unchanged on beer.

Overall the 1895 general election resulted in a landslide victory for the Unionists. They gained 110 seats, securing thereby a 152 seat majority in the new Parliament. This was the biggest electoral triumph achieved by any government since 1832. It concealed however some interesting cross-currents. Because of the large number of uncontested seats, the difference in votes between the two main parties was actually quite small: no more than 123,000 votes out of a total poll of 3,617,000.[19] Despite the strength of the national reaction against them, the Liberals actually managed to gain 20 seats in 1895, thereby demonstrating the continuing importance of local issues in politics. 5 of their gains were made in Scotland, against a loss there of 13 seats; and 2 were in Ulster, where the Liberals had paid money to the hard-up Anti-Parnellites to let them contest certain seats, in an arrangement which drew much adverse comment both from the Unionists and the Parnellites. The Liberals also regained 6 of the 9 seats they had lost in bye-elections since returning to office in 1892. The general election also attested to the continuing viability of the Liberal Unionists, who won 28 seats as against a loss of 5, and of the Parnellites, who gained 5 seats and lost 2. Finally it is important to mention the 35 Labour candidacies, half of which were in Lancashire and the West Riding. None of these proved successful, and arguably I.L.P. intervention prevented the Liberals from picking up one or two doubtful seats in Lancashire. Against a background of depression and unemployment, it was the Unionists more than anyone else who made the running on questions of social reform in 1895. Still, the I.L.P.'s showing in this year was a portent of some significance for the future. Several promising results were obtained, with Tillett garnering 23% of the vote at West Bradford, and with Labour candidates doing as well at Preston and at Halifax, Leicester, Gorton, East Bristol and South West Ham as Liberal or Conservative candidates had done ten years earlier. The total Labour vote in 1895 amounted to some 51,000. This did not seem much until it was remembered that the French Socialists had mustered only 90,000 in 1889, and that by 1895 they were in a position to make and unmake governments.[20]

The Liberals found a ready explanation for their humiliation in the hostility and machinations of vested interests. The 'triple alliance' in Radical demonology, of bishops, brewers and landlords, enabled the Liberal party to avoid a more searching examination of its own deficiencies. Drink was made a particular scapegoat, from the moment of Harcourt's defeat at Derby. And the view that the 1895 general election was to a considerable extent fought and lost on the question of local option has continued to enjoy a certain respectability, as much if not more so than Gladstone's famous explanation of his 1874 defeat that he had been borne down in a torrent of gin and ale. Harcourt himself contributed faithfully to this version of events when he left Derby to fight (successfully) the constituency of West Monmouthshire, and blamed his previous setback on the corrupt collusion between church and public house. Privately, however, he admitted, as has largely been argued above, that "the main cause was bad trade".[21] Certainly the drink issue had cost Liberalism votes, especially where, as at Derby, the temperance party had taken to the streets in an aggressive manner and paraded an effigy of a working man, in tattered garb and with a painted red nose, as a representation of 'the trade's finished article'.[22] But there is evidence that where the drink interest itself adopted aggressive tactics, by way of self-advertisement, it tended to provoke a backlash against it in its turn.[23] The Local Option Bill did not dominate the 1895 general election to the extent that was subsequently suggested by Liberal propaganda. Compared to Welsh disestablishment, it had hardly been debated in the course of the 1895 session, and it had not even got beyond its first reading. But the Liberals had been guilty of mishandling the issue in a way that had proved damaging to their cause. They should never have introduced a measure which they had so little chance of proceeding with. But once having introduced it they should at least have taken the trouble to allay unnecessary fears and to have explained it to the country at large. So little was the proposed legislation understood, at the time of the 1895 general election, that it was usually referred to, even by generally well-informed commentators like Hamilton, as a Local Veto Bill. Though, in fact, the Bill of 1895, as distinct from that of 1894, was more properly a Local Option measure, designed as it was to allow a local referendum to reduce the number of public houses in a given area as well as to ban them altogether. As such it proposed to democratise the system of licensing by taking sole discretionary authority away from magistrates and owners of large estates; but this positive aspect of the proposed legislation was rarely stressed by Liberal speakers who preferred to ignore what they feared was an unpopular subject altogether. Harcourt, often so devastating in attack, made a poor defence on the hustings of the only social reform for which he ever felt much enthusiasm or commitment. By going on so much about the connection of crime and poverty with alcoholism, he contradicted the generally optimistic view of society which Liberals were otherwise trying to convey, and he seemed to suggest that the average working man could not safely be entrusted with responsibility for his own actions. By making his advocacy of temperance the excuse for a partisan assault on the brewers and licensed victuallers, Harcourt also denied himself the opportunity of finding common ground with the Unionists, many of whom were similarly exercised by the social problems occasioned by alcoholic abuse, and of achieving a 'truce of God' which might have allowed some measure of temperance legislation, just like the Factory and Workshops Act, to be carried into law.

"I believe the Conservative result", wrote Hamilton of the 1895 general election, "to be mainly due to the Liberal policy pursued during the last 60 years".[24] This was a more pertinent observation than he perhaps realised, for one of the most telling features of the election campaign had been the extent to which the Unionists, and particularly Balfour and Chamberlain, were able to lay claim to the Liberal inheritance of the previous half-century. The traditional appurtenances of British Liberalism—liberty, democracy, and a due concern for the rights of the underdog—seemed to have been appropriated by its ancient rival. The Local Option Bill was only one instance among several of the apparent transformation of political values; for it proposed to interfere with the poor man's liberty to enjoy a pot of beer, while leaving untouched the privileges of the well-off in their hotels and restaurants, not to mention those of the Irish whose country would not be affected by the intended legislation. A similar case could be made out against the Welsh Disestablishment Bill, which threatened, it was said, the endowments of the poor and the preservation of the "religion of their forefathers". Even the House of Lords could be defended on democratic grounds, as it made possible the reference of key constitutional questions to the electorate, thereby safeguarding the "heritage of the people for the people" against "the chance action of a stray majority".[25] Balfour and Chamberlain constantly hammered home the theme of the incompatibility of the old radicalism with the new. The old radicals, of whom Chamberlain was now presumably the living embodiment, had stood, it was claimed, for liberty and building up the country's institutions, whereas the new radicals of the post-1886 Liberal party were bent only on coercion and destruction. Finally, in one other respect in 1895 the Liberal party could be said to have lost its former crown. It was no longer considered the party of prosperity which it had seemed to be in the Gladstonian heyday. This transformation in its image had begun even in Gladstone's time. Hard times, higher direct taxation, and a growing belief that Liberal policies tended to undermine business confidence, caused a swing against Liberalism in urban England in 1885. The same factors, reappeared on an intenser scale, had a similar, nationwide effect ten years later.

The 1895 general election has too easily been interpreted as in some sense a reflection of the imperially-minded mood of the day. In the words of one historian, its outcome could be explained "mainly because England (though not Scotland, Wales or Ireland) had now been caught up into currents of political feeling and doctrine—those of expansive imperialism—with which the Unionists were ready to comply and most of the Liberals were not".[26] In fact the far-flung empire was hardly an issue in the 1895 election campaign. The Rosebery administration had been markedly solicitous for Britain's imperial interests. It had come into existence on a programme of naval rearmament; it had warned France off the Nile valley; and almost its last real decision had been to authorise the building of a railway to connect the newly acquired Uganda protectorate with the sea. There was little here with which the Unionists could quibble, and they did not try. Only Chamberlain among leading Ministers made much reference to the empire, mainly in connection with the remedies for domestic depression and unemployment that could, he argued, be found in the development of Britain's overseas estates.[27] It would be truer to say that the 1895 general election was marked by an appeal to the usually dormant spirit of English nationalism. Chamberlain, in particular, made the most of the extent to which both the Newcastle programme and the record of the Liberal Government had seemed directed to the interests of the Celtic fringe.[28] In so doing he neatly reversed the Liberal argument of 1886–92, that the Unionists, by concentrating so much on killing Home Rule with kindness, were denying themselves the opportunity of doing anything useful for the rest of the United Kingdom. Rosebery had predicted at the start of his premiership that the fate of his Government would be decided, electorally speaking, by the 'predominant partner'; and so indeed it proved in July 1895.

CHAPTER 5 NOTES

1 Speech at Doncaster, *The Times* 22 July 1895.
2 4 *Hansard* XXXV 262–71 (6 July 1895).
3 Speeches at Dalkeith and Doncaster, *The Times* 18 & 22 July 1895.
4 Speeches at Walsall, Stratford-on-Avon, and Birmingham, *The Times* 16, 17 & 20 July 1895.
5 Stansky, P., *Ambitions and Strategies: the struggle for the leadership of the Liberal party in the 1890s* (1964) pp.175–76.
6 Speeches to the Eighty Club and at the Albert Hall, *The Times* 3 & 6 July 1895.
7 Speeches at the Albert Hall, Carlisle and Leven, *The Times* 6, 9 & 10 July 1895.

8 Stansky, op.cit. pp.175–76.
9 Speeches at Derby and Nottingham, *The Times* 6, 9 & 11 July 1895. Massingham, H.W., 'The debacle and after', *Contemporary Review* August 1895.
10 *Leeds Mercury* 15 July 1895; *Manchester Guardian* 15 July 1895.
11 *Daily Chronicle* 19 July 1895; *Liverpool Daily Post* 27 July 1895.
12 *Daily Chronicle* 18 July 1895.
13 Massingham, op.cit.
    The Times 17 & 23 July 1895.
14 *Daily Chronicle* 23, 25, 26 & 29 July 1895.
15 *The Times* 12 & 15 July 1895; *Daily Chronicle* 22 July 1895.
16 *The Times* 22 September 1891.
17 *Leeds Mercury* 9 July 1895.
18 John Morley's speech at Stoneleigh, *The Times* 4 August 1891. Rosebery used similar rhetoric in his speeches at Devonport and, on the eve of the election, at the Albert Hall,—*The Times* 12 December 1894 & 6 July 1895.
19 Cooke, C. & Keith, B., *British Historical Facts, 1830–1900* (1975) p.144.
20 Garvin, J.L., 'A party with a future', *Fortnightly Review* September 1895.
21 Harcourt to Gladstone 16 July 1895, Gardiner op.cit. II p.371.
22 *Leeds Mercury* 15 July 1895.
23 For instance at the bye-election at East Leeds in late April 1895—see *The Times* 1 May 1895.
24 See above 1 August 1895, Add. Mss.48667.
25 Quoted from speeches by Balfour at Glasgow and Dalkeith, *The Times* 17 & 18 July 1895.
26 Ensor, R.C., *England 1870–1914* (1936) p.221.
27 Speech at Walsall, *The Times* 16 July 1895.
28 See also speeches at Lambeth, Birmingham and Hanley, *The Times* 8, 11 & 13 July.

The Diary of Sir Edward Walter Hamilton 1894–1895

Tuesday 20 February   The secret about Mr G. is oozing out gradually. There is a general belief that something is going to happen: some think it is immediate dissolution; others that Mr G. is really about to retire . . . I confess I wish this long spun out episode were closed. I am getting so tired of lying & trying to put people off. Were it not for Mr G.'s strong feeling anent the increase of the Navy I am sure he would not be going now. He feels so well; & there are no signs of mental decay; he spoke last night in the House of Commons in his best & highest of forms. His eyes no doubt constitute a great difficulty; but even without eyes he is still better than anybody else in the House of Commons.

Wednesday 21 February   When I went to see Harcourt[1] this morning; he said I was sure I should be glad to know that he & John Morley[2] were fast friends again, and that all—(he believed he might speak for his colleagues as well as himself)—were determined to pull together shoulder to shoulder; all personal claims and personal likes and dislikes were to be laid aside. Whatever might happen, I might depend on his introducing the Budget, hinting that it might be not as Chancellor of the Exchequer but as First Lord. Indeed he gave me to understand that he would make no difficulty about taking the second place—that is, the Leadership of the House of Commons without the Premiership. I learned however later on in the afternoon that Harcourt, though foregoing his right to the first place, had not climbed down nearly as much as he had led me to suppose. His terms as conveyed to John Morley were very stiff. He made 3 conditions. (1) That he should be empowered to take a decision in the House of Commons without any reference to the Prime Minister: (2) That all important F.O. despatches should be submitted to him: & (3) that he should have a fair share of patronage. The Leader in the House of Commons on such conditions would of course be practically in plenary power and Prime Minister *de faco*. Rosebery[3]—I went to see him this afternoon—would decline point blank to accept the Premiership on such terms, however much he might be pressed by his colleagues to form a Government if he had as Leader in the other House a man with whom he was in complete accord & in thorough sympathy. Of course Lord Kimberley[4] might take a different view of the position; but he had been to

110

R. this morning to tell him that, if by chance the Queen should, on constitutional grounds, send for him (K.) he should advise Her to entrust to R. the duty of forming a Government. He certainly is a wonderfully loyal & modest man. R. told me that even if this duty did befall him in the end he would prefer that the Queen should send for Lord Kimberley in the first instance, so that he (R.) might avoid the charge of being considered the Crown's nominee . . .

Thursday 22 February . . . As to the formation of a new Government, the difficulties are evidently increasing. They are entirely connected with Harcourt. If he had not to be reckoned with, everything would go pretty smoothly: the rest of Mr G.'s colleagues would rally round Rosebery: all the influential ones (Asquith,[5] J. Morley, Acland[6] & Lord Kimberley) have given their adhesion to him. It would not be a very strong Government; but Rosebery could carry on for a time, with Asquith or C. Bannerman[7] as Leader in the House of Commons. With Harcourt on the scene, however, everything is changed. He came into my room this afternoon and said that I must not infer from anything which either he or Loulou[8] had intimated to me, that he was willing to forego his claims to the first place in favour of Rosebery; and there is no doubt he will be strongly backed by the Radicals. So it comes to this—Rosebery won't take the head of affairs with Harcourt as his lieutenant in the House of Commons; & Harcourt won't serve under Rosebery. The alternatives therefore appear to be—Harcourt as Prime Minister, notwithstanding the protests of his colleagues that nothing will induce them to accept him in that post; or Kimberley or Spencer[9] as Prime Minister with Harcourt in the other House as practical head of the show; or Rosebery as Prime Minister with Harcourt excluded from the Government . . .

Sunday 25 February I went & had a long talk with Rosebery this afternoon . . . As to the situation in Cabinet circles, Asquith had been this morning to tell R. that Harcourt was beginning to "show himself in the open": he was dreaming of a Memm. pointing out that, ever since the days of Melbourne, there had only been one Liberal Prime Minister in the House of Lords—Lord Russell—& then only for a very short time; but intimating that he was willing to forego his own claims on the conditions which he had previously stated. There was also, Asquith had said, in process of being got up a "round robin" among the Radicals demanding that the Prime Minister should be a commoner. This movement was believed to be due to a hint from Loulou H. R. thought that Asquith seemed to be rather taken aback at this manoeuvre intended to force the hands of R.'s colleagues. It is of course becoming a trial of strength between Harcourt & R. I have not a doubt which will win in the long run;

for though Harcourt may have had a good many Radicals with him, yet Rosebery has all the other members of the Cabinet at his disposal, he inspires confidence generally even with many Unionists; he has Scotland at his back; he has won favour with London & with the Labour party; & he is immeasurably superior as a Leader of man. R. does not say that he will decline the task of trying to form a government, but he would much prefer remaining at the Foreign Office than being a mere puppet Prime Minister in the hands of Harcourt. At any rate it was much better that he & Harcourt both knew how each other stood. Had I learned anything on the point? I said I did not know whether I ought to tell him what Harcourt had given me clearly to understand the other day. Rosebery said he thought I was bound to tell him. Whatever Harcourt had said was not said to me to keep to myself; it was said to me as one behind the scenes in order that it might come round. So I told him. Whereupon he remarked "I see now it is war to the knife". . .

Wednesday 28 February . . . I have been writing to Sir H. Ponsonby[10] this evening to tell him how the land lies. The only questions—but very material ones—are (1) will Harcourt consent to serve under Rosebery? (2) Will Rosebery consent to serve over Harcourt? I have hinted that, though it was clear that Rosebery alone can form a Government—I don't believe that Harcourt could get 3 men to serve under him—yet it might be well that the Queen in the first instance send for Lord Kimberley, the Leader of the other House; in order there may be no impression or suspicion that R. is the Crown's nominee. I feel more sorry than I can say about Harcourt. Nobody has ever been kinder to me than he has been; and unless he is to be excluded and consequently become a done man, he will have to climb down considerably. He won't be able to dictate his own terms.

The Lords have got the Parish Councils Bill back again today; and though they have given way on most points, yet they have inserted afresh one or two amendments: the Liberal Unionists Peers for the most part having supported the Government. This won't make the Duke of Devonshire & Lord Salisbury greater friends. Lady Salisbury in commenting upon the Duke's conduct is supposed to have said: "Yes, the Duke has behaved disgracefully towards my husband; but what else could you expect from the man who betrayed Gordon?". . .

Thursday 1 March . . . Ronald Ferguson[11] came to see me this afternoon. He had been touting round to pick up the news at political clubs. He said that whatever was going to happen, an immediate announcement was indispensable. Otherwise all kinds of caves would be formed. As far as he could judge, though a few old radicals were adhering to Harcourt, the bulk of the Liberals of varied shades were all for Rosebery; and this feeling will I am sure become more & more predominant.

Mr G. made what will be his last speech from the Front Benches this afternoon. I am sorry I did not go and hear him. He does not however seem to have been at his best. It was a word of more than warning to the House of Lords; but the case for attacking them, is not strong, for the Lords have really behaved extremely well: indeed, I doubt if any first class measure of a radical character ever emerged from the Lords with fewer vital amendments . . .

Friday 2 March   To-day has been a very interesting day for me: but rather painful and awkward. Loulou Harcourt asked me to come & see him this morning. It was evident that his father, seeing that it was impossible for himself to be head of affairs, desired to climb down: though Loulou did not say as much. What he did say was that his father was much wounded by what Rosebery is supposed to have said: "I could serve under; but I could not serve over him". Harcourt has taken this to be a direct imputation on his loyalty as a colleague. Loulou further said that it had come round to his father—(everything comes round)—that I had repeated to R. what Harcourt had gone out of his way to say to me—that in waiving his own claims he did not mean that he would accept R. as Head of the Government. Loulou & his father did not blame me for repeating it: it was only natural that I should assume that it was intended for repetition. But Loulou wished to explain that his father did not mean it seriously: his temper had been roused and he had said to me more than he intended to say. Loulou also added that his father quite understood the delicacy & difficulty of my position, standing as I did between the the two men, the life long friend of one (R.), and likewise as well-wisher of the other (Harcourt). I thanked him and said that I felt for his father more than I could express in words, as I certainly do. Loulou moreover was careful to explain that he had in no way been doing anything that savoured of intrigue: he had confined his communications on behalf of his father to the Cabinet & Edw. Marjoribanks.[12] I told him that I of course took him at his word and that I admired the gallant fight he had made for his father. I then undertook to go and see R. I found that R. had driven down to Willesden cemetery;[13] but I caught him on his return. I told him the gist of my talk with Loulou. As to the phrase he (R.) had used about serving "under" but not "over" Harcourt it was a *bon mot* more than anything else; and he referred to the many times in which in recent years he had advocated Harcourt's claims to the first place. "But", he added, "it is all very well for you to defend Harcourt, but you have not been his colleague. We cannot easily forget how we have suffered from him in Cabinet". After luncheon, while driving me back to Whitehall, he shewed me the paper which he had shewn to most of his colleagues, stating what he considered his own position to be. The gist of it was, that he would only consent to be removed from the Foreign Office to the Premiership on its being made quite clear that there was an unmistakeable call for him on the part of his colleagues that he should form a Government, and that then he would have to make two conditions—one, that there must be complete accord between himself & the Leader of the House of Commons: the other, that he should select whom he pleased for the Foreign Office and should have an unfettered hand as regards foreign policy.

Saturday 3 March   Mr & Mrs G. went to Windsor last night, & he handed in his resignation to the Queen this morning. So that great man was made his final exit from public life. I confess that on the whole I view it with thankfulness. I have always so dreaded it might be attended with some fiasco. As it is, he makes his bow with becoming dignity. His last act has not been connected with defeat in the House of Commons or in the country: nobody can say that he has clung to office up to the last moment: he quit Downing Street with almost unimpaired mental powers.

I saw Edwd. Marjoribanks this morning. As usual he was in good spirits and was most hopeful that personal difficulties would be surmounted. The fewer the changes made in the Cabinet, the better; but he considered it to be a *sine quo non* that the Foreign Office should be filled by a Commoner, like Campbell Bannerman: it was impossible that the two highest places in the Government—the First Lordship & Foreign Secretaryship—should be held by Peers. He did not attach much importance to the movement which was being made by Labouchere[14] & other Radicals, protesting against there having been no consultation with the party, the imposition of a Peer as Prime Minister, and the supersession of Harcourt. I feel tolerably certain that this will all "fizzle out". Labouchere has very little influence now; and it is known that he is actuated mostly by personal dislike of R., because R. declined to *place* him.

I heard this afternoon that Ponsonby was with Rosebery, which of course meant that the Queen had commissioned him to form a Government. I did not like to go to Berkeley Square; but at 7.30 I received a note from him begging me to come to dinner. Fortunately I was able to obey the summons and I have been spending a very notable evening with him. I found that the Queen had opened communications with him yesterday; and that his reply had been to point out the many objections which he saw to his becoming First Minister, and his own very natural dislike to succeed to what he called (in his letter to Ponsonby) a "damnosa hereditas". But Ponsonby's mission this afternoon had been successful; & he had consented to try his hand at forming an Administration, provided his colleagues agreed to let him have his own way about the Foreign Office.

He must put into that place the man whom he considers to be most fit, meaning Lord Kimberley: in spite of the protestations of Harcourt & J. Morley that a commoner should be appointed. Indeed R. believed that J. Morley wanted the place for himself! R. had got over his interview with Harcourt. He had been to see him in Downing Street; and he said that Harcourt had been very nice and had behaved very well in the difficult circumstances. Harcourt had indeed admitted to him that he recognised that he could not form a Government himself. So all is practically arranged; and what I have for so many years longed for & worked for has come about. Rosebery is Prime Minister of this country. He proposes to assume the First Lordship & Lord Presidency of the Council himself: to put Kimberley at the F.O.; Fowler[15] at the India Office; & Bryce[16] at the Local Govt. Board. Unless he can bribe Edwd. Marjoribanks to continue as whip with a seat in the Cabinet—(for which there is something to be said, considering how often the whip is called into Cabinet but which might constitute an awkward precedent)—he will offer E. Marjoribanks the Chancellorship of the Duchy with Cabinet rank, though what E.M. aspires to is the War Office—rather too high an aspiration. I suggested that if a great fuss was made about the Foreign Office, on the ground that the Peers had got too many of the big loaves & fishes, R. should content himself with the Lord Presidency of the Council, give the First Lordship to Harcourt, & put Fowler into the Chancellorship of the Exchequer. While at dinner, a box came from Windsor saying that the Queen was highly pleased that R. had accepted his commission and was ready to see him at any time. All she hoped was that she should not be obliged to see much of Harcourt. We sat till about 10.45, when he ordered his carriage round to drive down to the City to see his old friend Canon Rogers.[17] "As I can't" he said, "offer him a Bishopric, I will pay him the greatest compliment I can by announcing myself as Prime Minister first to him". Before we parted, he asked me what I thought would have been said, had he declined the task? I said, it would be considered that he showed the white feather. I held that he had no choice but to accept what the Queen, the party, & the country expected him to do. "Perhaps so", he said, "but I call you to witness that I undertake this duty of forming an administration with the greatest reluctance. The Foreign Office was an ambition of mine, I admit. I consider it by far the finest post to occupy. But the Prime Ministership I have never coveted. In doing what I have done today, I consider that it is the most daring act of my life, unless I except what I did just 32 years ago, which was steering the 'Defiance' at Eton without ever having been on the river".

Sunday 4 March I wrote to Loulou Harcourt this morning. I feel more than I can say for him as well as his father & Lady Harcourt. I am sure however the party will fully recognise his having submitted to take the second place only. I believe he will do his utmost to behave loyally to Rosebery & the rest of his colleagues. The question is whether he will have self control enough to carry out his good intentions . . .

I have purposely kept clear of Berkeley Square to-day, knowing how Rosebery would be pressed. He had to see all his colleagues, none of whom have a right to continue in their places without being invited to do so by the new Prime Minister. Everything seems to be going smoothly; but one unfortunate occurrence has taken place. Lord Tweedmouth died suddenly this afternoon . . . This will materially upset Rosebery's plans: Edw. Marjoribanks will be a great loss to him in the House of Commons; & it will be much more difficult to find a suitable post in the Government for E.M.

I found a large party at Londonderry House this evening . . . Randolph Churchill looked better but his speech was not less thick. I had some talk with him after dinner partly as to Budget prospects. He said that if Rosebery could give the "go-by" to Home Rule, the Unionist party would support him; but if he persisted in Mr G.'s Irish policy, he would be opposed as strongly as ever. The formation of the new Government was of course freely discussed. People have made up their minds that J. Morley will leave Ireland & that Bryce will be his successor. It is most essential that J. Morley should remain where he is; & I shall think little of him if he presses his claims for promotion . . .

Monday 5 March   The unparalleled Session, which commenced on the 31 January 1893, & which has consequently sat for 13 months with very short interruptions, had been brought to a close to-day, Parliament being prorogued—& only for a week—by a very short Queen's speech. In spite of the length of sitting, only one first class measure—the Parish Councils Bill—has been added to the Statute Book. As to Parliamentary reputations, Lord Kimberley has greatly improved his position in the House of Lords; while Mr G. has shewn in this, his last, Session undiminished energy & debating power as well as extraordinary adroitness in managing the House of Commons; while Asquith has shewn himself a strong & capable Minister. Arthur Balfour has come out as a much more dexterous Leader in Opposition than on the Government side. As a Parliamentary speaker he is now in the first rank, second only in Opposition to Chamberlain, who has been brilliantly successful as a debater, but who from his violent activity has I believe contributed more than anybody or anything else to keep together the supporters of the Government: they were determined not to be beaten by him. Poor Randolph Churchill has gone down hill very much.

I dropped into tea with Mr & Mrs G. this afternoon. I am afraid the Queen's letter written to him after he left Windsor on Saturday was anything but warm. It was (I understand) merely an acceptance of his resignation and an intimation that she would have offered him an Earldom, if she had not known that he would decline it. If she lives, she will find out how staunch a friend he has been to all monarchial interests. He declines to express any opinion on the ministerial arrangements necessitated by his retirement. He spoke in high terms of Edw. Marjoribanks' services. He said E.M. was "*the best*" whip he has ever known in his long Parliamentary experience. He referred again to the Navy question, & denounced the proposals in as strong language as ever. "If", he said, "I stood alone in the world on this question, I could not be moved, so strongly am I convinced that this large increase to the Navy will lead to disaster in Europe—Europe is my watchword."

After sitting with Mr G. some little time, I went over to the Foreign Office to see the new Prime Minister. He of course had had his way about the Foreign Secretaryship, & had offered it to Kimberley, who throughout the crisis has behaved like a real gentleman always thrusting his own claims in the background, & expressing willingness to serve anybody in any capacity. J. Morley, R. told me, had been prevailed upon to retain the Irish Secretaryship, but not without some grumbling & evident aspirations for something better & more dignified than the conduct of Irish affairs; Fowler had been offered the Secretaryship of the State for India but had thought it necessary to ask for a night to think over the offer; & S. Lefevre,[18] the Local Government Board, while Ellis[19] was to become First Whip. R. had not made up his mind yet what to do with Edw. Marjoribanks:- possibly some high Household Office; for Lord Oxenbridge is to be got rid of somehow. R. has had a very satisfactory audience of the Queen this afternoon at Buckingham Palace; & had accepted the First Lordship of the Treasury & the Lord Presidency of the Council. This is the best of all combinations for a Prime Minister. The First Lordship is the traditional office for him to hold; while the Lord Presidency is most appropriate, inasmuch as the Cabinet over which the Prime Minister presides is a Committee of the Privy Council, and the office gives him befitting rank. R. decided on my recommendation to take Geo. Murray[20] as his first Private Secretary, & he then walked across the road with me to make the offer and to pay his respects on Mr & Mrs G. as Prime Minister . . .

Tuesday 6 March   It is most gratifying to see the chorus of approval with which R.'s accession to the Prime Ministership is hailed.

I have been looking up the ages to Prime Ministers of this century to see how nearly R. has been the youngest of them. This is the order in which they come.
1.   *Lord Liverpool* born in 1770 & became Prime Minister on 16 June 1812, aetate *42 years*

2. *Lord Goderich* born on 1 November 1782 became Prime Minister on the 8 Sept. 1827, aetate *44 years 10 mos. & 8 days*

3. *Lord Grenville* born in October 1759 & became Prime Minister on 10 February 1806, aetate *46 years & 4 mos.*

4. *Lord Rosebery* born on 7 May 1847 & became Prime Minister on 5 March 1894 aetate *46 years & 10 mos.*

5. *Sir Robert Peel* born on 5 February 1788 & became Prime Minister on 26 December 1834, aetate *46 years 10 mos. & 21 days*

6. *Mr Spencer Perceval* born on 1 November 1762 & became Prime Minister on 6 December 1809, aetate *47 years & 1 mo.*

I have been seeing Harcourt this afternoon. He was most kind & considerate about myself: thinking perhaps that I might be disappointed at not succeeding Welby[21] as Secretary to the Treasury. I told him that I considered it would be monstrous if Mowatt[22] were not put into Welby's place: he has strong prior claims both as regards age & service; he is much better fitted for the work; and I prefer infinitely my present post. He said however he should insist on its being made quite clear that I was *second* to Mowatt. He hardly alluded to the events of the last few days—so I was able to confine my remarks to saying how glad I was—and I sincerely am—that he was going to remain on as Chancellor of the Exchequer. We then talked over the Budget. I think he is on right & sound lines; but I am doubtful about the expediency of his project to propose a graduated Income Tax surcharge on incomes over £5000 at the rate of ½d to the £ on every successive £5000. I am afraid it will frighten people while the result to Revenue is a pure shot and may lead to very little. After leaving him I went upstairs to see Lady Harcourt. It was rather a painful interview, as she quite broke down with me. She said she could not talk of recent events; but hinted that Rosebery had not shewn her or her husband the consideration he might have done.

Wednesday 7 March . . . Edwd. Marjoribanks (Tweedmouth that is) has been squeezed into the Cabinet as Lord Privy Seal, and is said to be quite pleased. Bryce has been offered the First Commissionership of Works in succession to Lefevre transferred to Local Government Board; but he has declined it rather huffily. R. thought he would like a place of more work than the Chancellorship of the Duchy; but Bryce aspired higher—to a Secretaryship of State. I suspect the Foreign Office in his heart of hearts! It is quite extraordinary what exalted ideas politicians have of their own claims: Bryce has gone quite high enough; for he is little use in Cabinet or in the House: he is too donnish in appearance and priggish in manner. There has been an idea of relieving Herbert Gardner[25] of his place by conferring on him a Peerage, which I believe is what he has always set his heart on; but the idea has been abandoned, in order that too many seats may not be vacated just at this moment. As the Board of Agriculture is not to be vacant at once, Herbert Gladstone[24] is to be put into the Works.

I have been dining this evening at York House—where the Duke & Duchess of York have been giving their first dinner . . . Rosebery talked almost all dinner to Mrs G.; and I am glad to say went & conversed with Lady Harcourt after dinner, which I hope may have done much good to relieve the tension. R. & I came away together. He took me back to Berkeley Square. He told me that the Duke of York[25] had been talking to him about getting up a little constitutional history. R. said what was more important & would be more useful was the acquaintance with the *machinery* of Government, & suggested that H.R.H. should ask me to come & discuss the question with him. Of course I will gladly do what I can to help the Duke of York; but I am not very good at expressing myself orally & have had no experience of imparting knowledge.

R. seemed very well in spite of the amount of work he had to face; for he was not only Prime Minister but still Foreign Secretary. He had 52 boxes in his room which were waiting to be disposed of, & he had to write the Queen's Speech. He said J. Morley was in a bad humour, soured & grumpy. Asquith remarked the other day that though J. Morley might be very touchy & difficult to manage he was at any rate a perfect gentleman. "Yes" said R. "but I am not sure whether a perfect lady would not best describe him". He is certainly apt to be peevish, changeable & jealous.

Thursday 8 March   Rosebery held his first Cabinet to-day, & held it at the Foreign Office from which he is not yet finally uprooted. The Queen's Speech was approved. I hear he conducted the Cabinet admirably. Harcourt was rather sulky & said little. The Cabinet is now definitely constituted thus.

First Lord of the Treasury & President of the Council	Lord Rosebery *
Lord Chancellor	Lord Herschell[26]
Lord Privy Seal	Lord Tweedmouth *
Home Secretary	Mr Asquith
Foreign Secretary	Lord Kimberley *
Colonial Secretary	Lord Ripon[27]
War Secretary	Mr Campbell Bannerman
Indian Secretary	Mr Fowler *
Chancellor of the Exchequer & Leader of the House of Commons	Sir Wm. Harcourt
First Lord of the Admiralty	Lord Spencer

Chief Secretary for Ireland	Mr J. Morley
Chancellor of the Duchy of Lancaster	Mr Bryce
Secretary for Scotland	Sir Geo. Trevelyan[28]
President of the Board of Trade	Mr Mundella[29]
President of the Local Government Board	Mr S. Lefevre *
Vice President of the Council	Mr Acland
Postmaster General	Mr A. Morley[30]

The only men who have changed places are those against whose names I have put a star; and the only addition to the Cabinet is Edwd. Marjoribanks Lord Tweedmouth. The other ministerial changes consist of Herbert Gladstone's transfer from the Home Office to the First Commissionership of Works; George Russell's[31] transfer from the India Office to the Home Office; and the appointment of Reay[32] to succeed George Russell . . .

I have been dining this evening at John Morley's to meet Asquith and Miss Margot Tennant. The Edward Greys[33] were also there. Harcourt had held out a very big bribe to J. Morley viz: the Chancellorship of the Exchequer on of course the understanding that J.M. would support Harcourt's claim. J.M. actually admitted to me that in his opinion the Foreign Secretaryship was the best of all offices to hold, with an evident hankering after it himself.

Friday 9 March   Rosebery looked in upon me at the Treasury to-day. He was inspecting the Council Office as well as Downing Street. He will eventually sit at No.10, when Mr G. is cleared out; but this will not be for some days. He had been deluged with congratulatory letters & telegrams: it is worse, he says, than being engaged to be married. The letter that seems to have pleased him most is the one that the Duke of Devonshire wrote him.

. . . There has been very little going on in the social world this spring in the way of entertainment. The fact is, big dinners & parties are being supplemented by small dinners either at home or at restaurants and Theatre parties.

Sunday 11 March   Lord Ripon told Henry Primrose[34]—and he has had longer experience of Cabinets than anybody else—that he thought Thursday's Cabinet better presided over than any other Cabinet which he had attended.

The usual Parliamentary dinners took place last night. R. had the whole of his ennobled followers to dinner in Berkeley Square, and Harcourt entertained all the members of the Government in the House of Commons, including the latest addition to the Government—Arthur Brand as Treasurer of the Household *vice* Chesterfield promoted.[35] R. read the Queen's Speech *before* dinner, following Mr G.'s practice in this respect. At Harcourt's dinner the grave irregularity of toasts was committed, Harcourt himself proposing Mr G.'s health, & Campbell-Bannerman proposing Harcourt's. Lady Spencer gave a party last night to follow the Parliamentary dinners. She has, much against her will, moved to the Admiralty which is not a good substitute for Spencer House; but Lord Spencer professes to be very hard up in spite of the sale of his library. Rosebery on acceding to the Prime Ministership has only submitted one honour to the Queen, and that has been declined—he offered Lord Leigh an Earldom on the ground of his faithful adherence to Mr G.

It is difficult to imagine the reassembling of Parliament tomorrow with its great central figure practically removed. Mr G.'s Parliamentary career has at any rate been absolutely unique: 60 years in the House of Commons, about 27 years in the service of the Crown, four times the Queen's Prime Minister, and Leader of the House of Commons in his 85th year. No man in the century has ever exercised so commanding an influence or so mesmeric a fascination. The secret of that influence and fascination has been the extraordinary combination of qualities—the personal dignity of the man, the charm of his manner, the loftiness of his character, his courteous and deferential bearing towards high and low, rich and poor, his boundless enthusiasm, the versatility of his interests, the earnestness of his conviction, the grandeur of his voice, the magnificence of his vocabulary, his great powers of construction, his mastery of details and lucidity of exposition. To many the last chapters of his life will be reviewed very differently to the previous chapters; but I am sure of one thing, and that is that he was never more convinced of the righteousness and conviction of a cause than the cause of Home Rule . . .

Monday 12 March I committed this morning the grave impropriety of attending the meeting of the Liberal Party at the Foreign Office. I thought the special circumstances might be held to justify my witnessing Rosebery making his *début* as Leader. I sneaked in behind him. He was well received; & if possible Harcourt, who came in immediately afterwards, got even a still better reception; the party being evidently determined to show that they thoroughly appreciated his having submitted to take second place. R. made an admirable speech: it was dexterous, incisive, and resoluute. It was, he said, a change of men, not of measures. There was no new policy to expound. It was a question of "as you were". The "Newcastle programme" had to be got through, & Home Rule could not be shelved. He was a convinced Home Ruler, in spite of the many assertions to the contrary; but he hinted that as there were many roads to Rome, there were many ways to Home Rule. The present constitution of the House of Lords was in these democratic days an anomaly; and he referred to his having made the reform of that House a special study. His allusion to the House of Lords was what really elicited most cheering. It is evidently the question which the party has most at heart. Harcourt followed R. and got another hearty cheer; but his speech was rather lumbering & over-pompous. John Morley said a few words; and then one or two of the rank & file spoke—Pease, Whitbread (an old hand at these meetings) O. Morgan & Hunter.[36] It was a very harmonious meeting. As soon as it was over, I walked across with Rosebery to Downing Street. He had to attend a meeting of the new Board of Treasury, at which the Patent was read and the Parliamentary & Financial Secretaries called in. I then drove with him to Berkeley Square: a considerable crowd had gathered round his carriage and cheered him heartily. Hawkesbury[37] (C. Foljambe that was) came to luncheon, in order to have a few words with R. before seconding the Address this afternoon in the House of Lords. R. told me he thought of offering the Mastership of the Horse to Tweedmouth. But owing to information I received later, I suggested his sounding Lord Cork or Kenmare. I believe both are ready to take office under him.

Tuesday 13 March   . . . All went well in both Houses last night. The allusions to Mr G. on both sides were very nice. R. made a very good speech; but there was an impromptu sentence in it which promises to give trouble. He had expressed his agreement with what Lord Salisbury had said as to the necessity of converting England, the predominant partner of the United Kingdom, to Home Rule before any such measure can be carried. It is an obvious truism, but the Irishmen have taken offence at it, as involving too long a wait. Harcourt was very exercised this morning at the effect of R.'s speech, and said the fat was all in the fire. He (Harcourt) had been pleased by his reception in the House of Commons and told me that nobody had been kinder or more sympathetic to him than Goschen. The Address in the House of Commons was seconded yesterday by one of the Labour candidates, Fenwick;[38] & court dress was for the first time dispensed with on the occasion in his case.

Wednesday 14 March   There was an unfortunate *contretemps* last night in the House of Commons. Labouchere, by a majority of 2, actually carried his amendment for the Address, praying the Queen to stop the power which the Lords have of preventing Bills from being submitted for Royal approval. So the Address has been so amended as to contain a request for the practical abolition of the Upper Chamber. It was a very disagreeable joke to perpetrate, and as Addresses to the Crown are not documents in which jokes can be inserted, some steps had to be taken to reverse the decision of last night. A Cabinet was hastily summoned this morning; and the only way out of the difficulty, which suggested itself and which was agreed to, was to negative the original address and substitute a new one. This decision was communicated to the House this morning on its meeting at noon by Harcourt, who was in his most funereal and pompous of moods; and the procedure was adopted this afternoon *nem.com*, a procedure, however, for which I believe no precedent could be formed. It was a very unfortunate beginning for the new Whip, and no doubt the House was taken entirely by surprise, Labouchere having succeeded in taking a snap division. But it is the duty of Whips not to be surprised; and so it is not possible to acquit T. Ellis of blame. I believe he is a good fellow and not unpopular; but I doubt if he is man enough for the place. He is hardly known outside the House at all (I have never met him myself) and he cannot carry real weight. Besides being wanting in these respects, I am told he talks with a broad Welsh accent. I went to luncheon with Rosebery. He took the House of Commons proceedings very quietly. He attached little importance to Labouchere's joke. What he did not like was the disposition of the Irishmen towards him in regard to the sentence in his speech on Monday. He admitted that it would have been better left unsaid; but he would have an opportunity on Saturday next of explaining his meaning more clearly. He was to see Mundella this afternoon who has got into trouble, having been a director of some New Zealand Company, which has come to grief, and some of whose proceedings are likely to turn out to be very shady. Other M.P.s are in the same boat with him—Gorst, Sir C. Russell & Sir J. Ferguson. I am very sorry for Mundella as it may involve him having to resign office. Not that he will be any real loss to the Government, but he is a good fellow himself and delights in Ministerial life. At the same time it is high time that some example was made of men of position and standing who lend their names to the directorship of companies and who intentionally or unintentionally know so little of the conduct of the business that they are really guilty of criminal negligence, to say the least of it.

I received a summons to go to York House this morning; and I obeyed it. The Duke of York said he was anxious to act on Rosebery's suggestion and have some talks with me about Government machinery. He was reading Bagehot's book on the Constitution with a professor; but he found it difficult to follow and hardly gave him the information he wanted. I found him very easy to talk to, because he asked so many questions; and the easiest way of imparting knowledge is by answering questions. He confessed that he had read very little and knew very little. He could not remember what he read and he had no power of assisting his memory with notes. Our talk this morning mainly related to the powers of the Sovereign, the constitutional checks upon those powers which were now mainly nominal, the popularity of the monarchy, the influence which may and the influence which may not be exercised by the Crown. He also discussed the relative advantage of a King & a Queen and referred very sensibly to the difficulties which might have arisen, had the life of the Prince Consort been prolonged.

Thursday 15 March . . . Buckle has always professed great devotion to Rosebery; but he does not show it, now that he has the chance; for anything more disagreeable & mischievous than the articles in the *Times* on the change of Government could hardly be imagined.

A Cabinet was held this morning in No.10 Downing Street in the old Cabinet room on the ground floor. Rosebery intended to resume the holding of Cabinets in that room and to have meetings regularly once a week, whether or not there is any specific business to be done. Harcourt explained his Budget proposals to his colleagues who accepted them. The proposals came to this: The expenditure of next year on its present basis exceeds the estimated Revenue on its present basis by about 5 millions. By putting an end to the financial machinery of the Imperial and Naval Defence Acts he bridges over 2 millions of this deficit; and the remainder he meets (1) by his new graduated Estate Duty imposed on all property passing at death, which is expected to yield £1000,000 this year (2) by putting on an additional 6d per gallon on spirits and 6d a barrel on beer which ought to give £1500,000 and (3) by adding a penny to the income tax which after excluding the exemption & abatement to small incomes and making an allowance on Schedule A, ought to make ends meet. The Chanc. of the Exchequer has reluctantly abandoned his proposals to introduce an Income Tax surcharge, which was to be levied by direct assessment on all persons having £5000 a year from all sources: the surcharge being ½d in the £ on the first £5000 over £5000, 1d in the £ on the next £5000, and so on at the rate of an additional ½d in the £ on every successive £5000 up to £100,000. I am not opposed to the principle of a moderate surcharge like this; but I am glad it has been abandoned this year. I have always felt that the proposals would over-weight this Budget and that coupled with a graduated Estate Duty it would frighten people too much. Moreover A. Milner[39] found the difficulties anent the proposals were greater, the more he went into it, what with (1) the impossibility of framing an estimate of the yield of such a surcharge, (2) the liability to have it evaded, (3) the many provisions it would entail in the Budget Bill to make it operate at all (4) the inquisitorial nature of the proposal and the unpopularity of it together with the odium which it will bring on the Inland Revenue Department and the Government (5) the great addition it would involve to the Income Tax Staff. In view of these objections, it became a question whether the game was worth the candle. My own opinion is that, if there is to be graduation in taxation on the property of the living the tax that lends itself best to the principle is the House Tax.

Saturday 17 March (Ascott, Leighton Buzzard) Rosebery has gone to Scotland to make a speech in Edinburgh this evening. There is great excitement as to what he will say, more especially as to the meaning of his remark last Monday in the House of Lords about converting the predominant partner of the United Kingdom before Home Rule has a chance of passing.

Sunday 18 March (Ascott) There was a great rush to the papers this morning to read Rosebery's speech last night. On the whole it seems to have been dexterous; and (to judge from the remarks which Dillon[40] made after hearing it) it ought to have satisfied the Irishmen. Both the Opposition and Irishmen had interpreted his speech last to mean that before Home Rule would be proceed with there must be a majority in favour of it in England. I never thought he meant this. What I believe he did mean, and what he now says he meant, was that there must be a larger majority in the House of Commons ready to support Home Rule; that as Ireland, Scotland & Wales are already largely in favour of it it must be in England the predominant partner where the increased majority must come from; but that this did not necessarily mean an actual majority in England...The fact is, it was not a happy remark to have made. What everybody, especially the Irishmen, has to remember is that Home Rule has no chance when it is carried in the House of Commons by a very decided majority. A good many of the Opposition are disappointed that the Irishmen have not revolted straight away under R's rule. They preferred to imagine that with R's appearance as Prime Minister Home Rule would disappear *in toto*.

Tuesday 20 March Randolph Churchill insisted on raising the question last night in the H. of Commons, whether Rosebery's speech at Edinburgh was an infringement of the Standing Order against the interference of Peers at Elections in view of the Leith Election. He made nothing of it; & Harcourt's proposal to proceed & the order of the day was agreed to without a division. The fact is the Standing Order is out of date & ought to be allowed to fall into desuetude. But Randolph C. must now find an excuse to make a speech, & it is very difficult for Arthur Balfour to say he won't have it.

I was at the Bank today borrowing a million in Treasury Bills. Year's Bills went for £1-12-0! an extraordinarily cheap rate . . . Lidderdale & others whom I saw take a more cheerful view of affairs—trade is reviving, confidence returning, & employment for money will soon be forthcoming.

Wednesday 21 March   The Navy proposals have been very well received. The Opposition are satisfied: indeed the provision for ship building is larger than they expected; and there is no outcry against 'bloated armaments' here or abroad. The great difficulty ahead for the Government is the Budget; but I think it is on sound lines, and the opposition won't be very keen to incur the odium themselves of increasing taxation. The most contentious point in the Budget will I expect be the increase in the Beer and Spirit duties. Ireland and Scotland besides the brewers are sure to hollow out loudly.

Thursday 22 March   Mr G. has written a letter to his Chairman in Midlothian to say farewell. He puts himself unreservedly in the hands of his constituents, and makes a dignified reference to his past political career[41] . . . I went to see him this morning & found him in his shirt sleeves arranging his papers & turning out his drawers . . . He said he was astonished to see how quietly this vast addition to the Navy Estimates had been taken, and he broke out again on the subject in strong language. 'I regard it', he said, 'as the greatest & richest sacrifice ever made on the altar of militarism. It is absolute insanity. I can only apply my old phrase to the author of it "mad or drunk". I dread the effect which the proposals may have on Europe. The peace of Europe is my primary consideration. Financial considerations such as the sounding of the death-knell to the Sinking Fund are merely secondary!' I did not like to argue with him to-day: so all I said was that I hoped that in this instance he could prove a false prophet. Today was presumably the last occasion on which I shall ever see that great man inside the walls of Downing Street.

Good Friday 23 March (Waddesdon)   Francis Knollys[42] though devoted presumably to R. is rather annoyed with him just now. He says R. has never since he assumed the Prime Ministership told a thing or written a line to the Prince of Wales. He (F.K.) thinks this is slighting the Prince in a marked manner. I told F.K. that I had already reminded R. of the arrangement made by Mr G. whereby the Prince was sent the gist of the Prime Minister's report of the Cabinet proceedings to the Queen. I have not a doubt but that R. has already done this.

Tuesday 27 March   I came up from Waddesdon yesterday morning. As Harcourt had remained in Town, I did not like being away longer. We have been 'budgetin' together yesterday and to-day. As at present minded, he proposes in order to be made quite easy [sic] to graduate the House Duty on houses valued at over £150 or £200. I prefer this to the Income Tax surcharge; but I believe it will be wiser not to frighten people too much by graduation on its first introduction but to confirm the assertion of the principle this year to the Death Duties. Harcourt is well advanced with his Budget statement, and has rehearsed it to me. I shall be treated to many more rehearsals before he has done. I think he will make a very good statement, but he will mar it by the delivery, which is too funereal, sermon-like, & pompous.

Wednesday 28 March   Rosebery asked to see me before he went down to Newmarket . . . He was rather exercised in his mind about the Budget. He was afraid of the graduated Inhabited House Duty on top of the graduated Estate Duty. A double dose of graduation would, he thought, alarm people considerably, and scare away from the party the few wealthy men left. He viewed this contingency with great concern. He deplored the already tremendous one-sidedness of the classes; and always hoped that a few additional ones might be attracted back, now that their Gladstonian bogey was no longer to the front. Moreover if the Liberal party are to lose the entire support of the well-to-do, who is to find funds for electioneering purposes?

   . . . I was most of the morning with Harcourt & Jenkyns[43] going through the Estate Duty Bill. It is necessarily a terribly complicated measure; & I don't propose to be able to follow all the complications. Indeed, it is so difficult that I doubt if during the last century any other man but Harcourt, Mr G. & Goschen, could have tackled it at all. I got Jenkyns to hint at the graduation in the scheme being too high at the top. I was afraid if I broached the question he would suspect it was at the instigation of Rosebery. Harcourt taunts Milner with being too tender-hearted towards Landlords, and me with being too kindly disposed towards millionaires.

Thursday 29 March   I saw Rosebery on his return from Newmarket . . . I advised him to see Fowler about the Budget. It is of course very awkward for R. to fight Harcourt over it, what with his admitted ignorance of finance and the fact of his being an interested party in the matter of graduation. I have also been spending the evening with him at the Durdans . . . R. said tonight he was not the least more reconciled to the Prime Ministership. He was sure that the Foreign Secretaryship was not only much more pleasant, but really more powerful. Nobody could envy him now. Neither the Cabinet, nor the Parliament, nor the policy of the present Cabinet were of his own making . . . R. thinks the Government will probably come to grief over the Budget; and that Harcourt will wish to retire in any case after it, if by chance it should be carried. Though he could not well have formed a Government without Harcourt—the Radicals would have rebelled—he believes that Harcourt's retirement could be effected now at any time without causing a break-up.

Sunday 1 April—The account for 1893-4 was very nearly balanced on the right side yesterday. As it was the deficit only amounted to £170,000, which will be a very pleasant surprise to everybody; the deficit having been variously estimated from 1 to 2 millions. How to make ends meet for the new year is now the question; and we are able to do it without producing a graduated House Duty . . . this is how we now stand:

Estimated expenditure 1894–5[44]	£95,470,000
Estimated Revenue	£90,846,000
Anticipated deficit	£4,624,000
By knocking down the financial machinery in the Imperial & Naval Defence Acts we get relieved of charges to the amount of	£1,574,000
& we are able to add to our receipts	£549,000
Accordingly the deficit is reduced from	£4,624,000
by	£2,123,000
to	£2,501,000
It is proposed to raise by fresh taxation of	
(a) Death duties	£1,000,000
(b) Additional Beer and Spirit duties	£1,400,000
(c) Additional penny on income tax	£1,780,000
But we lose by	
(a) raising abatement on income tax under £400 from £120 to £180	£640,000
(b) giving new abatement of £100 on income of £400 to £500	£200,000
(c) allowing deduction of 10% on lands & 15% on Houses under Schedule A	£630,000
So we get out of the additional penny only	£310,000
Thus converting the deficit into a margin of	£209,000

Monday 2 April   The Budget went before the Cabinet again to-day. I saw Rosebery afterwards. He told me that they had had most of the Budget speech rehearsed to them; & with a little encouragement which was not given, they could have been treated to the whole of it. He is still a good

deal concerned about the graduation of the Death Duties. No Estates consisting of personalty under £25,000 are touched; they are subject as now to 4 per cent duty: but the scale is perhaps frightening. It is:

5% on estates from £25,000 to £100,000

6% on estates from £100,000 to £200,000

7% on estates from £200,000 to £300,000

8% on estates from £300,000 to £500,000

9% on estates from £500,000 to £1,000,000

10% on estates of £1,000,000 and upwards

The scale admits of being modified. At present it hits small estates from £25,000 to £50,000 too hardly; and a rate of 9 & 10 per cent on large estates will alarm too much & unquestionably give rise to great evasion. But it is Landed Estates which will be mulcted most heavily; for they are hit in three ways including small estates valued at from £10,000 to £25,000. (1) They are to be subjected to Estate Duty, the substitute for Probate Account & present Estate Duty. (2) They will be taken at their Capital value instead of at the life interest of the successor. (3) They will come under the graduated scale.

Tuesday 3 April   R. is pressing for an amendment of the scale & will meet with support. But he must not be too timid. After all, who is it that called for this huge naval expenditure? The propertied & commercial classes: so they ought not to complain if the bulk of the charge falls upon them. It would be impossible to raise the duties on articles of consumption more: so the only alternative are Death Duties & Income Tax; and of the two unquestionably Death Duties are to be preferred. They are paid in the lump, before the property comes into one's possession; they are not inquisitorial like the income tax; they only fall on capital, and therefore do not mulct incomes which are derived from salaries and other sources dependent on the life of the income-earner.

Wednesday 4 April   The Bye-Elections are practically over. There have been six fights. No seat has been lost by the Governnment. In three of them, the ministerial majority has been reduced; & in the other three it has been increased, though not proportionately as much.[45] There is nothing conclusive to be drawn from the results by the most ardent believer in

Electoral meteorology. More significant, however, is the attitude of the Redmondites.[46] At a meeting held in Dublin last night, they passed a formal vote of no confidence in the Government, intimating that what they must now strive for is an immediate dissolution.

Things moreover are not going well in the House of Commons for the Government. There was rather a hash made last night. It was arranged that a motion of Sir A. Rollit on Parliamentary procedure should take up the whole sitting: instead of which the debate collapsed at the dinner hour; and a notion in favour of Home Rule for Scotland came on and was carried by a majority of 10: the Government voting as they pleased. This is an indication that, if we are to have Home Rule, it will partake of the nature of 'Home Rule all round'; which I have always believed is most likely to be the ultimate solution of the problem. Harcourt was not best pleased this morning. He said he did not know which were the most troublesome—the Scotch or the Welsh. They were at any rate both worse than the Irish (anti-Parnellites).

Rosebery has written, & sent Harcourt, a memm. in favour of moderation in the matter of Death Duties. He disclaims being any financial authority; but what he fears is an aggravation of the present & unfortunate cleavage between "the classes & masses". He told me had Fowler & others on his side; but at the Cabinet they funked speaking out & standing up against Harcourt. All that Fowler did was to hand across a slip of paper to say he agreed (with R.), but he was dumb. I have never regarded Fowler as anything but rather weak & second class man. However he is not the weakest man in the Cabinet. That honour is reserved for poor Trevelyan. R. says he is lamentable as Secretary for Scotland, & that an effort must be made to get him to exchange places with Bryce. I suggested that a Peerage might solve the difficulty; but R. says Trevelyan would not take one; he poses too much as the advanced Radical. R. finds Lefevre improves on acquaintance; sensible-minded; & quite 'brushed-up' since he was moved to the Local Government Board. The fact is, he is a most handy man in any administrative post. Where he fails is in the House; because he carries no weight & is unpopular.

Thursday 5 April   There was a discussion yesterday in the House on old-age pensions. It is being taken up keenly by all the Conservative & Radical Socialists, headed by Chamberlain. It is extraordinary how politicians can in a light hearted way advocate proposals which would involve a colossal expenditure; and then they hollow out at having to pay the bill!

Dined tonight at Ferdie Rothschild's[47]—a little dinner in honour of Rosebery . . . I think Rosebery enjoyed it. He was full of fun. He told me he did not see how the Government could last much longer.

Friday 6 April   The Government certainly is going very 'groggily'. Last night in the House of Commons they were beaten by 1 over a private (London Water Supply) Bill; & later on in the evening they only carried the adjournment of the debate on the foolish proposal to refer Scotch Bills to a Grand Committee almost wholly composed of Scotchmen, by a majority of 15. The Redmondites abstained & some of the Anti-Parnellites did not turn up. Harcourt was not there, having lost his sister in law, Lady Susan Harcourt, & having (without any reference to Rosebery) devolved the lead on J. Morley . . . I believe myself that if the Government are resolute and stick to their guns, they will probably carry the Budget proposals. Defeat is more likely to come from some unexpected quarter, some less important issue.

Saturday 7 April   Harcourt was in a very bad humour this morning. One must never attach much importance to his blurtings out; but increased bitterness towards Rosebery was very marked . . . He sneered at R.'s memm. and prided himself at having in his reply torn R.'s arguments to pieces. Then he was evidently greatly annoyed at the decision about Uganda (which amounts practically to a Protectorate). To give him his due however, I believe this is one of the few questions on which he really has convictions & strong ones. He is a sincere disciple of Cobden and convinced of the risk of indefinitely extending the Empire. The fact is, as he admitted himself, he has not one single view in common with Rosebery. He thought the announcement of the decision on Monday would alienate several radicals; and if so, the Government might very easily be beaten on their proposal for taking more time of the House. 'I hope to God it will be so; & then there will be an end to the whole thing'. I hinted that he had his own reputation to consider as well as that of the Government. I think he is keen now to deliver himself of the Budget at any rate; so perhaps that will moderate his feelings of revengeful chagrin for the moment. Otherwise I think that what with his temperament—and I can see it is shared by Loulou who is the most important factor in Harcourt's calculations—and the want of cohesion among the various sections of the party, it is impossible for the Government to last much longer, and certainly not to survive the session. At the same time it is always the unforeseen that happens in politics.

Sunday 8 April   In Town for Sunday, which I never like but I thought Harcourt might want me. The graduated scale of the Estate Duty has been somewhat modified. It goes up in smaller steps and the maximum rate of duty is limited to 8 per cent. This will tend to diminish alarm . . .
. . . There is a good deal of political flutter to-day. It is thought that the Government may barely get a majority tomorrow on their motion for taking more of the time of the House on a motion which they rightly

consider to be equivalent to a vote of confidence or no confidence. But I expect they will pull through. Much of course depends on Harcourt himself. If people see that he has not got his heart in his work they will very likely break away; but otherwise I can hardly conceive that the various sections will carry their threat into effect and bring about a Dissolution . . . I have been dining this evening at Alfred Rothschild's . . . I sat between Lady Algy L(ennox) & Burnard (Punch). She is well informed about Cape matters. According to her, Labouchere's charges brought against the Chartered Company in connection with the recent campaign in Matabeleland are not so devoid of truth as Selborne and others try to make out; and Rhodes is a dangerous & unscrupulous man, who merely keeps himself in power by favour of the Dutch population, & would throw the country over in a moment if it suited his book.

Tuesday 10 April   I came across F. Maitland[48] at Brooks last night. I take him as a good reasonable Liberal member without crotchets. He hoped that Harcourt would not long continue to lead in the House. He commanded no confidence in the party; mainly because he lacked conviction. People could not take him seriously or trust him. This I expect is a widely prevalent belief. The fact is, a man to lead successfully must have *character*. Politics may be a game; but the game must be played seriously. He however did well in the House yesterday evening. He moved his resolution for more time of the House in a conciliatory & dexterous manner; and the Government pulled through all right, having a majority of 24. So they are put on their legs again for a while at any rate.

I went and had luncheon today with Rosebery. He was fully aware of Harcourt's frame of mind. He took it all very philosophically. He had always, he said, foreseen the impossibility of the situation. It was that which made him so reluctant to assume his present position. The fact was, Harcourt was not only not behaving loyally as a colleague, but he was not behaving like a gentleman. There was a general disposition on the part of the Cabinet to treat Harcourt generously & forbearingly; and what was the result? Harcourt complained of being surrounded with intrigue—a complaint for which there was no foundation. Poor Lord Justice Bowen is dead: a very remarkable man, a fine Judge, brilliant scholar and charming society. Sir C. Russell[49] has put forward his claim to succeed Bowen as a Lord of Appeal; and Rosebery is ready to appoint him. The Solicitor-Generalship was not, he said, quite so easy to fill up. The choice lay between R. Reid,[50] Lockwood[51] & Haldane.[52] Lockwood it is believed looks for promotion to the Bench & has an uncertain seat. Haldane is backed strongly by Asquith, and is probably the ablest man of the three; but he is an equity lawyer, and it would not do to have him as well as Rigby[53] for Law Officers. So the appointment will probably be offered to Reid; though

Rosebery said that he thought it a bad principle to reward a man who, like Reid, had shown a good deal of discontent.

Thursday 12 April   Harcourt's humour has slightly improved during the last day or two; and I can't help hoping that if his Budget is fairly well received he will put more heart into his lead.

Friday 13 April   John Morley introduced the Registration Bill this afternoon. It reduces the residential period of qualification, introduces half-yearly instead of yearly registers, abolishes the disqualification at present attaching to the non-payment of rates, holds all polls at a General Election on one day, & does away with the plural voter. It raises the battle of 'one vote, one value' *versus* 'one man, one vote' (which by the way is John Morley's *mot.*).

Saturday 14 April   The Budget is now all 'cut & dried'. Harcourt knows his lesson very well. There is more excitement about it than about any other Budget in my recollection. Of course it will be virulently attacked; but it is not easy to foretell what the line of attack will be—probably a tendency to confiscate property and to place too heavy a burden on realty. Its fate will be intensely interesting. The increased spirit duty will of course give difficulty in Scottish & Irish quarters; and the brewers will be up in arms.

Sunday 15 April   I went through this morning the Chanc. of the Exchequer's Budget notes or rather speech (for it is almost written out verbatim) for the last and about twentieth time. The statement will be rather long, but it is difficult to shorten. I think it is extraordinarily clear. I quite believe he may score a distinct success with it. I should be so glad on his account; to gain the name of a financier would go some way to compensate for recent disappointments; and success may conduce to keep him in a good temper and make him a little less anti-Roseberyite.

Monday 16 April   I was with Rosebery this morning. He was in too pessimistic a humour about the Budget, declaring that it would be the ruin of the country, by breaking up big properties & driving away capital: and he had to be a party to it! He is too timid. I have just returned from the House of Commons: and the first impressions of the Budget are distinctly favourable: The Radicals a little disappointed perhaps on the one hand; but on the other hand, no scare or cries of alarm from the Tories. Harcourt acquitted himself very well. It was universally admitted that his speech was most lucid and able. Of course the delivery of it was pompous and funereal-like; but the exposition was a distinct score. People have of course not taken it in yet; but in ministerial circles what is evidently apprehended most is the increase in spirit duties. Harcourt entertained all those concerned with the Budget at dinner in J. Morley's room behind the Speaker's chair. I had some talk with J. Morley after dinner this evening. He recognised to the full that Rosebery's great difficuty was Harcourt but it had to be faced & made the best of; so Rosebery must try & get Harcourt off his nerves. He must, J. Morley said, take a broader view of things; at the present moment his vision is dimmed by the Harcourt spectre. Then Rosebery (so J. Morley thought) ought to see more of his colleagues & followers: not necessarily by being in the Lobby of the House of Commons which is rather *infra dig* for him, but by sitting in Downing Street & letting it be known that he is accessible to any member of the party, official or otherwise. Looking ahead J. Morley evidently thought it more than probable that Harcourt would retire at the end of the session, in which case he could not see why Fowler should succeed him at the Exchequer as a matter of course. The succession is evidently coveted by J.M. himself.

Tuesday 17 April   The press today is fairly unanimous in praise of the Budget as a whole; and favourable comment comes from unexpected quarters. The Tories evidently think it is a difficult scheme to fight in principle. They will of course discuss it in enormous detail, & will in so doing be always quoting Mr G.'s remark that reform of the Death Duties would take up a whole session.

Thursday 19 April   . . . I found Harcourt to-day in good humour: but I am afraid he was in a very explosive state again yesterday. Rosebery had summoned a Cabinet yesterday afternoon in order that they might go through J. Morley's Evicted Tenants Bill which he is introducing to-day. "Why on earth was a Cabinet summoned? Who cared about the Bill? Are we never to be allowed to do anything ourselves in the House of Commons?" Such was the language Harcourt was holding yesterday. He has definitely got Rosebery on the brain, quite as much as Rosebery has Harcourt on his brain. I tell Rosebery that there are only two ways to manage Harcourt—firmness & tactness. It must be a judicious mixture of both. He (R) ought always to stand up against Harcourt, and at the same time ought never to lose an opportunity of showing him attention & flattering his vanity . . .

   . . . The Opposition have not shown their hands about the Budget. It has been so well received that they will dare not dare to try & wreck it. Their game will evidently be to try to talk *ad libitum* on it & thus prevent the passage of any other Bill. The Government will be very lucky if they get it through as well as the Registration Bill, which however the House of Lords will never allow to pass in its present form.

Saturday 21 April   Yesterday's sitting in the House was again wasted over the proposal for a Scotch Grand Committee. There never was a more unfortunate proposal; and heaven only knows why the Government let themselves in for it, except that Mr G. pledged the Cabinet to it. The Opposition can talk it out this week, & make great capital of conceding to Scotland where the Government have a majority what they refuse to give to England where they are in a minority. At the evening sitting there came on the Morton-cum-Labby[54] motion for putting an end to the second annuity of £10,000 a year granted to the Duke of Edinburgh on his marriage.[55] The Government thought they might be beaten over it; but all but 61 of their own side voted against it and . . . the motion was rejected by a majority of no less than 231.

   . . . I hear that [Mr G.] approves the Budget in the main. The only point to which he takes real exception is the extension of relief to small income tax-payers. I remember his holding forth on this point in 1876 when Sir S. Northcote had a similar proposal . . . He (Mr G.) approves weekly Cabinets in the circumstances: they being the only means whereby a Peer-Premier can keep in touch with his colleagues and with Parliamentary business.

Monday 23 April   . . . the debate on the Budget resolutions. Goschen[56] spoke at some length; but was not at his best. His criticism was not very damaging. Indeed none of the arguments brought forward by the opposition was very formidable. It looks as if the opposition will confine their attack to talk, of which the proposals lend themselves to any amount. Harcourt in reply made some very good hits and excellent defence: but he allowed himself to be on his legs too frequently, and his tone was too contentious. The fact is, he can never resist the temptation of drawing Goschen & making him wince.

   I hear he was detestable at the Cabinet today. He was in his worst of humours, declaring that a decision on some point of foreign policy had been taken behind his back. As a matter of fact, there was documentary proof that he had been consulted; so there was nothing for it but for him to cave in. He is becoming, I am afraid, more and more unbearable to his colleagues; & the very name of Rosebery is now the 'reddest of rags' to him. I regret it more than I can say, quite as much in the interest of his own reputation as for the peace & comfort of Rosebery & the Government generally. The worst of it is, Loulou. He is as anti-Roseberyite as his father.

Tuesday 24 April   . . . Fowler spoke well this afternoon. He is certainly very handy in debate. He handled figures with great dexterity & lucidity, and always spoke with a great amount of self-assurance. Of course the principal line taken by the opposition is the final ruin which in the present state of agricultural depression any increased burdens in the way of Death Duties will bring upon the landed interests. But the same thing was said in 1853, when Mr G. proposed the Succession Duty. Some properties no doubt are almost bankrupt: but if there is no net revenue derivable therefrom, they won't pay anything on account of the new Estate Duty; and some estates in land are greatly enhanced in value—owing to affinity to towns, residential value, increased sporting rights. My own belief is that landlords greatly exaggerate the effect of the Budget proposals. The Opposition seemed quite disappointed at being told that the increased burdens on agricultural land are only estimated to amount to about £300,000 or £400,000 a year; & then only when the new Duties are in full force. I saw Randolph Churchill at the House this afternoon. He expressed himself as not dissatisfied with the Budget proposals as a whole. He should neither speak nor vote against them. The fact is, he intended to reform the Death Duties in the same direction himself. He talked about the prospects of an increased output of gold, especially from South Africa and Western Australia, as the remedy for all present depressed industries.

Thursday 26 April   . . . I was with Rosebery this afternoon. Harcourt, who has given very evident signs in the House by loss of temper, of being overwrought, is going away for a day or two; but has said nothing to R. about it . . . Rosebery, I was afraid, was rather annoyed at the Queen's having conferred the Honorary Colonelcy of the Fourth Dragoons on the Emperor of Germany, contrary to the advice he had given to Her and the Prince of Wales. There had been no precedent for connecting Foreign Sovereigns with our army; and the Queen had already repaid the German Emperor for her Colonelcy by making him an Admiral of our Fleet. But Royalties love these complimentary attentions to one another.

Friday 27 April   Asquith last night introduced the Bill for disestablishing & disendowing the Welsh Church. He seems to have made an admirably clear statement. There is presumably no chance of its getting beyond a Second Reading, even if it gets as far as that stage. It is only meant for show.

   The House of Lords at the insistence of Lord Salisbury threw out yesterday, most injudiciously, a most harmless Bill brought forward by the Lord Chancellor for providing that intestate real estate should be disposed of like intestate personal estate. A similar provision was actually inserted in a Bill of the late government; but the Tories would not have it now, emanating as it does from a Liberal Government. The Liberal Unionists supported it; & perhaps if the Duke of Devonshire had been there (he was at Newmarket) the result might have been different.

Wednesday 2 May . . . I went . . . to luncheon with the Arthur Sassoons at Albert Gate. The Duchess of Devonshire took a good deal of exception to Rosebery's speech at the City Liberal Club where he had made an appeal to the Liberal Unionists to return to the fold; and hinted that though their leaders by being too much committed were past praying for, the rank & file of the party might take independent action. She thought this was rather a mean incitement. I sat next Lady Cadogan, who declared that party feeling was beginning to run very high again. The Death Duty proposals were monstrous; it was the last nail in the coffin of the landed gentry; & they were powerless to make much of a fight.

Thursday 3 May Rosebery spoke at Manchester last night. It was, for him, rather a bad speech: he is naturally afraid of letting himself go, and committing himself in his present position of great responsibility. He of course had to defend the Government programme. Society says: 'He can't really believe what he says and really sympathise with such radical measures'. What people forget is that they are face to face with democracy; that democratic proposals properly tempered ward off still more radical changes; that if men like R. were to leave the advanced party worse fate would be in store for the properties classes; that their real security, therefore, is the moderating influence of those who have the courage to swim with and not uselessly to resist the democratic tide.

Friday 4 May Rosebery whom I saw this afternoon—I often invade him now in Downing Street where he sits in Mr G.'s gold room (the corner one)—had a great reception at Manchester. He admitted his speech was rather dull; but he was all the more amazed how well the audience of nearly 10,000 had listened to it. There had been a Cabinet this morning. It was feared that Harcourt was going to give much trouble. He takes strong exception to some secret arrangement we have made with the King of the Belgians to lease a part of our Congo territories bordering on the French possession; mainly I believe on the ground that the arrangement would give much offence to France. But he argued his case very moderately, and met with a good deal of sympathy from his colleagues: so much so, that some concession is to be made to him.

Saturday 5 May The 2nd Reading of the so-called 'Registration Bill' was only passed last night by a majority of 14. The small majority was partly to be accounted for; but it was a bad omen. It is clear that the Bill, in its present shape, had not a chance of being passed even in the House of Commons: it will have to be materially lightened. The Unionists have no doubt a very strong trump card in their hands, by insisting that anything like 'one man one vote' is to be accompanied with a fairer representation of the 3 kingdoms. The moment the Tories have a majority, they propose to cut down the representation of Ireland by 23 members, which would go a long way towards settling the Irish question; and the proposal is a most difficult one to resist. I should like to see it done and also to see a general disfranchisement of all illiterate votes.

A Conservative member behind the front bench (Lawson)[57] has given notice to move the rejection of the Budget Bill; but it is not yet known whether the Unionists are going to support the amendment bodily. They may now pluck up courage to do so after last night's poor division.

There is no denying that a general feeling of disappointment & lukewarmness pervades the Liberal party and the many sections which split it up. And why? What did people expect? Did they think that Rosebery could work wonders which Mr G. could not even himself work? That all the wolves and lambs of the party would lie down peacefully together under a new & untried leader? that Home Rule would be discarded and the Irishmen remain happy? or that some new scheme of Home Rule would be produced which everybody including the Irishmen themselves would accept? . . . The fact is, there has been for a long time no enthusiasm for any measure. There was enthusiasm for an individual; & now that that individual has retired from the scene, there is no enthusiasm at all. It is not due to defects of leading, but to apathy on the part of the constituencies. The present lethargic state of things is in one sense satisfactory: because it may be taken as an indication that there is contentment generally and no burning desire for material chance.

Harcourt made a most amusing speech last night on Sir W. Lawson's[58] motion in favour of a statement of the services rendered in consideration of which any honour of the Crown is conferred.

Sunday 6 May (Durdans, Epsom)   I came down here about luncheon-time to-day. Rosebery had last night been speaking at the Academy dinner; and he seemed fairly satisfied with it himself. It was certainly jocose from beginning to end and evidently amused his audience but possibly it may be thought a little too flippant. He is rather apt to fly from excessive gravity to excessive levity, and vice versa . . . He has found Harcourt decidedly better humoured the last few days—much more reasonable & consequently deferred to by his colleagues. But no matter what happens now, Rosebery can never consider that Harcourt has behaved to him otherwise than the reverse of a gentleman . . . He has not yet completed his list either for dinner or honours on the Queen's Birthday. The Archbp. of Canterbury has actually accepted the dinner invitation, though the Government have introduced a measure to disestablish a part of his church. R. would like also to ask Cardinal Vaughan and a nonconformist dignitary; but possibly the Archbishop might not reciprocate the compliment and there is no accepted 'first man' in the Nonconformist world . . . R. would like to recommend Sir James Paget for a peerage; no doctor or surgeon has yet been ennobled; and some painter or musician might be honoured; though there are always many jealousies to reckon with. He would also like to do something for literature. The man who appeals to him most, personally, is T. Hughes, the author of 'Tom Brown'; but that might be awkward if such conspicuous men as Lecky & Froude were passed over...It will be immensely popular if R. succeeds in winning the Derby:—such hundreds of thousands have their bet and generally on the favourite. Some people indeed attach importance to the event from a political point of view...I can hardly believe there is anything in that; unless all electors were called upon to vote the day after the race.

Monday 7 May . . . The Opposition have plucked up courage, & determined to support the amendment of Lawson for rejecting the Budget proposals *en bloc*. It is a strong order of things, & I believe unprecedented, to move the rejection of the entire Budget Bill; but it is the only way by which the Opposition could secure a united party vote and also the vote of the Parnellites, who can make the proposed increase of the spirit duties a good excuse for going against the Government. The debate was rather tame, and the only good speech made was by the mover of the amendment himself (Lawson), who seems to be a promising man.

Tuesday 8 May The Budget discussion was continued this afternoon. Goschen spoke before dinner. His criticisms were as usual to the point; but he committed himself too strongly, & perhaps very inconceivedly against the principle of graduation and the relief of small incomes from income tax. Whatever he may say, there is the fact that he did himself introduce the principle of graduation by his own Estate Duty, and that if he had had a free hand he would have carried the principle still further. It is expected that by a combination of forces with the Parnellites the Opposition will run the Government very hard on Thursday, notwithstanding that many Unionists expressed themselves publicly as well as privately, in favour of the Budget proposals as a whole, when they were first propounded. They were in short received too favourably:—a too favourable reception of a measure at the outset almost invariably means trouble at a subsequent stage, when time has been given for the purpose of dissection.

Wednesday 9 May . . . I talked with Lord Kimberley for some time this evening. He admitted that he did not like the Foreign Office as much as the India Office. He considered the Secretaryship of State for India the best of all Cabinet offices. It did not of course bring you to public note like the Foreign Office; but about that he had never cared. The charm of the India

Office was that there was so much variety of work: in fact, it was a Government itself *in petto*; and there was hardly any interference to be feared from the House of Commons. If the Secretary of State and the Viceroy pulled well together; almost everything could be arranged between them.

. . . As to political prospects, he thought what was most wanted just now was encouragement to the party. He hoped that Rosebery & Harcourt would do something in this direction tonight at the National Liberal Club where there was going on a political *soirée*.

Thursday 10 May   Asquith was married to Miss Margot Tennant this morning at St George's Hanover Square which is now going quite out of fashion for weddings. I was too busy to go to the Church, intending to go to the breakfast about 1.30; but when I got to the door in Grosvenor Square, I found so great a crowd & so little chance of getting upstairs that I came straight away. No wedding probably ever drew a more varied collection of people together—political & social, smart and dowdy, artistic & literary . . .

Being done out of the wedding breakfast, I went on to Berkeley Square to luncheon with John Morley & Acland whom I am getting to know a little & like. There was also there Cooke, the Editor of the Westminster Gazette...R. was saying that a Government like themselves were always considering & often magnifying their own difficulties, while they generally forgot the difficulties, often still greater, of the Opposition? 'Yes', said Morley, 'most true, if we are turned out tonight the Opposition will be in the greatest straits. How is Ireland to be governed by coercion, unless the Government has a swingeing majority? And that would not be the only difficulty for the Unionists in Ireland—there is the Education question which is a horrible nut to crack.' Rosebery agreed & said 'what is more, if they beat us, they won't have the choice of declining to form a Government, as Disraeli did in 1873 . . .'

. . . I came away with J. Morley from Berkeley Square. He admitted that Rosebery had as Prime Minister been something of a disappointment: for instance, his personality, to which much importance had been attached, especially in the metropolis, had not told in Hackney[59] as had been hoped. But the fact was, he (R.) had had no real chance. 'His only chance would have been the most complete accord with the Leader of the House of Commons, such as Campbell-Bannerman or I (N.B.) would have given him'. Harcourt has no doubt been on rather better behaviour the last few days; but he was still most difficult; & he will continue to be so, more especially as Loulou H., in his present humour (which disappoints me much), rather aggravates than lessens the difficulty.

. . . The Government have succeeded in getting a majority in the Budget Bill, but only one of 14 . . . I may well be that the Opposition will find their hands hereafter much hampered by moving the rejection of the Budget proposals *en bloc*. They would, as Gorst[60] said to me this afternoon, be in a very awkward position if they come in. 'I don't know what we would do. We could only raise a loan or suspend the Sinking Fund'. But opposition is opposition.

14 May Mundella's resignation of the Presidency of the Board of Trade is announced to-day. I am very sorry for him; for few men have ever raised themselves so creditably as he has; but it was inevitable, & it is only a pity that the resignation was not accepted when the New Zealand Loan Company of which he was a Director, was placed on its trial. The Directors were accused by his own officer, the Official Receiver, of sanctioning the distribution of unearned dividends and of issuing debentures under misleading pretences.

Whit-Tuesday 15 May(Waddesdon) . . . a notable day with me. I received a very gratifying letter from Rosebery, saying he wished to recommend me for the K.C.B. in the list of 'Birthday Honours'. He is a master at writing nice letters. I can't help entering it here, though the terms of it are much too generous.
'My dear E.
I have many burdens & few compensations in this office; but you can give me one pleasure in connection with it.
Almost my first thought when I assumed my present post was to offer you the K.C.B. But I doubted on account of my affection for you; & I feared that I might be charged with favouritism. But these scruples have gradually melted away, and I don't see why you should suffer because of my attachment, and lose the due of your public service. Give me then this happiness. I have known you long enough to be sure that I can make no worthier appointment. It is near 34 years ago since we first stood together pale & awed in the school yard at Eton. Since then in joy & sorrow, in good report & evil report, you have been the truest of friends to me & mine, so I hope will not hesitate or deny this great kindness to
Your affectionate old friend
A.R.'
In writing to thank him—& my words very inadequately express my feelings of gratitude to him . . . I have said that I wish to know whether the proposal has Harcourt's entire concurrence—(he is my immediate master) . . .

Wednesday 16 May . . . My scruples about the K.C.B. are a good deal relieved. I find that Harcourt has, in a manner characteristic of his uniform kindness to me, pressed my claim strongly; and I should not like to stand in the way of Rosebery's complying with any wish of Harcourt's just now.

Friday 18 May I dined last night at the Marlborough *tête-à-tête* with Francis Knollys. He said that, in spite of the strong hints given by the Prince of Wales and H. Ponsonby, the Queen was not to be induced to show Mr. G. some little attention, such as asking him down to Windsor. She had even been annoyed at a (wholly erroneous) statement in some newspapers that her letter accepting his resignation had been worded in cordial & grateful terms . . . It appears she is becoming more & more difficult to manage. The latest matter about which she won't listen to reason is connected with the precedence of the Duke of Saxe-Coburg in this country. She actually wants to give him precedence as a Foreign Sovereign over the Prince of Wales. Can any thing more impolitic be conceived? Is not the only real *raison d'etre* of continuing one of the Duke's grants the consideration that he still remains a British Prince?

Saturday 19 May I have been this evening to hear Verdi's new opera— Falstaff—with Lady Kaye & the Devonshires. It is a wonderful work for a man of 80; the orchestration throughout being superb. It was fairly well received; but it is too light for grand opera, & it is devoid of any firm concerted numbers, duets or great melodies. The Duke told me he had this week been in correspondence with Harcourt about the Budget. It had been very friendly: but he (the Duke) had derived cold comfort from it. The Liberal Unionists are now beginning to feel the real effect of their having parted company with the Liberal party, being as it is without its former ballast and moderating influence.

Monday 21 May . . . The Queen had, I found, approved all the Birthday honours submitted to Her, with one exception; & that was a suggested peerage for Sir J. Paget . . . She disliked the idea of a medical or surgical peer; and R. does not intend to press it. She is finding, as I knew she would, that Rosebery as Foreign Secretary was one thing, and Rosebery as Prime Minister is another. She has been referring regretfully to his *once* having been such a "prop" to Her, and implying that he was no longer so. His letter gave him an opportunity of explaining again to Her the difficulties of his own position:—an inherited programme and an inherited cabinet for which he most reluctantly made himself responsible, without having had anything to do with the formation of either; a party split up into groups, some dissatisfied, others avowedly hostile; intrigue in certain quarters; and a Leader in the House of Commons so far from co-operating with the Prime

Minister, personally unfriendly, & disloyal to him and making no secret of it. His cup will be full, he said, if to crown all these difficulties he is to forfeit the confidence of his Sovereign. His communication apparently had some effect; for he had a note from Her this morning, begging him to come to Balmoral, if he was not too afraid (as he had put it himself) that the mice would play too freely in the absence of the cat. He evidently manages Her very well, in spite of her being more & more difficult to manage. He told Her at the same time that he hoped to extricate himself from politics altogether whenever the present Government came to an end—a threat, which I expect will be very difficult to deter him from carrying out. He thinks it is quite possible that a Ministerial crisis may be accelerated by Cabinet disagreements about his Uganda policy. It is more than possible that Harcourt will decline to swallow the proposals in their entirety; & R. admits that Harcourt has a strong case. Certain instructions connected with treaty making in that part of the world were given in August last, when R. was at Homburg; and they were never submitted to the Cabinet. He cannot & of course does not repudiate his own responsibility for the instructions; but the fact remains that not only on this occasion but almost throughout his time at the Foreign Office he acted off his own bat: it was he knew his only chance of carrying out what he believed to be a right policy, feeling strongly the disastrous precedent in 1880–5 of settling foreign policy by Cabinet. At the same time, such independent action was no doubt unconstitutional; & Harcourt may easily make capital out of it. R. talked about his coming speech at Birmingham. I advised him to avoid flippancy and too much personality, though he cannot help making references to Chamberlain in his Midland stronghold. I hoped he would throw out a strong hint that unless he was properly supported in the House of Commons he would not go on. If this contingency does arise, I am sure resignation will be preferable to dissolution.

Tuesday 22 May A committee of the Cabinet has been appointed to consider, along with the experts & draftsmen, the amendments to the Budget Bill, of which an enormous amount has already been given notice mostly by independent Conservatives & Liberal Unionists. They raise important questions of principle; & I told Rosebery I thought it was absolutely necessary that there should be such a Committee. Harcourt is himself evidently averse to making any concessions (some think he is bent on revenging himself on the landlord classes for the little attention that has been paid him by them of late): but I am convinced that he will never get his Bill through unless he shows himself to be tolerably reasonable & ready to make compromises.

Wednesday 21 May Ladas has scored another success to-day at Newmarket. Bar accidents it ought to be a certainty for him to win the

Derby. If only that can come off, I don't much care what happens. Rosebery will have achieved the greatest feat (in its way) of any Prime Minister: & perhaps then the sooner he is out of the present impossible & uncomfortable state of things, the better . . .

A nasty point of order was sprung upon us to-day connected with the Budget Bill. It was raised by T. Bowles,[61] who is an extremely sharp little Parliamentary ferret. He discovered that the Resolutions with which a tax bill has to be prefaced did not cover a claim in the Budget Bill which indirectly increases the Succession Duty. It was feared that this flaw in procedure might invalidate the previous stage of the Budget proposals: but fortunately the Speaker has ruled that the defeat can be remedied by a supplementary resolution, if moved before the clause is reached.

Thursday 24 May   Mr G. was operated upon for cataract this morning by Nettleship. The operation is said to have been completely successful. He was not put under chloroform or ether: the local application of cocaine is now found to suffice for an operation of the kind.

Rosebery spoke at Birmingham last night. He has felt bound to make a certain number of speeches in the country in order to assert his position, & in order that he may not be entirely eclipsed from being in the House of Lords. He was bound to tackle Chamberlain in his stronghold; but perhaps he elaborated too much his indictment against the inconsistencies of Chamberlain. It is always tempting to show up inconsistencies: but afterwards what does it all amount to?—that a man has changed his opinions but everybody has a right to do that.

Tuesday 5 June   I went yesterday to Carlton Gardens but I did not see Mr G. . . . Mary Drew[62] . . . was immensely interested by the Rosebery premiership; & she fully appreciated & sympathised with his difficulties at the present juncture. She had never believed that he was the ambitious man most people made him out to be, and she is quite right. Harcourt, she said, had, when he came to see Mr G. a day or two ago, been pouring out his griefs: he described his own position as one that commanded the confidence of the Liberal party in the House of Commons, but that excited the aversion of his immediate colleagues . . .

Rosebery attended the "4th of June" at Eton yesterday; and made a charming speech. Everybody is delighted with it. "If only", they say, "he could speak like that on the political platform!" But *they* are prejudiced, being mostly political partizans & would never be pleased with any political speech of his unless he threw over his own party and their principles. By the way he made a slip in his Eton speech. He said there were only 2 Eton men in the Cabinet against 3 Harrow men. But the account is really balanced evenly; Rosebery, Kimberley & Lefevre representing Eton, and Lord Spencer, Tweedmouth & G. Trevelyan representing Harrow.

Clause 1 of the Budget Bill was disposed of last night. The Opposition took a division on the principle of graduation; but they were at sixes & sevens among themselves. Goschen committed himself against the principle by going into the "No" Lobby; but Balfour & others abstained from voting.

Wednesday 6 June (Derby Day)   Ladas has won all right, so Rosebery has actually pulled off the great "double event". I am more delighted than I can say . . . I hear the excitement and enthusiasm was never surpassed at Epsom. . . . There was a motion yesterday for adjournment over to-day, but it was defeated. The Government having taken the day for its own business could not devote it to racing, notwithstanding R.'s having the "favourite" for the Derby.

Friday 8 June   It looks as if we were going to get into trouble with France over an agreement between the British Government & the Congo Free State, whereby we have leased to the King of the Belgians a bit of territory under our sphere of influence in that part of the world. It is the agreement which Rosebery made practically off his own bat, and to which Harcourt has always so strongly objected. I am imperfectly acquainted with the details; but the French make out that the arrangement is practically an act of piracy. The French Chamber have given vent to their *perfide albion* feelings.

Monday 11 June   I was with Rosebery this morning, . . . He was annoyed at a paragraph copied from some American newspaper purporting to report the speech he made at Marlborough House last week on the night of the Derby. He had referred in humourous terms to the horror with which he looked forward to his post the following day, which he was sure would bring him many resolutions from non-conformist bodies protesting against his racing & indirectly encouraging betting, & crowds of begging letters in not dissimilar handwriting. It only shows how careful he ought to be when he is on his legs, no matter where he may be speaking. Anything that gives currency to the belief that he is not a serious enough man for his present position is unfortunate; because he has already given offence by his turn for joking.

Wednesday 13 June   . . . It looks as if we were going to get into trouble with Germany, as well as with France, over the agreement which R. made with the King of the Belgians in connection with the Congo Free State. I hear that Germany has lodged a strong, if not insolent protest against the proceeding which she regards as an underhand *do* on our part. Harcourt, who is always averse to anything that has the smallest tendency to Imperial extension, naturally exults over any bothering results. He complains that he is kept in the dark about F.O. matters; and with some reason; for being the Leader of the House of Commons he has a right to know what is going on. But references to him mean a "do-nothing" policy.

Thursday 14 June The Duke of Devonshire has been making a speech at Buxton inveighing against the Death duty proposals, & pointing out (what he and others consider to be) the inevitable result of them. His contention is that when the proposals become law, enormous exactions will be imposed upon owners of large estates like himself, and that the consequences of such democratic finance will be, not the ruin of proprietors themselves, but a great change in the manner in which revenues are expended. There will thus be less spent on charitable & benevolent objects. But those who maintain that property has not hitherto paid its fair share will not be slow to argue that the Duke's argument is practically an admission that men like himself practice beneficence at the expense of the poorer community. I am afraid the speech was not over judicious. Harcourt thought it was most unworthy of the man. "It is the first time," he said this morning, "I have ever known Hartington say something unworthy of himself. I detect deteriorating influences around him". He also had a good growl over foreign affairs: they were, according to him, in a horrible mess; and there was nothing for it but a humiliating retreat which perhaps might put an end to the Government.

Friday 15 June . . . I am held (in society) partly responsible for this "iniquitous Budget": and therefore come in for a good deal of the landlords' complaints. The Alingtons tonight declared that on his death Crichel would have to be shut up for years: all men like himself or rather his successors, would be ruined; and those who would feel the consequences most are the poor retainers on such estates.

   The House of Lords had a close division tonight on the 2nd Reading of the Deceased Wife's Sister Bill. It was rejected by a majority of 9. I suppose it will pass some day; but there is no very strong cry or need for it. The Bishops mustered very strong in the Non-content lobby.

Saturday 16 June Harcourt has arranged to come to terms with the opposition as to valuing agricultural land, including country places. The valuation is practically to be taken at so many years purchase (never exceeding 25) at the amount at which the property is annually assessed for income tax. Without any such special proviso, I believe the landlords would not have been more heavily mulcted; but they know the worst now in black & white. The concession is a great relief to many a distressed landlord, and will grease the wheels of the Bills generally in Committee.

The present price of Consols is the highest on record. "Goschens" being now at over 101, stand at a price equivalent to old 3 per cent Consols at over 118. They touched 78 in 1847. It is a wonderful rise to have seen.

Sunday 17 June (Waddesdon)   Harcourt has been terribly exercised today about the Congo business. He talked at length with me this morning, and then went all over the ground again with Arnold Morey after luncheon. He declared that there could not have been greater mismanagement and incapacity. Though he fires his written shots at Kimberley, his denunciations are of course aimed at Rosebery. The position of affairs seems to be this. In the arrangement made in 1890 for partitioning Africa, Germany, France & ourselves were all given "spheres of influence"; and we all jointly recognised the neutrality of the Congo Free State in the centre of Africa under the sovereignty of King Leopold of Belgium [sic]. If at his death Belgium does not acquire sovereign rights over the state, France is to have the refusal of it. We have not been able, nor are likely, to occupy the whole of the territory under our sphere of influence—that is, the most northern part of it which adjoins the source of the Nile. So, as the Congo Free State wished for it and we did not wish to appear too much in the light of "dogs in the manger", we consented to lease the occupied part to the King of the Belgians, on condition that the Congo State would hand us over a small strip of land at the back of Germany's sphere of influence which would give us the missing link in the connection proposed to be made, mainly by the lakes, between South Africa and the Nile. The agreement was made; and then down came France & Germany upon us: France for our having leased a part of the territory, to which, in the absence of our occupying it ourselves, she aspired eventually to occupy herself; and Germany for our having cut her off from the Congo Free State, thus diverting trade which might come through her (Germany's) sphere of influence. Harcourt declares we *must* give up the article in the agreement which secures to us the strip of land for a connecting link; that having done this much for Germany, we should have made the same concession to France; and that in these circumstances we had better throw the whole agreement up rather than "eat dirt" in instalments. There never was, he says, such humiliation; and he is able legitimately to crow, because from the moment he heard of the existence of the agreement he was dead against it & wanted to put an end to it. It is a very unfortunate business to say the least of it, and cannot fail to do Rosebery harm.

Tuesday 19 June   I was with R. this morning . . . and he made somewhat light of the difficulties arising out of the agreement with the King of the

Belgians. He seemed to think an honourable compromise would probably
be feasible; though he again admitted, very reluctantly, that there had
been a certain amount of gaucheness in the conduct of the latest stages of
the business on the part of the F.O. They should have taken the German
Government more into their confidence. However, things can hardly be as
bad as Harcourt would make out,—for the Queen so far from being
annoyed is complimenting R. on the skilful manner in which he is steering
through the difficulties . . . Harcourt by the way intimated most distinctly
to F.R. (Ferdinand Rothschild) last Sunday that he would retire when the
Budget was through and the session over. I am still sceptical about his
going. If he does, his successor I am sure ought to be Campbell-
Bannerman.

Wednesday 20 June   Goschen referred to a passage of arms he had with
Harcourt yesterday, about some verbal amendment in the Budget Bill, in
which Goschen appears to have been entirely in the right. Indeed his
proposed alteration had been approved by the draftsmen. What Goschen
complained of in Harcourt was not only his display of temper and
reluctance to meet argument by argument, but his want of grasp of the
details of the Bill. He had got up his broad principles very well: but could
not stand cross-examination on the clauses. Goschen said that R. Reid was
doing very well as Solicitor General; and that progress would be much
more rapid if Harcourt would leave more to Reid and interfere himself less
frequently.

Thursday 21 June   There was a demonstration yesterday at Leeds, under
the auspices of the National Liberal Federation & under the chairmanship
of Dr Spence Watson, against the House of Lords. Labouchere and others
were for ending the hereditary second chamber; but the majority were in
favour of mending it by depriving it of its vetoing power. This does not
seem to be an opportune time for raising a cry against the House; and there
was a good deal of wild talk. One does not see how it is, at any rate as yet,
within the range of political politics. I can conceive a reform of the Upper
House; but the Radicals dislike the idea of reform for fear of its resulting in
the establishment of a more powerful second chamber.

   The question, which is being mooted freely and which of all other
exercises me most, is—has Rosebery been a success as Prime Minister?
The general impression, not confined to opponents, is (I admit) one of
some disappointment. This is partly due to them having been formed with
expectations from, and exaggerated consequences, of his succession to Mr
G. There was a general sort of idea that in him the country had found a
second Pitt, and that by him the discordant elements of the present
administration would be welded into a harmonious whole, while at the

same time the radical lions would lie down with the Unionist lambs! Could anything be more absurd? What he has done, & it is a great deal to have achieved, is to keep together up till now a very heterogeneous party and a Cabinet with at any rate one very discordant element in it. Moreover it must be remembered that what chiefly reaches one's ears in the way of criticisms upon him emanate from tainted sources—society and landed proprietors who are smarting, not without some reason, under the impending lash of democratic finance. At the same time, the smoke as usual proceeds from some fire; and what may be said with some truth is that his speeches have not been up to the mark. They have been a little too flippant, and made people think that, for a Prime Minister, he is not serious enough or sufficiently in earnest—that he is beating about for a lead and not giving the lead decidedly himself. Again, not without reason, his latest foreign policy has not turned out quite the success which it was expected to turn out. It is said "We willingly make allowance for his difficulties at home; but abroad we felt absolutely safe in his hands, and now we find ourselves subjected to a rebuff from Germany". This seems to me to be a fair, though rough and ready way of summing up the Rosebery position. What ought to be borne in mind is that Leaders of Parties and Prime Ministers are not made in a day . . . They must have experience. No better instance can be given of this than Arthur Balfour. When he commenced his lead, he was universally said to be a disappointment: and after the experience of two years he had become the most successful leader the Tory party ever had. There is one thing more to be said anent Rosebery; and that is, one detects, I think the drawbacks that so often attach to want of discipline in political life. He practically never served in the ranks; he was plunged all at once into the headship of the Foreign Office where he always had an entirely free hand, but if only he can have loyal support, and does not throw the game up in disgust, he will I feel certain leave in political history the mark which I always said he would leave.

I was amused this evening by a talk I overheard at Brooks' between two old-fashioned Whigs, who were holding forth about the downright confiscation of this Budget. "Well thank God, the Unionists will be in next year, & the first thing they will do is to repeal the accursed Act."

Saturday 23 June   I went & had a talk this morning with Harcourt, & congratulated him upon the progress he is making with the Budget Bill. He was in good humour, and admitted that he was pleased with the result of his labours. The opposition to the measure had come from one class only—landed proprietors. I took the opportunity of trying to sound him about the future, by saying that after so big a measure this year he would have to be content with something very humdrum next year. He did not at all meet my remark by declaring that next year was no concern of him. I don't think he really knows his own mind; but if I had to bet, I should bet he did *not* retire.

Reay came to see me this afternoon. He is much exercised about the Congo business. He knows the King of the Belgians pretty well and thinks him a most slippery fellow to have dealing with. Reay cannot understand—and no wonder—how the F.O. could have allowed R. to introduce into the Treaty with King Leopold a provision analogous, if not identical with, one to which Germany took genuine exception in Lord Salisbury's time.

I stayed in town tonight in order to be at Randolph Churchill's farewell dinner. . . . His party consisted of Arthur Balfour, John Morley, H. Chaplin, Francis Knollys, D. Plunket, Labouchere, E. Dilly, Lucy, G. Lewis, Edw. Lawson, Hicks Beach, Borthwick . . . Irving & Asquith were due; but Irving apparently forgot all about it and Asquith had been summoned to White Lodge at Richmond for the Duchess of York's confinement . . . I could not help feeling that the dinner, which was a very good one—(there never was a greater *gourmet* or more fastidious man than Randolph)—was a sort of funeral feast. It is quite tragic to think of the way he has broken down. He certainly went up like a rocket in the political sky & also came down like one. I had some conversation with John Morley . . . He told me Harcourt was still insufferable; though he himself agreed on foreign politics and their recent phases much more with Harcourt than with Rosebery. I was surprised however to find J. Morley apparently ready to swallow the Uganda Railway Bill. He told me that he had had enough of the Irish Secretaryship, and intimated that he would look to something better ere long . . . I had a few words with Hicks Beach . . . he has kept himself rather in the background over the Budget. It is supposed he did not approve the tactics of his party whereby the proposals were to be fought all along the line . . .

He was saying that of course this Session, occupied as it had been with so technical a subject as the Budget Bill, had been a bad Session for the ordinary M.P. to get on; but he was surprised that legal members had not taken greater advantage of it. The only two lawyers he thought who had distinctly improved their positions were Byrne and Butcher.[63] A third man had done well, but he was no longer at the bar, and that was Lawson who sits immediately behind the front Opposition Bench.

Wednesday 24 June I came down here after luncheon today to be *tête-à-tête* with Rosebery: and we had a good deal of interestiing talk. As to the Congo business, he admits that he was misled in some respects by the Foreign Office. He was not aware that Germany had strongly objected before to a proposal analogous to that in Article III of the Treaty about a

road at the back of her sphere of influence. Moreover the F.O. had
blundered in not communicating the Treaty to the German Government
before it was laid before Parliament. He told me he should not give in to
France, as Harcourt was urging should be done; and did not think the
French were in a specially unreasonable frame of mind. I felt sure, I said,
that the concession to Germany would be forgiven if it was not followed by
a concession to France. But what I felt more strongly about than the
handling of foreign policy was the handling of affairs at home. What he
ought to do was to make a speech soon again on rather different lines: it
must be serious & correct in tone, and it must be decided. He must give a
lead not wait for one; taking the line of 'That's my policy, gentlemen; & if
you don't like it, you may leave it'. He admitted that there was much to be
said in favour of this course: but he did not well see how he could take it
until the situation was first cleared—until in short, he knew what Harcourt
was going to do. It was impossible that the present state of things should go
on: the two leaders never seeing each other or communicating with one
another, except at Cabinet, and then being always in disagreement. 'Either
he or I must go,' he said; 'I am more than willing to make my bow, if
Harcourt can carry on. I am afraid it may come to a trial of strength of this
kind; for as I told R. I believe less and less in Harcourt's going of his own
free will and on no definite issue. It may be that Harcourt rather courts a
trial of strength, for, though the result is hardly open to doubt, yet it would
in some respects be easier for him to be driven out than to go out of his own
accord. R. was saying today that he was rather disappointed in J. Morley.
He professed allegiance to him (R.) but gave him little support in Cabinet.
This might tell against J. Morley in any future rearrangement of offices. R.,
as at present minded, would certainly wish to see Campbell-Bannerman
lead the House of Commons, if Harcourt should go. He told me that he
thought Herschell was perhaps the most helpful & therefore the best man
in Cabinet . . . R. told me that the demonstration against the House of
Lords at Leeds the other night was got up without consultation with any
minister, much less himself, and he evidently was not best pleased, as well
he might be, for nothing could be more ill-timed, and nothing could be
more hopeless than to raise the cry in that sort of way.[64]

27 June   The clauses in the Budget Bill imposing the extra duties on spirits
have been carried by an unexpected majority this afternoon by 55. But it
was a snatch division. The fact is, the debate collapsed; and the only
alternative to putting the question was to report progress, which Harcourt
naturally would not agree to. So by the help of the closure the Government
divided the House on the clauses. It is perhaps a little unfortunate that the
application of the closure has been resorted to at all in connection with this
Budget. But the opposition to the increase of the spirit duties is the least

wise part of the attack on the Government measure. It is the only indirect duty which can practically be touched. So the Opposition is tying its own hands as regards the future in a most inconvenient way; for it means that the deficit would only otherwise be made good by the income tax.

Thursday 28 June Rosebery's answer to Mr Hawke, the head of the anti-gambling league . . . has appeared in the papers. His reference to Oliver Cromwell's keeping race-horses is happy, but . . . is open to be misconstrued as a comparison of himself with that great man.

On the motion of a congratulatory address to the Queen this afternoon in the House of Commons on the occasion of the birth of a son & heir[65] to the Duchess of York, Keir Hardie[66] made a most ill-conditioned speech. They wanted to closure him; but Harcourt thought, & rightly so, that it was better for him to have his say *out*.

Saturday 20 June(Southill Park, Bracknell) I had a talk with Asquith before dinner. He evidently thinks Harcourt has no real intention of going . . . and he does not see what is to make matters mend between Harcourt & his colleagues. Asquith regards Harcourt as an impossible man. His colleagues do their best to pull with him: but all they get in return is accusations of intrigues behind his back & so on. He actually exploded in this way (at Clarence House the other night) to Lady Tweedmouth. He told her that her husband was nothing more than a 'fetcher & carrier' of Rosebery's; that there is no colleague whom he could trust and so on. I understand that Tweedmouth has had it out with Harcourt since.

Monday 2 July I met John Morley this afternoon & had a little talk with him. He told me he felt sure that Harcourt did not mean going, & that Rosebery was consequently much depressed. J.M. thought the only alternative now was to work to some RACCOMMODEMENT between the two men. He believed that Harcourt if properly approached might become amenable to reason, and if sufficently flattered might fall on R.'s neck. I doubt it myself. If anyone is to intervene, it should I think be Lord Spencer. Though Harcourt does view him with very little favour, yet his position as an old colleague would enable him to speak with greater authority than any other minister. J. Morley told me he had seen one of the members of the French Embassy this morning at the service held in commemoration of President Carnot,[67] and he said now was the time to make some concessions on the Congo Treaty affair..but he did not expect R. would view the situation in the same light. I met Herbert Gardner this evening at Brooks'and his opinion is that on the whole Harcourt's remaining on will be regarded by his own side of the House, certainly on the Front Bench, with a good deal of disappointment. This may be; but there is no denying that by means mainly of the Budget Harcourt is a bigger factor than he was when Mr G. retired.

Harcourt, by the way, last week (on Friday) committed an "unconstitutionalism". Part of the arrangements with the amendment of the Imperial & Naval Defence Acts by the Finance Bill was objected to strongly by G. Hamilton & Goschen as heterodox finance; & Harcourt's main defence was that it had the approval of Welby and me! The names of permanent Civil Servants should never be cited as advocates of any policy.

Tuesday 3 July   The Committee of the Finance Bill came to an end last night. The opposition had insisted on having the Bill re-committed on purpose to take another division on the Clause increasing the spirit duties; and they pressed the Government badly, the majority falling almost to a dozen. From a Parliamentary point of view Harcourt would have done more wisely, had he not contended that the incidence of the increased duty on beer and spirits would fall on the consumer; and the fact of its so falling was the main argument in favour of the proposal, in order that the increased taxation should be partly direct and partly indirect.

Harcourt has taken himself off to Malwood for a few days rest during the interval of the Committee and Report stages of the Finance Bill. He has had a very hard time of it, and is entitled to a respite. But on the whole he has done the Committee work very well. He was not sufficiently up in the details of the clauses: he did not know the meaning of every sentence & word in each clause as Mr G. or Goschen would: but he rarely blundered on his legs, he was fairly conciliatory, he showed great intellectual powers, and his management of the Bill generally was marked throughout by great abiity. He had distinctly improved his position inside and outside the House. He has carried a very big Budget, which is distinctly popular in the country except with the landed classes. I went & had a little talk with him before he started yesterday; and he did not fail to have a parting dig at Rosebery. According to Harcourt, the French were annoyed with R.'s speech the other night about Carnot's assassination, and the opportunity it afforded of adjusting differences between the two nations.[68] 'There was,' said Harcourt, 'no limit to the blundering and incapacity of Rosebery'.

I met Arthur Balfour this afternoon coming back from Lord's where he had been seeing the end of the Varsity match, the end having been greatly to the advantage of Oxford. One can never see him without being struck with the strides he has made recently. He is now the political darling of the Tory party; & he is the social darling of all the smart people. The Tory party have never had such a leader; London society has never seen so agreeable a man. This is probably not very exaggerated language. What is

exaggerated is the flattery showered upon him and the greedy way in which
he takes it all in.

Wednesday 4 July   . . . I dined this evening at C. Bannerman's; and came
away with Herbert Gladstone who was there. I asked him what the feeling
of the House was about the succession to Harcourt, should he go or have to
go. He himself evidently considered that J. Morley's claims were the
strongest, and that J. Morley would suit the radicals best: what they want is
a man of real earnestness and strong convictions. Campbell Bannerman
might, Herbert G. thought, be handier but he would not be serious
enough, or impress enough people with his own belief in the articles of the
radical creed; while Asquith has not had sufficient Parliamentary experience, and is being suspected a little of preferring society and amusement to
the House of Commons and work. Such was Herbert G.'s opinion: and he
said it was an unprejudiced one; for he had lost his real interest in politics
now . . . We went on together to Harcourt House, where there was a small
party for the Duke & Duchess of Saxe-Coburg, (who by the way have
given one or two dinners and a garden party at Clarence House in order to
justify their continued grant of £10,000 a year). There I met Lady Spencer;
and I only told her I was sure that Lord Spencer was the only man who
could tackle Harcourt with any chance of success. She doubted whether,
from being viewed with so much suspicion and treated so disparagingly by
Harcourt, Lord Spencer would agree to have it out with him; and even if he
did whether any good would come of it. Unless some better understanding
can be arrived at between Harcourt and his colleagues, there must be a
crisis soon, and it might be a very awkward one; for Harcourt's position is
different now to what it was when Mr G. retired and Rosebery is not on
that very high pinnacle on which he was placed at that moment. Harcourt is
aware of this; and is very likely awaiting a crisis. In short, if he does go, it
won't be of his own accord: and if it is not of his own accord, the split in the
party might be a formidable one.

Thursday 5 July   . . . At the election in the Attercliffe Division,[69] the
Government candidate has been returned by a considerable majority over
the Unionist; but a large number of votes were detached by the Labour
candidate. It is the Labour vote which is likely to be the great rock ahead
for the Liberal party. This and other rocks make the outlook very bad.
Indeed I should not be surprised if they had to adjust their differences for a
long time in opposition.

Sunday 8 July   Edgar Vincent[70] told me to-day that everything was
wonderfully quiet at the Porte, but our influence at Constantinople was not
great. The Sultan was very anti-English. The German position was

probably the strongest, and next came the French. He thought it was just as well that the projected visit of the Khedive to this country had been given up. He was not a man to be easily impressed by what he might see here; and the French would probably have made more fuss about him in Paris. The present Egyptian policy of this country was a very unsatisfactory & hopeless one. Some more decided step in one direction or the other was wanted. Anything would be better than the present 'hand to mouth' sort of policy. But I expect it will go on for many years to come. We can't annex; and we can't retire. Haldane who arrived today and who has helped Harcourt with the Budget, more *in camera* than in the House, thought very highly of the measure as a whole. Indeed, he believed it could rank as high as any Budget this century. He did not think the Opposition had fought it well. They had taken lots of piddling points, but had not conducted the fight on any broad principle. He was in favour of making some concession, as I am, about works of art and their liability to the new Estate Duty.

Tuesday 10 July . . . The Cabinet met to-day. They have decided to proceed with the Evicted Tenants Bill, the Scotch Local Govt. Bill (which has been for weeks before a Grand Committee, and the conduct of which by Trevelyan has I hear been lamentably weak), and the Equalisation of Rates Bill. Harcourt for a very good reason declined to make any announcement until the Budget Bill is out of the way; and the Opposition are, not unnaturally, getting very impatient.

Thursday 12 July I was at luncheon with Rosebery to-day . . . He considered Lord Salisbury's Bill for putting a check on alien immigration and grappling with anarchism very unfortunate and ill-advised. Lord Salisbury knew he would not pass his Bill. So the only effect would be to put the Government in difficulty with foreign powers. It was a thoroughly unpatriotic move . . . I also spoke to R. about the Deputy Mastership of the Mint which is about to become vacant. He proposed offering the place to Rob. Hamilton,[71] whom, he considered had great claims on the present Government . . . I said what about Loulou Harcourt? I found that R...was against considering his claim. He was willing to forgive a good deal; but the Chanc. of the Exchequer's behaviour had exceeded all bounds of decency towards him . . . Would it be credited outside, that, since the present Government was formed, the Leader of the House of Commons had never once been to confer with the Prime Minister, and had only written to him once? They never met except in Cabinet, and it is only to disagree or to agree to differ. R. now realised that Harcourt's real intentions were to remain on. He did not view with much favour the projected dinner to Harcourt in celebration of the passage of the Budget

Bill. R. had thought of having a dinner for some of his followers the same night; but I told him I thought this would be a great mistake.

Friday 13 July   The Budget is to be through the House of Commons on Tuesday next. Harcourt has arranged this with Arthur Balfour. Front Bench arrangements of this kind are becoming more & more common; but they are a good deal resented by the rank and file. It would have been well if Harcourt had made a few more concessions on the Budget Bill. From a reverse point of view, he need not be afraid of them nearly as much as of evasions, which are threatened right and left.

Tuesday 17 July   . . . No doubt, it is Harcourt who ought to make the first move towards a *rapprochement*; but I don't believe he will. Can anything be done? What I am so anxious for, is that R. should not put himself in the wrong. If R. is to be generous, *now* is the time to strike; as Harcourt with his Budget practically through . . . ought to be more amenable.

Wednesday 18 July   The Budget Bill made its final exit from the House of Commons last night. The opposition took a divisions on the 3rd Reading; but the Government secured rather a better majority (20) than was expected. Though weeks & weeks have been spent in discussing the Bill; it has really emerged with very little alteration. It is a great triumph for Harcourt to have carried it, and unquestionably his position both inside & outside the House is improved. But is he in any better or more conciliatory humour? . . . J. Morley's conversation did not make me any happier about R. Nothing could be more loyal to R. than he was; but he told me that, where he thought R. was to blame, apart from the Harcourt business, was that R. had not made the most of his opportunities as Prime Mnister; and from his being so handicapped in the House of Lords he could not afford to neglect any. In the first place R. (J.M. said) would never come to the House of Commons. He (J.M.) Asquith and Acland had several times suggested that R. should come & dine with them at the House. By that means he would learn and see more of the House of Commons than by any other means: but R. judiciously excused himself and had never once proposed himself. Then R. had not taken enough interest in the work of the different Departments. He was nominally head of the Education Office as Lord President; but never had once concerned himself about education matters. He even feared that R. would in disgust throw the Prime Ministership up. For a proud man, J.M. admitted R.'s position was not a wholly pleasant one. Harcourt, though he was in no better odour with his colleagues, had scored several times in the Cabinet over foreign affairs. In short R. was not absolute master in his own Cabinet. It would be, J.M. further admitted, almost impossible for R. to extricate himself. In the first pace, it would *do* for him completely. He would in that case go down to posterity as a second Lord Goderich.[72] He would moreover break up the Government which had weathered the storm of the Session; for out of mere self-respect his colleagues could not now serve under Harcourt; the treatment accorded by Harcourt to his colleagues could never be forgiven. I am not myself seriously afraid now of R.'s taking any suicidal step. It would be too great a triumph for Harcourt.

The Government have announced what measures they intend to proceed with—Evicted Tenants Bill, Equalisation of (London) Bill, & Scotch Local Gov. Bill. The Opposition declare that so huge a programme will never be got through; and that if it is persevered with, the Session will last till November. If the Government allow the Opposition to do as they please, they will probably talk out each one of the Bills; but none of the Bills as such need to be individually discussed, and the Government unless they stultify themselves must resort to drastic measures by taking a leaf out of old W.H. Smith's book & having a guillotining closure.

Friday 20 July Rosebery is quite unmoveable, and so I fear also is Harcourt. Neither will budge an inch. Harcourt is most unquestionably to blame; for he never should have accepted second place if he neither could, nor intended to, work loyally & cordially with R. But I can't acquit Rosebery of blame himself. He might have made more allowance for Harcourt, his weaknesses, his temper & his disappointment; shewn himself willing to be very civil to Harcourt; consulted Harcourt on honours & appointments; & occasionally flattered him. Nobody is more open to a little bit of flattery than Harcourt. R. had another opportunity yesterday of extending his hand. Harcourt had written to ask R. to give Karslake[73] the C.B.—a well-deserved honour; & R. might have written a cordial note back to him without losing his own self-respect; but all he said was that he had only one *C.B.* to give away & that was heavily mortgaged.

Tuesday 24 July . . . I had a long chat this morning with Harcourt. He has entirely ceased dropping even indirect hints about approaching retirement. He is certainly going to remain. I never thought he would do otherwise; but when he can't make up his mind, he gives out he is going to do what he is the least likely to do in the end. We talked a good deal about revenue prospects. He is too sanguine: just as he was too pessimist last year. We shall have to reverse our parts of last year: he will be the *Bull*, & I shall have to be the *Bear*. He never alludes to Rosebery. So he never gives one a chance of putting a word in about that disagreeable relationship between two men. He was saying to-day that what the country was suffering from was *too much* of everything: too much gold, too much produce, too much legislation, too much politics.

Thursday 26 July . . . C. Bannerman told me that Harcourt must be screwed up to proposing some drastic procedure for getting through the Evicted Tenants Bill and the Equalisation of Rates Bill. The Opposition were determined to fight both measures desperately, though they practically admitted in the Balfour Act the principle of the first measure, and accepted provisions of the second Bill last year. Indeed this afternoon the Bill was read a second time without a division. The tactics of the Opposition are really ill-disguised obstruction; and obstruction will continue to be practised by both sides so long as there is no real cry for any particular measure. The fact is the country is apathetic to the last degree about legislation, which is perhaps a good sign & a good thing.

I had a drive after dinner with Rosebery. He has got Harcourt on the brain more than ever; and refuses to budge an inch. I make full allowance for his *amour propre*; but I believe if he gave Harcourt a chance, Harcourt would not well disregard it; and at any rate this would be wholly on one side.

Friday 27 July The House of Lords read the Finance Bill a second time last night of course without a division. The debate did not extend beyond the dinner hour, and Lord Salisbury did not speak himself at all. The Duke of Devonshire spoke, in the same strain as he spoke last time (in the country) about the Budget proposals; but it was not a very judicious speech. There were rumours that Lord Salisbury was not going to allow the Bill to pass as easily as he did; but I never believed in them. It has become the unwritten rule, if not law of the country, handed down from time immemorial and infringed only on rare occasions, such as in 1860, when the House of Commons, without being able to bind the Lords, reasserted their own rights, that Finance Bills can only be framed & altered by the Commons.

Sunday 29 July(Wrest Park) . . . The season is over. I am never sorry: except that it is an unpleasant land-mark—the close of another London year. It has been much like any other season. In spite of bad times and everybody being supposed to be poor, there has been no appreciable falling off in dinners and other entertainments:- the same number of people go to the Opera and the same number of horses and carriages are seen to be about.

The Government have made up their mind to apply the guillotine to the Evicted Tenants Bill. It has become a disagreeable necessity: indeed no contentious Bill will ever now be got through without some such accelerating process. As to the Bill I don't pretend to know much about it. These perpetual Bills tinkering with Irish landlords & tenants are demoralising and unsettling; but it is generally admitted that the question of evicted tenants, however questionable and even criminal may have been the action of those who at the instance of their leaders joined the 'plan of campaign', ought to be settled. An attempt was made to settle it by the late Government in the Balfour Land Bill; but the provision had proved to be inoperative. If nothing is now done, the social peace of Ireland is involved. The principal objection taken to the present Bill is that the provisions are compulsory; but the principle of compulsion has often appeared in Irish Legislation before. What is certain is that the House of Lords will reject the Bill in the present shape; and what is to be feared is that the rejection will be followed by consequences similar to those which followed the rejection of the Compensation for Disturbance Bill in 1880.

Tuesday 31 July   Lord Salisbury made the 3rd Reading of the Finance Bill the occasion for making a very silly speech—so silly that it is surprising that a man of his great calibre should have made it. Being unable to interfere with the passage of the Bill, he set himself to prove by electoral statistics that it merely represented the preponderance of 150 votes at the General Election! and therefore had not much weight behind it.

I went down with Geo. Murray last night to dine at Dollis Hill. Mr G. looked well and was in very good spirits: but I am afraid the prospect of any good use of his eye from which the cataract has been removed is rather bad. There is to be a supplementary operation a few weeks hence . . . He is splendidly plucky and uncomplaining. He was full of talk at and after dinner. He was naturally very reserved in his reference to the Budget; but he made two admissions. One was that graduated taxation in principle was not unjust; & the other was that so long as this 'iniquitous abominable & accursed' military expenditure had to be incurred, it was permissible and even necessary. Some of the subjects on which he touched were Lord Ripon, whom he regarded as a model statesman of the second rank; Lord Palmerston's clerical appointments, which were all made by Lord Shaftesbury; Sir Robert Peel's want of knowledge on financial subjects, until he tackled the free trade question

This morning Harcourt had a flare up with Mowatt & me about impending appointments. Rosebery had sent on to him Mowatt's suggestions, inviting Harcourt's observations but not enclosing them himself . . . Harcourt took the strongest exception to the suggested appointment to the Mint and the Chairmanship of the Customs.[74] He declared that to promote the cousin of the Prime Minister and to give so choice a place as the Mint to the brother-in-law of another minister would be fatal to the Government. He said this was not only his own opinion, but the opinion of his colleagues, to whom he had, wholly unauthorised, shown the suggestions last night in the House. He should tell R. simply that as regards the proposed appointments they were in his judgement little calculated to promote the interests of the public service.

Wednesday 1 August I resumed talk this morning with Harcourt about the appointments. I explained to him that . . . to put a younger man in age and standing . . . over the head of Horace Seymour would make the position intolerable. Harcourt rounded upon me at once. Is that an argument that ought to be addressed to me? The difficulties were got over in my case. At any rate, a younger man has been put over my head. So why should not other people be treated like me? I did not like to say, as I wanted; that I should have thought the argument would specially have appealed to him, considering moreover how disagreeable had been the consequences in his own case.

Thursday 2 August The Harcourt dinner appears to have been a success last night. His followers were enthusiastic, and he made them a roystering speech. But the taste of part of it was certainly bad. If there is one time more than another when a man can afford to be generous, it is when he is being glorified himself; and yet Harcourt took the opportunity of holding his quondam friend and colleague, the Duke of Devonshire, up to ridicule for the speeches he had made about the Budget. They were perhaps not very fortunate speeches. Indeed much that the Duke said should have been better left unsaid by a man in his position; but this did not justify Harcourt's scathing & sneering remarks, the only result of which can be to aggravate the anti-class feeling. There was of course no allusion to Rosebery. This was more than could be expected.

Friday 3 August Harcourt is furious at a somewhat innocent application made by the Lord Steward, & swears that if it were entertained he would not hold his present office for a day longer. The Queen is exempt from all taxes, except the Income Tax which she regularly pays; & from time to time demands are put forward for a rebate of duty on spirits and wine. Owing to some oversight similar demands have not been made in respect of beer and tea. It was such a demand to which Harcourt now takes such strong exception. He declares that if it were known, it would be fatal to the Crown. It reminded him of Walpole's reply to the question put to him by George the Second, who asked what it would cost to enclose Hyde Park. The reply was: "Three *Crowns*, Sir". It is a storm in a tea-cup. If the Queen is allowed to have her spirits and wine free of duty, why not her beer and tea? The principle is the same. Moreover, the rebate on one dutiable article (Beer) would not be known publicly any more than the rebate on another dutiable article (spirits).

Sunday 5 August (Brighton) . . . I had a visit yesterday from Cromer. He said that the situation in Egypt was becoming more and more difficult, what with a stubborn Khedive, a hostile native population, and the cantankerous French. He could write an equally convincing brief in favour of evacuation and annexation. But he recognised that neither alternative was practicable. So the present 'hand to mouth' policy would have to continue to be pursued.

The Duke of Devonshire seems to contemplate the possibility of there still being a compromise over the Evicted Tenants Bill; but I doubt it. The conflicting parties are all half-hearted about it. They allude to a compromise with their tongue in their cheeks. The Government are afraid of the consequences of the rejection of the Bill next winter; but they dare not throw the Irishmen over. The Irishmen in their heart of hearts would probably prefer half a measure (a voluntary one) to a whole measure (a compulsory one); but the Nationalists are afraid of the ultra-reaction—the Parnellites. The Unionists don't quite relish the responsibility of out-&-out rejection; but they would not be sorry to see the Government face to face with difficulties in Ireland next winter, and forced either to put the Coercion Act in operation or to throw up the sponge.

Monday 6 August (Brighton) I have enjoyed my two days here. I feel all the better for 48 hours of sea air; and have made some progress with my Irish Finance treatise . . . The presence of the Duke & Duchess of Devonshire necessarily means unceasing card-playing; whist in the evening and bezique in the afternoon. The Duke's addiction to cards may easily do him political harm; but fortunately he need not take so much account of the 'non-conformist conscience' as Rosebery has.

Wednesday 8 August I met Trevelyan last night at Brooks'. He is, I am afraid, a great wreck politically. But, even if he has mismanaged the Scotch Local Govt. Bill, he has got it through. He was very eulogistic about Harcourt. It was, he said, very remarkable how much Harcourt had improved his position lately, and how powerful was his hold over the House of Commons. He could, Trevelyan believed, take greater liberties with it than Mr G. His Budget and the passage of it were strokes of genius. Whether or not it is owing to that, the Government have certainly got through the Session wonderfully well: & they will emerge from it with greater credit than they commenced it. It is the first time in my recollection that the Liberal Radical party has taken a leaf out of their opponents' book & really stuck together . . .

The Duke of Devonshire seemed to think there was now no chance of a compromise. O'Brien[75] made a most unfortunate speech yesterday. He turned on the wrong tap completely. But somehow or other there ought to

have been an understanding. It is partly the fault of J. Morley: but partly
the fault of the Irishmen who never seem to know their own minds two
days running: they first said they would rather have no Bill than a voluntary
measure: & then when it was too late hinted that sooner than have no loaf
they would take half a one.

Thursday 9 August   Lord Salisbury was at Oxford yesterday in his double
capacity as Chancellor of the University and President of the British
Association which meets there this year. He delivered a very interesting
and scholar-like Presidential address. No man could be better suited for
the task—what with his great intellect, and his knowledge of science...It is
remarkable that our last 5 Prime Ministers have not confined their power
to the service of the state. Each one of them—Lord Derby, Disraeli, Mr
Gladstone, Lord Salisbury & Rosebery—has been more than a politician:
they have contributed to literature or science.

Friday 10 August   I went down this afternoon to Herne Hill, which is the
best cycling course near London . . . It is wonderful to what perfection this
new sport has been brought; and the pace which they get out of their two
wheeled machines is marvellous. It interested me very much.

   I have been dining this evening at Horace Farquhar's[76]—quite a banquet
for this time of year—the Devonshires, Arthur Sassoons, Stanleys,
Gosfords, Miss Peel, A. Rothschild, H. Chaplin, H. Calcraft, and actually
Rosebery; who had been induced to come on its being held out to him that
Mrs Arthur S. would be there. I wish he would more often go into society.
It would be good for society—as well as for himself. I drove with him after
dinner. He admitted that there had been a good deal of mismanagement
about the Evicted Tenants Bill, mainly due I am afraid to John Morley. It
is, R. says, too late now to do anything as to bringing about a compromise
on voluntary lines. John Morley was, he said, very difficult to deal
with—he was so petulant, hysterical and wavering at times. He was as
malleable as clay in the hands of the Irishmen, who know exactly the length
of his foot. He was in short almost as difficult to manage as Harcourt the
main difference being that one behaved like a gentleman and the other did
not.

Saturday 11 August (Waddesdon)   . . . Harcourt seems in a fairly good
mood: as indeed he may well be; for he has scored over the legislative
programme. The House (it seems) will get through not only the whole of
the Bills which Harcourt announced and was laughed at about, but several
others besides. In short the Statute Book of 1894 will be a very fat one. The
Government have, in fact, got through the Session better than anyone ever
expected or its friends ever dared hope, in spite of the strained relations

between the Leaders of the two Houses. Arthur Balfour said the other day the Government was like the proverbial valetudinarian, who was always going to die, but never did, and outlived those with the robustest constitution.

Sunday 12 August (Waddesdon)   Wolff[77] who generally knows most of the political gossip in Tory circles says that there is an idea about—I confess I don't give much credence to it—that when there is a change of Government it will be Arthur Balfour at the head of it: thus getting over the difficulty about the conflicting claims of Lord Salisbury & the Duke of Devonshire, and securing the Prime Ministership in the House of Commons in contrast to the previous Radical regime. Wolff told me last night, for what it is worth, that it is quite a mistake to suppose that Lord Salisbury lived up in the clouds and kept no touch with what was going on in the rank and file of the party.

   Harcourt has been much put out to-day—or pretends to be—by the receipt of news about the latest development of the Congo Treaty question. France, it appears, has followed the suit of Germany and insists on the King of the Belgians cancelling the rest of the Congo agreement. Our choice apparently is to submit or to come to loggerheads with France. It is not an agreeable position: and I am afraid there is no doubt the question has been handled undexterously by the F.O. But after all, it will only involve our allowing King Leopold to withdraw from an engagement with this country; and the situation probably does not warrant all the hard things said about it by Harcourt. 'There never were,' he said to me this afternoon, 'two such incompetent men as Kimberley and Rosebery. The sooner they changed their present calling, the better for themselves and the country. I foresaw what would inevitably happen from the first. Indeed, when I am shown a Foreign Office despatch, I generally have to put my pen through it!' He of course exults over anything which is likely to reflect discredit on R.; and apparently takes special delight in exulting over it to me.

Tuesday 14 August   The House of Lords had the Evicted Tenants Bill under discussion last night, and are debating it again this evening. Lansdowne seems to have made the best speech last night; and according to what I have just heard the Duke of Devonshire acquitted himself extraordinarily well this afternoon. It is said to have been one the best speeches he ever delivered, and the best he has yet made in the Upper House . . . There have been no real offers of a compromise; though I believe that with a little better management something might have been done in that direction. But the fact is, neither side wanted a *transaction*. Had Lord Salisbury or the Duke insisted on converting the Bill into a voluntary measure, they would have put the House of Lords in a strong position and the Government in a great difficulty.

Wednesday 15 August   Rosebery wound up the debate last night on the Evicted Tenants Bill. He made a fairly good speech and retorted on his old foe—The Duke of Devonshire—with whom he specially enjoys crossing swords, but he is said to have been rather nervous, and did not manage his voice as well as usual. The supporters of the Bill only mustered 30 in the Division Lobby; while in the 'Non-content' Lobby there were over 200 Peers.

Thursday 16 August   The Ministerial 'Whitebait dinner' at Greenwich was revived last night. It had fallen into disuse for many years; ever since 1879 I think. I hear it went off very well. Edw. Marjoribanks (Tweedmouth) took the chair at Rosebery's request; annd acquitted himself very well. I understand almost everybody was made to get on his legs; and the speeches, with the exception of that of George Trevelyan, were all suited to the occasion.

Friday 17 August   I have been dining to-night with Rosebery in Berkeley Square; & had a pleasant evening. Only Sandhurst[77] & Hawkesbury besides. R. is always at his best in the company of one or two men. I hope that relations between him & Harcourt are for the moment a little less strained. They met and spoke when going down to Greenwich on the boat; and Harcourt has actually written about going abroad and thus absenting himself. There seems to have been plenty of fun, jokes and amusing speeches at the ministerial dinner. It is believed that it was on the last ocasion when a Liberal Ministry dined at Greenwich (in 1873) that Lord Granville called upon Lord Selborne for a hymn.

Monday 20 August   I went and dined at Brooks' this evening, where I found Haldane to dine with. He told me that he thought the Budget Bill had on the whole been got through very well. The opposition to it had not been well done; and the line taken by a man like Sir J. Lubbock (who was worthy of better things) was beneath contempt.

Wednesday 23 August   On Monday night there was a long and very late wrangle in the House of Commons about the House of Lords vote. The Irishmen and extreme Radicals were determined to mark their sense of disapprobation of the Upper Chamber's action by moving to cut their officers off without salaries. This was a childish way of raising a great constitutional question; but it shows how strong in certain, though limited, circles is the anti-House of Lords feeling. I am afraid it will give Rosebery great trouble. He will have to make a pronouncement; but any reform he could propose, while it might rectify to some little extent the ludicrous unevenness of the balance of parties in the Upper Chamber, would probably tend to give the House of Lords a still better claim to have a veto. Seeing that the ending of the Second Chamber is not practicable, the Radicals seem to be running for the imposition of a limit on the veto: that is, supposing a Bill were sent up a second time to the House of Lords, it could not be rejected. But the exercise of the veto ought to be to some extent dependent on the Majority which the Bill received in the House of Commons and the consequent extent of authority with which it was sent up to the House of Lords. It is a hopelessly difficult question. Notwithstanding the anomalous division of parties in the Upper House, it will probably go on much as it does now for many years to come; so long as the Lords are careful not to stand in the way of a measure which is unquestionably demanded by the country. At present the country seems to demand nothing; and the agitation against the House of Lords is not much more than beating against the air.

Friday 24 August I went this afternoon to say goodbye to Rosebery. He made up his mind at the last moment to take himself off to Paris for a day or two. He said he must get across over the channel for a few hours. He seemed in fairly good heart; notwithstanding that he has been a good deal abused of late even in ministerial papers for no particular reason. He must take a line of his own—a decided one—this autumn. I understand the Irishmen expect to have a pronouncement from him. What with the Irish question and the House of Lords, he has a very difficult course to steer. He talked about John Morley: the curious contradictions of which he was constituted. No doubt J.M. is in rather an overwrought state of mind; but with all the charm and honesty of the man, there is often an effeminacy, petulancy, and vanity about him which it is difficult to understand and disappointing to see: only the other day, he wrote to R. and said he thought Judge Matthews had strong claims for the vacant Justiceship of Appeal. R. said it was not possible to act on his suggestion: an equity man was essential. Thereupon J.M. was greatly huffed and threatened to resign. J.M. actually the other day hinted that the vacant Order of St Patrick might be conferred on himself. It was half a joke, and he admitted himself that it was not possible; but the fact that the idea how even crossed his mind shows him up in an unexpected light. Then again, he has managed to tread most heavily and even cruelly upon poor Hibbert's[79] toes of late—so much so that Hibbert, who has done most useful service to the Gov., and to whom the Government is under some obligations, has been privately threatening to resign his Secretaryship to the Treasury. John Morley has been jealous about Treasury interference with the Irish Board of Works, which though certainly one of the most important Irish Departments is always held to be more directly under the control of the Treasury than of Dublin Castle.

I found Asquith at Brooks' this evening to dine with. He was very pleased that at his insistence Rosebery has promised to appoint "the Bart" (Sir C. Tennant) to one of the vacant trusteeships of the National Gallery, though he already is a Trustee of the National Portrait Gallery. A. seemed to be rather aggrieved that Rosebery had not introduced a little fresh blood into the Cabinet e.g. Edwd. Grey. There were one or two weak vessels in the shape of ministers in Bryce, Trevelyan, and Shaw Lefevre, who always managed to tread on everyone's toes in the House of Commons, and whose conduct of the Rates Equalisation Bill had been very poor. Asquith spoke in the highest & most appreciative terms of Alfred Milner, whom he has known ever since Balliol days. He hoped that A. Milner might go higher than he was at present. The post for him was that of Finance Minister in India. Without A.M. this year at Somerset House, I don't know what Harcourt would have done: indeed without him, I don't believe the Budget would ever have been carried.

Sunday 26 August (Audley Wood, Basingstoke) . . . taken for the summer by the George Bentincks. It has been a lovely day and most enjoyable to have a glimpse of the sun again. It has been the most sunless August I ever remember.

The Session was brought to an end yesterday; and Parliament duly prorogued. The Government have unquestionably weathered the sessional storm better than could have been expected; and people may say what they like—& they say many hard things—but they never would have got through it as they have, had it not been that they have had Rosebery at the head of it. There is, I do not deny it, a feeling of some disappointment about him; but that feeling proceeds mainly from two sources—those who expected that he would take up a very different line of policy to Mr G., which was an impossibility; and those who do not make sufficient allowance for the difficulty of his position as a Peer-Premier which has been so much enhanced by the behaviour towards him of Harcourt. Harcourt has no doubt improved his Parliamentary position this session & he could not help doing so except at the expense somewhat of Rosebery. His having monopolised the whole time of the House by his own measure has been his good luck & his opportunity, of which he has availed himself to the full very cleverly. Arthur Balfour has improved his position in a still more marked manner. He has thrown himself heart and soul into his work; and he has displayed great debating talent, excellent temper, and uniform tact. Asquith has not had much opportunity for getting himself nearer to the front. Campbell-Bannerman has improved his chances of succession to the Leadership of the House of Commons, partly because of his own popularity and handiness & partly because John Morley has not exhibited greater qualifications for leading. Reid has fully justified his promotion to the Solicitor-Generalship. Edwd. Grey has done well; he always pleases the House when he is on his legs; he has spoken well; and he is dexterous in answering questions. The fire brands on the other side, who have taken best advantage of their opportunities, have been T. Bowles, Byrne and Lawson.

Wednesday 29 August   London is very deserted & I am looking forward to getting away from it at the end of this week . . . Henry James has written a letter to the Times which has caused no small consternation at Leicester. Leicester is one of the double-membered constituencies; and as both members were retiring, both writs were issued simultaneously. H. James questioned the legality of this proceeding at a bye-election; and it looks as if he had reason on his side. The writ is made out in terms requiring the return of a new member in the place of A.B. retired; and therefore it is not clear how the Returning officer can comply with the writ; for it is impossible to say which of the new members is returned in the place of A.B., & which in the place of C.D.

Thursday 30 August   The Leicester election has resulted in the return of the Radical members; Broadhurst being well at the top of the poll but the Liberal majorities have largely decreased, mainly owing to the candidature of a Labour-man.[80] The Labour men are likely to give the Liberal party great trouble at the next General Election.

Saturday 1 September (Mar Lodge, Braemar)   I arrived here this afternoon, after a successful journey; but I am afraid I am threatened with a return of my troubles in the left leg.[81] I cannot account for it in the least which makes it all the more serious . . .

Monday 3 September   My worst fears are confirmed. I am quite *hors de combat*. I foresee a long bout of lying up again. I am almost inclined to go straight back to London; but having come all this way, I don't like not to take some advantage of this fine air . . .

Fife[82] & Horace Farquhar have both got hold of a story which they declare to be well authenticated but for which there is absolutely no foundation. It is that Harcourt was pressed by his colleagues, or at any rate the majority of them, to remain on; and that it is in deference to that strongly expressed wish that he has not carried out his threats of retiring. So far from that being the case, there is not a single member of the Cabinet (at least of any importance) who would not have thrown up his hat, had Harcourt withdrawn from it. This feeling would of course not be shared by the party, who are necesssarily ignorant of the impossibility of his colleagueship.

Wednesday 5 September (Mar Lodge)   There is a great flutter in Irish circles about a hundred pound cheque which Tweedmouth has forwarded (with a similar one of his own) from Mr G. for the Irish Parliamentary Fund. It was in response to a circular issued apparently under the authority of Justin McCarthy;[83] but many of the anti-Parnellites appear to resent the subscriptions very much, lending countenance, as they will to the idea that the Nationalists, despite all their protestations about being independent of British money, are not above taking assistance from English purses. Of course the Parnellites can and will make much capital out of it. I am afraid it was an ill-advised move on the part of Mr G. and Tweedmouth; and will make the Irishmen more & more hopeless to deal with.

Thursday 6 September (Mar Lodge)   I had a long and very rambling letter from Randolph Churchill to-day who wrote from California. The handwriting and spelling of the letter were not such as to make one think he had much benefitted, so far, from his trip . . . He hazarded a certain amount of political speculation. He regards Harcourt as (what he calls) a "sown-up-man"—finished and done for. He is convinced that the next Government, unless it is wholly composed of Goschens, will largely reverse the Budget. If he is himself back in time and restored to ordinary health, he will leave no stone unturned to re-cast the measure completely. *Nous verrons.* I don't believe myself that the Act will be altered in any material respects by anybody. Governments don't undo the acts of their predecessors, and the next Government will probably be glad enough of the money. He entirely forgets of course that, when the budget was first introduced, he declared he should not oppose it. He expressed scarcely qualified approval of it to me at the time.

Sunday 9 September (Mar Lodge)   Chamberlain has been starring at Liverpool on Conservative platforms. He has made several speeches; and each has been, as usual, cogent, brilliantly clear, and piquant. He evidently wished to show that he has thrown in his lot finally & constantly with the party (whatever it may be called) which will oppose his quondam colleagues. He had nailed to his mast the colours of socialism or (what he would prefer calling for fear of alarming his present associates) social reforms; and the cue which he gives to his programme is old-age pensions—a very big problem to solve, involving vast financial consequences.

Thursday 13 September (Mar Lodge)   . . . I shall hope to go to Dalmeny before I leave Scotland; and to find that [Rosebery] has made up his mind to take and give a decided lead this autumn. I should like him to say: "Them's my politics; and if you don't like them, you can leave 'em." Of course by so doing he runs a chance of breaking the party, and if he broke up the party, it would be some reflection on his leading powers. But as the party must break up sooner than later, the damage he could do it would be comparatively little; and therefore it is worth running some risk for his own reputation.

Sunday 16 September (Mar Lodge)   Horace Farquhar has talked to me several times about his going into Parliament. He has been offered Marylebone—a very safe seat—and has accepted the offer. It is strictly speaking a Conservative seat: but he stands as a Liberal Unionist. His return therefore for the seat will give the Duke of Devonshire an additional follower. Horace F. declares that this has been one of the chief considerations which has induced him to enter the political fray; but I am sure that the main consideration of all is the hope that actual Parliamentary service will qualify him for further elevation which is his great ambition. It will no doubt enhance his claims; but I expect he will tire of House of Commons life, before he has made much of a Parlimentary record. It is moreover always a doubtful thing for a man who has been very successful in one walk of life, as he has been (in business) to embark on a new career at past 50 years of age.

Tuesday 18 September (Mar Lodge)   The sport here has continued to be very bad; the wind being persistently the same and in a bad (N.W.) quarter. Indeed it has been the worst stalking at Mar since 1870. Fife is rather disgusted but takes it philosophically. He keeps up his interest in politics; and were it not for Home Rule, which is his *bête noir*, he would (he declares) have remained a Liberal. All the same I don't believe either he or any other Liberal Unionist Peer would rejoin the Liberal camp, if Home Rule were thrown overboard tomorrow. It is really the advance of democratic measures, like this year's Budget, which scared the quondam Whigs. It is very short-sighted policy; for the more the "Haves" range themselves against the "Have nots", the more have the former really to fear in the long run. The latest declared convert to the Unionists is Hothfield. He makes the "iniquitous Budget" the excuse for deserting the Liberal cause. His desertion of itself is of no importance; but it is an indication of the throw overboard of a little more ballast. The real thing is that he has never been able to get over the vexaation of being left out of office two years ago; though the omission was entirely his own fault.

Thursday 27 September (Tulchan Lodge)   Rosebery had two more freedoms of Scotch Burghs conferred upon him yesterday, on his way south from Dunrobin where he has been paying a second visit. The short speeches he made were admirable.[84] He is always most happy doing that sort of thing:- he never fails to make a happy allusion or two, and his language is always so neatly turned. I have arranged to go and spend a few days with him at Dalmeny on Saturday.

Sunday 30 September (Dalmeny Park) I arrived here yesterday a little after 8 o'clock. I found Haldane, George Murray (who now suits Rosebery very well), and the 'domestic' Private Secretary, N. Waterfield . . . He (Haldane) is certainly a man of very remarkable ability, and though a thorough Radical, he does not indulge in wild notions, and reckless schemes. He is certain to make a name for himself at the bar and in Parliament.

I am glad to find myself back at Dalmeny again, in order to take the taste out of one's mouth of the disagreeable and sad associations connected with my last visit here, which is now 4 years ago. I was then getting very bad myself, and it was the last time I saw poor Lady Rosebery, who was just beginning to sicken for her fatal illness. My present break down is nothing compared to what it was in 1890; but even on this occasion people especially R. himself—have been most sympathetic. It is wonderful how long a way sympathy goes to make up for physical privations.

Monday 1 October (Dalmeny) I had some interesting talk with Haldane this morning before he went away. He has great confidence in R's future as leader; though he fully admits that up till now there has been reason for some disappointment. Haldane thinks it is just as well perhaps that R. should not at first starting have had a great success. Difficulties and disappointments are the best of schooling for him. Haldane knows his man perfectly. Give R., he says, time; and he has the requisite originality, cleverness, and indeed genius for working out a policy of his own. He (R.) is not the man to be content with other people's leavings. He is gradually seeing his own way, and how to steer through the shoals. Haldane is sure that the question to which the first place must be given is the House of Lords; and then Home Rule and social questions will take back place. He is not for ending the Upper House, nor for mending it by elaborate reconsutruction schemes. There must be no Bill, he says, nor cut and dried proposals. The reform which is the only practical one he says—and I believe he is right—must take the form of further limiting the veto of the Lords. It must become unconstitutional, as it has been with respect to money Bills, for the Upper House to reject other measures on certain understood conditions; (one of which in my opinion should have reference to the backing accorded to the measure in the House of Commons). The only way of proceeding in this direction is, in Haldane's opinion, by

Resolution, which when passed repeatedly by the Lower House will in time become recognised by the Upper House. It must be unwritten law: like so much else of our constitution is. Haldane also spoke very sensibly on another question which I am certain is one of the greatest cruxes ahead—how to raise revenue sufficient to cover the growing expenditure on the present colossal scale. We are now getting as much, I believe, as we ought to get, in ordinary times, out of direct taxation. I doubt if the Liberal party, with its free trade traditions, will be able to take the matter up. But the other party on the initiative of a man like Chamberlain, might do something in that direction—such as a small duty on sugar, and possibly on barley. It would not be done on protection grounds: but solely for fiscal purposes. Haldane spoke in the most complimentary terms of the Budget. He believed it had exactly given expression to what has been floating about in people's minds. They wanted something in the way of graduated taxation, and did not know what. What they have got now is the least harmful form of it.

This afternoon I went into Edinburgh with R . . . I told him how anxious I was that he should speak out, and speak out in no uncertain note. There are three subjects specially on which he must give a lead—the House of Lords, Home Rule, and the social questions, which perhaps are really the most important. I regretted his having implied in one of his recent speeches that he sought for "guidance and inspiration" from the electors on a question like the House of Lords. It was for him to guide and inspire. He said his words, perhaps not well chosen, had been misinterpreted—he merely wanted to give a hint that nothing could be done without popular support. He was quite ready to speak out clearly and intended to do so at Bradford a few weeks hence. He had purposely laid low since he became Prime Minister. He wanted first to feel his seat in his saddle, and also to wait and see the result of the Session and what it brought forth, referring specially to possible changes in the personnel of the Government which had not come about. He still indulges in the hope—and I am sure he is wrong—that Harcourt will not see the Government out, but will break away on some issue in order to break up the Government. He said he had pretty well made up his mind what to say. I think he is, as regards the House of Lords, somewhat on the same track as Haldane expounded this morning. He told me he has been not a little shocked by an application for a G.C.B. from the Colonial veteran—Sir G. Grey—whom he had already recommended for the Privy Council. There is nothing like being Prime Minister or connected with the Prime Minister for having one's eyes opened as to the frailty of mankind. One must never be surprised at anyone—(even apparently the most disinterested being and who one might think was above all self-seeking)—asking for anything.

Tuesday 2 October (Dalmeny)   R. was very much taken up this morning by telegrams and despatches brought down by special messenger. Japan is so flushed with victory over the Chinese, that it is thought she may fail to fulfil her undertaking to respect the port of Shanghai; and it is a question of sending instructions to our Admiral out there to take steps to serve the protection of British subjects there. R. did not quite like authorising the despatch of such instructions without the authority of the Cabinet. He was afraid they might think he was taking too much upon himself; & so after some hesitation he determined to have the Cabinet summoned for Thursday. A Cabinet in doubtful circumstances is always on the safe side. I took a drive with him in the afternoon . . . and [he] again alluded to his coming speech. It was no doubt the most difficult speech that he had ever had to make; but he thought he saw his way. He will I think on that occasion confine himself to the House of Lords question; but I begged him to speak out on another early occasion on the social questions—these absurd "collectivist ideas", which can only lead to enormous additional expenditure and increase of taxation, and on which guidance is sadly required. The Queen has written to ask when he intends coming to Balmoral. He wants if possible to get out of it altogether; but I think it would be well if he went for 2 or 3 nights. Fowler is there now in attendance. It must be a real delight to him. I understand he gets on at Balmoral very well. R. has announced his appointment of Dean Ritching to the great cathedral prize—the Deanery of Durham, which Dean Lake is about to vacate. He (R.) has certainly had a large share of patronage since he became Prime Minister—civil as well as ecclesiastical. Harcourt (from whom I heard today) was to start off early this morning with Loulou. So he will just miss the Cabinet summons. He is sure to think that this was done on purpose. I hear that on his way back from Switzerland the other day he went and had a long talk with C. Phipps who is in charge of the British Embassy in Paris, and gave free vent to his views on foreign affairs, of which he showed much ignorance. I also hear that lately he has been hectoring Lord Kimberley again. Lord K. takes it very well, and hands on the diatribes to R. Lord K. declines to be drawn from his retreat in Norfolk, and is leaving the F.O. in charge of Frank Bertie,[85] whom R. considers to be the best man really there.

Friday 5 October (Hawarden Castle)   I arrived here this afternoon a little before dinner. I met Arnold Morley this morning at Edinburgh Station . . . He thought that the Cabinet had been summoned somewhat unnecessarily. It had produced quite a scare in London. The summons was attributed to bad relations with France, coming as it did immediately on the appointment of a new French ambassador (M. de Courcel) in the place of M. Decrais who has been recalled. I found John Morley here. He called here for a few hours on his way back to Ireland after the Cabinet. He, too, thought the summons need not have been issued. He told me before he started off to join the Irish mail that he was getting more & more tired of the Irish Secretaryship. He had held the thankless post long enough. It was time he got something better like the Chancellorship of the Exchequer. It is all very well for him to talk in this strain; but he cannot leave Ireland of his own accord without passing some remedial measure for her; and the promised Irish Land Bill affords the opportunity. Moreover there is not likely to arise any chance of a shuffling of places.

Mr & Mrs G. both seem wonderfully well: he specially. The operation has after all turned out quite successful; the film having removed itself; and with glasses the sight is restored to the eye . . . they say he reads & writes as much as he ever did, never being idle for a moment. He seems thoroughly happy. I never believed that he would fret or be bored in retirement; & that belief is thoroughly verified. He told me tonight he never ceased rejoicing at feeling himself a free man. He made one remark with great emphasis, and that related to the "class-riddedness" of this country. He thought it was marvellous how the country had stood it.

Saturday 6 October (Hawarden Castle)   Mrs G. came & had a talk this morning. She wanted full particulars about my break-down; and was as kind & sympathetic as she always was. She said—indeed she almost complained—that Rosebery hardly ever communicated with or consulted Mr G. She implied that Mr G. would like to be kept *au fait* with what was going on, and would gladly give his advice if it was sought. He (Mr G.), she said, was quite alive to R.'s difficulties, and to the unfair & disloyal conduct of Harcourt towards him. On ecclesiastical appointments, she thought Mr G. might be of great use to R.

After luncheon I drove out with Mr G. He expressed great thankfulness at having escaped from political life as and when he did. The impending operation for cataract had been a God-send, as an excuse for retirement. Otherwise the greatest difficulties might have arisen; because he never could have been party to the "financial measures" of last Session. He meant mainly the great Naval expenditure, about which he felt quite as strongly as he ever did, and he applied the same strong epithets to it. He greatly deplored the reckless way in which both parties were plunging into public extravagance. In his early days one party vied with another in economy; now each vied with the other in spending right and left. Could there have been anything worse than the act of the late Government in carrying, contrary to their own convictions, free education, which meant already an annual outlay of 3 millions, and to which there would be no end? Of all the many Cabinet colleagues he had had, the two men whom he had found most difficult to understand, and most difficult to pull with, were Harcourt and Rosebery—than whom there could not be two more different men. In old days there was unquestionably much greater unanimity in Cabinets than now. Ministers now fought for their own hands and took lines of their own at the expense of ministerial solidarity. It was probably that the time had changed, more than individuals. Mr G. strongly reprehended Harcourt's conduct in the present Government. He had no business to take office under Rosebery, if he could not act cordially or loyally with him. He (Mr G.) thought it quite possible that even now Harcourt would upset the coach. According to J. Morley, Harcourt had said that he did not consider himself one of the principal supporters of H.M.'s present Government. Harcourt, Mr G. said, had no doubt a kindly heart and immense intellectual power. It was his insufferable arrogance more than this want of control over his temper that made him an impossible colleague. He (Harcourt) had moreover the worst judgement of men or measures that he (Mr G.) had experienced. One insistence of this was that when Mr G. proposed Ed. Marjoribanks as Whip, Harcourt declared that it would mean the upsetting of the coach in no time. He (Harcourt) had good financial instincts, no doubt; but the moment he was cornered or even pressed he gave way, & acquiesced in what he considered the inevitable. He had attributed the naval demands this year to Lord Spencer's weakness & obstinacy; but in Mr G.'s opinion, Lord S. was neither weak nor obstinate; though he was not perhaps best suited to being the head of a great spending Department. Mr G. alluded to the conduct of Sir A. Gordon or Lord Stanmore,[86] than whose conduct nothing could have been worse. He, Sir A. Gordon, had always been urging his claims to a peerage; and the moment the claim, such as it was, had been admitted, he, as Lord Stanmore had lied to escape from recording his vote in support of the Government. He (Mr G.) had given Lord Stanmore a bit of his mind, and had advised him to see that the youngest Peer (as he then was) should be as little heard of as possible.

Sunday 7 October (Hawarden)   Last night at dinner—(this is probably one of the few houses of laymen at whose table grace is still regularly said)—Mr G.'s talk was very interesting. I wish it could have been taken down verbatim. I can only give a brief summary of it. Talking of Sir R. Peel, Mr G. said, he (Sir R.P.) made a great tactical error in dissolving before he met Parliament in 1835. He ought to have first tried his strength in the House of Commons, though he was in a great minority, thus following the example of Pitt. A minister should always keep dissolution in reserve. I asked Mr G. how far he considered that Sir R. Peel's change of views on the Corn Laws was really influenced by the Irish famine. Mr G.'s reply was that Sir R. Peel had before the famine been convinced of the impolicy of those laws. What he intended to do was to announce his change of mind at the end of Parliament. The distress in Ireland forced his hands and accelerated the announcement. On this point Mr G. was very clear. He told me again that Sir R. Peel had really no great knowledge of finance and trade questions; but he had great power of acquiring and assimilating information. The man in that Government who had such knowledge and who really had instincts of free trade was Sir James Graham, who though dry and uninteresting was a very sound man. The Duke of Newcastle had described Sir J. Graham as "the best administrator but the worst statesman he knew". Mr G. had entertained a great opinion of Sir J. Graham's good judgement. He (Mr G.) had always consulted Sir J. Graham in his difficulties; & had always been supported by Sir J. Graham, notably on the questions of Fortifications, French Treaty, and Paper Duty in 1860. Looking back on his own Budgets, Mr G. said he ranked his Budget of 1853 highest. It cost him more trouble than any other; & he regarded it as his greatest effort in every sense. He believed he was the first Chancellor of the Exchequer who really took pains to master his subject. He much deprecated the present fashion of Chancellors of the Exchequers like Goschen & Harcourt who brought down to the House written out statements and reams of manuscripts. Talking of other former statesman, Mr G. said the present Lord Grey (who was the only Privy Councillor of older standing than himself) showed wonderful promise as Lord Howick; and had certainly ever since, with the exception of his tenure of the Colonial Secretaryship been a disappointment. Another Colonial Secretary to whom he referred had been Lord Glenelg—a competent but lazy man who was credited with slumbering most of the day at the Colonial Office. Apropos of this tendency, he remembered Lord Brougham making an amusing allusion to it. Lord Brougham was speaking on some Canadian question; & he referred to it as having, he feared, been the cause of many sleepless—days to the noble Secretary of State. Spring Rice Mr G. held in considerable contempt for incompetence and jobbing proclivities.

8 October . . . In saying good-bye to Mr G. this morning, I asked what was now mostly occupying his mind. "I have", he said, "been long engaged on a big work, & I want much to finish it before I die—it is a work on Olympian religion"! (whatever that may mean). It seems a great waste that he should be devoting his powers to so uninteresting & useless a subject. If only he would write some of his own reminiscences; what a mine of historical interest they would be!

Friday 12 October . . . Chamberlain has been holding forth again, unfurling the Socialist flag.[87] He seems to want the State to undertake everything. I hate these grandmotherly tendencies.

The latest account of the Czar's state of health are decidedly alarming; there seems to be little doubt that he has a mortal disease upon him ("Bright's" or something akin to it) which may develop rapidly at any moment. He has unquestionably been a great peace preserver, & as such his life is perhaps more important than that of any other individual...But it seems impossible to justify his cruel & illiberal treatment of the Jews in Russia. That must always be an indelible blot in his character & in his reign.

Sunday 14 October (Gunnersbury Park, Acton) . . . I have written to Rosebery to-day further as to his considering Stephen Gladstone's [88] name for the Deanery of Winchester. He has got quite average ability—indeed his father thinks it far above the average—and he is a very strong Liberal—in fact he is a Dis-establisher. The principal drawback to his being given preferment of that kind is his appearance which is certainly not pre-possessing.

The licensing Committee of the London County Council are making fools of themselves again. They decline to renew the license of the Empire Theatre, if the promenade & public bar are continued, on the ground of its being a resort for so many improper women. Can anything be more silly in their own interests & in the interests of the object which they have in view? They will write themselves down as a body wholly bereft of common sense and in so doing they bring the Council itself into disrepute; while if the women are turned out of their extremely well-ordered place, the streets will become still more crowded with prostitutes. It remains to be seen whether better sense won't prevail at the Council when they review the decisions of their Committee . . .

Thursday 18 October The election at Birkenhead,[89] caused by the succession of Bury to the Earldom of Albemarle, turned out to be a very close fight. The Unionist candidate won by only 100 votes & had a sensibly reduced majority. The reduction may be attributable to the relative strength of the candidates; but at any rate (so far as it goes) it shows that there is no material change of opinion in the country. I believe that, if there were a General Election tomorrow, the majority for the present Government such as it is might disappear, but that there would be no majority for the Unionists. The fact is there is complete political lethargy. The House of Lords question may interest & stir up the extreme left; but the immediate case against that House is a weak one, not much stronger than it was in the days of Lord Melbourne's Government, when there was much said against the Upper Chamber but nothing done. Nor will anything be done now. Apart from that question, neither side has got much else but dead horses to flog, and that is not calculated to stir the electorate . . .

Friday 19 October . . . I have sent my Memm. on Irish Finance to the Royal Commission; and (though I say it) it is not uninteresting reading. It covers a good deal of historical matter which has never been put together before; and I think it contributes a very complete brief for the Commissioners.

There is apparently going to be a keen fight over the coming School Board Elections. The Church party are not content with the working of the compromise effected by the "Conscience Clause" in the Act of 1870. The idea was that, while no dogma was to be taught nor any denominational formularies used, teachers might expound in their own language the story of the New Testament. The Church party now want to have the *t's* crossed and the *i's* dotted; & it looks as if the old controversy was going to be fought all over again.

Saturday 20 October (Charters, Ascot)   F. Lockwood's appointment to the Solicitor Generalship, *vice* R. Reid promoted to be Attorney General, is announced to-day; and I am very glad there is no doubt any longer about Lockwood's fate. The appointment will be very popular, for no man's promotion in the House of Commons will be more cordially welcomed by both sides. The Unionists at York have in the most generous manner determined not to fight him on re-election; and it would be a good thing if this good example were followed elsewhere, so long as that antiquated requirement about seeking re-election on the acceptance of office is allowed to exist.

Sunday 21 October   Froude the historian, who has had a long lingering illness, has succumbed at last. He will probably live in literature for the charm of style and his fascinating essays. Whether he will, or is entitled to, take a high place as a historian is more doubtful. It will be interesting to see what Rosebery does as regards Froude's successor in the Chair of History at Oxford. Lecky would seem to have first claims; and after him Gardiner.[90]

Monday 22 October   Harcourt has returned with Loulou from his second trip abroad . . . He is in very good humour & very good spirits: there are no more allusions to retirement, though he gives himself out to be only a partial supporter of the present Government. On financial policy he is heart and soul with them; but not on several other questions, such particularly as foreign affairs. He thinks it is rather strange that Rosebery should be going to make his pronouncement on the House of Lords without first summoning the Cabinet & committing them to what he proposes to say. However Harcourt himself professes to be very pleased that R. has decided, as he has, to take his own line on his own responsibility; because Harcourt has not the faintest idea what to advise or to say himself on so insoluble a problem. All he knows is that nothing will induce him to appear on a platform during the recess. He had heard that R.

was going to take the line of suggesting procedure by resolution in the House of Commons; and it seemed to him that the Peers would merely snap their fingers and treat any amount of such resolutions as waste paper. Harcourt had met Labouchere at Venice; but they kept clear of politics altogether.

Wednesday 24 October   The Government, or rather Rosebery himself, is being much taken to task for having moved too precipitately about intervening in concert with the other big Powers between China & Japan. The *Times* has written very unfairly on the matter, taunting R. with having succeeded in getting a rebuff administered to this counrty; and *Truth* is following the lead of the *Times*. Labouchere never loses an opportunity of running down R.

Friday 26 October   Rosebery spoke last night at the annual "Cutler's Feast" at Sheffield. It is a non-political gathering. He went there I think mainly to please & solace old Mundella. He spoke almost entirely on foreign politics, alluding gracefully to the Czar's condition, saying some civil things about the relations between France & this country, explaining what had happened about the alleged "intervention" fiasco, and commenting on the disappearance in this country of "Little England" ideas. It was a good speech—because there was a decided ring & definite note about it. But the speech I am anxious about is the one he has to deliver tomorrow at Bradford. By that he may, & probably will, make or mar himself. A rather clever article about him is in the current number of the *XIX Century*—called— The seven Lord Roseberys. Pembroke[91] . . . has been writing to me about the article. It seems to him admirably to express R.'s way of seeming to be all sorts of inconsistent & more or less admirable things without committing himself to any one of them. This attitude of his, Pembroke says, so fascinating to the popular imagination with its suggestion of all sorts of possibilities and perhaps of great statesmanlike qualities made consistent by a higher wisdom than what the common man professes, is impossible to maintain now that he is Prime Minister. He must to some extent declare himself and let the country know what he really is. P. believes in a real Lord Rosebery—a man patriotic & clear-seeing in Imperial affairs, perhaps doubtful of the channel into which democracy had better run, but quite convinced that it must rule, & will rule in what it believes to be the interest of the masses; but he dreads lest the socialist-democratic Lord Rosebery may swallow up all the others, except the Imperialist-patriotic one, with which it is not inconsistent.

Saturday 27 October   There has been extraordinary interest taken in a matter not very big of itself. The Licensing Committee of the London

County Council had, mainly at the instance of one or two prudes (female ones) refused to recommend the renewal of the licence to the Empire Theatre unless the promenade were abolished and intoxicating drinks were no longer sold in the auditorium; and yesterday the recommendation came before the Council itself to be confirmed or set aside. Contrary to general expectation, it was confirmed by a large majority—75 to 32; and it is probable that the Empire will close its doors. I believe it is a very foolish action for the Council to have taken. They can't put down vice. As "boys will be boys", so will men & women be men & women. All that will result is a shifting of the scene from one place to another, & the eventual driving of more "unfortunate women" to the streets, which are already the disgrace of the metropolis, and where temptation is placed in men's ways in a still more overt manner. You can hardly find a sensible man or woman of the world who does not consider such action to be a mistake. Moreover, it holds a great public body up to ridicule, by showing that they are void of common-sense. The Empire authorities appear to have fought their battle badly. They rather gave themselves away by declaring that the conditions which the Council would impose upon them would involve the shutting up of the theatre, and thus practically admitting that what really *paid* was the least defensible part of the place of entertainment.

A more serious piece of *Imperial* news, elsewhere, is announced to-day; and that is the dismissal of Count Caprivi (the German Chancellor) & Count Eulenburg (the Prussian Premier) by the Emperor. It has taken everybody by surprise; and the most inexplicable part of the Emperor's action is the simultaneous dismissal of both men who were respective representatives of conciliatory and repressive measures against Socialists.

Sunday 28 October   Rosebery evidently got a great reception at Bradford yesterday. The text of his speech was, as he determined some time ago, the House of Lords. The gist of it is this: The next election, not very far distance, must, he said, be fought on the question of the veto placed by the irresponsible Chamber on measures emanating from the Liberal party. Was this, he asked, an opportune moment to deal with that question? He thought yes: because it was a time of calmness and it was better to deal with constitutional questions in the absence of passion and a spirit of resolution. The change of circumstances must be taken into account. The Lower Chamber had become more & more popularised; while the popular element in the Upper Chamber was undergoing daily diminution. There was no balance of parties there any longer. A Liberal Government could only look to a meagre 5 per cent support; no matter how large was the majority in the representative chamber. This was a mockery: it was useless for the House of Commons to waste its time in sending up measures to the House of Lords. He himself was a Second Chamber man. The temptation of absolute power was as great for a body of men as for an individual. But when it came to a choice between a second chamber and the present House of Lords, one might hesitate to choose between the two. The present constitution of that assembly was a positive danger and an invitation to revolution. It was not a Second Chamber at all. It was merely a permanent party organisation. The Tory party knew they had the House of Lords in their pocket. Liberal legislation could only now be carried by menace; while Tory legislation might descend like the rain from heaven. This was a national danger. But the issue was no doubt *tremendous*, and the method of dealing with it most complex & difficult. Nor was the remedy obvious. You could not pass a Bill abolishing the House of Lords or its veto short of a revolution. But there were means of making the will of the country felt without violence or unconstitutional methods. We cannot, he said, move in a hurry as the recent conference at Leeds would have us do. It was too great a responsiblity. One swallow did not make a summer. So one conference did not make an overwhelming mass of public opinion. Moreover there was no mandate as yet:- there was no sufficient majority. Without a mandate & without a big majority, it would be reprehensible to cast the country into a seething whirlpool of constitutional agitation. No. You must be wary, persevering, and patient. You can't carry the House of Lords by storm or by a rush. The great constitutional forces which we possess must first be brought into play. First come the House of Commons; and that could only be brought into play by resolution, like on the question of finance more than 200 years ago when it asserted its full and uncontrolled right to represent the people in matters of finance. The House of Commons must now assert its right to be predominant partner. Irresponsible resolutions had been made before. A resolution now must be moved by the Government, thus representing the demand of the Executive Government as well as the House of Commons. The question would then enter on a new phase. It would be a new Charter, a new constitutional amendment, the first act of a new drama with probably many other acts to follow. But such a resolution would not be sufficient by itself. Behind it must be the strength which could only be afforded by the people of Great Britain and Ireland. The Government would appeal to the country on such resolutions; & it was for the country to say whether they would support it. We shall then, he said, ask for a direct popular reference as to whether a revision of the constitution is desired or not. We fling down the gauntlet: it is for you to back us up.

I have been thinking much of the speech to-day, & I have come to these conclusions. It must be considered from a party point of view & from a statesman's point of view. I believe the party, except the unreasonable Laboucheres & Co., will be satisfied with the speech. It is a clear indication from their leader that the present state of things is indefensible, and that some change, gradually made, must be introduced in our constitution, in order to bring the second Chamber more into harmony with the first Chamber. He has spoken out decidedly & strongly—more strongly indeed than many expected, for instance Arnold Morley . . . The speech will thus probably establish R.'s position more firmly than it has hitherto been established, as Leader of the Left Party. It will probably make members of it more enthusiastic about him than they have been before. He will therefore have a more powerful hold over them. From the other point of view, the speech appears to me to be statesmanlike and unstatesmanlike. It may be said, Is it wise to raise a great constitutional question when the case is not strong, and when the only solution that can possibly be offered is somewhat feeble & impotent? Might it not have been wiser to take the line of saying "The House of Lords is on its trial: the real test will come when measures have been sent up to it which have been endorsed by great majorities. Will the Peers then defer to the clearly expressed wishes of the people's representatives? Let the House of Lords first place themselves flagrantly in the wrong". On the other hand, it must be remembered that a man in R.'s position must control as well as lead. He believes that the only question which at present interests electors is the House of Lords. If he declines to deal with the question, the result will be that the party will run riot, may get on totally wrong lines, and if left to themselves may run a revolutionary muck against the Peers. Is it not therefore wise for R. to put himself *en rapport* with the feeling of the masses; & tell them boldly. "You can't do away with the House of Lords or their veto. You can only clip their wings very gradually & slowly by bringing public opinion to bear upon them. Don't be carried away with wild & revolutionary notions. You must walk warily & patiently. You must consider the questions calmly. We must take time by the forelock & deal with the question before pistols are at our hands." If he can succeed in making people weigh these considerations, and in preventing them from being carried away anywhere or nowhere, he will have done the act of a statesman. Of course his opponents will charge him with goading on the masses to do away with the House of Lords; but what can be milder really than his proposal.

Monday 29 October I met Lockwood—very pleased to be Solicitor-General—in the Park this morning. He thought R.'s speech would do very well, and was what was wanted. The captious article in this morning's *Times* had done most to confirm him in this opinion.

I was dining *tête-à-tête* with R. this evening in Berkeley Square. He is beginning to face his house with stone which may involve his turning out for a time and seeking temporary shelter in Downing Street. He was very much pleased with his reception at Bradford, and said the audience was most attentive and intelligent. There were rather long faces drawn when he pointed out the great difficulties of dealing with the House of Lords question; but they seemed to appreciate the difficulties. Those who were on the platform with him were apparently satisfied and were very complimentary. I told him what I thought of the speech. I never saw him more convinced that the line he had taken was the right one. It was, he felt, quite impossible for him to defend the present state of things. The question was bound to be faced; and his proposal would, he hoped, help to guide public opinion on a safe track. It would lead to a minimum of harm at any rate; was in his opinion a really conservative move. He had always made up his mind to make the House of Lords his own question; and had therefore propounded his ideas on his own responsibility. He must of course stand or fall by his speech. Judging from the precautionary telegrams he had received from the Queen, he might expect somewhat of a jobation; but he had a complete answer for Her, which was that if he fell she would have a worse alternative to face. "Society" would very likely be up in arms with him; but what was Society to him? If he had put the drag on, he could afford to face with equanimity the scathings of the Conservative Press and the *classes*. He admitted that his speech would easily be answered—he would gladly have the answering of it himself; it was obvious—that a resolution or dozens of resolutions aimed by the Lower House against the Upper House could have no immediate effect, and therefore Peers could quietly wait till such expressions of opinion had assumed the force of immemorial custom.

Tuesday 30 October   Harcourt came up this afternoon for the Cabinet tomorrow. He was in an amiable humour. He said nothing disparaging or uncomplimentary about R.'s speech; though he would express no opinion upon it, until he had seen how public opinion took it—a safe alternative to assume—meanwhile he had already begun to turn over in his mind the form of the famous Dunning Resolution, moved & carried in 1780, that "the influence of the Crown has increased, is increasing, and ought to be diminished".

Wednesday 31 October   The Cabinet appears to have been an amiable one; & Harcourt greeted Rosebery quite cordially. He rather sneered at the proposed Resolution; and told me that he believed there was in the Cabinet a majority of anti-Second Chamber men, of whom he was one himself. Rosebery had, he said, been apparently rather taken aback by his (Harcourt's) having pointed out that no resolution could be moved in the House of Commons on the responsibility of the Executive Government without the previous concurrence of the Sovereign. Fortunately, however, Harcourt is never very accurate in his statements. Rosebery is of course aware of the A.B.C. of constitutional Government; and told me that there was evidently a clear majority in this Cabinet ready to accept his (mild) proposals: though of course the terms of it might be not a little difficult to frame. John Morley, R. said, seemed to be in one of his captious and cussed moods. He thought I might say a word to J.M. I shall have a good opportunity, as J.M. is staying with me for a night or two.

Rosebery was at Bristol yesterday unveiling a statue of Edmund Burke and receiving the freedom of the city. His speech about Burke was as good as it could be; but that on being made a citizen of Bristol was rather flippant—too much so, for a Prime Minister.

Harcourt this afternoon made me the offer, in the kindest of terms, of the Comptroller-Generalship of the National Debt Office, from which Rivers Wilson is about to retire. But I told him that I infinitely preferred staying where I was: I held the most interesting post in the Civil Service; the National Debt Office would be very dull and I should feel that I was shelved. He said that he was only too glad that I should remain on as "his right hand man"; but he felt bound to give me the refusal of the post. Loulou has, he told me, made up his mind not to take the post. He (Loulou) knows his father could not get on without him; that therefore so long as his father remains on in public life, he will not look at outside employment. This is most creditable to Loulou; and I confess I think it is a wise decision; for though he is perfectly competent for the post, there might be disagreeable things said about his being placed at one bound into so big an administrative office . . .

Thursday 1 November John Morley & I dined with Arnold Morley last night at the Savoy . . . I have had some talk with John Morley. He is sore at Rosebery's references in his recent Sheffield speech to the virtual disappearance of "Little Englanders". He (J.M.) was a "Little Englander" himself; and he determined to remain so. Now that Jingoism was the declared policy of the Radical Leader, and Home Rule (which he believed in more than he ever did) was practically placed on the shelf, he thought he had better retire—(not that he will). He would like to spend his "declining years" in writing a political history of the last 8 years: though of course that was not feasible. He was moreover tired of his post in Ireland. In fact, he is in a discontented frame of mind. I deprecated this; and told him that whatever might be his feelings he was rather hard to vent them upon Rosebery, who was in the same boat with him, and who would be quite as glad to "slip out" of his place as he (J.M.) was; only he knew he could not. Moreover he might remember how attached personally R. was to him. J.M. admitted that he had not always been very considerate.

He and I have been dining again at the Savoy tonight. Asquith entertained us: also the Ribblesdales,[92] Haldane and Acland. We had a most pleasant dinner, and we have been foregathering in my rooms afterwards. The more I see of Acland, the better I like him. He is pleasant in conversation and cheery. J. Morley has a high opinion of him. He says Acland has great political acumen; & that moreover he has the power of initiating and constructing. Asquith, according to J.M., is deficient in these respects; & often has to depend on Acland. These three ministers, when the other had gone, discussed the political situation and the "plan of campaign". They seemed to think that on the whole they ought not to let their hands be forced at the commencement of the Session: that, while the Opposition would of course try to stop everthing, they ought to plod on with Welsh Disestablishment and the Irish Land Bill, not moving the House of Lords Resolution till the end of the Session. Then they must dissolve, unless they first tried to run a Registration Bill through at an Autumn Session. The House of Lords would certainly reject Welsh Disestablishment and any Registration Bill: so they would be piling up the agony. It might be otherwise with the Irish Land Bill, if Ulster, as seemed likely, supported it. Might not the passage of that Bill, I asked, cut away the ground a good deal from the feet of the House of Lords agitators, and make the case against the Peers still less strong than it was now? Acland said it was not a question of the rejection of this and that measure, and the acceptance of a third (probably in a modified form). What agitated the public mind was the fact of a permanent and big majority against the Liberal party in one of the Legislative Chambers. The Radical electors felt that one party of the State was under the present state of things perpetually handicapped with severity; this was not fair play; and what they were bent on was to get at any rate fairer play.

The Czar (Alexander III) is dead. He seems to have met his end with great fortitude & calmness. His death is not likely to have any immediate effect in political or financial circles. It has already been discounted. The new Emperor (Nicholas II) is said to be a well disposed young fellow. I have heard him spoken of in high and affectionate terms by the Duke of York whom he is singularly like in appearance.

Saturday 3 November . . . I have not yet heard anything very savage said in society about Rosebery's. The impression in Tory and social circles seems to be that it was a clever move from a party point of view; and that the placing of the House of Lords at the head of the Liberal programme has for the first time made a Liberal majority possible at the next General Election. The Queen's remarks were quite moderate. She knows R. will not stand anything strong or abusive. Lord Salisbury by the way replied to it at Edinburgh a night or two ago; and of course was able to make his reply effective and pungent. But he was a little over-violent, especially when he came to deal with R.'s undeniable allegation that the majority in the House of Lords was at the beck and call of the Conservative Leader. R.'s statement was not really more than what one of Lord Salisbury's present colleagues said of the Upper House in 1885—I allude to Goschen—when he called it (I think) "a Conservative Committee". Pembroke is, as I expected, considerably exercised over the speech. He is vexed to see a man like Rosebery fanning an agitation which can lead to no good. He ought to know better than to appeal to the people to attack the House of Lords—"in the spirit of Cromwell's ironsides"! without attempting to foreshadow what he is going to do when he passes his Resolution, and if he gets a majority in the country . . .

John Morley has returned this evening to Ireland . . . It is mistrust of the conduct of foreign affairs which exercises his mind. When Rosebery became head of the Government, he (J.M.) had only reluctantly agreed to Lord Kimberley as Foreign Secretary on the assurance of Lord Spencer that Lord K. belonged to the old-fashioned school on foreign policy. He (J.M.) had held out as long as he could for the Foreign Office to be in the hands of a Member of the House of Commons, like Campbell-Bannerman; and he had given way because he thought that Lord Kimberley was a man who could be relied upon and who would take his own line. Instead of this Lord Kimberley proved to be as malleable as clay in the hands of R.; and R. was practically Foreign Minister as well as Prime Minister. He (J.M.) feared now that mischief was brewing with France". . .

John Morley had been much amused by a talk he had with Fowler. Fowler had come back from Balmoral quite the courtier and fascinated by the Queen and her graciousness towards him. "You must really, Morley, cultivate Her Majesty's acquantance. I can assure you. She is worth knowing. You are just the man to suit Her." J.M. admitted that, being less fortunate than his favoured colleague, he knew little of the Queen; but he did not quite see how he was to know more. He could hardly invite himself to Windsor or Balmoral.

Sunday 4 November (The Durdans) . . . Rosebery and I have had a *tête-à-tête* evening. I have told him the gist of J. Morley's conversations with me. He thought J. Morley rather unreasonable; especially about foreign affairs. What he said, can men like Harcourt & J. Morley know about such a subject of which they have had no actual experience? I told R. this evening, a propos of his speech to the Bristol citizens, that he must try and drop the flippant style as Prime Minister, and also references to his holding the office of Prime Minister so "unworthily", which have the appearance of much-humility. He admitted the force of the criticism and took my remarks very well. He was rather exercised about his coming Guildhall speech. He did not know what to say. He rather thought he might take as his text the State and the limit to its functions—certainly an excellent text on which to preach on these days, when everybody wants to thrust everything on to the Executive Government. Referring to the conduct of business in Cabinet he said the only men whose voices were as a rule heard were Harcourt, Lord Kimberley, Herschell, and J. Morley. He thought it a great pity than men like Asquith & Acland did not assert themselves more in Cabinet deliberations: & that he had a right to expect more support from them. As to the future, which was more than usually uncertain, he expected the dissolution would have to come sooner rather than later. It seemed to him that the Opposition after clamouring for an appeal to the country could hardly help using every effort to force the hand of the Government . . .

Mr John Walter's reign in Printing House Square has come to an end, and Arthur Walter, or "Jupter" Walter (as we used to call him at Eton—I do not remember why) reigns in his stead. The *Times* has certainly been a Press wonder under the late Proprietor; but latterly it has become so partisan that it has lost its former weight for impartiality and independence. I have heard it said that he would never die happy until he had ruined Mr Gladstone . . . I am afraid therefore his death could not have been a wholly happy one; for Mr G. has survived all the violent attacks upon him in the *Times* and likewise survived the proprietor.

Tuesday 6 November I met Natty Rothschild[93] this afternoon. He declares that Rosebery's speech is going to give the Unionists a clear majority of 120! and that that is not only his opinion but that of Lord Salisbury. He denies that there is any strong feeling in the country against the House of Lords; and that what is going to tell against the Government is the action of the Progressives in the London County Council. N.R.'s judgement is so often at fault, that I am beginning for the first time to think that the Unionists may not get any majority at all at the next Election. The real card for Lord Salisbury or the Duke of Devonshire to play is undoubtedly to introduce a measure themselves for reforming the Second Chamber. A reform, on such lines as having a certain number—say 200 or so of Peers elected and adding to them some Life Peers and others with ex-officio seats in the second chamber, might not be relished by the Radicals but it would be acceptable to many moderate men and would go a long way towards taking the wind out of the sails of any House of Lords agitation.

This evening Tweedmouth and I dined together at Brooks'. He had just come from Hawarden. According to him Mr G. approved the idea of proceeding by resolution on the House of Lords question. He (Tweedmouth) had been speaking at Manchester and had an excellent meeting. The Second Chamber was the only topic that really interested the audience. He thought the Government outlook would be fairly good, were it not for one great crux ahead: and that was the difficulty about Labour candidates. Unless certain seats were given up to them, they would be standing at many elections, with the result that many seats would be lost. The only chance was to get a few Labour men accepted by Liberal Associations. He told me that all the cheques sent in response to the circular, which the Irish party now disown, have been returned to the senders except Mr G.'s. They thought it might be a slight upon him. These Irishmen are certainly very curious about money affairs—mainly from fear of the suspicion attaching to taking English gold: he had actually offered them on his own account a cheque for £33,000 when they were in considerable difficulties pecuniarily a few months ago. The offer was made through Blake[94] but it was declined straight away.

Thursday 8 November Fife . . . talked to me a good deal, very confidentially of course, about the Queen & Rosebery's speech . . . She was, he said, much exercised not in anger but in sorrow, and felt much hurt. She had not understood the letter which he had written to prepare Her for a pretty strong speech; and could not gather from his speech what he was really driving at. Was he or was he not a Second Chamber man? She was much attached to R. personally; & therefore was all the more distressed at the prospect of losing one of Her few remaining confidants. One cannot help feeling very much for the Queen's isolated position—with no one to consult or advise Her. Her surroundings are almost wholly Tory and she knows nothing but Tory gossip and Tory views . . . I am all for R's doing nothing to imperil his friendly relations with the Sovereign: so I suggested that in Her present frame of mind a further civil and softening-down letter should be sent Her. He sat down and wrote a very nice one, which he showed me as well as the others previously written. He emphasises his distress at giving Her trouble, and would gladly resign if it was thought that it would help Her. But she has to remember that the majority of the party & perhaps even of his colleagues are anti-second chamber men. The declarations therefore he has made are the least possible that can satisfy his followers. Had he said less, they would have broken away from him, & the extremes would undoubtedly get the upper hand.

I confess myself I cannot well comprehend how sensible men can seriously advocate the abolition of the House of Lords and the establishment of a single chamber. There is hardly a constitution in the world without two chambers; and the inevitable result would be to call into activity the veto of the Crown.

Saturday 10 November (Waddesdon) . . . I went last night with Ferdie Rothschild to see the new piece at the Haymarket. Beerbohm Tree has enticed Mrs Patrick Campbell away from St James' Theatre. She is certainly a very fascinating actress. She again takes the part of an impropriety. In fact, improprieties constitute now the leading parts of most modern plays on the English stage. The most striking feature of the present stage are the increased *breadth* which is not only tolerated but which appears to be thought necessary in order to draw; and the great improvement in acting. The standard of actors & actresses is now quite a high one which is more than can be said of the standard of play-wrights.

While we were at the Theatre last night, Rosebery was making his first appearance at the Guildhall as Prime Minister. He seems to have got an excellent reception in spite of the Tory audience . . . Even Harcourt referred to-day to the success of the proceedings at the Guildhall. I went & had luncheon with him. He was quite like a child at the thought of his being able to put on his Exchequer robes on Monday on the occasion of the pricking of the sheriffs at the Law Courts.

Sunday 11 November (Waddesdon)   The *Spectator* is very much down on Rosebery; and takes the line of his being a fiasco as Prime Minister. No doubt R. has not come up to general expectation. But what did people expect? Or (perhaps what is more to the point) what had they a right to expect. They seemed to think the political millennium was coming; that the Liberal party would be forthwith reconstituted. Home Rule was to be placed definitely on the shelf; and the Government were, notwithstanding, to become all the stronger. Could anything be more absurd? If Home Rule had been abandoned, I doubt if one single Liberal Unionist would have returned (as it is called) to the fold. Certainly *no individual member of that party*, great or small, ever made the smallest advance towards R. when he was forming his Government. They knew in their heart of hearts that Home Rule could not be given up. Indeed had R. ever dreamt of this, he would have been practically admitting that he had held office under false pretences for a year & a half; and the Irishmen would have turned out the Government the moment it had been formed. No: there may have been some reason for disappointment about his speeches until lately; but the fact remains that in spite of inherent difficulties and the behaviour of one particular colleague towards him he has kept the party together, which is no small feat to have achieved. He is now endeavouring to keep them together on the one question of all others which is said to interest the electorate—the House of Lords. At present there does not seem to be any great response to his speech; but I expect this is to be attributed to the fact that he has not gone far enough to please the extreme section, and it is from them that the response would naturally come. Of course what he wants to do—but he may not succeed—is to prevent the idea of a single Chamber from getting hold of the party too strongly. On the other hand, had he taken up the *non possumus* line or emphasised too strongly the *mending* of the House of Lords, he would have lost his hold over the party. They would (and even now may) break away from him; and with him would go almost the last piece of ballast in the Liberal ship. A moderate paper like the *Spectator* serves its own cause badly by running a tilt against Rosebery. Curiously enough it was in its columns that R.'s claim and natural capacity to succeed Mr G. was I believe first advocated. It must have been 1887 or 1888 that it broached the subject.

Tuesday 13 November (Longleat, Warminster) I had a talk with Harcourt—it was *Harcourt benignans*—about Budget prospects. I expect we ought to have a surplus this year of something like ¾ million. The real question is, will ends meet next year? Will the increase of Revenue be equal to the increase of expenditure? Most depends on the Admiralty demands. Harcourt declared that nothing would induce him to impose additional taxation again to meet those demands. He thinks (& rightly so) that we have come to the end of our taxation tether in times of peace. If therefore the Naval cost cannot be cut according to the financial cloth some other Chancellor of the Exchequer must provide the necessary ways & means. His family solicitor had been to see him, and told him that there were no very palpable steps being taken to evade the Death Duties. Out & out gifts were the only possible evasion; and people would be deterred from this by the inherent love of possession.

I travelled down in the train this afternoon as far as Chippenham with Lansdowne. He spoke strongly against the present state of things with respect to Land Legislation in Ireland. Nothing could be worse. The incentive of the tenant to become his own landlord by buying his holding no longer existed; and nothing could be more intolerable than the present position of the ordinary landlord. The Land Courts had, he said, worked great injustice. They might have been necessary to prevent the raising of rents; but now they were a synonym for lowering rates. There was no standard of valuation. The judicial rents were fixed all haphazard according to the whim of the local commissioner who had probably little agricultural knowledge & much political bias; and now according to the Morley Committee the rents were to be revised every 10 years. The only solution, in his opinion, now was to make all the landlords rent-chargers. They would probably be content with a low rent-charge. Anything was better than the present uncertainty, and the present half & half system of landlordism. If the rent-charge were once fixed, then there would be inducement to the tenant to buy. He won't buy now, beccause he is in constant expectancy of further reductions of rent.[95]

Thursday 15 November (Longleat) Bath[96] is as Tory as ever. He looks upon Lord Salisbury with great suspicion and on Arthur Balfour with little less. Lord Salisbury seems, he says to be always fighting; and admitting that he is fighting, a hopeless battle. Bath told me something about Sir Rob. Peel which he heard on the authority of Lord Derby (the great), and which I had never heard before. According to Bath, Lord Derby said that Sir Rob. Peel was a man who naturally had a great sense of humour; but that he studiously repressed it, because he had seen how much harm Canning had done himself by giving play to a similar sense.

. . . I have read Rosebery's speech at Glasgow last night; & on the whole I am well pleased with it. The two main points he made were (1) to warn the party that it was impossible to proceed *pari passu* with the measures which each section regards as indispensable; and (2) to emphasise his own individual position as a Second Chamber man. I believe a single chamber, especially in democratic days, to be impossible as well as impracticable; and would result eventually in the downfall of the throne, because the only alternative to a second Chamber would be the vetoing power of the Crown, and the revival of that power would never be stood.

Sunday 18 November   I am afraid from what I gather, that Rosebery's speech at Glasgow won't help to minimise ministerial differences. His emphasising so strongly his predilections for a Second Chamber was perhaps rather bold and honest than judicious. The fact is—strange though it may seem to be—there is I believe a distinct majority of the Cabinet in favour of a Single Chambered constitution, or who at any rate profess to be willing to dispense with a Second Chamber altogether. It may be therefore that R. has said too much and the party may break away or break up on the question of the House of Lords.

The floods in the Thames Valley especially about Eton and Windsor have been higher than they have been known to be during this century. Eton was flooded out, and the school has had to be broken up . . .

The School Board controversy and the impending elections are not creating any great excitement, but they occupy a deal of space in the newspapers. The position of affairs seems to be this: when Forster's act was passed in 1870, whereby School Boards were established and schools placed under those Boards were to be maintained wholly out of rates and Exchequer money combined, the teaching of creeds was naturally to be excluded from the regular tuition in Board Schools. The Bible was to be taught like any other book of history in a non-controversial manner; while the clergymen of the Established Church and Ministers of all denominations and sects were to be allowed access to the schools to supplement the religious teaching by explaining their particular dogmas and articles of faith. This was a very reasonable arrangement to make; for as were are a professedly Christian nation, it was natural for the state to say "we will teach Christianity in the broadest sense of the term and nothing else". The system worked well enough, and seemed to give pretty general satisfaction at any rate in the country at large. Unfortunately however in London some few ill-judging teachers produced the impression that they were giving a sceptical version of the story in the old and new Testaments. Thereupon, the Church party who have a majority on the London School Board took a still more ill-advised step by issuing a circular which pointed out that the faith of Christendom involved the acceptance of the three mysteries of the Trinity, Atonement, & Incarnation. So it has now become a fight between (what many would hold to be) dogmatic or sectarian teaching advocated by the Moderates, and pure secularism advocated by the Progressives. It is thought that the Church party or Moderates will win the day, because they are on the side of economy and because many strong Churchmen (like Edward Otley), though they prefer pure secularism to diluted Christianity, do not like to record their votes with the Progressives against the Church.

Wednesday 21 November   I am regularly laid up again, confined to bed. This time my troubles taking the form of an attack of phlebitis in my left leg. With their return comes a renewal of kindness from one's friends. Rosebery who returned from Scotland looked in upon me last night. He did not seem particularly disconcerted at the prospect of to-day's Cabinet. The Forfarshire election,[97] resulting in the return of the Unionist candidate Ramsay (poor Dalhousie's brother) and consequently in the loss of a seat to the Government was (he said) of course a nasty slap in the face; but it would make the supporters of the Government a little more wary & less inclined to be recalcitrant, while the Unionists would probably be unduly elated and become more reckless. Harcourt who is never behindhand when a friend of his is *down*, kindly came over this evening and sat with me for an hour, making himself very pleasant. He now of course talks less of political affairs with me than formerly; but there was nothing disagreeable in any of his remarks or insinuations. It is curious that he should be content to lie low all this time, allowing Rosebery to put himself *en évidence* and effacing himself entirely. Presumably he knows that he would not speak his mind out, without showing that he and the Prime Minister were little in agreement; and as that would not be decent, he probably thinks his best chance is to play a waiting game, on the chance of R,'s "putting his foot" into it. Reggy Brett was here to-day. He agreed that the outlook for R. was not rosy. R,'s principal mistake had been want of clearness. People could not make out what he was driving at as regards the House of Lords. The House of Lords was on no account to be abolished. Therefore there must be a Second Chamber, and a Second Chamber with some vetoing power: otherwise it would be an absurdity. Then was it to be a reformed House of Lords which he was advocating? In that case, let him say so. A reformed House of Lords might be more evenly balanced as regards parties but it could hardly fail in some respects to be more powerful than the present Upper House.

Saturday 24 November The School Board elections have resulted very nearly in a tie, which means that the Progressives have gained sensibly. The old Board consisted of 34 Moderates, 19 Progressives, 1 Independent, & 1 Roman Catholic. In the new Board the Progressives number 26 and the Moderates 29. The poll was a heavy one; and the relative growth of the Progressive Vote remarkable; for while the Moderate Vote increased from 471,000 to 672,000, the Progressives vote increased from 392,000 to 818,000. Moreover, though the Progressives are in a minority on the new Board, the aggregate Progressive vote exceed the aggregate Moderate vote by nearly 150,000 & so much for the cumulative vote and proportional representation! The Church party headed by Mr Diggle ought to have had a lesson read to them by the Elections, and if they are wise we shall hear no more of the Church Circular. One feature of the elections worth noting is that the Socialists and Labour party were nowhere in the contest.

What is going to become of Consols, I can't say. Here are the 2¾ per cents up at 103¼, as high as the old 3 per cents were, when we undertook the conversion! and all other first class or "gilt edged" securities are correspondingly high.

Monday 26 November John Morley came to see me this afternoon. I at once taxed him with being a "single chamber" man, & he did not deny it. Indeed, "why not?" he said, "Is there any real danger attached to it? and as regards that power, does it not for all intents & purposes already reside in one Chamber—the representative Chamber? Has there been any great abuse of that power, which the veto of the House of Lords would have checked? Moreover, when the Tories are in power, is not the House of Commons then practically supreme? Have the House of Lords ever rejected or even maimed a Bill sent up by a Tory majority in the House of Commons?" However, he admitted that such arguments were not of much avail, because the idea of ending the House of Lords is not practicable. What the Cabinet had to do was to try and carry out Rosebery's original proposition, which was to "adjust" the relations between the two Houses. How that was to be done, he said, was not easy: possibly by Bright's plan of limiting the vetoing power to one session. I said I thought the limitation ought, if possible, to be to some extent regulated by the support which had been accorded to the Bill in the House of Commons, as represented by the majorities with which it had been carried. J.M. was not averse to that in principle (as far as I made out); but strong exception was taken to the idea on the ground that it involved too great a departure in principle from our constitution. He was also favourable to what was generally termed the

"Rosebery Relief" reform; that is, giving Peers the option of sitting in the Lower House. He told me he was much engrossed in the preparation of the Land Bill. After having had two legislative failures, he was determined to make this Bill one to pass; and if only the Irishmen had a little more pluck he believed he could pass a measure which could be accepted by & acceptable to both landlord & tenant. He had just returned from visiting the Waterfords, and found him most reasonable and sensible. If only there were a few more landlords like him in Ireland, the land question would not be difficult to solve. Waterford apparently says that the present chance was a good one and one which might not recur. I told J. Morley what Lansdowne's views were, as I understood them to be; and I think he would like to confer with Lansdowne as well as Waterford. If only he could bring those men face to face round a table with Dillon & Healy.[98]

Tuesday 27 November   Rosebery looked in this afternoon. He did not remain long & was not particularly communicative. He was not dissatisfied with the Cabinet decision; but the "resolution" business was still very "chaotic". He seems, I am glad to say, to take the criticism and abuse of the Press much less to heart than I feared he would . . . Arnold Morley also paid me a visit. He is apparently not very decided in his views on the House of Lords question. In principle I gather he favours a Single Chamber; because he doubts if any practicable scheme can be worked out which would make it impossible for the House of Lords to reject permanently or persistently measures approved by the House of Commons. But any change whatever it may be will take years to be brought about; and so it is not necessary to have immediately any cut and dried views. As far as he could gather, the political tone seemed to be not at all bad. He had had several meetings lately at Nottingham; and he had never had more enthusiastic ones. He had just come from the Cabinet Committee on the Temperance Bill. Harcourt was quite reasonable; and he thought he now saw his way to provide for Local Option as well as for Local Veto.

Wednesday 28 November   I have had several visitors today. Loulou Harcourt looked in about noon. His father and Lord Spencer are having a battle royal again about the Navy Estimates for next year. Lord Spencer threatens a further increase of two millions; but Harcourt insists that the increase must depend on the amount of revenue which he can spare the Admiralty. Nothing, he declares, will induce him to be a party to an expenditure on shipbuilding next year which will entail the imposition of further taxation . . . Tweedmouth looked in later. He is practically a single-chamber man; though of course he recognises that end can only be achieved very gradually by limiting the vetoing power of the House of

Lords. Rosebery, he thought, had been impolitic in emphasising his own
personal predilection for a Second Chamber: it had placed some of his
colleagues in considerable difficulty; & it would put the back up of the
out-&-out Radicals. He talked a good deal about Harcourt who was not in
an unreasonable frame of mind. He thought Harcourt's game was to ride
for a fall. He (Harcourt) wants the Government to be beaten on the
address and to resign, forcing the other side to dissolve, and leaving
himself in Opposition to "rule the roost". Tweedmouth however doubts if
the Opposition will or even want to throw the Government out
immediately, though much no doubt, will depend on the electoral reports
which they receive at the beginning of the New Year. It must, he said, be
remembered that on the Bills with which they intend to proceed, like the
Welsh Church & the Irish land Bills, the Government would probably get
more than their normal majority. Though there was perhaps no enthusiasm
& certainly no *wave*, yet wherever he had been he had found the party in
good heart.

Thursday 29 November   Haldane paid me a visit this afternoon. He
thought things were a trifle on the mend politically. The effect of
Rosebery's too emphatic declaration of his own views on the House of
Lords question was wearing off. The fact was, the supposed differences in
the party on that question were greatly exaggerated. There were no real
"single-chamber" men, because abolition of the House of Lords was out of
the range of practical politics. The whole party could & would accept some
limitation of the veto. R. (he said) was not always quite happy in the
selection of his phrases. He would have to acquire more thoroughly Mr
G.'s art of guarding himself. The real thing that would put Rosebery & all
his colleagues in a hole would be if Lord Salisbury or the Duke of
Devonshire came forward with a plan of reform themselves. I believe this
too; but I am pretty sure there is no fear of their playing this trump card.
At least I think I can answer for the Duke. I got someone to draw him on
the point the other day; & he said "Certainly not: my move in the direction
of reforming the House of Lords from the Unionist party now would have
the appearance of being extorted by fear". It is curious how family history
like other history repeats itself. Among the books I have been reading
since being laid up has been Wraxall's memoirs; & his description of the
5th Duke of Devonshire (husband of the famous Duchess Georgiana)
would almost apply *totidem verbis* to the present Duke (Vol.III p.344).
Wraxall writes of the 5th Duke as "a nobleman whose constitutional
apathy formed his distinguishing characteristic. His figure was tall &
manly, though not animated or graceful, his manners calm & unruffled. He
seemed to be incapable of any strong emotion, and destitute of all energy
or activity of mind. As play became indispensable in order to rouse him

from this lethargic habit & to awake his torpid faculties he passed his evenings usually at Brooks' engaged at whist or faro. Yet beneath so quiet an exterior, he possessed a highly improved understanding . . . Inheriting with his immense fortune the hereditary probity characteristic of the family of Cavendish, if not a superior man, he was an honourable & respectable member of society. Nor did the somnolent tranquility of his temper by any means render him insensible to the seduction of female charms". Substitute 'The Turf Club' for 'Brooks', and 'bezique' for 'faro'; and you have a not unfaithful character drawn of the present Duke, though it would give an inadequate idea of his political position and solid abilities.

Friday 30 November   I have had a visit this evening from Reay. He gives a very good account of Elgin[99] in India. Elgin & his wife have not been social successes but as an administrator he has given complete satisfaction at the India Office . . . Reay says that Fowler lacks decision as Secretary of State and does not handle his Council very tactfully. He is far better in the House of Commons than as Head of a Department. I understand that he loses no opportunity of letting it be known that he is in high favour at this moment. It is curious how the Queen generally prefers second class men, like Fowler & Cross.

Thursday 6 December (Hotel Metropole, Brighton)   I have come down here for a few days to recruit . . . George Murray writes that he found Harcourt the other day at Malwood in excellent spirits. He (Harcourt) has, it appears, been writing some violent letters to Lord Kimberley about the alleged Armenian atrocities in quite a new style—waving the flag & beating the big drum. This is because he thought the Foreign Secretary & Prime Minister were treating the matter too mildly.

Saturday 8 December (Brighton)   . . . Fife has taken a house down here for his children. I went to luncheon with him to-day . . . Fife talked at great length politically. He appears to be willing to sacrifice everything to the maintenance of the Union, so strongly does he feel about the disastrous consequences of Home Rule. I believe he greatly exaggerates any dangers that could come from it; and what is far more important & dangerous is the growing tendency of the classes to range themselves against the masses. He is concerned at Rosebery's position. He maintains that Rosebery has been a disappointment as Prime Minister; and is losing his hold over Scotland: principally because he has not spoken out distinctly enough, and that he does not seem to have his heart in the policy which he advocates . . . Now comes the loss of the Election in the Brigg Division of Lincolnshire.[100] Succeeding so closely the Forfarshire election it is more of a blow than the loss of an ordinary seat at a bye-election; because it looks as if the policy which he has announced about the House of Lords is falling flat, and that if that question which is supposed to be the one that excites keenest interest falls flat, it is not unfair to assume that the days of the present Government are numbered. Moreover, the loss of the seats is of itself a serious consideration when already the majority of the Government is hardly a working one; and it is probable that the Opposition will take heart & force the hands of the Government at the commencement of the next Session. Perhaps the sooner the present administration comes to an end the better for R. himself and everybody.

Monday 10 December   I came up from Brighton this afternoon; I think I shall be able again to resume my ordinary life. I found Haldane at Brooks' this evening. The Brigg election, he admitted was bad: because it appeared to indicate the beginning of the end. On looking back Haldane thought that Rosebery would perhaps have done better had he declined to take the head of affairs without having *carte blanche* to start afresh—with a reconstructed Government and a fresh programme. Had he failed, he would still have been the "mystery man", to whom unlimited powers of statesmanship might have been attributed. Had he succeeded his boldness would have justified the risk

Tuesday 11 December   Goschen came & paid me a visit this afternoon at the Treasury . . . He agreed with me that finance was & must be one of the greatest problems ahead. The worst of it was, he said, there were so few public men who had really studied the question. He attributed this to a great extent, to the over-shadowing authority of Mr G. as a Financier. So long as he was to the front, his own side felt it useless to take the matter up; while the other side was shy about tackling the question, when the chances were that they would only be knocked down by Mr G. . . .

I went to see Lady Gosford this afternoon . . . [She] takes the ordinary line of Society about Rosebery. They all regard him as a disappointment and profess to take it quite to heart. They look upon him as a trimmer—as a sort of fallen angel. If he had only, they say, taken a decided line of his own, the very boldness of the step would probably have commanded the respect of his own recalcitrant followers and also of the country at large. People forget that personal interests have sometimes to be sacrificed to public considerations. The real task that R. had before him was that a man of his position, stake in the country, and abilities, should keep the ill-assorted bundle of sections together, in order that they might not get into dangerous and unscrupulous hands.

Wednesday 12 December   I have been dining this evening with Rosebery *tête-à-tête* in Berkeley Square. He was rather exhausted and hoarse after his effort last night at Devonport. He had had a very good reception; and seemed fairly satisfied with his speech which was mostly devoted to the House of Lords again. No matter how much pains he takes to define his position, he is always misunderstood and misrepresented. I do not say that this is not partly his own fault. Notwithstanding however all the harsh things said about him, he seemed in fairly good heart. I thought he had unnecessarily emphasised the intention of the Government to proceed with their legislative programme next session, no matter what happens. He said he was obliged to make this intimation on the ground of tactics, and implied that he was equally at liberty to dissolve or resign if the Government were run really close. He had had another of J. Morley's letters of vanity and petulance, implying that no Chief Secretary had ever had such a record before and that he (J.M.) was the only man who had been a real credit to the present Government . . . of the many duties which a Prime Minister has to perform, there is one which R. has fulfilled without raising a single cavil; and that has been his ecclesiastical appointments. The last two have given satisfaction. They have just been the right man in the right place—Gore, of "Lux Mundi" fame, as Canon of Westminster, and Stephen (Dean Hook's son in law) as Dean of Winchester.

Friday 14 December   I dined tonight at the Reform Club with Alfred Milner . . . and he asked me what was going to happen at the General Election. I said that if I had to make a prophecy, I should predict a majority of from 30 to 40 for the Unionists. There is no appreciable revulsion of feeling; but there seems to be great apathy, and when that is the case the Liberals & radicals are sure to lose ground.

Harcourt had Lord Spencer with him to-day to discuss Naval Estimates. The Admiralty ultimatum is a further increase of $1\frac{3}{4}$ millions next year. Harcourt wisely declined to committee himself. It is impossible for him to agree to a sum which will involve an increase of taxation. It can't be done. He had been amused by Fowler's account of his recent audience at Windsor. According to Fowler, he had discussed with H.M. the House of Lords question; and he had implied that it was the first time she had really had it explained properly to Her.

Sunday 15 December   . . . I saw Jenkyns yesterday. He told me that Harcourt-'s new Liquor Bill was a great improvement on that of last year. He believed it could almost be carried if it were given a decent chance. Harcourt had thrown himself into it thoroughly well, argued it out entirely & was quite master of it. Jenkyns, whom I always regard as a specially level-headed man, was commenting on the want of response to Rosebery's appeal. His speeches were wonderfully well thought out & well arranged while the matter was good and the language first rate; but they failed to inspire any enthusiasm. He (Jenkyns) could not understand it. I attribute this mostly to the entire absence of any interest in any political subject: all classes seem thoroughly apathetic; though I admit that the recent School Board poll gave decided signs of animation.

Tuesday 18 December   I am laid up with a bronchial attack . . . With his usual thoughtfulness, Rosebery on hearing that I was shut up came at once & paid me a visit. He had been amused by Chamberlain's absurd letters to the "Times" about his (R.'s) speech at Devonport. (R. had alluded in grave jest to the frequent allegations that the Liberal party was now wholly divorced from the intellect & indeed education of the country; & Chamberlain had taken it or pretended to take the statement as serious.) R. could hardly believe his eyes when he read Chamberlain's first letter; and in the second letter he (Chamberlain) had given himself away over the first . . .

I saw a letter in yesterday's *Times* which is fairly representative of the puzzle-mindedness in which people are or profess to be with respect to R.'s attitude on the House of Lords question. What is he driving at? they ask. He says he is a second-Chamber man: therefore he can not mean the abolition of the House of Lords. He says he is against reducing the House of Lords to a nullity; therefore he can not mean to propose that they should be deprived of all vetoing power. Lastly, he says he is against reforming the present Constitution of the Upper Chamber: therefore he can not mean to *mend*. If he does not mean mending or ending, what does he mean? One would imagine that those who hold this language had exhausted all possible alternatives. They entirely forget that there is another alternative which is evidently what he is making for; and that is, to put some limitation on the present vetoing powers of the House of Lords, such as was advocated by John Bright whom the Unionists are now so fond of quoting.

Friday 21 December   There has been the marvel of a cricket match in the antipodes: the Australians *versus* Stoddart's English team. The Australians scored 586 in their first innings; and the English 325. The English team had of course to follow on; and they put together the respectable score of 437, thus leaving the Australians 177 to get to win. The Australians failed to win by 10 runs. Rain had made the wicket almost unplayable on the last day; and so the English were materially assisted in that respect; but still it was a wonderful up-hill game to have won. I believe no team ever was yet beaten after making nearly 600 runs in their first innings.

Saturday 22 December   Saturday's financial papers make one think of the marvellous price of Consols. "Goschens" had recently been standing at the equivalent of old Three per cents at 122, taken on the simple basis of interest and allowing for the terminable character of the additional ¼ per cent to 1903.

Arthur Balfour was speaking in Scotland yesterday.[101] He naturally, and not ill-naturedly, had a fling at Rosebery's House of Lords project. He said that R. had driven his first ball into a bunker, and had ever since been trying to get it out with the result that it was in a more hopeless position that it was at first. It is the fashion of course to compare the two men, to the disparagement of R. People forget that it is comparatively child's play to lead the Conservatives. A.B. has only to open his mouth, and the respnse is a chorus of "Hear, Hears": whereas, whenever R. speaks the many captious "Oh, Ohs" go some way towards drowning the "Hear Hears".

Tuesday 25 December (Chatsworth) I came down here yesterday to spend Christmas . . . The Duke says that the Derby people have made up their minds that Harcourt is going to take a Peerage: his silence on the House of Lords Question has probably given rise to this belief. He (the Duke) referred to Rosebery & the House of Lords question. In his opinion R. had alluded to one point that seemed tangible and sensible—something in the nature of a representative conference between the two houses; but he had no sooner referred to it than he had apparently run away from it. The Duke thought that the beginning of the end of the present Government was visible.

Sunday 30 December (Mentmore)   It was Mr G.'s birthday yesterday; he has thus entered on his 86th year. He celebrated it by making a speech on the Armenian question. An Armenian deputation came to present Hawarden Church with a chalice, and he took the opportunity of speaking some very plain words on the alleged activities in Armenia, which seemed to be worse and better authenticated than the Bulgarian atrocities 18 years ago, against which he led such a campaign. He spoke out very strongly; but counselled the Deputation and others to suspend judgement unti! the horrors were corroborated, and expressed confidence in the action of the Government. This emergence from privacy will of course make people say that he intends after all to return to public life.

Monday 31 December The year 1894 is just drawing to a close. It will always be a notable year in my annals, having landed as it has Rosebery in the position of Prime Minister of this country. It is the fashion in both Government and Opposition circles to disparage his leadership. But after all he has succeeded in keeping the heterogeneous party together for the best part of a year. What more really could have been expected of him? No man could have done more; few men as much. Whatever mistakes he has made have been due to the inherent difficulties of an impossible position.

On the other hand, he has shown great pluck in coping with those difficulties; his speeches have shown ability of a high order, and though they have not evoked real enthusiasm, yet he has often acquitted himself as no one on his side could have done. What one cannot help feeling, and feeling with commiseration, is the loneliness of his position. He might perhaps take more into confidence than he does some of his colleagues; but few of them are really congenial to him; and the few that might be, such as J. Morley, Asquith & Acland, do not seem to have rallied round him as they ought to have done.

The year has been rather a mixed one for me. I have had more than one breakdown, and I have had several domestic anxieties which have worried me a great deal. On the other hand, I have had more than my due in other respects: what with having the K.C.B. bestowed on me, and securing not a little kudos from the memorandum I wrote for the Financial Relations Comm. Adieu to 1894.

1895

Tuesday 1 January   . . . The new year is pretty certain to see a change of Government. It is impossible to say how long the present administration will stagger on. It may end its existence at the commencement of the Session, and it may drag on its existence throughout the Session. But if I had to bet, I should lay even money that the change will come about half way—probably on some unforeseen contingency.

Thursday 3 January   Harcourt has come up to Town, to talk over budget matters. He is rather staggered by the prospective increased demands all round for next year; and . . . he is careful to emphasise the fact that the principal feat of the "Rosebery Government" has been, or rather will be, to have added some 6½ millions to the annual expenditure. But the less he says about this the better; for on whom does the responsibility for this mainly rest but on the Finance Minister of the day? He says that in his position the opposition will be playing a bad game if they try conclusions with the Government over the Address. The more they endeavour to force the hands of the Government, the more will its supporters stick together. He hears that their electoral accounts are very good, having greatly improved during the last few months. He says he has it on the highest authority that, whereas the Unionists could not in September see their way to getting a larger majority than 20, they now are able to put it at 70. Henry James told Loulou H. the other day that in his constituency—Bury—which he regarded as a typical constituency, no less than 500 Gladstonians had recently sent in their adhesion to the Unionist cause: the change being attributable according to H. James to the dislike of the Trades Union programme at Norwich, and apprehensions about the threatened House of Lords campaign.

. . . India. I am afraid there may be some trouble there about accompanying the import duty on cotton goods with an Excise duty, though it is to be a restricted one. But it appears that Fowler & Herschell (who advises on Indian Finance matters) could not bring themselves to countenance an import duty by itself. It looked too much like a violation of free-trade principles; and it would have offended too greatly the Lancashire manufacters.

It has been decided to appoint Monkswell[102] to succeed Sandhurst at the War Office. Rosebery found that Campbell-Bannerman and most of his other colleagues, bar Asquith, considered Monkswell's claims far better than those of Ribblesdale. Monkswell had stuck to the Liberal party through thick & thin in its darkest days and had had very little recognition (a lordship in waiting): whereas Ribblesdale had only joined the Liberal party latterly after much shilly-shallying, and had received a fairly high Household place. I am afraid there will be much disappointment in Tennant circles, and not a little ebullition on the part of Asquith who is apt to think he is in a position to dictate his own terms and who cannot stand being thwarted in any way.

Friday 4 January Harcourt has had his talk with Lord Spencer, who appears to be quite reasonable. He recognises the impossibility of the imposition of any fresh taxes; and all he will have to do is to induce his Admirals to submit to a reduction of their demands to the extent of about a quarter of a million or so—an infinitesimal reduction on about 19 million . . . Notwithstanding the satisfactory result of the talk, Harcourt insists on having a Cabinet next week. It is really unnecessary; but he evidently want to deliver to his colleagues a financial lecture. Moreover he says it is high time that his colleagues came to Town.

In the afternoon Sir J. Stokes and Austin Lee[103] came to see me about the Suez Canal Shares payment . . . I took them down to see the Chanc. of the Exchequer. He questioned A. Lee about the present feeling in France towards this country. Lee could not admit that the tone of the French Press had really improved; though the French Foreign Secretary (Hanotaux) and the new French ambassador here (Courcel) seem to be less anti-English than most Frenchmen. All our difficulties with France, Harcourt said, were attributable to one canal in Africa. If we could only *swamp* Africa, we should be on the best of terms with everybody. As to the Suez Canal shares, they had no doubt turned out to be a very fine investment; but the advice he would give to every English Government is "Don't do it again".

We might perhaps have made a venture in the Panama Canal instead of the Suez Canal; and then, where should we have been?

Horace Farquhar gave a dinner to-night . . . I was treated to a long bi-metallic lecture from H. Chaplin.[104] I admit he talks on the subject very plausibly, and has got it up from his own point of view very creditably. But tampering with or degrading our standard is too great a leap in the dark. His main points are that the great fall in prices commenced simultaneously with the disappearance of bi-metallism; and that, as the greatest of our industries—agriculture—is already ruined and other industries are on the verge of following suit, we could not be worse off under bi-metallism than under mono-metallism and we might do better. Therefore why not try it? Bi-metallism according to H. Chaplin is gaining converts every day, and it is only the narrow-mindedness and prejudice of the City and the Treasury that stand in the way. As to political prospects, he did not seem at all keen about the return of the Unionists to power, owing to their having no settled programme.

Monday 7 January Poor Henry Ponsonby has been struck down by paralysis . . . It is impossible to exaggerate what his loss will be to the Queen & Ministers. He may not have had as much influence over the Queen as he might have acquired; but he knew Her exactly—knew how far he might & might not go with Her. He has done much of late years to grease the wheels of the ministerial coach; & he has been a perfect repository of ministerial confidences. He has in short been little less than a sort of permanent Cabinet Minister; and it will be almost impossible for the Queen to replace him.

I have been dining this evening with the Harry Gladstones to meet Mr & Mrs G. who are passing the night under this roof previous to their departure to Cannes. He seemed wonderfully well; but was much concerned to hear about Ponsonby. "I have" he said, "long regarded that man with feelings approaching to veneration. His breakdown will be little short of a national calamity". . . . Going back to old days, he recalled his reminiscences of the Duke of Cumberland who was quite a *character*. He remembers the Duke's attending St James' Church, where he was supposed to make running comments in an audible voice as the service proceeded. "Thou shalt do no murder". "No, it was not me; it was my brother Ernest". "Half of my goods I give to the poor". "No: that's too much. I don't mind a *tithe*". The Duke was sometimes made use of as a sort of go-between by political notabilities. He was asked to persuade the Archbishop of Canterbury (Howley) to move the rejection of a Tithe Bill in the House of Lords—I think in 1837. He was given to express himself in strong language; and his account of his mission to His Grace was that he (the Archbishop) "would be damned to hell if he did not move the rejection of the damned Bill".

Mr G. has been receiving T.P. O'Connor[105] & some other Irishmen this afternoon; and he took the opportunity of enjoining them to unite and not to blurt out to the rest of the world their differences & jealousies of which there are signs of a revival. This discussion among themselves is one of the considerations which are tending to make the grant of Home Rule more & more difficult. Indeed, there is no denying the fact that the cause is on the decline for that reason and others. The other reasons to be taken into account are (1) That Mr G. himself has retired (2) That the more the question is examined, the greater is the difficulty of devising a practical scheme on Mr G.'s lines. (3) That the British electors are more & more callous about and tired of the Irish question. (4) That the financial crux grows; for Great Britain will refuse to grant to Ireland what alone would make her solvent, and Ireland will never agree to accept what Great Britain would be induced to offer; (5) That contrary to what was predicted, Ireland has admitted of being governed under the present system, without the necessity of resort to the exercise of coercion. (6) That the Irish party is short of funds.

Wednesday 9 January　Harcourt arrived this afternoon. We had a long talk on financial prospects together; and later A. Milner came & joined us. He takes a more gloomy view of them than I do. The income tax assessments, he says, are turning out very badly; and then there is the great unknown quantity—the yield of the spirit duty. There is no doubt that as the time for the Budget approaches, the distillers and publicans will keep their stocks down to the lowest possible point in the belief that the extra duty imposed last year will come off. It would, no doubt, have been impossible to carry the Budget proposals without the concession; but the result has shewn that a temporary tax on a commodity ought never to be proposed.

Shaw Lefevre came into Downing Street while I was there. He wanted to broach the question of making loans to British landlords for improvements. He said he believed it was the only practical suggestion which the Agricultural Commission would be able to make. Harcourt threw the coldest of water on the proposal; and said that landlords who wanted loans must wait till the other side came in. But I daresay he will view the idea with less disfavour another day. In such times of agricultural distress, it seems to me that landlords have a very just claim to some consideration from the Government. In Ireland land improvement loans have been made for years; & we have lost hardly anything over it. The British landlord has certainly quite as good a title to such assistance as the Irish Landlord; and the only loans of the kind made in Great Britain—the Drainage loans—were repaid in full.

Thursday 10 January   The Cabinet seems to have gone off very smoothly. Harcourt undertook to place at Lord Spencer's disposal an additional million and a half for ship-building purposes—probably £200,000 this year and £1,300,000 next. Lord Spencer thinks he will be able to keep his Admirals quiet with a sop to this amount. Harcourt was in the best of humours, even with Rosebery. He (Harcourt) was much pleased at R.'s having written him a note from Osborne on Tuesday giving the latest account of poor Ponsonby. It was just one of those little attentions which go a long way towards making Harcourt amenable. I said to R. this afternoon that, if during the last few months he had only written Harcourt a friendly line of that kind from time to time, things would have been very different. R. replied that, in view of Harcourt's present mood, he was seriously considering whether he would not do something in the way of trying to ameliorate the relations between them. I do hope this will come about . . .

I am afraid there will be an explosion on the part of John Morley. It appears that some weeks ago, he casually mentioned to Harcourt that a little money might be wanted to provide potatoes in certain districts for seed supply in Ireland; & Harcourt raised no difficulty. On the strength of what passed, there arrived to-day two official letters from Dublin Castle stating that the Government had *agreed* to an expenditure of £70,000 or £80,000 on relief work, & to a Bill empowering loans to be made for potato seeds. Harcourt being taken by surprise at such big demands wrote off to Morley hinting that he ought to have come over for the Cabinet to-day if he wanted money, and that as the *mot d'ordre* was to cut down expenditure as much as possible there could be no money forthcoming for relieving Ireland. I fully expect John Morley will tender his resignation by return of post. I tried to stop the letter: but it was no good. There seems to have been some misunderstanding on both sides.

Friday 11 January   I was present at the meeting of the Cabinet Committee this morning on Navy Estimates: besides Harcourt & Lord Spencer, there were Lord Ripon, Campbell-Bannerman, & Fowler. Lord Spencer was evidently willing to acquiesce in the proposal which was made to the Cabinet yesterday; but said it would be a very tight fit and it would be no easy matter to cut down the Admirals' demand by even a quarter of a million—(very little really on so gigantic a sum as 19 millions). Besides the increase to the Navy Estimates, the Admiralty want a loan for works at Gibraltar and harbours at home. I believe a loan is justifiable for works of that nature; and to grant it may help to safe-guard the Sinking Fund, which I feel sure will soon be imperilled. Harcourt of course harangued his colleagues on all these "preposterous demands": we should soon be told we wanted a navy equal to that of the rest of the world, & so forth.

Moreover, the Admiralty demands were not the only ones necessitate by all this latter-day Imperialism: "Jewels of the Crown" like Uganda & Cyprus were going to cost big sums besides. What was to be the end of if all? The others of course did not agree with him: they allowed him to blow off steam *ad libitum*.

I had a visit this afternoon from Lord Wemyss,[106] looking more wonderful for his age than ever—such a contrast to his weakly sons! He wanted to have some mercy shown towards his own little harbour. That was the real object of his visit; but he descanted on his pet hobby, which I call "anti-socialism" for want of a better word. We were, he said, reverting to barbaric times: there would soon be no such thing as individual liberty: he supposed that as rents throughout the kingdom would soon be fixed by a Court, as they already are in Ireland, so we were within a measurable distance of having it decreed what we should pay for our food and clothing; in short there would be judicial prices as well as judicial rents!

Saturday 12 January (Mentmore)   Down here for the Sunday, the only others being the Sutherlands.

John Morley has not exploded as I expected in consequence of Harcourt's letter pointing out to him that his proposals to relieve distress in Ireland had not been considered & much less approved by the Cabinet, and that there was no available money. The proposals will of course have to be entertained. It is one of those demands that cannot be resisted.

Rosebery seems in fairly good spirits. He likes both the Duke & the Duchess. It is a great thing for him to have such nice additions to his friends, of whom he has not too many, because he shuns society so much .
. .

Sunday 13 January (Mentmore)   I went out sleighing this morning with R. and we had some talk. I strongly urged him again to make some move himself that will bring about a *rapprochement* with Harcourt. This is a favourable opportunity. Harcourt is in good humour; and R. himself is less unwilling to take action. All that he need do is to write a friendly line to say let bye-gones be bye-gones; and let us start afresh with the new Session. He has practically promised to do this. I feel sure that he will never regret doing it. When he looks back on this eventful time, it will be a great thing if he cannot charge himself with want of generosity. I believe Harcourt would respond favourably, unless indeed Loulou H. urges his father to keep the breach open. I asked R. what amount of truth (if any) there was in N. Rothschild's alarmist story which he told me the other day that we had been within an ace of seeing a European war. Italy was, according to N. Rothschild, to declare war against France, and had appealed to the Emperor of Germany, who had responded to the extent of making certain representations to Paris about the Dreyfus trial. R. said it was the grossest of exaggerations, but he did not conceal from himself the fact—and indeed had said so in the Cabinet—that Italy in her present bankrupt condition was a danger or might become a danger to the peace of Europe out of sheer desperation. R. was in fairly good spirits about himself. He thought those who had abused him had rather overstepped the mark, and there were signs of the natural reaction. At any rate he had the satisfaction of feeling that we had not for a long time occupied so favourable a position *vis-à-vis* with the other European powers as we were now occupying. Russia was most friendly—Germany was in much better humour—we were on good terms with Austria and Italy—and France, owing to the supposed understanding between Russia & this country, was less inclined to make herself disagreeable.

The *Observer* to-day has inserted the following letter which I sent yesterday to the Editor. I could not resist the temptation of saying a word, however feeble it may be in R.'s defence; the line he has taken about the House of Lords has been so wilfully misunderstood.

To the Editor of "The Observer".

Sir,—It is always pleasant to read anything that comes from Mr Edward Dicey's pen. There is a welcome absence of partisan asperity from his writing, and he evidently wishes to be fair and just towards those with whom he is not in political agreement. The letter which he addressed to you a week ago on "Lord Rosebery and the Lords", was couched in his accustomed language of courtesy and friendliness but I venture to think that in his concluding remarks he does (it may be unwittingly) an injustice to Lord Rosebery.

Mr Dicey makes an appeal to the Prime Minister to "drop the agitation against the Lords" "because, in his opinion, it "has died stillborn". "The spirits," he says, "which Lord Rosebery called from the vasty deep have declined to come, and the public remains utterly and profoundly indifferent to the spectacle of Liberal Bills being rejected and mutilated by the House of Lords . . . The sooner this agitation is buried out of sight the better for the country, for the Liberal Party, and, above all, for its author".

I submit that in making such an appeal to Lord Rosebery, Mr Dicey raised considerations of doubtful political morality. He tells the Prime Minister of the day, who has deliberately put forward a proposal of great gravity, that, as the country is utterly and profoundly indifferent to it, he should drop it. I do not pretend to say whether this utter and profound indifference prevails; but whether that be so or not, Mr Dicey implies that Lord Rosebery must have merely advocated an adjustment of the relations between the two Houses of Parliament, in the hope that it would raise an agitation, to catch votes; and therefore, finding that the proposal had not caught on, he should quietly abandon it.

Now I cannot believe that a man of high principle and honour like Lord Rosebery should have raised a great constitutional question merely as a *ballon d'essai* for electoral purposes. It seems to me to be only fair that he should be credited with higher motives. He has probably convinced himself—indeed, I feel sure that he must have convinced himself—that the present state of things, in which, when one political party is in power, the "predominance of partnership" rests or may rest with the House of Lords, is one which is indefensible, which, being indefensible, is fraught with danger to the State, and which, being fraught with such danger, ought to be remedied.

Impressed with such convictions, Lord Rosebery foreshadows a proposal which is (at least as I read his recent speeches) not to "disestablish" or "overthrow" a great institution, or to deprive the Second Chamber of all its powers and privileges, but one whereby he hopes, by constitutional, and thus by necessarily slow means, to bring the relations between the two Houses of Parliament into better harmony with the spirit of the present democratic times.

Is he to renounce his convictions merely because the country, possibly not having his foresight, remains indifferent to his proposals? Surely not. He must stand or fall by them, whether the response to them is favourable or unfavourable.

In these days, when our statesmen are too apt to follow instead of leading public opinion, I for one admire the man who has the courage of his opinions, and who, in impressing them on the public, does what he believes to be best calculated to serve the true interest of his country, whether he is or is not to reap for himself or his party any immediate political advantage.

I am, Sir,
Your obedient servant.
Jan 12 1895   SPECTATOR

Monday 14 January   Poor Lady Leconfield has lost her eldest son, who succumbed to an attack of typhoid after a few days. Rosebery has taken it greatly to heart on his sister's account and wants to get off going to Cardiff this week; but I am afraid this is an impossibility. It is not merely a local meeting; but a meeting of members of the National Liberal Federation who will assemble from all parts.

I met Haldane this evening. He said he thought things looked very bad. Rosebery had not defined his position about the House of Lords with sufficient clearness. He (R.) had not got up the constitutional history with enough accuracy; and had failed to give the idea that he was really in earnest about the question. Haldane wanted to see R. to beg him to say something more at Cardiff. I told Haldane that perhaps he had better try & have an interview; though I do not feel sure that his judgement is of the best. Scotland, Haldane said, was gradually turning Tory. London might in time assert its radical preponderance; but at present there were a great many metropolitan districts which were very Conservative. The Londoners were apparently more interested in municipal than Imperial affairs.

The Lancashire people are greatly up in arms about the import duties on cotton in India. They declare they are being sacrificed to India; while India with much greater reason declares that by being required to impose a corresponding excise duty on certain cottons she is being sacrificed to Lancashire. The Lancashire folk are so exercised in their minds that they have actually gone the length of advocating an Imperial grant to India in lieu of the import duties.

Wednesday 16 January   Professor Sir J. Seeley is dead. He had, I believe, been hopelessly ill for a long while. He will be much missed at Cambridge as Regius Professor of Modern History; and will long be remembered as the author of "Ecce Homo" and "Natural Religion"—two books which made a great stir some while ago, and the anonymity of which was kept for a very long time—and also of a third and very charming book, published under his own name—"The Expansion of England".

There was a Cabinet to-day. Rosebery was himself absent from it: he had gone to see his sister at Petworth.

France is again undergoing one of her periodical political crises; only on this occasion, it is a more serious one than usual; for not only has Brisson's Ministry resigned, but also the President himself—Casimir Périer, for causes as yet not satisfactorily explained.

Shuttleworth[107] came to see me to-day to have a talk about Navy Estimates. I have promised to do my best to get another £100,000 out of the Chancellor of the Exchequer for the Admiralty next year, in order to help in extricating them out of their difficulties. But there seems to be no end to this Naval expenditure: the maw of the Admiralty is insatiable. They are not content with an increase of 1½ millions on their Estimates: but they must have a loan of some 8 millions for works—harbours, fortifications, & docks. A loan, I believe, to be defensible in the interests of maintaining the Sinking Fund, whose fate is sealed, I feel sure, in the near future.

Thursday 17 January   Poor Harcourt is in trouble. His boy Bobby is down with typhoid. He could hardly speak when I went to see him this morning, and he very nearly broke down. There never was greater parental devotion than his, which is quite touching. He managed to attend the Naval Committee of the Cabinet which met this afternoon at the Treasury to consider the Admiralty proposals for permanent works. I was present part of the time. He gave a very reluctant consent to the project of a loan; he said he would be a passive instrument in the matter, but no more. The Palmerston precedent of the Fortifications loan is to be followed: and what a precedent! There is not a scrap of the work then undertaken which is of the smallest use—so rapidly has modern warfare changed . . .

M. Faure has been elected President of the French Republic this evening over the head of Brisson; and thus the election of the more moderate candidate has been secured. He has now to get some one to form a ministry, which promises to be no easy task.

Friday 18 January　Arthur Balfour has been making several speeches at Manchester. He has certainly improved in his speaking in a wonderful manner. He emphasised before a very sympathetic audience his leanings or rather his convictions on bimetallism which finds more favour in Lancashire than anywhere else. These convictions may give rise to great difficulties ahead; for he may quite likely be himself Chancellor of the Exchequer and a bimetallic Chancellor will be indeed a new departure.

I went to luncheon to-day with Lord Spencer to tell him that Harcourt would "go one (£100,000) better" for him next year; but that must be the ultimatum. Lord Spencer was grateful for this addition: but said he should have the greatest difficulty in curring his naval coat according to the cloth meted out to him.

After luncheon I went down to the Bank to have a talk with the Governor—mainly about Exchequer Bills, which the Chanc. of the Exchequer wants to extinguish if he can. There are great difficulties; and I think we shall have to wait till the Bills mature and then let them die a natural death. The Governor told me that according to the latest and most prudent estimate that could be formed the Baring Estates would show a surplus of £800,000; but that of course included the personal estates of the partners—their lands, houses and effects—and I gathered that of this sum probably about £200,000 only represented surplus cash.

Harvey, Manager of Glyns of whose opinion on City affairs I think highly, came to see me this afternoon. He said he did not believe that in London at any rate bimetallism was making any real way in commercial circles. His Bank, which means Bertram Currie, would fight to the death in the interests of a gold standard.

Monday 21 January　I was summoned to Salisbury on Saturday. Affairs there worry me greatly; but I hope some little good may come of my having gone down and seen sundry people.[108]

I went over yesterday to Wilton to see Pembroke. He seems to be at any rate holding his ground; and is more cheerful about himself. He is one of those who has always advocated a moderate reform of the House of Lords; but he regards the campaign on which Rosebery has entered as dangerous, & if not dangerous as futile. He told me that there have been serious thoughts on the part of many Peers to make reprisals against the Commons—such for instance as declining even to consider Bills which had been closured in the House of Commons.

Rosebery's speech at Cardiff on Friday night was mainly devoted to Disestablishment. I hear from more than one quarter that he made an excellent impression on his audience in Wales, was in very fine voice, and help them throughout his speech—in short it was considered by those who heard it to have been the best he has delivered since he was Prime Minister.

Thursday 22 January   I had luncheon with Rosebery to-day, for the first time in Downing Street, where he has so far established himself as to have a few servants there. In the present uncertain state of things, I doubt if he will have a bed-room fitted up there for him. Berkeley Square is not very habitable, but he will probably go up & down for the present at any rate from the Durdans. He has moved into "No 10" his great picture of Pitt, which hangs there with great appropriateness, considering how long that great man lived in the First Lord's official residence. There are unfortunately no traditions as to what room he occupied. I found that R. had never got his promised letter off to Harcourt. He did write one last week: but it went into argument which is not what is wanted; and Geo. Murray very rightly dissuaded him from sending it off. The shortest of notes to the effect of saying "let byegones be byegones and let us start the new Session on friendly terms" is all that is needed. I feel much disappointed at his not having fulfilled his promise. He is certainly a difficult man to manage . . .

Wednesday 23 January   Bobby Harcourt is going on favourably so his father was able to go to Derby yesterday to make his speech there tonight. He will make it under somewhat depressing circumstances; for the Evesham Election has gone badly for the Government.[109] The Unionist candidate has not only retained the seat but has about doubled the Unionist majority. Coming just at this moment—on the eve of the opening of Parliament—the result will have a considerable effect.

Asquith spoke last night at Hull, and put the House of Lords case, on the Rosebery lines, very forcibly and clearly. It is curious how people have misunderstood or rather refused to understand Rosebery's meaning. They make out that he has contradicted himself and that one speech has been inconsistent with the other. But there are none so dense as those who decline to understand. People seem to expect that he would come out with a cut and dried plan, but he does not seek to make any change in the statutory law. It is the unwritten law of the realm which he hopes gradually to see altered.

Thursday 24 January Harcourt's speech last night was nothing very remarkable. I thought it read rather dull. There were no good hits, such as he usually makes. I went to see him on his return from Derby, where he had got a great reception which had evidently gratified him. Referring to the Evesham Election, he said it was "actum est" with the Government. But how, I asked, was the Government to be got out? On the address. But who would vote against them? He professed to know that some of the Irish Nationalists would not come up to the scratch. "And that", he said, "would be the best thing that could happen to us. Mr G.," he went on to say, "has indeed much to answer for. No statesman ever so gratuitously smashed up a party as Mr G. did by his precipitate action in 1886. The Liberal Party will never get over it".

So it is all over at last with poor Randolph Churchill. He breathed his last about 6 o'clock this morning; and thus there is ended a very remarkable career. It was meteor-like in the rapidity of the rise and fall of the man. He undoubtedly may be classified as a *genius*—and a more than usually erratic one; and there are few public men belonging to the last quarter of this century who will probably afford greater interest to the future student of political history. His principal characteristic was perhaps his audacity. From the moment he asserted his position in the House of Commons, he rushed in where angels feared to tread. Between 1880 and 1885 he monopolised almost the whole of the opposition. What he preached and likewise practised was that it was the duty of the Opposition to oppose, and to oppose in relentless fashion. He used always to hold up to scorn what he considered to be the mildness of the tactics pursued by Mr G. & his colleagues while in Opposition during Lord Salisbury's second administration. He had great and good political instincts. He may be said to have invented the democratisation of Conservatism. He saw that in these democratic days the Conservative party was bound to have something more than a negative policy; and to him was mainly due the Liberal lines on which the Conservative or Unionist party has acted since the last Reform Bill. He was one of the principal organisers of the Primrose League, which has become a powerful factor in modern politics despite the ridicule which its inception evoked. On the other hand, he had little and bad political judgment. The way in which he wrecked his own career by making (ostensibly at any rate) a stand against "bloated armaments", and the advice which he tendered in 1893 that the Home Rule Bill should be allowed to pass practically unopposed in Committee, were striking instances of his want of political judgment. In Parliament he showed great acumen. No one, as I have heard Mr G. say, could feel the pulse of the House so quickly as he could. It was an instinct with him. His vocabulary was an extraordinary one. He had always at his command a copious supply of expletives. He daubed on his colours in the coarsest fashion; but what was depicted on the canvas, though often presenting the appearance of vulgarity, rarely failed to strike the imagination. It was the forcible manner in which he put his case that made his public-speaking such an excitement to his audience. He was very intolerant of crassness and want of perception in his colleagues. His nervous system was too highly strung to stand the wear and tear of ministerial responsibility; and had he not resigned when he did, after holding for barely six months the Chancellorship of the Exchequer, he would I feel certain have broken down very shortly, even if he had not broken off with his colleagues on some other subject than that of military armaments. It is quite a mistake to suppose that anybody at the Treasury influenced him in the decision which led to his downfall. It has always been said—and I believe correctly said—that it was his social ostracism due to his behaviour towards the Prince of Wales 20 years ago or more that first made him bent on asserting himself in politics and determined to have (as it were) his revenge. He felt that he had a power in him and he had only to put it forward to attain pre-eminence and triumph over those whom he had offended—a feeling which subsequent events fully justified, by his attaining the extra-ordinary position of Leader of the House at an earlier age than anybody else had attained it, since Pitt himself. On the attainment, however ephemeral, of that position he always prided himself upon and comforted himself with when he was latterly conscious that power had slipped away from him. In private life there was much that attracted his friends and disarmed his opponents. To this his frankness amounting often to great indiscretion considerably contributed. He was, ever since his time at the Treasury, most kind to me; and I feel that I have not only lost a friend but have one less interest in public life.

Saturday 26 January (Sandringham) . . . Before leaving London yesterday I saw Rosebery . . . I found that R. has still not written what I want him to write to Harcourt. He said he had paid a friendly visit to Harcourt; but that is not the same thing. He had taken my hint and was in communication with the Dean of Westminster about having a Memorial Service in the Abbey for Randolph Churchill . . .

Sunday 27 January (Sandringham) . . . The Bishop of Peterborough seems to be a very practical pleasant man, genial and a very free smoker. He spoke last night about the possible successor to Seeley's Professorship at Cambridge, & I have reported his conversation to Rosebery. He says

the man from whom the University pray to be delivered is Oscar Browning
. . . Leslie Stephen would be a fairly good appointment; but probably Lord
Acton (provided he is qualified) would be the best appointment . . .

Monday 28 January   I came up from Sandringham this morning by the
early train, in order to be able to go to the Memorial Service in
Westminster Abbey . . . It was a remarkable gathering—so representative
of all classes & all parties, from Rosebery & Lord Salisbury (looking very
old) downwards. Poor Randolph Churchill would have been himself, I am
sure, highly gratified by the number who attended the service in his
honour. He once said, speaking of Mr G.'s courtesy towards his opponents: "The old man will certainly see me out. I can see him now sitting
down to write a beautiful letter to my family suggesting my interment in
Westminster Abbey". One calls to mind too R.C.'s famous reference in
1886 to Mr G. as the "old man in a hurry". It very soon afterwards proved
to be the "young man" who was "in a hurry", when he tried to measure
swords with Lord Salisbury.

This afternoon I sent with Jenkyns to the Admiralty to discuss the lines
of the Naval Works (Loans) Bill with Lord Spencer, Shuttleworth &
Robertson.[110] Their programme involves an expenditure of 8 millions,
mainly on Gibraltar, Portland & Dover Harbours. Owing to awkward
speeches made by Harcourt & Fowler which may be brought up against
them, the Cabinet have decided to have an annual Bill, so that Parliament
may exercise a control every year on the doings of the Admiralty. There
are considerable administrative & difficulties connected with an annual
Bill; & what Jenkyns & I propose is that there shall be one Bill embodying
the whole programme and giving the requisite borrowing powers but that
they shall only be exercised to the extent to which authority may be given
by a resolution of the House of Commons each Session.

After the Admiralty conference, I went to meet John Morley at No.11
Downing Street to discuss his proposals for dealing with Irish distress.
Harcourt was in one of his most sulky humours; but he had to acquiesce in
the Irish demand, involving an expenditure of about £80,000 on Relief
works and a loan for providing potato seeds in distressed districts. The
hope which he professes to entertain of getting the Irishmen or some of
them to vote against the Government & turn them out will not be realised.
For, according to John Morley, the last thing the Irishmen want is to face a
dissolution, for the best of reasons that they have no money with which to
fight an election.

I saw the Devonshires this afternoon. He was talking of Goschen and
commenting on the silence which Goschen had maintained all the autumn.
This silence confirms me, as I told the Duke, in the impression that
Goschen for some reason or other does not aspire to return to the

Exchequer, if indeed to any other office. I expect he foresees the possibility of financial difficulties and heterodox proposals.

Tuesday 29 January   There was a Cabinet to-day. The Queen's Speech was approved, not without some discussion. Lefevre's proposal to make proposals to landlords for permanent improvements as a means of relieving their dire distress was knocked on the head: those ministers who are landlords themselves being most averse to it, on the ground (I believe) that it would only encumber estates already over-burdened with charges. It was also decided, mainly by Rosebery and Harcourt, but contrary to the rest of the Cabinet, not to have a Party meeting before the opening of Parliament. I believe the decision to be a mistake. Such meetings, though attended with some risk, almost invariably do good: they put the party in good heart, and the malcontents blow off steam with advantage. John Morley is said to be in a bad humour generally. Harcourt & he can't agree whether the Local Veto Bill or the Irish Land Bill shall have precedence. It is curious how difficult John Morley is to manage in spite of all his charm. He is often petty: for instance, he won't attend the State functions at Dublin Castle, because he would have to carry the Sword of State before Houghton.[111]

Thursday 31 January   I had some talk with Fowler . . . he is a tolerably shrewd electioneer; & he evidently thinks that the Government must be defeated whenever the Dissolution comes, whether sooner or later. If the Government get through the Address, he does not see why they should not go on for some little time, perhaps through the session—(I doubt this myself). He was sure that the main reason why prospects were so bad was that people had become alarmed by the Leeds & Norwich programmes. The extremists had overshot the mark. I fully believe this is so; and I should not wonder if the Liberal party were in Opposition for a consider-able time to come, unless the Unionists play false with the currency system or with free-trade. In other words I shoud not be surprised if the best chance of re-uniting the Liberal party on safe and sound lines were retrenchment & the maintenance of the fiscal & monetary *status quo*.

. . . Asquith & John Morley have been making speeches at Newcastle. John Morley was able—and legitimately so—to pride himself on the present well-ordered state of Ireland under his administration: the country being according to the statistics more free from crime that it has been for the last 50 years.

Sunday 3 February (Brighton)   I came down here yesterday afternoon to spend Sunday with the Arthur Sassoons. The Devonshires are also here...The Speaker[112] (not looking very well) came to luncheon to-day: also

Miss Peel and Maguire to whom she has engaged herself. The Speaker seemed to anticipate a stormy opening of the Session, and feared that questions of privilege about the Tweedmouth cheque & other matters might be raised. Privilege was, he said, the most difficult of all things to define; but he endeavoured to limit the definition as far as possible. The Duke of Devonshire thought that little could be made of the cheque: much depended on the date when it was offered to the Irishmen. It was, as I know, in April 1894 when Edwd. Marjoribanks had become Lord Tweedmouth, and it came not out of party funds, but out of his own pocket.

5 February . . . I had a talk with Rosebery yesterday. He quite expects that the Government majority may be run down to a single figure—(the wish may be father to the thought)—in which he should consider himself at liberty to reconsider his position, notwithstanding his former pronouncement that he would go on with a majority of even two. It is absurd trying to force through Parliament big measures, when the Government, on the assumption that the Parnellites will vote against them, have at best a majority of only 15.

Thursday 7 February The Opposition are going to try conclusions with the Government by an amendment in the sense of a want of confidence. But it has not yet made its appearance on the Notice paper; nor is it yet known who is to move it. I don't believe that the Government will be landed in a minority or will be run close enough to warrant resignation or an immediate dissolution; but I confess I should on the whole like to see a termination of the present unsatisfactory state of things. Rosebery can get no credit out of a continuance of them, and a rickety Government is bad for the country. The country is evidently apathetic; and that being the case, a Government uncommitted to constitutional changes and free to take up social questions is more suited to the times; though how in the world any Government is going to set the great agricultural interest on its legs and deal with the 'unemployed' difficulty appears to be tolerably chimerical . . . The intensely cold weather continues. In the Midland Counties there have been some record registrations: the thermometer in certain places having registered 36 degrees of frost. The view from my windows is quite Siberian: the river being almost blocked with ice flows, which move up and down with the tide in most picturesque fashion.

Saturday 9 February Thursday and last night were devoted in the House to debating A. Jeffreys'[113] amendment reflecting on the Government for not announcing more measures calculated to relieve the distressed agriculturalists. They apparently turn up their nose at the idea of Light Railways which, they say, only means an increase of the rates. The agricultural industry is no doubt in a most serious condition; and there are hardly any practical suggestions forthcoming. To all those that have been made there are strong objections; at any rate the difficulties connected with any one of them are immense and the result of their adoption could be most doubtful—a further relief of rates on land, protective duties, bimetallism, and loans to landlords. But the agricultural case against the Government is a plausible one. "We are on the point of ruin", they say; "and instead of *trying* to do something, you (the Government) are bringing upon us the last straw which will break our backs, what with the increased death duties, parish councils which will indubitably further burden the rates, and your projected Light Railways". The Government were pressed hard in the Division Lobby: they only secured a majority of 12. Harcourt made a very telling speech—according to accounts from both sides, one of the best speeches he ever made in the House. He thoroughly enjoys putting Goschen on the rack; and Goschen who spoke first yesterday and appeared to be making a bid for a return to the Exchequer gave Harcourt a good opportunity of crushing him by telling hits and making humourous points. Goschen is not popular on his own side—and the Opposition seem to have shared in the enjoyment of the fun.

Arthur Balfour's book on "The Foundations of Belief" has made its appearance, and will no doubt create a stir. He writes with extraordinary power. He is really a philosopher first, and a politician only second.

11 February I went over yesterday to Wilton to see Pembroke. He is always interested in Rosebery. He was saying Rosebery had had the double misfortune of first being over-rated and now of being greatly under-rated. I came up in the train last night with Folkestone, who told me he expected a hard fight in his Division (Wilton) of Wiltshire.[114] According to him, the only question that really interests this agricultural constituency is an amendment of the Poor Law—anything that promises deliverance from or substitute for the workhouse.

Naylor-Leyland has given immense offence to the Tories by resigning his risky seat at Colchester just at this moment, on the ostensible ground that he is in disagreement with them about the House of Lords. I expect there is more than meets the eye about his resignation and conversion. Meanwhile, one would imagine from the language in which his conduct is arraigned by the Unionists that no one had ever 'ratted' before.

. . . I congratulated [Harcourt] on his speech; and he said "Well, Goschen and others bowled some very bad balls, & so I went in for slogging and made I believe a good score" . . . Harcourt still declares that the Government is going out at once. He should, he said, spend a pleasant March . . . I hinted in reply that he was generally a bad political prophet. But I admit that if the Leader of the House has not got his heart in the fight, the chances of coming to grief are greatly enhanced.

I have been with Ferdie Rothschild to see Oscar Wilde's new Play at the Haymarket. "An Ideal Husband". I liked it. It is well written and well acted.

Tuesday 12 February The Government got rather a better majority—20—last night in the House on Redmond's amendment in favour of an immediate Dissolution. Harcourt took a night off and left John Morley in charge of the House. He does not, somehow or other, suit the House as Leader. It is curious how little way any one of three men in the Cabinet who forsook their pens for politics make in Parliament. J. Morley is only a *succès d'estime*; while Bryce and Trevelyan are more or less failures. I have been dining this evening *tête-à-tête* with Francis Knollys at the "Marlborough". The Prince of Wales . . . came into the club before we left. He told me he was much annoyed with Chamberlain who had disagreed with everybody on the Aged Poor Commission (on which the Prince has been serving), who had nearly killed the Chairman, Lord Aberdeen[115] by his contentious attitude. Chamberlain, the Prince said, had been merely playing for his own hand throughout the inquiry; and it was entirely due to Chamberlain that the Report had not kept clear of contentious matters. The Prince would not be able now to sign it himself.

Thursday 14 February Harry Chaplin expects that when the Dissolution does come, there will be a great swing of the pendulum, and the Radicals will be crushed. This may be so; but there are no very evident indications of such a result, though I do not doubt for one moment that the Unionists will secure a fair working majority. I told him that I believed the great danger ahead for the Unionists when returned to power will be finance and currency. Any great exhibition of heterodoxy would probably split them. He made light of this; and said he foresaw a difficulty, if not a danger, of another kind. If a Unionist majority were returned, the Peers would find themselves in a unique position—an appeal to the country for limiting their powers and the response being one in favour of their veto. Lord Salisbury, contrary to the general belief, had had difficulties enough as it was with his Conservative friends in the Upper House; and it was more than likely that, if the country apparently supported their past action, they would be fools enough to lose their heads and become quite unmanageable. There is I think a good deal in this view.

Thursday 14 February . . . At the Cabinets lately, Rosebery said Harcourt had been very rude to his colleagues; and what was worse he talked loudly in the House before everybody about the coming downfall of the

Government to which he wished a speedy end. Such language is of course very hard on the Whips; for if anything were to happen in the shape of a catastrophe nobody would come down on them with a heavier hand than Harcourt himself. I told Rosebery that I feel sure the great party crux ahead is economic questions. It will be (what is still considered) orthodoxy versus heterodoxy: & he ought to study these questions. It does not do to meet them with a mere *non possumus*, and to tell bimetallists & others they are mere fools, as Harcourt does.

Sunday 17 February . . . Chamberlain moved his "confidence amendment" to the address on Friday afternoon. It was to the effect that it was contrary to public interests that the Government should take up the time of the House with measures which they have no chance of passing. His speech was not considered to be up to his usual mark. It was taunting the Government with having a primary policy—Home Rule—which they set aside, for their secondary policy—House of Lords—and this in turn they had abandoned for a tertiary policy of what had been called 'filling up the cup' of the Hereditary Chamber—a phrase Asquith in his very telling speech showed that Chamberlain was himself the author of in old days when he was running a tilt against the House of Lords. Harcourt told me yesterday that he considered Asquith's reply to Chamberlain was one of the greatest Parliamentary successes he had ever remembered. The speech will give a distinct fillip to Asquith's Parliamentary position. Harcourt still believes that the days of the Government are numbered. The next rock ahead will be, he thinks, his motion to take for the Government the greater part of the time of the House. All will of course depend on the terms of such a motion which has not yet been determined. So long as Harcourt prophesies the speedy down fall of the Government, so long shall I believe it to be safe. He is always the worst of prophets.

The cold is less intense, but there are no signs of anything like a break-up of the frost, which is said to have penetrated about a foot and a half into the ground in this part of the world—a bad look out for the remainder of the hunting season this year.

Monday 18 February Lord Acton's appointment as Regius Professor of Modern History at Cambridge is announced today. It is regarded as a new departure. I believe he is the first R.C. that has ever held an University Professorship; but the extraordinary erudition of the man seems to be held to justify such a departure.

Tuesday 19 February The debate on Chamberlain's amendment was brought to an end last night. The government had a majority of 14; though when Harcourt moved the closure the majority fell to 8. Dilke made a very nasty speech with all kinds of disagreeable innuendoes about Rosebery; and no one on the ministerial bench got up to defend R.—an omission which produced a bad impression. A Cabinet was summoned hurriedly this morning. I have not seen R.; but I fully expect from what I have heard in 'subterranean' circles that he gave the Cabinet a piece of his mind and told them that unless he was firmly supported by his colleagues he should not remain any longer head of the administration. I believe outspoken words of his may do good. His colleagues know perfectly well that they could not get on a day without him.

Wednesday 20 February There was a foolish debate last night in the House of Commons which Howard Vincent[116] brought on by moving to prevent the importation of foreign goods (like brushes) made by convict labour. Nothing could be more futile than the idea contained in the motion. How in the world can the identity of the manufacture of a brush which arrives in this country be established? . . . Bryce . . . offered a committee of inquiry as a means of shelving the resolution; but Chamberlain interfered and deprecated the acceptance of the committee with the result that the House passed the resolution with a discussion. This is a small matter in itself; but it shows how demoralised the House of Commons is with a dissolution impending; everything is done with a view to electioneering. I am sure that on public grounds the continuance of the present state of things is most undesirable. At the same time, it is not easy for a Government to take the step of committing suicide; and it often happens that the more Governments 'ride for a fall' the better they get over their fences.

I have just returned from dining with the Fifes. Rosebery . . . consented to dine out from home: but he was very reserved about what had happened during the last few days . . . E. Stanley[117] told me after dinner that he believed the Government may be beaten tomorrow on the Indian Import duties question which Henry James is going to raise on behalf of Lancashire by moving the adjournment of the House. The Government could not be beaten on a better issue; but I can hardly think the Opposition will be fools enough to allow this to happen. According to Stanley, bimetallism has taken strong hold of the Lancashire people; and so also, in a more marked degree, has protection. He professes to be a strong free-trader himself, but what answer was there to the contention that though latterly wheat has fallen 30 per cent in price nobody can buy a loaf of bread one farthing cheaper? As certain as I am writing now, we are going to have a revival of the tariff question, coupled with some currency experiments.

Thursday 21 February I saw Harcourt just as he was starting to go down to the House this afternoon. He said "Well, it is going to be all over at last.

We are to fall, and we shall fall lightly—on cotton wool". I told him I did not believe a word of it. From what I had heard on fairly good authority the Opposition were becoming alive to the fact that their tactics were mistaken from public and party points of view equally.

Friday 22 February   The expected of course never happens in politics. There never was a more complete upsetting of political calculations than took place last night. So far from the government being even pressed, Henry James' notion was negative by a majority of 195—a nice respectable working majority. The Opposition at the last moment had sense enough (as I expected they would) to see that they could not challenge the Government on a worse issue. India ought to be the last place chosen for political battle-grounds; and the case which the government had was overwhelmingly strong. If they were to be blamed at all, they were to be blamed rather for sacrificing India to Lancashire than Lancashire to India. Henry James apparently made a poor and ineffective speech; and he was completely demolished by Fowler, who spoke quite admirably. It is wonderful how plausible and effective he is on his legs in the House of Commons. He is actually not overburdened with courage; but when he can once be brought up to scratch, he states his case with such lucidity and self-assurance that he produces the impression of being unanswerable. Almost the whole of the front Opposition bench turned tail. A. Balfour was (fortunately for himself) away unwell; and the only man on that bench who spoke in support of H. James was Geo. Hamilton,[118] who, according to Harcourt, not only cut the poorest of figures himself, but lugged Lord Salisbury into the fight. Goschen behaved with considerable pluck and spoke for the Government. The result of the night was that contrary to the original hopes both of the Government and the Opposition, the Government remains *in*: indeed it has been put on its legs again temporarily by the division.

Sunday 24 February (Ascot)   Rosebery is the latest victim to the renewed outbreak of the influenza epidemic, which seems to be as rife as it ever was, only of a milder type. Broadbent is attending him, and had great difficulty in finding two nurses for him, so great is the demand for them just now. R. is not allowed to see anyone. It seems to be a moot point whether the influenza is infectious or contagious; and indeed whether it is either or both. Harcourt was full of kindly inquiry for R. yesterday. Trouble always brings to the fore the kindly disposition which characterises the man *au fond*.

Monday 25 February   Harcourt talked to me this morning about the bimetallic debate which is to be brought on tomorrow evening by Everett.[119] The resolution to be moved is a very mild one, evidently drawn to be accepted; & I told Harcourt I could see no reason why he should not accept it. It merely declares that the constant fluctuations in the relative value of the two metals is to be regarded with increasing apprehension and urges the desirability of co-operating with foreign countries in an international congress for considering whether the evil can be mitigated. It may be bimetallic in its inclinations; but it is minus bimetallism in terms. I found that Harcourt was prepared to accept the resolution as it stood. I am sure he is right. It does not do to pooh-pooh bimetallity. The more a question of that kind is thrashed out the better; with the result, as I believe, that the more impracticable will any change in the standard of this country be shown to be.

I went afterwards to the Bank of England, and drove down to the City with Mr Evan Spicer, the Chairman of the Finance Committee of the London County Council. He thought a few seats might be lost by the Progressives at the coming election, which would be a good thing as it would make the two parties less unevenly balanced: but he did not believe there would be any sweeping change. He told me he regarded Chamberlain's scheme of splitting up London into separate municipalities as out of the question: nor did he think that vestries of District Boards with a central council practicable. Men who could attend to their District Councils and likewise to a Central Council were not to be found. Though nominally belonging to the Progressives he is a moderate-minded man; and said that few people outside had any real notion of the amount of sterling good work which the present County Council got through. It is certainly wonderful hw so many busy men will give their service gratuitously to municipal work in this country, out of which so little honour and glory is to be got.

I borrowed on Treasury Bills today at phenomenal rates—the average for a million being only a little over 1 per cent. Our tender was for £200,000 at ½ percent, which of course brought down the average, but which I think must have been made in error.

Rosebery is still very seedy—can see no one and attend to no business. The worst of it is that he cannot sleep.

Wednesday 27 February   The bimetallic debate went off successfully yesterday . . . Harcourt . . . made a very good speech in which he pronounced himself very strongly against any alteration in the monetary basis of this country . . . Anything that will put an end to the present agitation, which of itself must be harmful to trading prospects, will be a distinct gain.

While I was with Harcourt this morning, a note arrived from the Speaker to say that he had made up his mind that he must resign . . . there is really no replacing him. The party would resent the proposal of any Unionist;

and it would be hard for any supporter of the Government to be elected at the tag end of this Parliament with the probability, if not certainty, of being superseded in the next Parliament. The man who seems to be most eligible on the Government side is Arnold Morley. Another man who might be suggested in certain quarters is Haldane. I have been dining this evening with the Tweedmouths; and he had no other name to suggest. If the Unionists had to propose a man, he thinks they would be pretty certain to take Mat. Ridley.[120] He does not believe Courtney[121] will be in the next Parliament.

Friday 1 March   The Government steered clear last night of the last rock that was immediately ahead, and carried their resolution for taking more time of the House by a majority of 25. They might now go on at any rate until Whitsuntide, and unless the unexpected happens (as it probably will) they may now even get through the Session. Harcourt admitted this morning, with some groans (mostly feigned) that the last chance of immediate escape from office was gone . . .

I have been dining this evening with the Horace Farquhars. He has taken immense interest in and pains with London municipal matters. He has got a Union or League to counter-act the Progressives. As regards tomorrow's elections, he thinks the Moderates are sure to gain seats. He hopes for 15, but will be content with 10.

Saturday 2 March   I was with Harcourt a long time this morning . . . [He] regards the result of Tuesday's bimetallic debate as very satisfactory. He believed it had set back the hands of the bimetallic clock, no matter what the bimetallists said; but the mono-metallists ought to exert themselves, and not leave the whole of the talking & argument to their opponents. He has asked H. Chaplin when the invitation to an International Conference would come, as he was greatly looking forward to writing the reply to it. H. Chaplin said it would not come at all. So Harcourt concluded that the bimetallists were going to await political events—a change of Government in this country and possibly another Chancellor of the Exchequer whose reply to an invitation would be drawn in diferent terms. Harcourt told me that he had been to see Arthur Balfour (who is still laid up with influenza) about the Speaker's determination to resign; but they were not hopeful about it, though the Speaker had undertaken to postpone announcing his resignation till near the Easter recess. Harcourt and Arthur Balfour are on friendly chaffing terms. They could (Harcourt said) only think of one man whom all parties would accept: and that was Mr G. Harcourt had told Arthur Balfour that the tactics of his side had been very bad—that they ought to have got the Government out by this time, if they had played their cards well; and he had congratulated Arthur Balfour on his providential absence from the House on two such awkward questions as Indian Import Duties and Bimetallism. Harcourt was—& with good reason—much annoyed at not having been consulted by Lord Ripon about the appointment of Sir Hercules Robinson[122] to the Governorship of the Cape. He had, he said, made it one of the conditions of his accepting the lead of the House of Commons that he should have a voice in important Government appointments—a very reasonable condition, considering that the defence of any appointment that might be challenged would devolve upon him. This was an instance; because it was more than probable that exception would be taken to Sir H. Robinson, owing to his being mixed up with South Africa, & a Director of the Chartered Company. I understand the selection of Sir H. Robinson to be successor to Loch[123] was made on the ground that it was absolutely necessary to have some one out at the Cape for a short while who was thoroughly well versed in South African affairs.

Chamberlain will not easily hear the last of his "strategic movement to the *rear*" when he disappeared so mysteriously in the Lobby on the occasion of the Division on the Indian Import Duty motion. It has made him ridiculous. Henry James too has suffered from the part he took in the matter. He avows that he acted independently of his party, and merely as a Lancashire M.P.[124] It is plucky of him to take the responsibility on his own shoulders; but it is difficult to believe that sitting next to Chamberlain in the House he did without Chamberlain's cognisance and concurrence.

Sunday 3 March . . . The frost is dying hard. It cannot make up its mind to go. Last night there were 14 degrees of frost here, and this morning the ground was covered with snow.

Most of the London County Council Elections were disclosed last night & are known today. The "Moderates" have won all down the line. They have gained already about 20 seats, which nearly wipes out the 'Progressive' majority; and the votes recorded in favour of the Moderates have largely increased. I believe the result is on the whole a good thing. The extremists on the Progressive side have had it clearly shown to them that London is neither socialist nor collectivist; and the Moderates will find that they will have to spend quite as much as the late Council have spent. Of course the Tory Journals will regard the County Council Elections as a great Unionist victory; but I doubt if such political significance is to be attached to them. There are still at present no signs of any swing of the pendulum. Even the "Times" in a series of articles on the political situation cannot make out that the Unionists could have a larger majority than about 30.

Monday 4 March   The London County Council Elections have ended in a tie; each party having secured 59 Councillors. The Progressives will still have a majority; because of the 11 aldermen who remain for another 3 years, the Progressives have 8. The exact balance of parties will depend on the election of the 9 new aldermen; and these will probably have to be evenly divided as the election is in the hands of the councillors.

Rosebery is I fear making very slow progress towards convalescence . . .

Tuesday 5 March John Morley introduced his Irish Land Bill last night. To judge from the reception accorded to it, it looks as if it may pass the House of Commons at any rate, but it is certain to be discussed *ad nauseam*.

The two men principally spoken of in Cabinet circles for the Speakership are C. Bannerman & Arnold Morley. The first might be accepted by both sides; but the nomination of the second would pretty certainly be contested; and there are strong reasons against taking a Cabinet Minister which would involve a departure from precedent. So it is quite likely that Courtney may be put up; he is not popular with any side of the House; he is moreover lacking in presence and has not too plentiful a supply of H.'s; but he has had great experience as Chairman of Committees, and the Unionists could hardly oppose him. Further than this the Government majority is so small that the ministerialists can ill afford to spare a man from their own ranks.

The question of making some provision for the exercise of the powers of the Sovereign during the Queen's absence abroad this spring has been engaging the attention of the Cabinet . . . Precedents are in favour of appointing Lords Justices; but considering the Prince of Wales' position, the idea has been to make him Guardian of the Realm. I gather that there is a precedent for this in the time of George II. But the Cabinet appears to think that this would mean too large a devolution and to fear that such a proposal might invite a discussion which would be derogatory to the monarchy. So the latest idea seems to be that there should be no general devolving power; but that if any specific bit of business has to be done like the holding of a Cabinet on the signification of the Royal Assent to a specific Bill, the Queen should issue a Commission empowering the Prince of Wales to act for Her *ad hoc*, and *ad hoc* only. It looks as if Harcourt has taken this line to curry favour with the Queen.

8 March I have seen Rosebery to-day for the first time . . . He attributed his illness, or at any rate his predisposition to becoming ill, to the harassing time he had had in seeing all his colleagues individually, & hinting to them that he must be better supported. His interview with Harcourt was evidently not pleasant & far from cordial. He had instanced to Harcourt as wanting confidence in himself Harcourt's threats of resignation towards the end of last session, which were certainly very frequent and outspoken.

Harcourt wholly denied them to R. The fact is Harcourt says so many things which he does not believe himself that he disowns the paternity of them subsequently and not without ingenuousness.

Sunday 10 March . . . The secret about the Speaker's resigning is out—the 'Times' got hold of it . . . and had a leader upon it yesterday morning. It is very unfortunate: for the longer the question is discussed, the more awkward and difficult will be the solution . . . Harcourt [has] evidently made up his mind in favour of Courtney. He objects to nominating a minister to the Chair; not only because it would be contrary to all precedent, but because it could mean reconstruction of the Government, and reconstruction of a tottering Government, possibly involving the loss of a seat as well as the vote of the nominee, was out of the question. These difficulties naturally incline the Opposition to regard with favour Campbell-Bannerman, whose removal from the Government would be a very palpable weakening of it.

. . . A case of some disagreeable interest came before Newton, the Police Magistrate yesterday. Queensberry had left an insulting card the other day on Oscar Wilde at his club. O. Wilde now desires to bring an action for libel against that eccentric peer; and the case was committed for trial. Queensberry with some reason objects to the intimacy between one of his sons and Oscar Wilde, and in giving expression to his objections he used some opprobrious epithet which can be more easily grasped than written. Oscar Wilde was of course bound to take notice of the insult, and Queensberry declares that he intends to stand by what he said, no matter how difficult it may be to prove justification.

Monday 11 March The premature announcement of the Speaker's resignation and its possible consequences are already beginning to create flutters in ministerial circles.

. . . I paid Rosebery a visit. He had been down to Windsor to see the Queen. He was naturally very tired by the visit . . . He had summoned a Cabinet for tomorrow to discuss the question of the new Speaker—rather a delicate one to handle, considering that there are at least two ministers (C. Bannerman & A. Morley) who are aspirants to the place. R. himself is decidedly in favour of Courtney. The great thing is to avoid a contest; but it is not at all sure that the Unionists could accept Courtney's nomination. There have been only three contests for the Speakership during this century. Littleton was put up against Manners-Sutton in January 1833, but was rejected by a majority of 210. Abercromby was (as everybody knows) nominated against Manners-Sutton in February 1835 and carried by a majority of 10. H. Goulbourn was put up against Abercromby in May 1839, but rejected by a majority of 18. It is curious that there has been no

Speaker taken from the Conservative ranks for the last 60 years; that is, since Manners-Sutton.

Tuesday 12 March   I gather that at the Cabinet to-day a self-denying ordinance was passed to the effect that no ministers should be proposed for the chair; but Campbell-Bannerman who is unwell was absent and therefore did not subscribe to the ordinance. It is pretty well understood that he wants the place and will press his claim to it.

I had some Budget talk with Harcourt this morning. He seemed rather to wish to take off half the additional Beer duty put on last year as well as the additional spirit duty; but he won't be able to do this as far as I can see, and I am dead against his thinking of it. It would be a fiddling proposal: Beer can perfectly well bear the present duty; and the great thing to avoid is constant change of duties, which so demoralises the trade.

. . . The mania of society at the present moment especially among the ladies, is bicycling and skating at "Niagara" which up till now has proved a very successful venture.

Thursday 14 March   . . . At the first meeting of the new London County Council on Tuesday, 4 "Progressive" Aldermen and 4 "Moderate" Aldermen were elected, the 9th man being Godfrey Lushington who was taken to be neutral. The Progressives showed some greed in monopolising the Chairmanship, the Vice-Chairmanship and Deputy Chairmanship, which under the circumstances seemed a mistake. They might well have given the Vice-Chair to the Moderates.

I was with Harcourt almost all the morning. He was considerably annoyed with Hibbert for having foretold the probable surplus of this year at a public dinner the other night. It was not judicious: but I pleaded with Harcourt that he should not deal harshly with Hibbert, who does his work very well at the Treasury. We had some Budget talk: both this year & next year will turn out about exactly as I anticipated more than 2 months ago. Harcourt told me he was going to sound Courtney about the Speakership. Will he accept, in view of threatened opposition to his nomination in Unionist circles? I am afraid Campbell-Bannerman is very disappointed; but Harcourt said that self-abnegation on the part of the Cabinet was absolutely necessary. Anything that involved reconstruction would be fatal & he declined point-blank to be a party to it himself. A re-assortment of places would greatly weaken the Government; and John Morley would be pressing his claims for a Secretary-ship of State.

I have been dining this evening at Harcourt House. I came away with Paulton M.P.[125] and asked him what the general feeling on the Government side of the House was about the Speakership. He said the nomination of Courtney would be very unpopular. People below the gangway would even prefer Ridley to Courtney. The general wish was that the best man for the post should be appointed, irrespective of politics. But *is* Ridley the best man? Why would there be such unanimity about him? His position in the House is not great; he is irregular in his attendance; & not widely known. He was once singled out for the Chair; and on the reverse principle of "Give a dog a bad name and it will stick to him", Ridley's supposed qualifications for being Speaker have always stuck to him—right or wrongly. It has been most unfortunate that the secret about the Speaker's intention to resign should have been prematurely divulged. It seems that the correspondent of the *'Times'*—a man named Pitt—overheard some indiscreet remark dropped in the lobby by some one who ought to have maintained special reserve, and at once challenged the Speaker's Secretary—Edw. Ponsonby—on the truth of the report. He (E.P.) being taken by surprise was apparently not ready with a categorical denial; and the "*Times*" man thereupon was sharp enough to infer that the rumour was authentic.

Friday 15 March   George Peel[126] has been asked to stand at Warwick as his father's successor; and is minded (I am afraid with injudicious haste) to give up his post in the Treasury at the instance of Chamberlain, who not only claims the seat as a Liberal Unionist one (as to which there seems to be some doubt) but has induced A. Balfour to admit the claim, notwithstanding that there has been a Conservative candidate—M. Nelson—long in the field.

It appears that Courtney, whom Harcourt has sounded for the Speakership, declines to allow himself to be put in nomination. The Conservatives with whom he is not popular would, he believes, oppose him, and he is not sure even of the support of his own Liberal Unionist party, to say nothing of some Radicals. The Government are put in difficulty by Courtney's refusal; for the only man on their side who could be carried without opposition is Campbell-Bannerman and he cannot be spared—a fact which the Unionists in promising to support him have naturally taken into full account . . .

Sunday 17 March (The Durdans)   I came down here yesterday. I don't feel comfortable about Rosebery. The acute insomnia with which he is afflicted shows no sign of subsiding. Sir W. Broadbent,[127] who is spending Sunday here, says he has never seen a more acute case. R. barely gets 2 hours of sleep at night; but nothwithstanding he is cheerful, shows marvellous patience, never says an irritable or complaining word, and looks less pulled down & worn than one might expect. Broadbent seems to be positive that he knows the cause of mischief—a want of nervous muscular power in the stomach which in consequence fails to fulfil its functions properly. He accounts for this stomachic derangement by R.'s being given to take his meals alone and to read while eating, with the result that nervous power has gone from the stomach to the brain. R. has been spending most of the day with Campbell-Bannerman who came down after breakfast to talk over the matter of the Speakership, on which he himself has apparently set his heart. Indeed, he had thought of resigning if his claim to the Chair was passed over. However he seems to have behaved wonderfully well and R.'s talk with him has smoothed him down. He is thoroughly loyal to R. R. took the line with C.B. of saying that he was indispensable to the Government, of hinting that the next lead of the Liberal party in the House of Commons would be assured to him, and of pointing out that the chorus of approval at the idea of his being nominated to the Chair was far from being disinterested. I feel sure he will on consideration waive his claim under the circumstances. R. is just as strong as Harcourt about the inconvenience, if not fatality, of any ministerial reconstruction. If Harcourt carried out his threat of resigning, J. Morley would probably follow suit from mortification at not receiving the lead which certainly would not fall to him. So C.B.'s nomination to the Chair might deprive the Government of the services of three of its foremost members. So far, R. & Harcourt are agreed; but where they differ is as regards the alternative to C.B. Harcourt is now strongly in favour of M. Ridley but R. thinks that it would be a grave reflection on the party if the Government had to resort to the front Opposition Bench for a Speaker. The man whom R. seems mostly to favour is Lockwood; whose nomination however Harcourt regards as one *pour rire*. He (Lockwood) is undoubtedly popular; but he is not supposed to know much about House of Commons affairs, and his caricaturing propensities might be considered ill-fitted for the dignity of the Chair. Another man mentioned as a possible nominee is Gully Q.C.[128] whom I do not know. It is unfortunate that this worry should come upon R. just now.

Monday 18 March   Rosebery had another very bad night last night & Broadbent this morning was very disappointed. I made bold to suggest to him that, for his own satisfaction and the satisfaction of the public at large, he should call in a second opinion. He took this suggestion very well; but said he did not know whom it would be worth consulting. The difficulty no doubt would be to induce R. to consent. I stayed behind this morning in order to take a drive with R. The weather was heavenly. He was certainly depressed, though wonderfully uncomplaining & plucky. He said it could not go on: if he did not break down in body, he would certainly break down in mind. Moreover, how long was he justified in retaining the head of affairs without being able to attend properly to his duties? He was pleased with his interview yesterday, with C. Bannerman. Nothing, he said, could have been more loyal & nicer than C.B. was. C.B. will evidently submit to remain on in his present post; but the difficulties anent the Speakership were not at an end; for R. was as strongly opposed to, as Harcourt was strongly in favour of, the claims of M. Ridley. He (R.) could not subject his party to the humiliation of seeking a nominee from the front Opposition Bench, more especially as the Government had already proposed one man outside their ranks (Courtney) and that proposal had met with no success. R. talked about Reggy Brett's application.[129] He (R.B.) wants the vacant Commissionership of Woods and in doing so places R. in a position of some delicacy and difficulty. He does not like to refuse to oblige a friend; and yet thinks the appointment might give rise to awkward comments. R. Brett has had no training and professes no special qualifications. Moreover Harcourt, though the friend of R.B., is not a little averse to the idea. The last thing a man ought to do is to apply to a friend for a post: it is not fair; and I am surprised that R. Brett has not seen it in this light. I am afraid too, that if R. gives an appointment to Reggy Brett, it will make it more difficult for him to promote another friend (and relative) to the Chairmanship of the Customs, which must be vacant soon as poor Robert Hamilton cannot live much longer, and for which Henry Primrose is very well qualified.

Tuesday 19 March   There was a Cabinet this morning. R. was able to come up to attend it. Campbell-Bannerman seems to have behaved well, as indeed he was certain to do. He withdrew his claims to the Speakership in deference to his colleagues. It now seems to be a choice between Ridley and Lockwood or some such less prominent a man as Gully; but any further action is to be postponed for a week or so. Harcourt was very well satisfied with the decision for the time being. He is convinced that the more the matter is freely discussed on both sides, the more certainly will Ridley become "Hobson's choice".

R. went back to the Durdans after luncheon. Broadbent came and offered himself to call in a fresh opinion: but R. refused to entertain the idea.

I have been dining this evening with the Ripons . . . Paul M.P.,[130] was on my other side; and I had a good deal of talk with him. I found that he held the view like Rosebery, that the Liberal party would resent the nomination of a real Tory. If Courtney only had had the pluck to stand, he would (according to Paul) be elected by a large majority; & he still thought that this might be the best solution.

Wednesday 20 March   Yesterday and again to-day Harcourt took pains to make it clear to me (in order to be conveyed to Rosebery) that, if unfortunately the state of R.'s health should compel him to reconsider his present position, nothing would induce Harcourt to attempt to carry on without R.: Harcourt's fate must be understood to be bound up with R.'s. He (Harcourt) greatly hoped that R. was sensible of there being improved relations between them lately; he had done his best to effect this improvement, or at any rate to show what his intentions were.

The electoral squabble over the seat at Warwick does not promise to be settled amicably. The Conservative candidate refuses point-blank to withdraw; and the Liberal Unionists are equally minded to run George Peel. It appears that Arthur Balfour gave way too soon to the dictation of Chamberlain: the Tories are a good deal annoyed. They will not improbably have enough of Chamberlain before they have done with him. The seat at Warwick would not strictly speaking fall within the compact of 1886; because it was not fought then & the present Speaker never declared himself in decided terms.

I have been dining this evening with the Harcourts. Mrs Asquith was there: maternal expectations seem to be near realisation.

The second Reading of the Welsh Church Disestablishment Bill was moved yesterday by Asquith—in a speech which (according to John Morley whom I saw last night) was the best he has ever delivered in the House. The Church party was evidently going to fight the Bill very hard. All I go upon is that, if representation is to be taken into account, a case is surely made out for Disestablishment in Wales, inasmuch as 30 out of 32 Welsh representatives are committed to it. It will be long before a corresponding majority of English representatives are returned in favour of putting an end to the State Church. So English Churchmen need not be greatly alarmed.

Courtney seems to be somewhat redivivus for the Speakership. An official communication has been made to the Unionist Press denying that if he should be nominated the Liberal Unionists would oppose his election. He has again been approached: Whitbread has been told to speak to him, & J. Morley has had a talk with him. Harcourt would still accept this solution of the question.

I have just received a letter from Rosebery. I had sent him extracts from my Journal about the appointment of the last Speaker which have interested him. He admits to feeling decidedly stronger, but he cannot say that his sleeping powers have much improved. I had been asked to bring to his notice the name of Jack Horner[131] for the Commissionership of Woods, and I believe he would fill the appointment very well. R. says he will certainly consider the claim if he decides to set aside Reggy Brett. He (R.) alludes to Harcourt in his letter. He readily and joyfully recognises that the relations with Harcourt have greatly improved of late; and that, although they differ materially on the Speakership. If he is to go away, he has the choice of more than the three proverbial courses—the Queen wants him to come out to Her at Nice; Sutherland has offered him Dunrobin; the Admiralty have placed their yacht "The Enchantress" at his disposal, & Hanotaux, the French Foreign Minister wishes France to have the credit of restoring him to health.

Saturday 23 March   A motion in favour of the payment of members was carried again in the House last night. I would gladly see provision made for any member who declared his inability to keep up his position in Parliament on his own means; and I cannot see that such a declaration need be considered to be invidious. Why should a man be ashamed to own his own poverty? But to give every member a payment of £200 or £300 a year, whether he wants it or not—and nine out of ten men returned to Parliament have more than enough means of their own on which to maintain themselves—seems to be a wanton waste of public money, and to tend to lowering the standard of our representative system. It is true that the principle of payment prevails in our Colonies & in foreign countries; but we have always prided ourselves on being superior to paid public service. Indeed, honorary service in this country has always been one of its distinguishing features . . .

Sunday 24 March   Mr & Mrs G. were brought back from abroad by the faithful Armitstead. They are under this roof, staying with the Harry Gladstones.[132] Mrs G. looked in upon me this morning; and according to arrangement I went at 5 o'clock this afternoon to pay them both a visit . . . Mr G. had been reading a French Book called "Notes sur Londres" which had interested him. There were in it allusions of rather a disagreeable nature to the Prince of Wales' private affairs and insinuations about help from doubtful sources, in which (as I told Mr G.) I did not the least believe. But Mr G. said that there was the fact that when he assumed office in 1880 and again in 1882-3 intimations were conveyed to him that something would have to be done; and yet somehow or other the crisis was tided over—he never knew or understood how. The book seems to have commented on the curious anomaly that this country of all countries should have allowed itself & willingly allowed itself to be ruled by a man who was so much of an impostor as Disraeli. There was, Mr G. said, no life which required so much to be written as that of Disraeli and which it was so difficult, if not impossible, to write with any approach to faithfulness. He had tried to incite Lord Derby (the late Earl) to put on record his impressions of the man, but he feared nothing had been done . . .

Tuesday 26 March   The Liberal Unionists met yesterday to consider the question of the Speakership. The conclusion at which they (or rather presumably Chamberlain) arrived was that as their allies, the Conservatives, had determined to nominate Ridley, they were against the nomination of any man of their own party. Thus Courtney is finally put out of court. It may now be best for the Government to pocket their feelings of pride and accept M. Ridley's candidature. Indeed, it is doubtful whether they could carry one of their own side against Ridley. Lockwood is believed to be averse to the idea of being nominated: & the only other man now at all in the field is Gully Q.C.

I went this morning and had a talk with Mr G. . . . He went *seriatim* through his objections to Courtney (1) Courtney was not gentleman enough for the purposes of the Chair. (2) He was wanting in sound judgement & a faddist. (3) He was overweeningly self-confident. (4) He neither would, nor indeed would he know how to, consult with others. (5) He had on one occasion shown a tendency to run not quite straight—an allusion to his failing to support Mellor[133] on a ruling of his (Courtney's) own. The man whom Mr G. thought would do admirably for Speaker was Balfour, the Lord Advocate;[134] but as he is understood to have the largest practice on record at the Scotch bar, it is not the least likely that he would consent to be nominated, especially as there could be no guarantee of his being re-elected in the next Parliament, nor would a pension be justified after so short a term of office. Mr G. said it was impossible to forecast the future fate of a man nominated to the Chair now. If he acquitted himself well as Speaker, it would be a very strong order of things to pass him over, notwithstanding present threats. Moreover, that consideration assumed— and it was from a party point of view a demoralising assumption to make—that the Unionists would command a majority in the next Paliament. In the whole of his long experience, Mr G. said, there was only one instance of the displacement of a Speaker—the notable one in 1835 when the Liberals having a majority carried Abercromby against Sir R. Peel's nominee, Manners Sutton. Mr G. remembered seeking explanation of this action of the Whigs at the time; and he believed it was due to the suspicion, if not knowledge, that Manners Sutton had intrigued with the King about the dismissal of Lord Melbourne's Government in the previous autumn. His authority for this belief was Sir C. Wood. The Whigs, it must be remembered, especially retained Manners Sutton in the Chair after the Reform Bill, though they had an overwhelming majority. They did so of course because they thought that in a newly reformed Parliament it was a great object to have a Speaker of tried experience and authority.

During this evening . . . I met Chamberlain, who at this moment seems not to be in particularly good odour with the Conservatives and who undoubtedly has indirectly been the means of keeping the ministerial party together. He referred among other topics to the laches of the Government in not getting Jabez Balfour extradited. It looked as if they were not over-anxious to have him back for fear of disclosures affecting members of the Government, alluding to Woodall[135] & Sir W. Foster,[136] who were apparently once mixed up with some of his bubble companies . . . Chamberlain said he must raise in the House of Commons the question of Sir Hercules Robinson's appointment at the Cape, which he regarded as most objectionable, if not scandalous. It was an appointment to which only Americans would stoop, regard being had to Sir Hercules' connection with South African financial institutions.

Thursday 28 March I have been dining this evening with the Harry Gladstones to meet Mr & Mrs G.—George Russell & Algy West[137] were the only others there. George Russell by the way made quite a brilliant speech the other day on the Welsh Disestablishment Bill. He will always be making flashes occasionally; but I doubt his ever assuming a high political position. He is indolent and does not command confidence. Referring to it, he said that in following Plunket[138] he had followed one of the most eloquent speeches he had ever heard. Alluding to the times of the Palmerston Government, Mr G. said he had some very curious letters for a Prime Minister to have written to his Chancellor of the Exchequer. Indeed there was one in which Lord Palmerston had told Mr G. that if there was an adverse vote on the Budget—the Budget I think of 1861—he (Lord Palmerston) would not consider it a vote of want of confidence . . . Talking confidentially to me in the evening about the future of the present Cabinet, I ventured the remark that curiosly none of the three literary men in the Cabinet, alluding to J. Morley, Bryce & Trevelyan, would in my judgement ever attain real political pre-eminence. Mr G. expressed surprise at my allusion to J. Morley whose administration in Ireland he (Mr G.) regarded as a remarkable performance. I admitted that John Morley stood far higher than the other two men, but he could never be a Parliamentary leader. He did not suit the House; and he had not sufficient confidence of the party. I did not add that J. Morley was proving himself to be a most difficult colleague, and was constantly referring to his own claims for better office. I had no wish to dispel Mr G.'s illusions about J. Morley, for whom in spite of his little weaknesses & effeminacy I have the sincerest regard. Reverting to the Speakership—(Mr G. is less chary about speaking to me on the subject than to his late colleagues)—Mr G. held the view that it was not fair to exact from a member of the Cabinet such a sacrifice as that which had been exacted from Campbell-Bannerman. He was certain that C.B. was eminently fitted to occupy the Chair, and he made light of the difficulties about reconstruction of the Cabinet which the appointment would involve. He little knew that one of the greatest difficulties would be connected with J. Morley, who would be certain to press for the vacant Secretaryship of State. The resolve of the Cabinet about C.B. is, I am certain, fixed; and though nothing is to be settled for some few days, it looks as if the candidature of M. Gully Q.C. will have the best chance. He is too little known; and there will probably be disagreeable allusions made to his antecedents or rather the antecedents of his grandfather who was a prize fighter and his father (a Doctor) who was mixed up in the Bravo case.[139] Indeed it is already said that if Gully is elected Speaker, the time-honoured exclamation of "Hear, Hear" will disappear, and the word "*Bravo*" will be substituted. But he is said to be a very level headed man, a good lawyer, of good presence, and dignified bearing.

Friday 29 March   Edward Grey made a speech last night about France and the poaching appearance of her marauding expeditions in Africa in the directions of the Niger and Nile, which will no doubt create somewhat of a flutter on the other side of the Channel, but which has given general satisfaction here except to Harcourt and John Morley, the solitary "Dodos" of Cobdenism, who seem to be a good deal exercised over it.

Saturday 30 March (The Durdans, Epsom)   Came down here this afternoon with Rosebery accompanied by Broadbent. There was a long Cabinet this morning which was occupied entirely by the consideration of foreign policy—Edwd. Grey's speech and its consequences. It seems to have gone off better than might have been expected, and R. notwithstanding having had so tiring a day was wonderfully cheerful and indeed quite like himself at dinner in spite of his continued "short commons" of sleep. Broadbent marvels at R.'s being as he is, and is fairly reassured about him . . .

We have closed the Exchequer books to-day for the year and have come out with a surplus of £766,000, about £200,000 better than I expected. It is very satisfactory. We shall be able to get rid of the additional 6d on spirits imposed last year and make ends meet all right in 1895–6, which will be a pleasant surprise to the Irishmen.

Sunday 31 March (The Durdans)   Rosebery had a very bad night last night. He only got about 2 hours sleep; but he was wonderfully uncomplaining this morning, and took me for a long drive, during which he talked all the time. He cannot make up his mind about the appointment to the vacant Commissionership of Woods. He does not like disappointing R. Brett, but wishes he had not pressed his claim. Harcourt is not favourable to it, though Loulou (who has backed up R. Brett) is not conscious of this. It is a delicate question. Harcourt is quite right in saying that nothing affects Governments so much as appointments. As to the Speakership, it is (as R. says) "Aut Gully aut nullus"; and it is now almost certain to be Gully. R. sees no reason why Gully should not be quite as efficient in the Chair as M. Ridley who is crammed down every one's throat as an ideal

Speaker. R. fully recognises that Harcourt has behaved much better of late. Indeed he believed if it were not for Loulou, he could get on fairly well again with the father. The improved relations are due to R.'s having "had it out" with Harcourt before he fell ill, and to R.'s illness itself. The nice side of Harcourt always comes out when there is trouble. R. feels that the Government is appreciably stronger than it was at the commencement of the Session, and that his own position has improved lately; the improvement being partly due to the natural course of reaction. There is only one rock ahead; and that is the Local Veto Bill; and why on earth Harcourt by insisting on bringing it forward is bent on running his head against such a brick wall, I can't conceive. I told R. I wondered why the Cabinet had not put *their* veto on such a Bill.

Tuesday 2 April   The Welsh Disestablishment Bill was read a second time last night by a majority of 45. Only two Liberal Unionists voted in the "Aye" Lobby—Chamberlain himself & C. Corbett:[140] 21 voted against it: 10 paired against it; and 15 were absent unpaired. It seems really absurd to keep up the figment of 2 parties—Liberal Unionists and Conservatives. Unless the Liberal Unionists have divested themselves of every shred of Liberalism, one would have thought they would have supported a Bill of this kind. When they were on the ministerial side as they were last Parliament, they had a very legitimate excuse of voting with the Tories, because they were bound to do nothing to jeopardise the existence of an Unionist Government. But they have no such excuse now. They might have donned Liberal colours *ad hoc* without favouring Home Rule an inch. I dined with Asquith to-night at Brooks'. He considered that the debate had been of quite a high order (notably the speeches of D. Plunket, G. Russell and Birrell)[141] and was pleased with the Division. He has himself done very well this Session.

Thursday 4 April   There was a Cabinet yesterday; and it was finally decided to support nomination of Gully as Speaker. I presume he will be carried; but his candidature and that of M. Ridley will probably be a close one. The fear is of course that if Gully is elected the Opposition will do their best to put him in a hole in order to be able to say "I told you so—if you had only taken our man, things would have been very different". A still greater fear is that this is the commencement of having Party Speakers according to the majority of the House whenever an election has to be made. It would however be very awkward & contrary to all precedent for the Government of the day to support the candidature of a man on the front Opposition Bench; and it is tolerably certain that it is the last thing which the Conservatives would do had they a majority in the House. To judge from a man like Paulton . . . Gully's nomination may be acquiesced in, but not heartily supported, by the rank & file on the ministerial side.

There was another meeting yesterday of the Bimetallic League in the City. Arthur Balfour was the principal spokesman, and is thus committing himself more & more to so great a leap in the dark as any change in our currency system must be.

The Oscar Wilde case is proceeding; and some horrible disclosures are being made. It seems impossible that a British Jury can do otherwise than acquit Queensberry of defaming O. Wilde's character by imputing to him the character of "posing as" an unmentionable creature. The net seems to be closing round the brute; though he certainly is a very clever one, and has given utterance to many smart sayings in his cross-examination by Carson[142] who is conducting the case for Queensberry with great skill.

I had a long Budget talk with Harcourt this morning, who had submitted his proposals to the Cabinet yesterday and in so doing told them that so long as we were the principal disturbing power not only in Europe but in every quarter of the globe they cannot expect good budgets. Of course the proposals are very simple. All that can be done is to avoid renewing the additional spirit duty.

Friday 5 April The Oscar Wilde case came to a somewhat unexpected end this morning. Queensberry's Counsel—Carson—was proceeding to discuss the miscreant's relations with the young men, when Sir E. Clarke[143] intervened, and announced that those who were prosecuting felt that, what with the literature involved in the case and O. Wilde's own admissions, they could not expect a verdict. Accrdingly the prosecution was withdrawn and a verdict of "not guilty" given; the Jury finding that a plea of justifiction had been proved and that the alleged libel had been published for the public benefit. The Public Prosecutor was at once communicated with, and a warrant was granted this afternoon with the result that O.W. was arrested in an Hotel in Sloane Street—(he seems to have been acquainted with innumerable London Hotels)—and taken to Bow Street. He is said to have been aware that the Police has been watching him for some time, and that he took proceedings in the hope that he would win in the action which he brought against so crack-brained a man as Queensberry, and that he would thus stave off Police proceedings.

Saturday 6 April I spent some time this morning with Harcourt . . . He prided himself—and legitimately so—on the progress which the Government will have made with business by Easter (next week). He has certainly led the House this Session with great skill; and in spite of the drawbacks to the individual, there is no doubt he is the *biggest* man in the House of Commons now. As to the Speakership, the election for which is to come off next Wednesday, he seemed doubtful about the result. It will be a very close race between Gully and Ridley. The Government will not treat the Division as one of confidence; but, he said, they must not give this out.

Monday 8 April   Rosebery came up to Town for a while to-day. He seems to me to make no way: there being hardly any improvement in his sleeping powers. I cannot say I feel easy about him. Downing Street has been cleared and smartened up for him; and he intends to come and reside in No.10 after Easter. He has appropriated the whole of the first floor—the same rooms as Disraeli occupied.

Tuesday 9 April   Harcourt introduced his Local Option Bill yesterday. It can only be regarded (to use a favourite expression of his own) as a "Bill *pour rire*". There are two options in it: (1) total prohibition of the liquor traffic at the end of 3 years after the commencement of the Act if a resolution be carried by a majority of two thirds on there being taken a poll at the requisition of 1/10th of the parochial electors in a defined area; (2) a reduction in the number of licenses to the extent of ¾ if a resolution be carried by a simple majority . . . I can't conceive what object can be served by bringing the proposal forward now, even from an electioneering point of view, for the temperance party all vote radical as it is; so while no votes may be gained many may be lost. He has brought the Bill forward entirely, as it seems, on his own responsibility: and it is to be presumed that the Cabinet will say now—"Thus far and no farther"; unless he is bent on wrecking the Government and there could not be a worse rock on which to effect a wreck.

The Vote of thanks to the Speaker was moved this afternoon. Harcourt seems to have spoken well, but to have been more than usually ponderous and pompous, though the matter was very good and put into eloquent language. His habit of reading out his set speeches deprives them entirely of spontaneity . . . Thus ends to-day a remarkable Speaker's reign. Arthur Peel has certainly added lustre to that illustrious Parliamentary name. It is only to be regretted that his retirement was not effected with a little more consideration for the House and for the Government.

Wednesday 10 April   The proceedings so connected with the election of a new Speaker which resulted in M. Gully's being carried by a majority of 11 votes were not got through this morning in as seemly a manner as was to be wished. Whitbread proposed and Birrell seconded the nomination of M. Gully. Birrell spoke well testifying by intimate personal knowledge to the excellence of Gully's qualifications; but Whitbread with some want of tact at a moment of tension struck (unintentionally as he subsequently avowed) a note of discord by asking whether it was still necessary to select the occupant of the Chair from the landed interest classes. M. Ridley was proposed by Mowbray[144] and seconded by Wharton[145] in a speech that impressed people with the idea that he would have made a good Speaker himself. Then followed according to custom brief speeches from both candidates, at the end of which the House should have proceeded to divide. Unfortunately however, Arthur Balfour thought it necessary to intervene, though Harcourt had strongly impressed upon him the expediency of their both following the precedent of 1839 and saying nothing. Arthur Balfour not only dilated strongly on the want of Gully's Parliamentary experience, in which respect he undoubtedly compares unfavourably with M. Ridley who has served on many Committees and been Chairman of a Grand Committee, but for some reason or other in so dilating he completely lost control of himself and his temper with the result that he necessarily laid himself open to a crushing retort from Harcourt, who was able to remind the House not only that much the same sort of thing had been said (outside) when Mr Peel was elected, and that if the Government had had their own way they would have suggested and supported the nomination of a man with a unique experience of Parliamentary procedure belonging to the party who opposed the Government—to wit, Courtney. While Harcourt was speaking, Arthur Balfour looked white, and Chamberlain green, with rage; and at the end of the speech, the House was so worked up that it was with great difficulty that Arthur Balfour got a hearing at all to make a personal explanation in which he apparently wished to intimate that not he, but somebody else (meaning of course Chamberlain) was responsible for the setting aside of Courtney's candidature. So far as one can judge, Arthur Balfour's intervention and the manner of it are regarded as a great mistake by his own as well as by the other side. The worst of it is that to-day's proceedings are likely to lay the seeds for making in the future the Speakership a party appointment, which is greatly to be deprecated. In returning thanks Mr Gully seems to have impressed the House very favourably by his manner and appearance . . . It seems odd, however that the Speaker-elect should be a man whom one does not even know by sight.

There is no doubt that at the present moment the relations between the Conservatives and Liberal Unionists are a little strained. What has taken place and what has been said about the Speakership and the late Speaker's seat at Warwick clearly indicates a tension. But . . . the Unionists are certain to close up their ranks fast enough . . . and still less necessary is it for the Liberal Radical party to crow and prophesy serious differences in the enemy's camp.

Friday 12 April (The Durdans)   Rosebery seems to have made little or no progress; the last 3 nights have been very bad again; and meanwhile

Broadbent does nothing and tries nothing. He promised me more than a week ago that he would try douching; but as yet nothing has been done. R. is beginning to think himself that Broadbent's periodical visits are becoming a farce; and he is thinking of taking his own line and putting himself on board some ship for a short sea-voyage. He is certainly more depressed about himself than he was—and no wonder. He says he can quite appreciate the feelings which prompt suicide, when night after night he lies awake. We drove together this morning and dined *tête-à-tête* this evening. The negotiations for peace between China and Japan are in a very critical state: & he is rather fussed at the absence of Lord Kimberley from the Foreign Office just at this moment. It is difficult for us to put any real pressure on Japan to make her reasonable in her demands, for we can't be expected to back up diplomatic pressure by threats of force. R. says that Lord Kimberley makes an excellent Foreign Secretary: but he is apt to take things too easily and he lacks initiative power. I find that Harcourt has asked to be made a Trustee of the British Museum: and it is the one thing he covets. Of course R. will appoint him and will do so gladly; but considering what the relations of the two men have been, at any rate until quite recently, it seems strange that Harcourt should of his own accord have begged a favour of R. It appears that Lefevre always takes copious notes of the proceedings at the Cabinet—(I remember Lord Derby used to do so)—and R. has written to ask Mr G. whether this is not contrary to etiquette & tradition and whether notice may and indeed should not be taken of it. R. has made up his mind that it won't do to give the vacant Commissionership to R. Brett: the appointment would not be easy to defend if it were challenged, and might give rise to disagreeable remarks. He proposes to offer the place to Jack Horner . . .

Easter Sunday 14 April (Malwood, Lyndhurst)   I came from the Durdans yesterday morning and on here in the afternoon to combine a little Budget work with Easter holiday . . . I brought a note from Rosebery about the Woods appointment; & Harcourt acquiesces in the suggestion of Horner. We have said very little about it: for it is delicate ground for Harcourt, inasmuch as he never liked the idea of Reggy Brett for the post in spite of his being backed by Loulou. Harcourt seems a little knocked up after his recent excitement in the House of Commons. He prides himself—& legitimately so—on having scored last Wednesday unintentionally; for he would have kept silence, had Arthur Balfour consented to do so. Harcourt cannot understand what possessed Arthur Balfour to do what he did; he genuinely regrets it on public & personal grounds. They had both acted most harmoniously up to the last day. Harcourt had taken A.B. into confidence at every step and I can answer for Harcourt's having been from the first bent on doing his utmost to keep clear as far as possible from party heat and feeling. Loulou has an idea that Arthur Balfour was annoyed at finding when he came down to the House that he could not carry Ridley, who had only consented to stand on being assured that he would be elected. But I don't believe this. I feel sure Ridley was ready to take his chance. He had nothing to lose and much to gain. The division was certainly in doubt up till the night before the election; but Ridley's friends could never have thought that they had more than a good chance. Harcourt admits that he had to "lobby" a good deal and to use all his diplomatic powers in order to prevent defections; but he says he might certainly have spared himself that trouble had he known Arthur Balfour was going to make the speech he did, which at once pulled the supporters of the Government together. In fact, in Harcourt's judgement, A.B. for the first time produced an impression such as Chamberlain has often produced this Parliament. There is one point on which Harcourt feels strongly—and I know Rosebery feels the same—& that is, that the importance of the Speakership and the difficulties of filling it competently are absurdly exaggerated.

Thursday 16 April (Malwood) We have got through a good deal of Budget—in fact I have got very little more to do or to suggest. Harcourt is most laborious over his Budget, more so than any other Chancellor of the Exchequer with whom I have had to do. He takes my brief—and that is practically an invention of my own, at least in a complete form—and from it writes out verbatim what he intends to say. When he has finished it after a good deal of re-writing and corrections, he has it type-written, tables and all. Fancy Pitt or M.G. composing a Budget like that! They would have scorned almost to have a brief given them. Harcourt certainly takes great pains with whatever interests him and he also generally takes very good points connected with the subject. Talking of the succession to the Exchequer, he thought that Goschen was more in the running than he was some little time ago. I agree certainly his chances have of late materially improved what with his having put himself more to the front, Arthur Balfour's having committed himself more deeply than ever to bi-metallism, and Chamberlain's not being in particularly good odour with some of the Tories who would take fright at his socialistic programme if he had the purse under his own command with which to carry it out. Failing these three men, Beach of course might become Chancellor again; & he would probably make a very good one. Harcourt has a high opinion of him: he is so straight; & Harcourt believes he (Beach) is one of the very few real free-traders left in the House of Commons; the others being himself, Mundella & Fowler. Harcourt declared again to-day that he always felt as if he were sitting on a volcano, what with Kimberley at the F.O. and Rosebery behind him. To hear him talk in one of these moods, one would imagine that those two men together were on the verge of going to war in all parts of the world, and that he (Harcourt) alone by himself kept the peace! The latest thing, according to his own account, he had stopped were our jointly with Russia threatening Japan with force unless she moderates her demands with China, and our bombarding the principal port of Nicaragua for some sort of "Don Pacifico" *replica*. The real fact is, one must never take seriously what Harcourt says. After dinner this evening he got on the subject of Chamberlain. He did not feel at all sure that Chamberlain will himself take office in the next Unionist Government. Much as Chamberlain loved power, he did not care for office. All he liked was having "his own regiment" under his command with which he could turn the fortunes of the day. I believe that so far Harcourt is right about Chamberlain. But I feel sure that, whether Chamberlain wishes it or not, he will have to assume ministerial responsibility. He can't separate himself from the Duke of Devonshire; and it seems to be quite a recognised thing that the Duke will join the Unionist Government whenever it comes to be formed.

Friday 19 April I left Malwood on Wednesday morning . . . I saw Rosebery to-day . . . The peace negotiations between China & Japan were, he said, still in rather a ticklish condition. The Cabinet were not yet in receipt of any authentic statement of the terms. He was anxious to compensate in some way with Russia and was suggesting that this country & Russia should jointly demand an explicit account of what was really proposed and agreed to by the belligerent powers of the Far East. Anything further in the direction of joint pressure with Russia on Japan was of course out of the question.

Sunday 21 April (Ascott, Leighton Buzzard)   Came down here yesterday afternoon . . . Stanley talked about the view taken by the Opposition of the Gov. Front Bench. The man they like most is Campbell-Bannerman, becuase he is such a good fellow & so excellent a Secretary of State for War; and the man they like least is Asquith: he gives them the idea of not being quite to be trusted. The man they have the most contempt for is poor Herbert Gardner; they look upon him as a sort of Minister of Agriculture *pour rire*.[146]

A somewhat new & rather doubtful departure from the traditions of the Civil Service taken by Bryce, has proved a success. He made Courtenay Boyle[147] arbitrate between the employers & employed in the Boot trade at Northampton, where there has been a formidable strike and terms have been arranged; the arrangement being apparently to a great extent due to his ability & tact. The fact of his being charged with the duty of arbitrator is a good instance of the enormously increased responsibility which has of late been thrown upon heads of Departments.

Tuesday 23 April   There was a Cabinet to-day mainly to consider House of Commons business. Harcourt I hear was in a bad humour; on this occasion he was sullen by way of a change from hectoring & bullying. He wants precedence given to the 2nd Reading of his Local Veto Bill[148] over the committee stages of the Irish Land Bill and the Welsh Church Bill. I imagine, from what J. Morley told me, that Harcourt got little support. The fact is nobody wants & still less likes his Bill. Heaven knows why he is pushing it so himself unless it be to ride for a fall. J. Morley, I understand, is in a very petulant mood just now. He has apparently got the Irish Office on the brain. In the few words I had with him to-day, he said in answer to my enquiries how he was: "How can any one he well in such a thankless office as I am in, and from which I am apparently never to be relieved?"

Poor Robert Hamilton's lingering illness came to an end yesterday; and by his death the State has lost one of its most valuable public servants . . . I well remember being called into the Cabinet which was summoned on the eventful Sunday after the Phoenix Park murders in 1882 and being asked my opinion of his as a successor to poor Burke. It was decided that the Under Secretaryship for Ireland should be offered to him; and he accepted at a moment's notice the post which was one of special responsibility and even danger . . . He did extremely well in Ireland; but what with his Home Rule proclivities and his unpopularity in legal circles in which he had attempted to effect much needed economical reforms, the Salisbury Gov. felt that he was not the man for them to entrust the carrying out of a coercion policy. He was accordingly sent out as Governor of Tasmania. One had hoped that having returned and being appointed Chairman of Customs he would have rendered valuable public service for some years to come; but that horrible disease—cancer—laid hold of his liver and of course proved fatal. I must have already recorded his connections with the inauguration of Home Rule, towards the solution of which he wrote, evidently at the instance of Lord Carnavon (Lord Lieutenant in the autumn of 1885), a statesmanlike memorandum. I think his place will go to Henry Primrose. Rosebery will have scruples about it, but I expect he will not allow his relationship to stand in the way of his cousin's well deserved promotion a second time.

Wednesday 24 April   . . . The new Speaker is said to be very nervous in the Chair; & to show a considerable want of familiarity with the ordinary forms of the House; but he ought to be able and probably will learn his apprenticeship quickly enough. The outlook for George Peel at Warwick as Liberal Unionist candidate for his father's seat seems to be a very bad one. The Conservatives are prepared to support a Liberal Unionist chosen by the locality but not George Peel sent down at Chamberlain's dictation. He will, I am afraid therefore, fall astride the Parliamentary & Treasury stools.

The mid-Norfolk and Oxford elections[149] have gone badly for the Government. They had shown a remarkable growth of Unionist votes polled; and though in both cases the Unionist candidates (Gurdon and Valentia) were better than their opponents, the results seem to indicate the shadows cast before by coming events—the General Election. In Tory circles and in the Tory Press one hears much about the "revolutionary policy" of the progressive party. It is the old old story. One has only to read the memoirs relating to the Melbourne Government and one finds similar language; while I remember it being said in 1869-73 and again in 1880-5, when a good many of the Unionists were aiders & abettors in "blunders & plunders";[150] though nowadays one certainly hears more of "plunder" than "blunder" for the present "revolutionary" Government has kept singularly clear of administrative "blunders". What is never sufficiently taken into account is that administration is far more important than legislation; and in this respect the present Government has like its predecessor been on the whole very successful.

Thursday 25 April I had luncheon with Rosebery to-day in Downing street and I have been down to dine with him too this evening at the Durdans. He is certainly better. If he . . . sleeps fairly well . . . he is much less depressed about himself. He regards the present situation of foreign affairs as one of the most interesting situations that have taken place this century. It may be the commencement he thinks, of a great change in the powers of the world, which may possibly end in a combination of the yellow races—Chinese & Japanese— against the white races. He believes that France and stilll more Germany had acted very foolishly in joining Russia in making a protest against the terms of peace which Japan seeks to impose upon China. R. talked about his colleagues a good deal. He felt that they stood too much aloof from him, and that the Cabinet did not co-operate enough. Each minister went his own way. Owing to Mr G.'s great age the present Government began as a "Government by Departments", and it has never been able to shake off this habitude. For instance John Morley never gave R. an inkling of what was going on in Ireland, & never consulted him. Harcourt never went near him (R.), and his other colleagues hardly ever volunteered to come & see him. I think it is partly R.'s own fault. Charming & winning as his manner can be if he likes, he is often rather "stand-offish" . . . He asked me how I thought he stood in the estimation of his colleagues. I was, as I told him, at some disadvantage about giving him a reply; for I had come across so few of them lately; but I had no reason to think that the feeling among those who were not his friends—indeed all but Harcourt & J. Morley—was otherwise than quite cordial & grateful towards him for having persevered with so thankless a task.

Saturday 27 April (Compton Place)   George Peel has had to retire from
the Warwick contest as I feared, and is consequently stranded. It was
evident that the constituency would not have him. So he had no choice . . .
It is believed that Alfred Lyttelton is to be chosen in his stead as the
Unionist candidate. I am sorry he should be standing as such, in his Uncle's
life-time; it seemed unnecessary more especially as he remained Liberal
until so recently.[151]

I dined last night at Brooks', when owing to the House having been
counted, I found Arnold Morley & Herbert Gardner as well as Tweedmouth. We all went on to the Palace Theatre with its miscellaneous
programme. I gave a hint that colleagues might rally round Rosebery a
little more than they do.

Tuesday 30 April   The government carried by a majority of about 20 last
night their Resolution for further time to be placed at their disposal. The
Standing Orders must soon be altered. It is absurd any longer that the
Government should only have two nights a week allotted to them.

I was with Harcourt some time this morning. He has got his Budget quite
ready. What is now much more in & on his mind is his Local Veto Bill. He
told me he had just received what he considered an important notification,
which was that the Church Temperance party had decided to support his
Bill. But the importance he attached to this announcement was not very
consistent with his subsequent professions of a longing to fall upon it. I said
I could not conceive a worse thing on which to fall. He told me I knew
nothing about it: he was convinced that temperance was the only question
which really interested the electors. I am afraid I was not convinced; for all
the temperance people or the bulk of them, as it is, vote Liberal. He went
on to say that what would suit him better still would be if the Cabinet
declined to let him proceed with the Bill, meaning that he would then retire
from the Government. I don't take this profession seriously. I can quite
imagine that he would not be sorry to bring the Government to an end
soon and to go into opposition where he would be relatively to his
colleagues a bigger power than he now is; but I cannot think he will run the
risk of leaving the party on his own hook and give the choice of letting
some one else step in as Leader of the party in the House of Commons.
Rosebery came into my room this afternoon. He believes that Harcourt's
views about temperance & the Local Veto Bill are shared by no other
member of the Government unless it be John Morley, with whom just now
R. is a good deal hurt. He showed me a letter he had had from R. Brett
about Jack Horner's appointment to the Woods. It evidently showed
disappointment and was wanting in nice feeling, hinting that R. had been
influenced in his choice by Mrs Asquith and others which is absolutely
untrue: indeed if she or anybody like her had spoken on Horner's behalf I

am sure R. would never have made the appointment. He particularly resents suggestions and applications. He likes to make appointments of his own creation. He is more sensitive about this than most Prime Ministers. Indeed as an instance of this, he sent for Archdeacon Farrar the other day after he had appointed him Dean of Canterbury and told him point-blank that, glad as he had been to make him the offer, he had almost been deterred from so doing by the application of his injudicious friends. The scruples of the Queen about the appointment of Eyton to succeed Farrar at Westminster have by the way, been surmounted.

The Government have actually scored an electoral success—having in one of the seats at Leeds[152] secured a considerably increased majority.

Wednesday 1 May Rosebery's horse "Sir Visto" ran third to-day in the "Two Thousand" . . . several horses who on former occasions took the same place as "Sir Visto" have been Derby winners. So Rosebery has still a chance of carrying off the "Blue Riband" of the Turf two years running; but his interest in "Sir Visto" is small compared with that which he took in "Ladas" last year.

I dined to-night at Brooks' with F. Lockwood. He is a really loyal friend & supporter of Rosebery in the Government. He believed that R. had done better than anybody could have imagined, considering the difficulties with which he has had to contend; and it was absolutely certain that nobody but R. could have kept the Government together for over a year. What had struck and even surprised Lockwood so much was the great pluck which R. had shewn: the more R. had been abused the more determination had he displayed—and this notwithtanding his recent illness. I encouraged Lockwood, who is a very modest & unself-asserting man, to volunteer occasional visits to R. R. I know would like to see more of him; & Lockwood would be a very good Parliamentary barometer for R. The man in whom Lockwood has most confidence, apart from R. himself, is Campbell-Bannerman.

Thursday 2 May There was a Cabinet this morning—I believe it was chiefly occupied with the Armenian question. Harcourt declared he should stay away—Cabinets, he thought, ought not to be held on Budget days—he should be occupied in putting finishing touches to his Statement; but there was nothing to finish: it has all been cut and dried for days past. I verily believe he has spent as many weeks over the preparation of it as Mr G. would have spent hours, considering the character of it. However, as a matter of fact, Harcourt did join the Cabinet soon after it met.

The Budget went off quite quietly this afternoon. It was known there would be nothing very exciting about it; and so the House was not at all full. Harcourt was longer in delivering his Speech than I expected;—indeed he spoke, or rather read, for nearly two hours. He managed, to his credit, to make his statement more interesting than the paucity of materials warranted. There was a good deal of laughter at the "cogent reasons" for letting the extra 6d on spirits expire and retaining it (for a year) on beer. But I don't think the Budget proposals can give rise to any serious opposition. He might with advantage have brought home to the House more seriously than he did the formidable fact that unless this country is prepared to take a new fiscal departure we shall soon be unable to cope with our huge & increasing expenditure. I am certain that finance is going to be the crux ahead for the Government of the day in the near future.

Friday 3 May   Blackie Hope is very anxious to succeed Henry Primrose at the Office of Works, & I believe he would do very well there. I hinted at this to Rosebery this afternoon; but he did not respond favourably to the idea. He said he could not forget that Blackie Hope had gone out of his way to become a "faggot-voter" in Midlothian. I confess I thought this was rather petty of R.: politics have no business to stand in the way of the promotion of a civil servant. R. had dined and slept at Windsor last night to see the Queen on Her return from abroad. He found Her a good deal excited at the set which is being made by the *Times* and other newspapers against the retention of the Commandership-in-Chief by the Duke of Cambridge.[153] I am told that the *Times* is determined not to let the matter drop. The retention of the appointment was condemned by the "Hartington Committee" and is supposed to stand in the way of any reform in the organisation of the War Office. I don't believe the old Duke will budge an inch. The greater is the outcry against him, the more determined will he be to remain on. I expect he is saying—"I will see them all damned first". R. thinks Harcourt, *as at present minded*, is really bent on trying to bring the Government or himself, or both, to grief over the Local Veto Bill. I feel certain that, even if Harcourt did break away, R. would hold on with Campbell-Bannerman as Leader of the House of Commons.

One's fears about George Pembroke have alas! been realised. That beautiful life—for such it was—came to a premature end this morning . . . He was thoroughly worn out by a varied illness of over two years and a series of complications . . . Of all my contemporaries, I think I may say without invidious comparisons, he was the one whose nature was most perfect . . . The trend of his mind, especially in early life, was essentially Liberal; but during the last 20 years of his life or more he was strongly Conservative. This may have been partly due to his political start, which Disraeli was clever enough to give him. Of all young men whom it was an object to Disraeli to capture Pembroke was probably the one on whom Disraeli set most store. It is always supposed that Disraeli was more in awe of Sidney Herbert than of any other political opponent and consequently hated him most. Small wonder then was it that in his days of triumph Disraeli should have exerted himself to secure among his supporters the son of his brilliant opponent. Disraeli went very cleverly to work about it. I so well remember the letter which he wrote Pembroke in forming his Government in 1874. It was of course almost fulsomely flattering to the effect that though the places in the Cabinet were assigned there was one place outside it of great importance which he would place at Pembroke's disposal—the under Sec'ship for War. I was lunching at Herbert House on a Sunday; and we walked down together to Whitchurch Gardens afterwards, when Pembroke accepted the offer verbally. I was of course keen about his entering political life, no matter on which side he was. His health very soon could not stand the combination of official grind & being in love; and he had to resign his Under Secretaryship.

Thursday 9 May   There was an assembly last night at the National Liberal Club; and Rosebery, who having already appeared again in public was bound to show himself, came to a full stop in the middle of his speech. Something put him off & he lost completely the thread of his thoughts. It must have been most painful for those who were present; but his pluck came to his rescue, and he went on again in better voice than he ever had before. I have not seen him to-day: but I understand he [is] neither annoyed nor anxious about himself. His courage in adverse circumstances has contributed not a little to his enhanced popularity of late.

At yesterday's afternoon sitting the Irishmen again brought in a Bill for repealing the "Coercion Act". It was supported in an injudicious speech by J. Morley; but the 2nd Reading was only carried by a majority of 14, though last year the majority was more than three times as large. So long as the so-called coercion powers are only put into operation when absolutely necessary I cannot see why they should not be kept in reserve.

Monday 13 May   Rosebery, I am glad to say, has gone off to-day with Lord Spencer in the Admiralty yacht "Enchantress". I hope it may do him great good. The Queen I understand is fussing a good deal about the Duke of Cambridge. She is I believe beginning to see that his early retirement is best for his own interests and Her own. If she helps the Government to get the old Duke to resign, she will probably be able to make better terms as to the succession. She attaches immense importance to the retention (nominally at any rate) of the post of Commander in Chief; for without a Commander in Chief, she says, what becomes of *Her* army? She hopes too, presumably, that if the post is retained the Duke of Connaught[154] may be appointed to it some day for a limited time; but I doubt if Her hopes will ever be realised.

Wolmer[155] is going to contest the question of his eligibility to continue to sit in the House of Commons, notwithstanding his succession to the

Earldom of Selborne. His contention is going to be that though a Peer of the realm, he is not necessarily a Lord of Parliament unless & until he accepts the writ of summons to the House of Lords—a distinction (I expect) without difference in the eye of the constitution (so to speak). Harcourt is going to give a Committee of inquiry: but nothing can come of it. Wolmer's action seems rather foolish & looks almost like a bit of self-advertisement. If he & other elder sons want to be freed from the disability of sitting in the House of Commons, there is only one practical way of settling the quetion, and that is by legislation, which will take a long time.[156]

Wednesday 15 May   Campbell-Bannerman sent for me to-day to talk about his War Office arrangements . . . he wants a new Accountant General. It will be no easy matter to find the right man for him.

At the Committee of Public Accounts this afternoon I rather lost my temper with Mr Cleophas Morton who is a perfect pest on the Committee. He asks questions which are not the least cognate to matters of account, in order to be enlightened in the rudiments of public finance, and thus to be able to display his financial knowledge in discussions in Committee of Supply. The Chairman (Sir R. Temple)[157] & other members seemed quite pleased that I should have stood up against such a bore.

Partly owing to the recent bye-elections, and partly owing to the congested state of business in the House with which no progress is being made, the Government are going rather more groggily. I believe it would on many accounts be best to bring things to a head and dissolve, if it were not that such a step would have the appearance of giving in too much to the daily imprecations of the "Times" which is always telling the Government that they are in a "humiliating" position and should appeal to the country, taking it for granted that the ministerial party would be utterly routed at a General Election.

I had to dine this evening with the Association of Bankers at the Metropole (Whitehall rooms) which now has the monopoly of public dinners . . . I had to return thanks for the guests. It was my first appearance as a public speaker. I was rather nervous before I got up; but I got on better than I expected. Indeed, I spoke quite fluently.

Friday 17 May   . . . Yesterday evening the sitting of the House was devoted to the 2nd Reading of the Budget Bill, or (as it is now called) the Finance Bill. There were several amendments mostly aimed against the retention of the additional 6d on Beer; but they were withdrawn and the Bill was read a second time without a division. Indeed the threatened opposition completely collapsed, which is not to be wondered for there was nothing in the financial proposals to oppose. The discussion was good humoured and friendly. Goschen was very fair, and deprecated the idea that the basis of taxation could not be broadened. Harcourt spoke several times with much tact. Indeed, throughout the Session, he has shown great Parliamentary tact & has, in consequence, greatly improved his Parliamentary position. He was very pleased this morning with last night's proceedings. He was saying what an excellent Budget he & Goschen would concoct together; if it were not for infernal political considerations, they could raise the duty on tea; in fact, he did not know what they could not do in co-operation. It is pretty clear from last night's discussion that the tax against which the next tilt is going to be made is the Land Tax. But how it is to be turned to the relief of the agricultural interests exclusively remains to be seen.

Monday 20 May Rosebery has returned from his little cruise on the "Enchantress". I have not seen him; but I think it has done him considerable good from what I hear.

I understand that the Queen quite recognises the expediency of the Duke of Cambridge's retirement and of his announcing it soon. It is now mainly a question of dates. The one most favoured is 1st November. The "Times" is evidently determined to force a reform of war office administration, of which the first step is the Duke's retirement, and suggests to-day that there should be a Commission appointed by Parliament to which should be delegated the task of evolving a scheme of reform, and on which it is suggested that among others I should serve.

Bonhatzell of the Russian Embassy came to see me to-day about the subjection of the late Czar's holding of Russian Bonds deposited here to Estate Duty. It is clear that the property is under the law of the land liable to pay the duty; and no exception has been made in the case of any foreign sovereign. I undertook to bring the matter before the Chancellor of the Exchequer. It is a case in which it may be for State reasons desirable to wink at the law.

I have been dining this evening with the Bischoffheims—a large dinner. Sir Robert Peel—or "Sir Peel" as he was familiarly called—used to be a habitué of Bute House; which reminds me that I have not noted his death. He died quite suddenly. Indeed I saw him making his way to St James' Club to dinner about 12 hours before he was found dead in his bedroom. He was a most agreeable man socially, and might have made a great public mark for himself. No one ever had a finer start—a great name, good abilities, fine presence, magnificent voice, a good fortune, & a handsome wife; and no one ever made a greater mess of his life. Gambling ruined his fortune; extravagance of behaviour & bearing, his position; and latterly political wobbling, his political chances.[158]

Tuesday 21 May   Harcourt told me this morning that come what may, he, J. Morley & Fowler were agreed on one point, and that was, they were determined not to appeal to the country on the House of Lords question. He would never stand up in the House of Commons & move the promised Resolution. He was, he said, still convinced that Local Option was the question on which to stand or fall. At any rate a large section of the community were enthusiastic about it (which I take leave to doubt); while the reform of the Upper Chamber was a dead letter.

I went this afternoon to York House to resume talks with the Duke of York. The question which was mainly discussed was Local Option. He is easy to talk to on public affairs because he asks so many questions, & generally intelligent ones.

The Oscar Wilde & Taylor cases have been brought forward again; & unless there is some cantankerous jury-man a verdict is confidently expected this time. A verdict of guilty would remove what appears to be a wide-felt impression that the Judge & Jury were on the last occasion *got at*, in order to shield others of a higher status in life.

Friday 24 May   To day I have been cross-examined by the Financial Relations Commission. The cross-examination was left to the O'Conor Don,[159] who took the chair in Childers'[160] absence. (Mrs. Childers is said to be dying) —and to Barbour. The O'Conor Don cross-examined with much intelligence & fairness. Sexton[161] was no doubt inclined to put posers to me. My great object is to be strictly impartial & to hold the balance evenly between Great Britain & Ireland. The question is a very great crux. There is no doubt that relatively to Great Britain Ireland is taxed more heavily, but how the inequality can be adjusted I confess I do not see. The line which according to latest indications the friends of Ireland are likely to take is not any differential rates of taxation which would be impracticable, but the expenditure of more public money in Ireland on some reproductive service or other, as for instance the buying up of the railways and the reduction of the charges by the state, which is a very big order of things of a very doubtful expediency.[162]

Saturday 25 May   The Queen's birthday being kept to-day, I took the orthodox holiday, and spent it by going down the river with Arnold Morley who had a party on board the Telegraph Ship "The Mermaid" . . . On our return I met F. Lockwood at the station (Charing Cross). He had just won his case and was very triumphant over it. Oscar Wilde & Taylor have each got 2 years with hard labour. I am more glad than I can say about the verdict; for I never had a shadow of doubt about the guilt of the two beasts, and there was I am sure a very prevalent suspicion abroad that the Government were trying to hush up the case in order to screen certain people of higher rank in life.

To-day's birthday honours have been well received—even by the Times. They are catholic and even the stage comes in for its first recognition, in the shape of the bestowal of a Knighthood on Irving—a step which has given general satisfaction, & one which I remember Mr G. wished to take more than 10 years ago. The accustomed "Birthday Dinners" took place to-night; and I dined with the Chanc. of the Exchequer. Owing to Lady Kimberley's recent death, the Foreign Office was of course not opened. Rosebery entertained the ambassadors with others in Downing Street; and the Tweedmouths gave the evening at Brook House. All the Royal Princes were there; but no Princesses, bar Princess Louise (of Lorne). It seems impossible to get the Princess of Wales to go about anywhere now. It is a great pity: for in time it may tell on her wonderful popularity. The second son of the Amir of Afghanistan—Shahzada Nasrullah Khan—who arrived yesterday, was of the party. He seemed very much bewildered as well he might; for a ring was formed round him in one of the drawing-rooms and he was stared at in truly English fashion by the assembled crowd. A ring of ladies with bare arms & necks must have struck his oriental eye as a very curious sight . . . George Curzon,[163] having been the guest last autumn of the Amir, was of course much to the front, and introduced his wife (the American Miss Leiter that was) who looked remarkably well, and who I expect is bent on cutting a good figure in London society.

Tuesday 28 May   Rosebery seems better. He held a Cabinet to-day as well as yesterday, mainly it seems to discuss the policy which is to be pursued in Uganda and the making of a railroad. It is one of those questions about which there is far from being unanimity in the Cabinet; but those who dislike the forward policy in Africa have to give way. They know in their inmost hearts that it would be a very unpopular point on which to break away from Rosebery. Harcourt I hear acquiesced without making much difficulty. He professes now to be ready to make any sacrifice in order that he may promote the great object of his life—the lessening of the curse of drink—which he won't serve much by his Local Veto Bill, even if he could carry it, which he cannot do. John Morley gave way with much less grace: he becomes more & more difficult to manage; and another man who seems to have given quite as much if not more trouble is Asquith. Is he playing his own game? and is he running quite straight with Rosebery, though he was foremost in encouraging Rosebery to take the helm? I sometimes have doubts which are shared by others who know him better than I do. . . .

Wednesday 29 May   I have actually been to the Derby to-day. It is many years since I witnessed the race; and being unable to go last year I was determined to be present when Rosebery had another, though less good, chance of pulling the race off. I was more than rewarded: for his horse "Sir Visto" won, and he thus achieved the extraordinary feat of winning the Derby two years running as Prime Minister. No wonder the Afghan savage, when he saw the Prince of Wales win one race and the Prime Minister the next & the biggest, thought the whole proceeding was a got-up affair . . . R. did not get anything like the reception he got last year; and people will say that this is evidence of his dwindled popularity; but excitement has much more to do with the horse than with the owner, and this is sure to be much greater when the winner is first favourite and consequently so many more people win their money. Rosebery was himself—& naturally so—not nearly so pleased as he was last year, when it was his first Derby triumph, and when he had a horse like *Ladas*. This year's horses are all said to be a very second class lot. I am glad that he should have this fillip just now when he has been so much tried. It is a reward for all the pluck he has shown during the last 4 months . . . He told me this morning that he had had the greatest difficulty with John Morley, who appears to be unable to acquiesce with grace even when he had made up his mind to acquiesce. After the Cabinet yesterday, R. tried to soften J.M. down by saying "Well, if we are obliged to agree to differ now, we shall I hope be as good friends as ever when we are no longer colleagues in a Cabinet"; and all that J.M. said in response to this in leaving the room was "Perhaps". It is true that J.M. tried to take the taste out of R.'s mouth of the "perhaps" by a friendly note written a little later in the day when there had been a little more time for reflection; but the incident shows what a difficult man J.M. is to pull with. He has indeed disappointed me greatly. I was always under the belief a year ago that he would somehow or other be R.'s staunchest colleague. R's theory of Harcourt's acquiescing in the Uganda business is the delight of seeing J.M.'s being over-ruled and making a fool of himself; he (Harcourt) never having forgiven J.M. for burking the "Malwood compact" about a Peer as Prime Minister. R. is thinking of going yachting at Whitsuntide & offers to take me with him. I shall love that.

[Hamilton spent the period from 1 June to 11 June 1895 on a yachting cruise with Rosebery]

Tuesday 11 June   I landed at Weymouth yesterday morning & got back to London about 2.30; the Whitsun recess being at an end. Rosebery went on in the yacht to Southampton, intending to return to Town this morning; but a Cabinet seemed necessary to-day & so he came up last night.
[R.] told me the Cabinet went off very amicably this morning until just the end, when Harcourt, *à propos* of nothing, flew into one of his tantrums.

W.G. Grace has been surpassing himself this season in the cricket field. He has already got 10 centuries this year and has achieved the feat of being credited with his hundredth century. A public testimonial is being started for him. He is nothing short of a cricketing marvel.[164]

Thursday 13 June . . . Russia seems to be scoring a success with China. She has undertaken to guarantee a Chinese loan, which is to be subscribed for jointly by France & Russia; and if the arrangement is carried out, the latter power will no doubt get her foot into Chinese territories or at any rate exercise a commanding influence over that country. The French as well as the English Rothschilds have stood aloof from the loan, ostensibly on the ground that this country has been left out in the cold.

. . . The Cabinet met again to-day. They were, I believe, unanimous in their decision about Chitral which is to be evacuated, notwithstanding that the Government of India take the opposite line. If left to themselves, that Government would always be for a forward policy; at least I hardly remember an instance when it was not so. It was also settled that the Uganda railway is to be taken in hand. So the "Little Englanders", principally consisting of Harcourt & J. Morley, have been over-ruled, & Rosebery has had his way. Harcourt professes to be willing now to sacrifice anything and everything, if only he is allowed to proceed with his great Local Option Bill! He has however had his way about procedure in the House of Commons. There is to be no "gag". The Government are to go on pegging away at the Welsh Church Bill till it is through Committee. The prospects of all legislation seem very hopeless, more especially as while annexing the whole time of the House, the Government proposes to devote one evening a week (Fridays) to Supply. But H.'s Parliamentary judgement is of the best, and I expect he is right in not trying to force down the throats of the Government a Bill, like the Welsh Church Bill, in which only Welsh members are keenly interested.

Saturday 15 June . . . The Government are not going any more strongly since the House reassembled. The Committee of Supply have succeeded in reducing the Vote for the House of Lords buildings by £500—by way of marking their sense of the continued occupation of many rooms in the Houses of Parliament by Black Rod who has been unable to attend to his duties for 2 years—an arrangement which is becoming rather a scandal. The Government have also had a shave over the vote for erecting a statue to Cromwell. It looks as if they may any day find themselves in a minority. If it were not for the shrieks and abuse of the *Times*; I believe the most dignified course to pursue would be resignation, before defeat is actually inflicted.

Sunday 16 June (Ch: Ch: Oxford) . . . The place has looked glorious to-day. This morning I attended the University sermon which was preached by Scott Holland, and which in spite of his pulpit fame did not, I confess, greatly impress me; there was too much verbiage and too little practical common sense.

. . . The Invernesshire election, declared yesterday, is another blow to the Government. The Unionist candidate—J. Baillie (who married Miss Bass)—has been returned and returned by a large majority, which means the loss of another seat, the still futher reduction of the Government majority in the House of Commons, and indeed the worst slap in the face which the Government have yet had.[165]

Tuesday 18 June   The Cromwell statue business came up again last night in the House of Commons on report. It was decided in the morning that the Government should stand by their guns; but finding or fearing that persisting with the Vote would end in defeat, the Government at the last moment, without any communication with Rosebery, faced right about, and "chucked" the business. Rosebery whom I saw in the Park early this morning was not a little provoked; & was almost minded to take the line of saying that if Cabinet decisions were reversed at the last moment without his cognisance he would not be responsible any longer for the head-ship of affairs. He might almost be justified in doing this, though the matter of immediate issue is perhaps too small: but what I believed—& I told him so—he was much more justified in doing was to bring the present unsatisfactory state of things to an end, not by his own resignation but by the resignation of the Government. He said however he must go on till he was beaten. He had stated so, publicly & emphatically; and turning tail without being actually defeated would, I admit, look as if he were showing the white feather.

Wednesday 19 June   Another bomb—a good deal exaggerated—has been exploded by the *Times* at the door of the Government. It has been discovered that Mr G.'s permanent pair with old M. Villiers[166] has been taken off. "So even Mr G.", it is said, has at last thrown over the Government. They have "lost his moral support. This ought to be the finishing nail in their coffin". The facts are these: There are one or two details in the Welsh Church Bill to which Mr G. has always taken exception; and some time ago he gave the Whips to understand that he intended to hold himself free on these points. As it was not possible to pair him for this provision in the Bill and unpair him for that, the Whips ought to have taken off the pair some time ago. Instead of which, they kept the pair on till they reached the moot provisions; and now that the pair is broken, the Opposition naturally assume that Mr G. has suddenly broken with the Government. This is not the case; but any breach with Mr G. on details, however unimportant, is a serious matter . . .

Friday 21 June . . . The *"Times"* continues to clamour for the ousting of the Government. Until they are beaten, they are from a constitutional view strictly correct in remaining on. They are powerless to pass any measures; but, though I should welcome an end of the administration from which R. can get no credit, the *Times* & Co. always forget that the first duty of a Government is to govern, and that the legislation of which you have more than enough is a secondary consideration. Whatever people may say, the present Ministers have on the whole been decidedly successful as adminis-trators: that is to say, they have not only made no or few blunders, but they have given evidence of considerable administrative capacity. The latest administrative score has reference to the old Duke of Cambridge. He has consented at last to resign as from the 1st October, and the news was, I believe, to be announced in the House this evening. The Queen is I understand quite satisfied. All she cared for was that the title of Comman-der in Chief should be retained. The appointment is to be a 5 years' appointment: and she believes that the Duke of Connaught may get his turn of holding it in due course, which is what she has primarily in view . . .

Saturday 22 June (Panshanger, Hertford) I little thought last night that there was a crisis going on at the House of Commons. The Government were beaten; and my first knowledge of it was when I opened the *Times* this morning. As was to be expected, it was the unexpected which happened. The House were in Committee of Supply considering the War Office Vote. C. Bannerman had made his announcement about the Duke of Cambridge, which apparently gave much satisfaction; and then St John Brodrick,[167] in order to draw attention to the alleged inadequacy of the supply of cartridges, moved to reduce the salary of the War Secretary by £100. The motion for the reduction was carried by a majority of 7; and there was naturally great jubilation over the defeat of the Government in Tory quarters. C. Bannerman at once moved to report progress. There cannot be a more distinct way of carrying a vote of want of confidence in a Government than a motion to reduce a Minister's salary; and by a strange irony of fate, it was the reduction of the salary of by far the most popular Minister in the House of Commons, and of the man who has not only been long considered to be the best Secretary of State the War Office ever had, but one who had just announced his intention of carrying through the most important reform in military administration that has been taken in hand during this generation. There has of course been great excitement to-day; but when I came away from Town this afternoon, no definite decision had been taken though the Cabinet had sat all the morning and were then holding an adjourned meeting. From the moment I became aware of the ministerial defeat, I have never doubted what the best tactics were. I am sure what the Government ought to do is to resign instantly. It was of course a snap division; & I have no doubt last night's vote would be reversed by a considerable majority if the House had the chance of doing so. But what was wanted was a chance of getting out: and here is the opportunity and under the circumstance a good one. I met Rosebery driving into the Park this morning: and I found that he was of the same opinion as I was—that resignation was to be preferred to Dissolution. I have always heard Mr G. say that the Government should not dissolve if it could resign—that Dissolution should always be kept in reserve as a last card to play. He did not himself act on this dictum in 1886. He held at the time that the circumstances were exceptional—the Government had been defeated on a question which had not been put before the constituencies; but he subsequently admitted to me that his tactics had been wrong. The Cabinet met this morning at 11; but had come to no definite decision by luncheon time, when they adjourned the meeting till 4 o'clock. I met J. Morley, Acland & Tweedmouth in Downing Street about 3.30. They asked me what my view was; and I told them it was unhesitatingly for resignation. I found from them that up till then there were only 4 ministers for that course—Rosebery himself, Harcourt, Lord Ripon, & Tweedmouth; two were for remaining on; the others for Dissolution. When I came away the Cabinet were still sitting; but there seemed to be a prevalent opinion that resignation would carry the day.

Sunday 23 June (Panshanger) . . . We know nothing more to-day. I forgot to ask that a telegram or note should be sent to me announcing the Cabinet decision. Among the tactical advantages which resignation has, the difficulty connected with the promised House of Lords Resolution will be got over. It is tolerably certain that the Cabinet would disagree over its terms. Moreover the "go-by" will be given to the vexed question of proceeding with the Local Veto Bill

It has been a lovely day; but this place like all others, is terribly burnt up by the prolonged drought.

Monday 24 June   It was decided at the adjourned meeting of the Cabinet on Saturday afternoon that it should be resignation: and Rosebery, who was going in any case down to Windsor, tendered the resignation of himself & his colleagues immediately afterwards. The Queen accepted their resignation; and Lord Salisbury has been sent for. It is not certain whether he will accept the task for forming a Government in the present Parliament. I expect he will: but if he declines then Rosebery & his colleagues will be in a better position; for they will be able to resume office and dissolve at the time most convenient for them, disregarding small majorities or even adverse votes.

Harcourt announced the resignation of the Government in the House of Commons this afternoon, and in doing so said some dignified "parting words" about his relinquishing the lead of the House, which seem to have erroneously been construed to indicate his intention to retire from public life. Rosebery likewise announced in the House of Lords the resignation of his ministry: they could not separate themselves from their colleague—Campbell-Bannerman—who had been censored by the House of Commons.

Later. There are still rumours of rumours; but it is understood that though Lord Salisbury has not actually kissed hands he has determined to take upon himself to form a Government. The difficulty—but I think it is exaggerated—is the question of supply and ways & means. The Army Votes—or authority to spend on military services—will run out about the 10: prox:; and so also will money or "ways & means" available to meet all supply expenditure. So a further Army Vote must be immediately taken, and a further Ways & Means Bill immediately passed. Neither of these steps can be taken without a responsible ministry: and if Lord Salisbury decided to dissolve at once, there must first be taken Votes on Account for Army, Navy, & Civil Services, and there must first be passed an Appropriation Bill, not merely a Ways & Means Bill.

Tuesday 25 June Lord Salisbury is forming a Government. The only appointments yet known are those of Arthur Balfour as First Lord of the Treasury and of Chamberlain as Colonial Secretary. The Duke of Devonshire presumably takes the Lord Presidency of the Council, and Lord Salisbury himself resumes the Foreign Secretaryship with the Premiership. If the new Ministers in the House of Commons are not opposed on the re-election—and they are not likely to be—they ought to be back in the House in time to get through the necessary financial procedures by the required dates. They seem to apprehend obstruction & delay in Supply; but these apprehensions are groundless, at any rate so far as responsible members of the Opposition (that will be) are concerned.

I have been dining this evening with Arnold Morley. Mr & Mrs G. were there . . . Mr G. was very reticent about the crisis; but even from the little he said I could infer that the course which he would have taken would have been to disregard the snap adverse Vote of last Friday and to go on; but he admitted that the difficulties which had of late surrounded the Government were very great and that he might be unable to appreciate them to the full. A little episode to-day anent the crisis was naturally discussed at dinner. Lord Salisbury sent Schomberg McDonnell[168] (his Private Secretary) this

morning to Campbell Bannerman asking whether it would be convenient
for him to hand over his seals to his successor in the course of the day. C.B.
replied that the course proposed seemed to him an irregular proceeding,
but that if Lord Salisbury & Rosebery had agreed to the proposal, he
would fall in with it. S. McDonnell admitted that Rosebery had not been
communicated with but pointed out that direct transference of seals had
frequently occurred. C.B. said he was not aware of that, and at any rate
must first consult Rosebery. He went off at once to Rosebery, who of
course agreed that it would be improper for C.B. to surrender his seal to
anyone except the Sovereign. Such a blunder of tactics is hardly
conceivable. Indeed Mr G. said it was only because it was a *fact*, that such a
request as had been made to C.B. could be credited. It always appeared to
him (Mr G.) that Lord Salisbury was imbued with less constitutional
principles than any other public man. This disregard of constitutional ways
by the Conservative party was, he believed, due to Disraeli; "and to Joe"
added Lord Spencer. There was another point on which Mr G. expressed
himself as unconstitutional; and that was, an attempt made in the House of
Commons this afternoon to move the writs of Arthur Balfour & Chamberlain by themselves. He held that the writs of incoming ministers should
according to precedent be moved *en bloc* and not in driblets.

Wednesday 26 June   The additional appointments known to-day are those
of Goschen as First Lord of the Admiralty and of Hicks Beach as Chan: of
the Exchequer. I am sorry not to have Goschen back again at the Treasury;
though, until lately, I had long been under the belief that Goschen would
prefer another place. I know that he had the refusal of the Chancellorship;
and I expect the reason why he declined the office was that he feels that a
reduction of the Sinking Fund is inevitable, that his reputation as a
financier had already suffered from the reduction which he made in 1887,
and that he could not be responsible for proposing a further reduction
himself.

    Lord Salisbury sent for me this afternoon, in order to have the financial
situation explained to him. I took with me a programme according to which
I believe everything can be got through in time, provided that by the
middle of next week he can get a sufficient number of Ministers on the
Treasury Bench. He said however he was bound to assme the *role* of
pessimist. He had no reason to suppose that the outgoing Ministers would
put him in a difficulty; but they would be unable to control their
irresponsible followers, and there might well be serious obstruction. He
wanted therefore to know what measures there were to which he might
resort in the event of there being obstructive tactics and in view of his being
powerless to stop them. Could Army & Navy payments be postponed? I
doubted if postponement of any appreciable amount was feasible.

Moreover I pointed out that in my humble opinion it was neither possible nor expedient to assume obstruction beforehand. Could he, then, borrow from the Bank or get money from elsewhere to carry on? I said it was not a question of our running short of money; it was that if we exhausted the ways & means placed by Parliament at the dispoosal of the Executive Government, the Comptroller & Auditor General who held the key of the Exchequer would decline to unlock it. If the worst came to the worst, Lord S. went on to say he must stop services & salaries & everything. This, I submitted was so serious a step to take that I hardly liked to contemplate it; but I promised to ascertain whether there were any contracts at the War Office or Admiralty which could be postponed. Nothing could have been more courteous to me than he was or more charming in manner; but I could not help thinking what a shock it would have been to Mr G. if he had heard such revolutionary ideas propounded—and they were propounded seriously. Lord Salisbury commented on the complications of the financial procedure, which were such that they were able to stand in the way of an appeal to the country. On leaving Arlington Street, I went to the War Office & Admiralty, & I found that what could be done in the way of postponing payments to contractors for a few days was infinitesimal. I therefore wrote to Lord Salisbury and at the same time suggested that, if his pessimistic fears were realised and the new Government were driven into a corner, they might take an *ad interim* step by setting to work on Army Estimates and running an ordinary "Ways & Means Bill", into which they might insert Votes already passed but as yet uncovered by a Money Bill. They would then have several days on which to debate Army Estimates before Army supplies ran out, and in the meanwhile they would be taking power to obtain further ways & means.

I have been dining with the Harcourts this evening. He is quite ready to turn out off Downing Street; but he finally admits that he has thoroughly enjoyed his time as Chancellor. He has liked the work and those he has worked with. I confess I shall be very sorry to lose him. I am afraid that I cannot forgive him for his behaviour towards Rosebery which has been shabby & even ungentlemanlike; and his *tantrums* have at times been not a little trying; but no Minister has ever treated me with greater consideration and kindness than he has. It may at times be a disagreeable exterior; but is a very kindly interior *au fond*.

Thursday 27 June . . . Harcourt showed me to-day a letter which he had received from Hicks Beach and which had pleased him greatly. Beach is, I imagine, not a man to gush; but in expressing a hope that Harcourt did not mean by what he said that he was going to retire from the Front Bench, Beach wrote that he could honestly say he considered Harcourt had been the best Leader of the House in his (Beach's) experience.

Rosebery took Lord Salisbury to task this afternoon for the extraordinary message sent to C. Bannerman on Tuesday; and Ld. S. in the end apologised for any apparent rudeness. It was not really so much rudeness as such as a want of constitutional etiquette. Of course there have been occasions on which Ministers have not surrendered their seals in person to the Sovereign. There was the case of Lord North & Fox in 1780 [sic], and of Randolph Churchill in 1887. In those cases the seals were sent (by Deputy or messenger) to the Sovereign; but they are instances in which the Minister has left office in more or less disgrace. The object of trying to get a new Minister of war appointed at once in advance of other Ministers was that there should be someone installed at the War Office to direct the postponement or even stoppage of military expenditure.

. . . I have just returned from a midnight drive with Rosebery . . . I had been anxious to implore him to take no decisive step about the future. I was afraid he might have committed himself this morning when he & his colleagues had an informal meeting in Downing Street to talk about the future. He admitted that he had intended making an announcement to the effect that he could no longer pull with Harcourt and was quite willing to stand aside. But he found everybody so amicable and so friendly to him that his heart failed him and he had to allow matters to slide for the present. I told him tonight I thought he was quite justified in making any stipulations he liked, and in continuing leader on his own terms only, but it would never do for him to throw up the sponge now. He can't extricate himself from public life; and it would expose him to the charge of cutting & running as soon as he had lost the glamour of the highest office. He was in quite a reasonable frame of mind—delighted to have escaped from the Premiership and to have effected as good an escape as he has. He told me that on receiving his submission of the name of Aberdeen for the vacant Thistle—(he could not just now submit Tweedmouth)—the Queen had expressed the wish that it should be bestowed on him. He does not care much about having a second riband; but he cannot well refuse the compliment intended to be paid to him by the Queen on Her own motion; the Thistle used to be held by his family; and it is important that after taking a strong line about the House of Lords he should have some visible token of the Queen's confidence. He will be the only subject with both Orders (Garter & Thistle), with the exception of the Duke of Argyll . . .

. . . I had dined at Brook House; and there were Mr & Mrs G. again . . . Mr G. was in very good spirits and talked much at dinner. He gave rather an amusing account of what really took place at a Cabinet meeting just before the Crimean War, at which according to Kinglake Ministers slept peacefully despite the gravity of affairs. Mr G. said there was foundation for the sleep: but none for the importance of the meeting. The fact was that everything connected with policy had been settled beforehand; but at the meeting which was held at Pembroke Lodge, Richmond where Lord Russell was living, the Duke of Newcastle insisted on reading out interminable & worthless despatches. He always, Mr G. said, was a man who bored his colleagues by his love for details.

Saturday 28 June   I had a little talk with Hicks Beach yesterday. I have very little doubt I shall get on with him & like him. He is a gentleman, a very straight man, & has no *fads* or heterodox notions. I told him that while I thought he would find the Chancellorship of the Exchequer by itself an easy administrative post, it would prove to be probably the most difficult; finance being the great difficulty ahead. What of course he will wish to take in hand first is something in the way of relieving the burdens of agriculturists. The mere handing over of the Land Tax won't go nearly far enough.

. . . The Cabinet is now supposed to be complete:

Lord Salisbury	Prime Minister & Foreign Secretary
Duke of Devonshire	Lord President (with nominal powers of Commander-in-Chief & Lord High Admiral)
Lord Halsbury	Lord Chancellor
Lord Cross	Lord Privy Seal
Mr. Chamberlain	Sec: of State for the Colonies
Lord Lansdowne	Sec: of State for War
Lord George Hamilton	Sec: of State for India
Sir M.W. Ridley	Sec: of State for the Home Office
Sir M.H. Beach	Chancellor of the Exchequer
Sir Henry James	Chancellor of the Duchy of Lancaster (with Peerage)
Mr. Balfour	First Lord of the Treasury & Leader of the House of Commons
Mr. Goschen	First Lord of the Admiralty
Lord Cadogan	Lord Lieutenant of Ireland
Mr. Ritchie[169]	President of the Board of Trade
Mr. Chaplin	President of the Local Government Board
Lord Ashbourne	Lord Chancellor of Ireland
Lord Balfour (of Burleigh)	Secretary for Scotland

Seventeen in all; but there are rumours that Akers Douglas[170] may be added to the Cabinet, soon if not immediately. Londonderry[171] was offered the Privy Seal, and declined it on the ground that he wanted administrative work. Nothing apparently could have been more foolish. People who go in for political life must learn that they can't pick & choose places for themselves; they must take what they are given. Presumably in consequence of his refusal, Cross has been resuscitated. Lord Salisbury tried by means of Viscountcies & pensions to put Lord Cross on the shelf 10 years ago: but he was not to be got rid off then, partly owing to the favour in which he is with his Sovereign, and he is not to be got rid of even now. I admire his tenacity.

It is a strong Cabinet no doubt; but I do not know that man for man it is really stronger than the late Cabinet. If one makes a classification, the comparison does not seem to me to be to the disadvantage of the latter.

Lord Salisbury's present Cabinet	*Lord Rosebery's late Cabinet*
First Class	
Lord Salisbury	Lord Rosebery
Mr. Balfour	Sir W. Harcourt
Duke of Devonshire	Lord Kimberley
Mr. Chamberlain	Mr. Asquith
Mr. Goschen	Lord Herschell
Second Class	
Sir M. Hicks Beach	Mr. J. Morley
Lord Lansdowne	Mr. C. Bannerman
Lord Halsbury	Mr. Fowler
Sir Henry James	Lord Spencer
Lord Balfour	Mr. Acland
Sir M. Ridley	Lord Ripon
Lord Ashbourne	Mr. Bryce
Third Class	
Mr. Ritchie	Mr. S. Lefevre
Mr. Chaplin	Mr. A. Morley
Lord Cadogan	Sir G. Trevelyan
Lord George Hamilton	Lord Tweedmouth
Lord Cross	

The fact is the late Government was a very successful administrative body. I never knew a better. It was (especially) "a Government by Departments"; but a very strong Government viewed as such. There were some weak members of it—notably G. Trevelyan and S. Lefevre; but there were never more efficient or more popular ministers at the War Office & Admiralty than C. Bannerman and Lord Spencer; Fowler was excellent at the India Office, at any rate so far as being India's spokesman in Parliament was concerned; Asquith was a first rate Home Secretary; Lord Herschell an excellent Chancellor and man in council. Arnold Morley was a good Postmaster General; Acland did well at the Education Office; & John Morley administered affairs in Ireland with success, disappointing though he was in many other ways. Harcourt has left his mark on Finance, and is admitted to have led the House of Commons with conspicious dexterity and ability. As to Rosebery, perhaps I may be not impartial. In many quarters he is said to have been a failure and disappointment as Prime Minister and to have shown less political nerve than was expected. But I am convinced that, if the difficulties with which he has had to contend—namely, the taking over of a ready made Cabinet & a ready made policy, himself a Peer, and under strained relations with the Leader of the House of Commons—are properly appreciated, the wonder is that he managed to carry on with the success he did for over 15 months. Whatever may be said against him, it is as clear now as it was when Mr G. retired that he is the only possible Leader of the Liberal party, and that surely is saying a great deal. To have had his own way in foreign policy is alone a sufficient answer to the assertions of his being infirm of purpose; and time will I believe show that in domestic policy he has been not only right to give a preference to the House of Lords question over the variegated "Newcastle programme", but also that he is more far-seeing than most of his colleagues, and thus has real statesman-like qualities of the highest order.

Sunday 30 June   I confess I am not best pleased with the principal honours which Rosebery has conferred on leaving office. Had he had a perfectly free hand, he would I know have consistently refused to make any Peerage recommendations. He found however that there were two men—of whom the less said the better—S. Stern & Williamson[172]—to whom Mr G. had at the insistence of A. Morley committed himself, and having reluctantly to redeem these pledges, he thought he might as well extend the list somewhat. To these extensions no reasonable objection can be taken— namely Earldoms to Carrington[173] & Houghton and new Baronies to H. Loch (whose public services amply justify a Peerage) and Herbert Gardner (whose case is peculiar).[174] Among the Baronetcies, there is one which is specially odious and disagreeable; and that is the one conferred on Naylor-Leyland, whose only qualification for an hereditary honour consists in his having deserted the Tory party. I believe that, here again, the responsibility mainly rests on Arnold Morley; but I think Rosebery might fairly have declined to have had anything to do with so discreditable a bargain. It is bad enough—both sides are equally bad in this respect—to make honours a matter of *sale*; but it is worse still when it is a question of *barter* as well as sale. Among other honours, none is better than Alfred Milner's K.C.B. on which Harcourt insisted.

   In connection with the change of Ministries, Harcourt raised the question of Letters Patent for Secretaries of State; they held formerly by Letters Patent as well as by seals; how came Letter Patent to be dispensed with? The matter has been looked up: & it has been found that Letters Patent fell into disuse about 30 years ago. The Warrant directing the issue of Letters Patent for the appointment of Mr Spencer Walpole as Home Secretary was drafted, but never signed. When at the Home Office himself, he declined (in 1867) to sign the letters to the Law Officers for the preparation of Letters Patent in the case of other Secretaries of State, as in his opinion that form of appointment was unnecessary; and it is on record that Mr Gathorne Hardy when he succeeded Mr Walpole concurred in his predecessor's action, from which date no Patent appointing a Secretary of State has been issued. This is curious & not generally known.

Monday 1 July   The only further appointments definitely announced are those of George Curzon to the Under Secretaryship of the Foreign Office and Hanbury to the Financial Secretaryship of the Treasury. Both are to be sworn of the Privy Council. George Curzon is quite entitled to the honour, for his abilities entitle him to Cabinet rank; but the Privy Councillorship for Hanbury, who is quite new to office, seems unnecessary. Hanbury may find it rather awkward to defend what he has always been attacking—the Civil Estimates.

I dined with Haldane tonight. He has always been staunch to Rosebery. He believes that R. may be well content for the moment to regard with satisfaction three very considerable achievements, which he has attained by his own individual influence in the late Cabinet; that is to say that it is to R. & R. alone that (1) the Liberal party has acquiesced in an Imperial policy abroad, (2) a strong Navy become an accepted item in the Radical programme, and (3) the House of Lords question has been placed in the forefront.

Tuesday 2 July   No appointments announced—only rumours. The House met *pro forma* yesterday and to-day the Committee of Supply passed all three Votes on account (Army, Navy, and Civil Services) with very little discussion. I never believed that there would be any Parliamentary difficulties—still less in Lord Salisbury's pessimistic views.

I went and had luncheon with the Harcourts to-day, who do not clear out of Downing Street till the end of the week . . . I verily believe that, had Loulou taken a somewhat less offensive line towards Rosebery, matters might have been not a little different in the relations of the two Leaders. Loulou has disappointed me greatly in this respect: one had always looked to him to tone down his father; instead of which in the matter of Rosebery he has continuously done his best to keep the *raw* open.

Wednesday 3 July   The following further appointments are announced:

Akers Douglas	First Commissioner of Works
Walter Long	Minister for Agriculture

both with seats in the Cabinet, which now consisting of 19 members is the largest on record.

Gerald Balfour	Chief Secretary for Ireland

(which is quite a surprise and a commendable experiment),

Duke of Norfolk	Postmaster General
Sir J. Gorst	Vice President of the Council
W. Walrond	Whip, as Patronage Secretary of Treasury
Austen Chamberlain	Civil Lord of the Admiralty
Jesse Collings	Under Secretary at the Home Office
St. John Brodrick	Under Secretary at the War Office
Selborne	Under Secretary at the Colonial Office
T.W. Russell	Secretary to the Local Gov. Board
Powell Williams	Financial Secretary at War Office

Chamberlain has certainly opened his mouth pretty widely and (what is more) has had it handsomely filled. Bar Sir Henry James, Chamberlain has secured places for six of his own immediate followers—his faithful henchman "Jesse", Macartney, Austen Chamberlain, Selborne, T.W. Russell & P. Williams (of whom I know nothing).[175]

It looks as if Chamberlain will try and air some of his own fads as well as find places for his own lot. I gather from a conversation, which he has had with R. Meade,[176] that he (Chamberlain) is seriously contemplating the possibility and expediency of giving colonial produce a preference over foreign produce.

Everything is going quite smoothly in the House of Commons—as I expected and contrary to the pessimistic prognostications of Lord Salisbury. All Supply has been reported to-day and the Appropriation Bill introduced. Parliament ought now to be prorogued on Saturday and dissolved on Monday next.

Thursday 4 July I went & paid Harcourt a little visit this morning. He and Rosebery are taking their own & separate lines. Rosebery (who spoke to the "Eighty Club" on Tuesday) is putting the House of Lords in the van of electoral questions and preaching on the sensible text of "one thing at a time". Harcourt on the other hand considers Rosebery's tactics absurd. If the Liberals get a majority, they would, under R.'s programme, have to deal first with the House of Lords, which (Harcourt says) would involve a further dissolution. He (Harcourt) intended to stick to the old programme & the whole of it: it would never do to disappoint Irishmen, Welshmen and "Local Optionists" all alike.

From a little talk I had this morning with the new Chancellor of the Exchequer, I gather that he has no intention of being responsible for reopening the Death Duties question; though of course he will be willing to consider any necessary administrative amendment of last year's Finance Act.

I met Redvers Buller this evening (dining with the Manners). He told me that this cry against War Office administration had been instigated in the *"Times"* by A. Walter himself and conducted mainly by Chesney.[177] He evidently considers that it was high time for the Duke of Cambridge to resign; but as to any extensive reorganisation of military administration, it was neither necessary nor possible.

Friday 5 July   Some more (minor) appointments were made known this morning, viz

Anstruther	
Hayes Fisher	Junior Lords of the Treasury
E. Stanley	
W. Walrond	Patronage Secretary
Onslow	Under Secretary at the India Office
Dudley	Parly. Secretary to Board of Trade

and two Household appointments—Sidney Herbert (I can't call him Pembroke) is to be Lord Steward, and Lord Lothian is to return to the office of Lord Camberlain. I wonder that Lord Salisbury should have made any appointments beyond those that were absolutely necessary. The more he makes, the greater must be the number disappointed and the more will be placed—in both cases electioneering will be dampened. I am very glad about Sidney H.; and also that Stanley should have *run* to a place.

We are getting very near the electoral fight. The present position of parties is as follows:-

Liberals	267	
Nationalists	72	348
Parnellites	9	
Conservatives	272	321
Liberal Unionists	49	
Liberal Majority	. . .	27

The loss of 14 seats, therefore, on the Liberal side will give the "Unionists" a bare majority. All kinds of shots are made about the result of the General Election. The Unionists are given majorities from 0 to 100. I don't believe it possible to forecast it with any certainty: but I put the Unionist majority myself at 37, which has as good a chance of being the right number as any other. Everybody takes it for granted there is to be a majority of some kind for the Unionists. There would certainly be something "very comic" in the situation, as Mr Goschen said to me on Wednesday at the Clarence House Garden party, if there were no such majority at all.

I went & bade farewell to Harcourt this morning. He is off to Derby. He said there were only two matters about which he felt very strongly; and these were (1) the maintenance of the gold standard, and (2) the keeping up of the Sinking Fund. He has told Beach this.

Sunday 7 July (Southill Park, Bracknell)   My Birthday & I am spending it at the Hayters' place.[178] He has gone off to Walsall to commence electioneering. They are evidently very sore, at not having got the Governorship of New South Wales. The offer was not made to them because his seat was risky, and the late Government felt that it was impossible to risk the loss of a seat. The defeat of the Government so immediately afterwards, when his not standing again would have mattered very little, has enhanced the mortification. I am sorry; for they have been very loyal to their party and done much for it.

Our little Sunday party consists of the Yarboroughs, Henry Oppenheims & Mrs Adair. I have been talking all the afternoon to Mrs Oppenheim. She is a good deal exercised at the alleged refusal of Lord Kimberley to give her second boy a nomination for the Diplomatic Service on the ground of his Jewish name & blood. I believe there is some Foreign Office prejudice about admitting into the service men of Jewish origin: but I don't believe for one moment that Lord Kimberley knowingly did a slight to the Oppenheims. If he did, it was an inconceivable blunder to make in the case of the Proprietor of or rather chief shareholder in the Daily News. H.O. & his wife have always adhered steadfastly to the Liberal party.

We had an electioneering "sweep" to-day; each of the party putting his forecast down. I stuck to my number of 37.

Rosebery had a great meeting in the Albert Hall on Friday evening; and he seems to have got through it very well. Mr Arthur Sassoon who was present told me yesterday that he was in splendid voice and only once hesitated at all when his notes got out of order. Asquith also spoke and seems to have acquitted himself wonderfully well. I am thankful to think R. is out of it. I understand he is in the best of spitis; & no wonder, for I doubt if any one ever quitted office with a greater sense of relief. The little matter of the Naylor-Leyland Baronetcy is doing him I am afraid considerable harm. I believe Arnold Morley is the principal culprit: but R. ought to have put his foot down and declined point blank to fulfil any pledge of so disgusting a kind given without his own authority. I am rather surprised that the Queen did not put her pen through the name in the list of submissions.

Monday 8 July   All Ministers being away, work slackens off. A General Election always brings easy times to the hard-worked official; and until the new Government are firmly seated & know for certain that they are to remain where they are, Ministers naturally eschew work. It gives one an opportunity of working off arrears, and of setting one's *shop* in order. I must among other things write a report on the Savings Bank position which is really a very serious one. It is not only, or so much, that it is difficult to invest Savings Banks money at a remunerative rate, but to find investment for it at all. I calculate that in the next year we shall have to lay out about one hundred millions: and it is tolerably obvious that Consols to that amount won't be able to be had at any price.

I went up for a while this afternoon to see Gentlemen & Players at Lords. Cricket—I mean high class cricket—draws bigger crowds every year. In spite of golf & other athletic rivals, cricket still holds the field in English pastimes.

Francis Knollys & I have been dining together this evening at the Marlborough. He told me one or two little interesting things connected with the political crisis. The Queen was not a little annoyed about the demand made on C. Bannerman to deliver up his seals; and requested an explanation of the circumstances. A memorandum was drawn up saying what was intended and what took place: and she noted upon it that it was "not satisfactory". When Lord Salisbury was sent for he put the Foreign Office at the disposal of the Duke of Devonshire. The Duchess, strange to say—for her judgement is generally so good—urged the Duke to accept the offer; but his wiser counsels prevailed, and he declined. The post would never have suited him. He has never given great attention to foreign affairs; and apart from his being an indifferent French scholar, the grind of the Foreign Office would not only have been distasteful to him, but would probably have broken him down. The appointment to which Londonderry aspired was that of Chief Secretary for Ireland with a seat in the Cabinet. It is hardly credible, for the post has I believe never been held by a Peer, and the last person for filling it would be a pronounced Orangeman & Irish landlord like Londonderry.

Wednesday 10 July . . . Webster has consented to become Attorney General again; and Clarke is supposed to be going to be Solicitor General; but he is still haggling over terms. The new Government appear to be willing to make some change again about the remuneration of the Law Officers: that is, instead of a salary to cover all business, it is to be a salary for contentious business, but they are not to be allowed to practice privately. There are necessarily a good many left out in the cold—notably Knutsford (who is to have a step in the Peerage) and Matthews (who is to be made a Peer); Courtney, who after being unacceptable for the

Speakership is passed over for ministerial office; (he is very unpopular and an awkward colleague); Heneage (who I understand is very wroth); C. Wortley (whose case is rather a hard one); Ashmead-Bartlett (who is a good riddance);[179] and Howard Vincent (who presumably has counted on high office, but at whose disappointment there is general rejoicing).

I went to Lord's again to-day to see the last day of Gentlemen & Players; and owing to the lively play of the last two Gentlemen wickets—Fry & E. Smith—it looked almost as if Gentlemen would pull the match out of the fire. As it was, they only lost by 30 runs.

I hear Chamberlain says that the Liberal-Radical party do not realise how crushing is the defeat in store for them. He counts on a majority of at least 75. It may be so; but I cannot at present see where it is to come from, unless some great surprises are pending.

Friday 12 July I went to see Lady Londonderry yesterday afternoon. She professes to be quite satisfied with his refusal of office. The only good arument however which she could adduce in favour of Londonerry's decision was the strong line which he had taken up about the Irish Land question and the difficulty he might have in being charged with the conduct of a new Land Bill in the House of Lords. It would look as though he were throwing over his friends; for as Lord Privy Seal he was to be in charge of Irish business in the Upper House . . .

Sunday 14 July The result of the first day's elections has been startling. The Unionists have not only gained 7 seats on balance yesterday, but they won both seats at Derby, thus ousting Harcourt & his highly respectable Colleague (Sir T. Roe)! There never was a greater upset. Three years ago Harcourt had a majority of nearly 2000 and now he is beaten by 1100. The man who headed the poll was a popular local man & he carried with him G. Drage who acted as Secretary to the Labour Commission, more cleverly than judiciously.[180] This successful start for the Unionists will have a considerable moral effect on the Election generally: and if the result of the first day is a fair criterion of what is to come, there must be a regular swing of the pendulum in store for us, and the Conservative majority may be a very big one—far bigger even than the most sanguine Unionists have expected . . .

Tuesday 16 July (Cowes) The new Chancellor of the Exchequer being away, I took the opportunity of coming down here yesterday for two days . . . The Elections yesterday again went very favourably for the Unionists. It looks as if the tide were going to flow with a vengeance for the Conservatives; and as if what was expected to be a Liberal defeat will be become a Liberal rout.

Wednesday 17 July   . . . Unionist victories continue to flow in. Arnold Morley, Lefevre, and Hibbert have met the same fate as Harcourt. He has been offered a seat in West Monmouthshire, Mr Warmington Q.C. having retired in his favour; and he has accepted the offer. I believe his defeat was mainly due to his Local Veto Bill. I always believed it was the most unpopular of measures; but he on the contrary always maintained that Temperance Reform was the only question that interested the electors! I am personally very sorry that he should have met with such a fall at Derby; but the perverseness he showed about his pet Bill, contrary to the judgement of the most level-headed of his colleagues, may be a not wholly undeserved lesson to him.

Thursday 18 July   The Elections are still going on steadily in favour of the Unionists. It is not only that they have won a great many seats; but they have increased greatly their majorities in places which they held before, while the Liberals have almost universally maintained their seats only with largly reduced majorities. John Morley is the latest victim, having been rejected for Newcastle;[181] and one wonders whether he will take this opportunity of returning to his first love—literature—by retiring from the political fray altogether. I believe it might be best for him to do so in his own interests; but I doubt if his vanity will permit him to give up Parliamentary life. George Leveson Gower[182] & Arthur Brand have also "gone under"; as has also poor Arthur Hayter, whose defeat at Walsall will be the culmination I fear of his mortification.

  The great Liberal reverse probably due to a considerable extent to the combined causes of three "B's"—Bible, Beer and Bad Trade, and also the absence of the great figure-head which has stood the party in such wonderful stead for nearly 30 years—Mr G. But one must recognise as the primary factor a very remarkable wave of conservatism which has come over the country, which is a satisfactory as well as significant sign of the times, indicating as it does an absence of discontent and a wish to be let alone. Home Rule does not seem to have been much thrust to the front; and unless the Irishmen can reunite, it may well be that the question is indefinitely postponed . . . London society is naturally more than jubilant at the result of the Elections.

Friday 19 July   It was fully expected that Asquith would also lose his seat; but so far from doing this, he has increased his majority.[183] Curiously enough the two men whose seats were considered to be most in peril were Asquith & Mr Speaker Gully; and both have been returned triumphantly.[184] So much for political prophecies. It will be curious to see what the Government will do about the Speakership. If they nominate M. Ridley, it will undoubtedly be the commencement of making the Chair a party place, which is much to be regretted. They would I am sure be well advised to forego the passing over of M. Gully. Flushed with victory, they can afford to be generous: but I doubt if the rank & file of the Conservative party will allow wiser counsels to prevail. They will want another place and demand the fullest possible share of the spoils . . .

Saturday 20 July . . . According to the latest returns, the Unionist majority has very nearly reached 100 already; and they are likely I expect to increase it to no less than 130. The Liberal Unionists are I think getting a little uneasy at the magnitude of the majority; for the Conservatives will be able to dispense with their support;—not that I expect they will, at any rate for some time to come. This Election has been devoid of all good squibs & caricatures, with one exception, & that is the "Westminster Gazette" which has produced daily a first rate set of cartoons drawn by Gould of Lord Salisbury & Chamberlain. He has swept the midland counties, & has been the most conspicuous figure in the fight. His speeches have been far the most telling . . .

Tuesday 23 July . . . The Unionist tide still flows on in the most marked manner. The Liberal party is simply annihilated for the time being. It has been a regular *débacle*. Conservatives will apparently have a majority independent of the Liberal Unionists. The question is what will the Government do with its majority? They have given plenty of promises— agriculture is to be set on its legs again by extensive relief of rates; trade is going to "leap & bound" again: voluntary schools are to be freely supported; the aged poor are all to receive pensions; artisans are to be enabled to become owners of their own cottages; & Ireland is to be made happy and contented by remedial legislation. I went to see Mrs Asquith this afternoon (she has at last fairly recovered); and she told me that Matthews was convinced the Government would not hold together long. He spoke in no bitter tone; because he never expected to have an offer of office, and had one been made he would not have accepted it.[185] But the Cabinet was too much of an *omnium gatherum* to last—there were bimetallists & monometallists; freetraders & Protectionists, socialists and antisocialists; spendthrifts & economists. They must, he said, "fall out".

The "Times" I am glad to say is appealing to the Government not to put aside M. Gully; but to be magnanimous and re-elect him as Speaker. But I think Arthur Balfour has committed himself too strongly . . .

Thursday 25 July . . . One of the many peculiarities of this Election has been that most of the seats which were vacated during the last Parliament and won by the Unionists have now gone back again to the Liberals.[186] So much for the basis of political meteorology. After what has happened, I think that even Mr G. must be shaken in attaching importance to bye-elections. Mr G. has been *drawn* occasionally during the Election and has emitted a few electioneering letters; but spoken without responsibility they have not told much; though what I feel sure has told much has been the want of his active lead in the contest. The electors have shown very good sense in one respect, and that is in declining to re-elect the principal bores and faddists who belonged to the last Parliament.

Friday 26 July   . . . Willie Grenfell[187] . . . becomes more & more a fanatic about bimetallism and more & more of a pessimist—pessimism seems to be part of the creed of bimetallists. He wanted to bet—and I was quite willing to do so—that unless there was a change of currency in the next 7 years the whole of our foreign trade would be gone. All our industries, he said, were on their last legs; and this not withstanding the startling figures relating to imports & exports and the Income Tax returns. I, on the contrary, maintain that, in the absence of any great catastrophe like a war, we shall 7 years hence be still more flourishing that we are now, *unless* (which is very improbable) there is any tampering with our currency system.

Sunday 28 July (Compton Place, Eastbourne)   . . . The Unionist majority is 152! I think the Duke [of Devonshire] seems almost appalled at its size. It will be very interesting to see what the Government will do with such a majority and whether they will hold together for any length of time . . .

Tuesday 30 July   . . . I am sure that among the contributory causes to the Unionist triumph is the *fashion* of Conservatism. The Upper Classes of recent years have become much more Conservative, and the fashion which they set filters down from one class to another.

Being convinced that the great rock ahead for the Government may be finance, I have prepared a paper to show that, as present taxes do not submit of being screwed up, they may find themselves confronted with great difficulties, unless the brake is applied to the present spending propensities of the State, which with men like Chamberlain & H. Chaplin seem boundless.

Wednesday 31 July   Rosebery came south a day or two ago. I caught him this evening at Brooks' where he was dining with his boys, previously to his joining his yacht in Scotland with them. He seemed in excellent spirits, and admitted that he had been sleeping better. He made no allusions to "cutting and running", as I feared might be the case. On the contrary, he said he should make a point of showing himself on the meeting of Parliament. He was certain that what had happened had all been for the best. The greater the reverse the better the lesson read to the Liberal party; which, if ever it is to become powerful again (and it will), must give up some of its fads. If the party stick to him, I believe he will stick to them. Harcourt's personal reverse will probably make him more tractable and less disposed to ignore the recognised Leader of the Party. Not Temperance reform on moderate lines, but Harcourt's particular Local Veto & Local Option, will have to be put on the shelf, along with several recent measures.

Thursday 1 August   The General Election is now practically over, the only undecided contest being that for Orkney and Shetland, which may be assumed to remain Liberal. So it is now possible to give a final return of the composition of the new Parliament. Thus:

Unionists	{	Conservatives	340	
		Liberal Unionists	71	411
Liberals & Radicals	{	Liberals	177	
		Irish Nationalists	70	
		Parnellites	12	259
Unionist majority				152

How does this majority compare with other majorities since the Great Reform Bill was passed? The comparison is shewn in the following table; the figures being taken from the Political Handbook of Acland & Ransome, and the Peelites and Irish Nationalists being reckoned as part of the Liberal party.

Year	No. of Conservatives	No. of Liberals	Conservative Majority	Liberal Majority
1833	172	486	–	314
1835	273	380	–	107
1837	310	348	–	38
1841	367	286	81	–
1847	331	325	–	6
1852	299	355	–	56
1857	287	366	–	79
1859	305	348	–	43
1866	294	361	–	67
1868	265	393	–	128
1874	350	302	48	
1880	243	409		166
1885	249	421	–	172
1886	394	276	118	
1892	315	355	–	40
1895	411	259	152	–

The majority of 152 is no doubt in excess of the proportion of votes given to the Conservatives; but owing to the remarkable number of uncontested constituencies it is impossible to arrive at what that proportion of Conservative representatives ought to be. Such calculations moreover are useless. We must take our constitutional system as it is with all its anomalies & all its inequalities. The fact remains that the Conservatives have gained the largest victory they have ever achieved since 1832; and I believe the Conservative result to be mainly due to the Liberal policy pursued during the last 60 years. All crying inequalities have been redressed, and the country is happy & contented. Hence people wish to be let alone. If the Liberals & Radicals play their game well and exercise patience, their time will come again & perhaps sooner than is generally expected.

Friday 2 August . . . The only news is that is practically announced that the Government are not going to put up M. Ridley or anybody else in opposition to the present Speaker, and they have thus avoided making a great blunder at the outset. But it is only fair to say that the decision is more of a necessity than a virtue; for, had they proposed to nominate anyone else but M. Gully, they would have found themselves confronted by a formidable cave headed by men like J. Lowther,[188] and nothing could be worse than to start with a *cave* . . .

Sunday 4 August (Brighton) . . . The weather has not been holiday-like to-day. One has been able to get out but little. In King's Gardens card-playing had to be resorted to in the afternoon. The fashionable game now is a game called "Bridge", which is a sort of development of whist and which seems likely to supersede that time-honoured game.

Friday 16 August . . . The new Parliament commenced business last night, opening with more than usual formality. Rosebery seems to have made a good speech. He always speaks best in Opposition, as indeed do most public men. There was a little less want of liveliness in the House of Commons owing to the misconduct & consequent suspension of Dr Tanner,[189] who seems to be generally "mad or drunk" (to use Mr G.'s epithets). The Queen's Speech was confined to foreign affairs. No hint of any domestic measures was given. This was only natural. The Session is necessarily to be confined to getting through Supply and the new Government must have time to develop their home policy, which will be no easy matter if such promises like better trade, improved agriculture, higher wages, & more employment, which were pretty freely given at the General Election, are to be fulfilled . . .

NOTES

1   Harcourt, Sir William (1827–1904): M.P. Oxford 1868–80, Derby 1880–95, West Monmouthshire 1895–1904; Solicitor-General 1873–4; Home Secretary 1880–5; Chancellor of the Exchequer 1886 and 1892–5; Leader of the House of Commons 1894–5.

2   Morley, John (1838–1923): M.P. Newcastle-upon-Tyne 1883–95, Montrose Burghs 1896–1908; Chief Secretary for Ireland 1886 and 1892–5; Indian Secretary 1905–10; Lord Privy Seal 1910–14; created Viscount Morley of Blackburn 1908.

3   Primrose, Archibald, from 1868 Earl of Rosebery (1847–1929): Under-Secretary of State for Home Affairs 1881–3; First Commissioner of Works and Lord Privy Seal 1885; Foreign Secretary 1886 and 1892–4; Prime Minister 1894–5.

4   Wodehouse, John, from 1847 Baron Wodehouse and from 1866 Earl of Kimberley (1826–1902): Under-Secretary of State for Foreign Affairs 1852–6; Lord Lieutenant of Ireland 1864–6; Lord Privy Seal 1868–70; Colonial Secretary 1870–4 and 1880–2; Indian Secretary 1882–5, 1886, 1892–4; President of the Council 1892–4; Foreign Secretary 1894–5.

5   Asquith, Herbert Henry (1852–1928): M.P. East Fife 1886–1918, Paisley 1920–4; Home Secretary 1892–5; Chancellor of the Exchequer 1905–08; Prime Minister 1908–16; created Earl of Oxford and Asquith 1925.

6   Acland, Arthur (1847–1926): M.P. Rotherham 1885–99; Vice-President of the Council—with responsibility therefore for the controversial subject of education—1892–5.

7   Campbell-Bannerman, Sir Henry (1836–1908): M.P. Stirling Burghs 1868–1908; Chief Secretary for Ireland 1884–5; War Secretary 1886 and 1892–5; Prime Minister 1905–08.

8   Harcourt, Lewis (1863–1922): private secretary to his father, Sir William, 1881–1904; M.P. Rossendale 1904–16; First Commissioner of Works 1905–10 and 1915–16; Colonial Secretary 1910–15; created Viscount Harcourt 1917.

9   Spencer, John, from 1857 Earl Spencer (1835–1910): M.P. South Northamptonshire 1857; Lord Lieutenant of Ireland 1868–74 and 1882–5; President of the Council 1880–2 and 1886; First Lord of the Admiralty 1892–5.

10   Ponsonby, Sir Henry (1825–1895): private secretary to the Queen 1870–95.

11   Munro–Ferguson, Ronald (1860–1934): M.P. Ross and Cromarty 1884–5, Leith Burghs 1886–1910; private secretary to Rosebery 1885

and 1894; Junior Lord of Treasury 1894–5; Governor-General of Australia 1914–20; Scottish Secretary 1922–4; created Viscount Novar 1920.

12 Marjoribanks, Edward, from 1894 Baron Tweedmouth (1849–1909): M.P. North Berwickshire 1880–94; Parliamentary Secretary to the Treasury 1892–4; Lord Privy Seal 1894–5; First Lord of the Admiralty 1905–08; President of the Council 1908.

13 Where his wife Hannah, who had died in 1890, was buried.

14 Labouchere, Henry (1831–1912): M.P. Middlesex 1867–8, North-ampton 1880–1906; a diplomat in his youth, and subsequently a prominent journalist; a bitter critic of Rosebery, especially after the latter had refused to appoint him British ambassador at Washington in 1892.

15 Fowler, Sir Henry (1830–1911): M.P. Wolverhampton 1880–5, Wol-verhampton East 1885–1908; Financial Secretary to the Treasury 1886; President of the Local Government Board 1892–4; Indian Secretary 1894–5; Chancellor of the Duchy of Lancaster 1905–10; created Viscount Wolverhampton 1908.

16 Bryce, James (1838–1922): Regius Professor of Civil Law at Oxford 1870–1893; M.P. Tower Hamlets 1880–5, Aberdeen South 1885–1907; Under–Secretary of State for Foreign Affairs 1886; Chancellor of the Duchy of Lancaster 1892–4; President of the Board of Trade 1894–5; Chief Secretary for Ireland 1905–07; British ambassador at Washington 1907–13; created Viscount Bryce 1914.

17 Canon William Rogers (1819–1896) was a Prebendary of St Paul's and a social reformer, who had helped to interest Rosebery in problems of London government. He had officiated at Rosebery's wedding.

18 Shaw Lefevre, George (1831–1928): M.P. Reading 1863–85, Brad-ford central 1886–95; Postmaster-General 1884–5; First Commiss-ioner of Works 1892–4; President of the Local Government Board 1894–5; created Baron Eversley 1906.

19 Ellis, Thomas (1859–1899): M.P. Merionnethshire 1886–99; Parlia-mentary Secretary to the Treasury 1894–5.

20 Murray, George (1849–1936): private secretary to the First Lord of the Treasury 1892–5; Permanent Administrative Secretary 1903–07, and afterwards Permanent Secretary to the Treasury; knighted 1899.

21 Welby, Reginald (1832–1915): Permanent Secretary to the Treasury 1885–94; created Baron Welby 1894.

22 Mowatt, Francis (1837–1919): Permanent Secretary to the Treasury 1894–1903; knighted 1893.

23 Gardner, Herbert (1846–1921): M.P. Saffron Walden 1885–95; Presi-dent of the Board of Agriculture 1892–5; created Baron Burghclere 1895.

24 Gladstone, Herbert (1854–1930): M.P. Leeds 1880–85, Leeds West 1885–1910; Under-Secretary of State for Home Affairs 1892–4; First Commissioner of Works 1894–5; Liberal chief whip 1899–1905; Home Secretary 1905–09; Governor-General of South Africa 1910–14; created Viscount Gladstone 1910.

25 The Heir Presumptive, later King George V.

26 Herschell, Farrer (1837–99): M.P. Durham 1874–85; Lord Chancellor 1886 and 1892–5; created Baron Herschell 1886.

27 Robinson, George, Marquess of Ripon (1827–1909): M.P. Huddersfield 1853–7, West Riding of Yorkshire 1857–9; War Secretary 1863–66; Indian Secretary 1866; President of the Council 1868–73; Viceroy of India 1880–4; First Lord of the Admiralty 1886; created Earl of Ripon and de Grey 1859, and Marquess of Ripon 1871.

28 Trevelyan, Sir George (1838–1928): M.P. Tynemouth 1865–8, Hawick district 1868–86, Glasgow Bridgeton 1887–97; Chief Secretary for Ireland 1882–4; Chancellor of the Duchy of Lancaster 1884–5; Scottish Secretary 1886 and 1892–5.

29 Mundella, Anthony (1825–97): M.P. Sheffield 1868–85, Sheffield Brightside 1885–97; President of the Board of Trade 1886 and 1892–4.

30 Morley, Arnold (1849–1916): M.P. Nottingham 1880–5, Nottingham East 1885–95; Liberal chief whip 1886–92; Postmaster-General 1892–5.

31 Russell, George (1853–1919): M.P. Aylesbury 1880–5, North Bedfordshire 1892–5; Under-Secretary of State for India 1892–4 and for Home Affairs 1894–5.

32 Reay, Baron (1839–1921): Governor of Bombay 1885–90; Under-Secretary of State for India 1894–5.

33 Grey, Sir Edward (1862–1933): M.P. Berwick-on-Tweed 1885–1916; Under-Secretary of State for Foreign Affairs 1892–5; Foreign Secretary 1905–16; created Viscount Grey of Fallodon 1916.

34 Primrose, Henry (1846–1923): Rosebery's cousin, Secretary to H.M. Office of Works, and after 1895 Chairman of the Board of Customs.

35 Brand, Arthur (1853–1917): M.P. Wisbech 1891–5 and 1900–06; Treasurer of H.M. Household 1894–5. The Earl of Chesterfield was promoted to be Captain of the Corps of Gentlemen-at-Arms.

36 Respectively M.P.s for Barnard Castle, Bedford, East Denbighshire, and Aberdeen North.

37 Foljambe, C., created Baron Hawkesbury 1893 and Earl of Liverpool 1905, was M.P. for North Nottinghamshire 1880–5 and for Mansfield 1885–92.

38 M.P. for Wansbeck 1885–1918.

39 Chairman of the Board of Inland Revenue 1892–7.

40 Dillon, John (1851–1927): M.P. Tipperary 1880–5, East Mayo 1885–1918, a leading Anti-Parnellite; Chairman of the Irish Parliamentary Party 1918.

41 Gladstone's letter, *The Times* 22 March 1894, referred to the "discrepancy of sentiment between the two Houses of Parliament", and, in a manner typical of his later years, noted that "another period had opened . . . of great ordeal for those classes which are now becoming largely conscious of power, and never heretofore subjected to its deteriorating influences".

42 Knollys, Francis (1837–1924): from 1870 private secretary to the Prince of Wales, later King Edward VII. Created Viscount Knollys 1911.

43 Jenkyns, Sir Henry (1838–99): Parliamentary Counsel to the Treasury 1886–99.

44 This figure does not include the annual sum of over £7 millions in grants-in-aid to local authorities, most of it added to the Treasury's commitments during Goschen's period as Chancellor of the Exchequer.

45 Seven bye-elections in all were held at this time, in late March and early April 1894. The results were as follows:
Berwickshire—Liberal 2,722: Unionist 2,157 (1892 Liberal majority 748).
Hawick Burghs—Liberal 3,203: Unionist 2,566 (1892 Liberal majority 365).
Leith Burghs—Liberal 5,823: Unionist 4,692 (1892 Liberal majority 1,643).
Mid–Lanarkshire—Liberal 3,965; Unionist 3,635; Labour 1,221 (1892 Liberal majority 1,122).
Montgomeryshire—Liberal 3,440: Unionist 3,215 (1892 Liberal majority 815).
Romford—Unionist 7,573: Liberal 6,890 (1892 Unionist majority 1,182).
Wisbech—Liberal 4,363: Unionist 4,227 (1892 Liberal majority 122).

46 The nine Parnellite M.P.s, led by John Redmond (1856–1918), M.P. for Waterford, and later Chairman of the reunited Irish Parliamentary Party.

47 Ferdinand, Baron Rothschild (1838–98) was Rosebery's wife's cousin, and the owner of Waddesdon in Buckinghamshire.

48 M.P. for Brecknockshire.

49 Russell, Sir Charles (1832–1900): M.P. Dundalk 1880–5, Hackney South 1885–94; Attorney–General 1886 and 1892–4; Lord Chief Justice of England 1894–1900.

50 Reid, Sir Robert (1846–1923): M.P. Hereford 1880–5, Dumfries 1886–1905; Solicitor-General 1894; Attorney-General 1894–5; Lord Chancellor 1905–12; created Baron Loreburn 1905 and Earl Loreburn 1911.

51 Lockwood, Sir Francis (1847–98): M.P. York 1885–98; Solicitor-General 1894–5; caricaturist and contributor to *Punch*.

52 Haldane, Richard (1856–1928): M.P. East Lothian 1885–1911; War Secretary 1905–12; Lord Chancellor 1912–15 and 1924; created Viscount Haldane of Cloan 1911.

53 Rigby, Sir John (1834–1903): M.P. Wisbech 1885–6, Forfar 1892–4; Solicitor–General 1892–4; Attorney-General 1894.

54 Morton, Alpheus Cleophas (1840–1923): M.P. Peterborough 1889–95, Sutherlandshire 1906–18; a voluble Radical backbencher.

55 The Duke of Edinburgh was the Queen's second son, who had succeeded as Duke of Saxe-Coburg and Gotha in 1893.

56 Chancellor of the Exchequer 1887–92.

57 Sir John Grant Lawson, M.P. for York 1892–1906.

58 Lawson, Sir Wilfrid (1829–1906): M.P. Carlisle 1865–8, Cockermouth 1868–85, 1886–1900 and 1906, Camborne 1903–06; Radical and temperance advocate.

59 The result of the Hackney South bye-election, held in early May 1894, was—Liberal 4,530; Unionist 4,338 (1892 Liberal majority 1,146).

60 M.P. for Cambridge University, formerly Financial Secretary to the Treasury 1891–2.

61 M.P. King's Lynn 1892–1906 (Conservative) and 1910 (Liberal); a vigilant guardian of the public purse, who won a case against the Bank of England in 1913 which forced the Government to pass an Act to make legal the provisional collection of taxes.

62 Gladstone's second surviving daughter.

63 M.P.s for Walthamstow and York respectively. (Hicks Beach, M.P. for Bristol West, had been Chancellor of the Exchequer 1885–6.)

64 A special conference of the National Liberal Federation passed resolutions in favour of severely curtailing the veto of the House of Lords.

65 The future King Edward VIII.

66 Hardie, M.P. for West Ham South, prophesied that the young prince would be sent on "a tour round the world, and probably rumours of a morganatic alliance will follow"—4 *Hansard* XXVI 463–4 (28 June 1894).

67 President Carnot had been assassinated by an anarchist on 24 June 1894.

68 Rosebery expressed the hope that "international complications may

by that tomb abate some of the strenuousness"—4 *Hansard* XXVI 205–07 (26 June 1894).
69   The bye-election result at Sheffield Attercliffe was—Liberal 4,486; Unionist 3,495; Labour 1,249.
70   Governor of the Imperial Ottoman Bank, later M.P. for Exeter and Lord d'Abernon.
71   As Under-Secretary for Ireland 1883–6, he had advised on the policy which culminated in the first Home Rule Bill.
72   The hapless prime minister of 1827–8, whose son, the Marquess of Ripon, had been born in Downing Street in 1827 and was now Rosebery's cabinet colleague.
73   Controller of Succession Duties 1886–99.
74   Horace Seymour and Henry Primrose.
75   M.P. for Cork City, a leading Anti-Parnellite and agrarian agitator.
76   M.P. for Marylebone West 1895–8.
77   Ambassador at Madrid, former Tory M.P.
78   Liberal Unionist M.P. for London University, later Lord Avebury.
79   Hibbert, Sir John (1824–1908): M.P. Oldham 1862–74, 1877–86, 1893–5; Financial Secretary to the Treasury 1884–5 and 1892–5.
80   The result of the double election at Leicester was—Liberal 9,464; Liberal 7,184; Unionist 6,967; Labour 4,402 (1892 Liberals returned unopposed).
81   The vascular disease which had begun to afflict him in 1889.
82   The Duke of Fife was son-in-law to the Prince of Wales through his marriage to Louise, later Princess Royal. Mar Lodge belonged to him.
83   M.P. for North Longford, chairman of the Anti-Parnellite party 1890–6.
84   At Dornoch and Tain.
85   Later British Ambassador at Paris.
86   Son of Lord Aberdeen, Prime Minister 1852–5; an old friend of the Gladstone family, he was created Baron Stanmore in 1893, but then earned Gladstone's displeasure by his lukewarmness over Home Rule.
87   Speech at Birmingham, *The Times* 12 October 1894.
88   W.E. Gladstone's second son, Rector of Hawarden 1872–1904.
89   The result of the bye-election was-Unionist 6,149; Liberal 6,043 (1892 Unionist majority 604).
90   Rosebery appointed Frederick York Powell.
91   The thirteenth Earl of Pembroke, son of the Peelite, Sidney Herbert, the Under-Secretary of State for War 1874–5.
92   Baron Ribblesdale was Master of the Buckhounds 1892–5. Like Asquith, he was married to one of the daughters of Sir Charles

Tennant, industrial magnate and former Liberal M.P.
93 Baron Rothschild of Tring, head of the family firm.
94 M.P. for South Longford, leading Anti-Parnellite, and former Leader of the Canadian Liberal Party.
95 The Marquess of Lansdowne had been Viceroy of India 1888–92 and was a major Irish landowner. In 1894 John Morley had set up a select committee to examine the Irish Land Acts of 1870, 1881, and 1887.
96 The fourth Marquess, a former diplomat.
97 The result of the Forfar bye-election was—Unionist 5,145; Liberal 4,859 (1892 Liberal majority 866). The thirteenth Earl of Dalhousie, referred to here, had died in 1887 at the age of forty.
98 M.P. for North Louth, later Governor-General of the Irish Free State.
99 Bruce, V., Earl of Elgin (1849–1917): Viceroy of India 1893–9; Colonial Secretary 1905–8.
100 The result of the Brigg bye-election was—Unionist 4,377; Liberal 4,300 (1892 Liberal majority 427).
101 Speech at Haddington, *The Times* 22 December 1894.
102 Under-Secretary of State for War 1895.
103 Respectively a director of the Suez Canal Company and a diplomat.
104 M.P. for Sleaford and spokesman for the agricultural interest.
105 Nationalist M.P. for Liverpool Scotland.
106 Formerly Lord Elcho, the Adullamite.
107 Kay-Shuttleworth, Sir Ughtred (1844–1939): M.P. Hastings 1869–80, Clitheroe 1885–1902; Chancellor of the Duchy of Lancaster 1886; Secretary to the Admiralty 1892–5.
108 Probably a reference to family problems, involving one of Hamilton's ne'er-do-well brothers.
109 The result of the Evesham bye-election was—Unionist 4,760; Liberal 3,585 (1892 Unionist majority 580).
110 M.P. for Dundee and Civil Lord of the Admiralty.
111 Crewe-Milnes, R., Baron Houghton and later Marquess of Crewe (1858–1945): Lord Lieutenant of Ireland 1892–5; President of the Council 1905–10 and 1915–16; Indian Secretary 1910–15; Colonial Secretary 1931.
112 Arthur Peel, Speaker of the House of Commons 1884–95.
113 M.P. for Basingstoke and spokesman for the agricultural interest.
114 Viscount Folkestone, M.P. for South Wiltshire, later Earl of Radnor.
115 Formerly Lord Lieutenant of Ireland 1886.
116 M.P. for Sheffield Central, founder and secretary of the United Empire Trade League.
117 M.P. for the Westhoughton division of Lancashire.
118 M.P. for Ealing, and Indian Secretary 1886–92 and 1895–1903.

119   Liberal M.P. for Woodbridge.
120   M.P. for Blackpool, Home Secretary 1895–1900.
121   M.P. for Bodmin, Chairman of Committees and Deputy Speaker 1886–92.
122   Governor of Cape Colony 1880–9 and 1895–7.
123   Governor of Cape Colony 1889–95.
124   Sir Henry James had been M.P. for Taunton 1869–85, and was M.P. for Bury from 1885 until 1895, when he was created Baron James of Hereford.
125   M.P. for Bishop Auckland 1885–1910.
126   The Speaker's son, a Clerk of the Treasury, subsequently Liberal M.P. for Spalding 1917–18.
127   President of the Neurological Society 1895–6, Physician Extraordinary to Queen Victoria 1898–1901.
128   M.P. for Carlisle 1886–1905.
129   Brett, R., from 1897 Viscount Esher (1852–1930): M.P. Penryn and Falmouth 1880–5; Secretary to H.M. Office of Works 1895–1902; permanent member of the Committee of Imperial Defence after 1905. The objections to Brett's promotion in 1895 had to do partly with his uncertain political allegiance; he had been Hartington's private secretary 1878–85.
130   Liberal M.P. for Edinburgh South 1892–5, and for Northampton 1906–10.
131   Sir John Horner was Commissioner of Woods and Forests 1895–1907; he was also a close friend of the Asquith family, and his daughter was later to marry Asquith's eldest son, Raymond.
132   H.N. Gladstone, W.E. Gladstone's third son, was Hamilton's neighbour at 4 Whitehall Court, S.W.
133   M.P. for Sowerby, Deputy-Speaker and Chairman of Ways and Means 1892–5.
134   M.P. for Clackmannan and Kinross; Lord Advocate 1881–5, 1886, 1892–5.
135   M.P. for Hanley, and Financial Secretary to the War Office 1892–5.
136   M.P. for Ilkeston, and Parliamentary Secretary to the Local Government Board 1892–5.
137   W.E. Gladstone's private secretary 1892–4.
138   M.P. for Dublin University.
139   Gully's father was a celebrated physician. His name had been frequently mentioned at the sensational inquiry, in 1876, into the death of a barrister named Charles Bravo, whom, it was suspected, had been poisoned by his wife, herself an intimate friend of Gully's. In consequence Gully's name was removed from all the medical societies and journals of the day.

140 M.P. for Glasgow Tradeston, he rejoined the Liberal party in 1909.
141 Birrell, A. (1850–1933): M.P. West Fife 1889–1900, Bristol North 1906–18; President of the Board of Education 1905–07; Chief Secretary for Ireland 1907–16.
142 M.P. for Dublin University.
143 M.P. for Plymouth, Solicitor-General 1886–92.
144 M.P. for Oxford University, later Father of the House of Commons 1898–9.
145 M.P. for Ripon.
146 This may have had something to do with the fact that he was rumoured to have been put in charge of agriculture by Gladstone because of his work in translating Virgil's *Georgics*.
147 Permanent Secretary to the Board of Trade.
148 This should really be styled the Local Option Bill.
149 The Mid-Norfolk result was—Unionist 4,112; Liberal 3,904 (1892 Liberal majority 470). The Oxford City result was—Unionist 3,745; Liberal 3,143 (1892 Unionist majority 120). Of the successful candidates, Gurdon had been M.P. for South Norfolk 1880–5 and for Mid-Norfolk 1885–92, and Valentia was to be M.P. for Oxford 1895–1917.
150 "Plundering and blundering" was a phrase used by Disraeli in October 1873, in an open letter to the Conservative candidate in the Bath bye-election, purporting to describe the policy of the Gladstone administration. The somewhat intemperate language was believed to have cost the Conservatives victory in the contest at the time.
151 Gladstone's wife's sister, *née* Mary Glynne, had married into the Lyttelton family. Alfred Lyttelton himself (1857–1913) was a former test cricketer who later became Colonial Secretary.
152 The result of the bye-election at Leeds East was—Liberal 3,999; Unionist 2,868 (1892 Liberal majority 827).
153 The Duke of Cambridge (1819–1904) was the Queen's cousin and had been Commander-in-Chief of the British Army since 1856.
154 The Queen's third son, in command at Aldershot 1893–8.
155 Liberal Unionist, M.P. for East Hampshire 1885–92 and for Edinburgh West 1892–5; later First Lord of the Admiralty.
156 In fact until 1963.
157 Conservative M.P. for Kingston-upon-Thames.
158 The eldest son of the Prime Minister of the same name, formerly M.P. for Tamworth, he had been in turn Peelite, Liberal Conservative, Conservative, and, from 1886, Liberal.
159 Formerly Liberal M.P. for Roscommon 1860–80.
160 Formerly Chancellor of the Exchequer 1882–5.

161 M.P. for North Kerry and one of the ablest Parliamentarians among the Anti-Parnellites.

162 The Financial Relations Commission had been set up in 1893 to examine whether Ireland was over-taxed, and in 1896 was to report that it was.

163 M.P. for Southport, and subsequently Viceroy of India 1899–1905.

164 It was during the 1895 season that W.G. Grace, then aged forty-five, accomplished the feat of scoring 1,000 runs in May. Only two other men have matched this achievement, though others have managed it before 1 June.

165 The result of the Invernesshire bye-election was—Unionist 3,164; Liberal 2,514 (1892 Liberal majority 329).

166 M.P. for Wolverhampton South. First elected in 1835, he was Father of the House of Commons 1890–8.

167 M.P. for Guildford, later himself War Secretary 1900–03.

168 Schomberg Kerr McDonnell, son of the Earl of Antrim, and Salisbury's Principal Private Secretary from 1888–92, 1895–9, 1900–02.

169 M.P. for Croydon, subsequently Home Secretary and Chancellor of the Exchequer.

170 M.P. for St Augustine's, Kent, and Patronage Secretary to the Treasury 1885–6 and 1886–92.

171 Londonderry subsequently became Postmaster-General 1900–02 and President of the Council 1903–05.

172 The two men were generally believed to have contributed heavily to Liberal party funds for their peerages.

173 Lord Chamberlain of the Household 1892–5, formerly M.P. for High Wycombe 1865–8.

174 As the illegitimate son of Baron Gardner he aspired to acquire a peerage in his own right.

175 Of the Liberal Unionist contingent, Austen Chamberlain was M.P. for East Worcestershire, Jesse Collings was M.P. for Birmingham Bordesley, and Powell Williams was M.P. for Birmingham South. T.W. Russell, a keen advocate of Irish land reform but an opponent of Home Rule, was M.P. for South Tyrone. Macartney, M.P. for South Antrim, became Parliamentary Secretary to the Admiralty.

176 Permanent Under-Secretary at the Colonial Office 1892–6.

177 Chesney, author of *The Battle of Dorking* (1871), had been M.P. for Oxford from 1892 until his death earlier in 1895. Lieutenant-General Sir Redvers Buller (1839–1908) had been Campbell-Bannerman's candidate to succeed the Duke of Cambridge. He was later to command at Aldershot and in South Africa.

178 Sir Arthur Hayter was M.P. for Bath 1873–85, and for Walsall

1893–5 and 1900–05. He had held minor office in Gladstone's second administration.

179   Heneage, M.P. for Great Grimsby, had been Chancellor of the Duchy of Lancaster in Gladstone's third administration before resigning in opposition to the Home Rule Bill; Stuart-Wortley, M.P. for Sheffield Hallam, had been Under-Secretary for Home Affairs 1886–92; Ashmead-Bartlett, M.P. for Sheffield Eccleshall, had been a Civil Lord of the Admiralty 1886–92.

180   The result at Derby, a two-member constituency, was:
Bemrose (Unionist)—7,907   Harcourt (Liberal)—6,785
Drage (Unionist)—7,076   Roe (Liberal)—4,475

181   The result at Newcastle, a two-member constituency, was:
Hamond (Unionist)—12,833   Morley (Liberal)—11,862
Cruddas (Unionist)—12,170   Craig (Liberal)—11,154
Hammill (Labour)—2,302

182   M.P. for Stoke-on-Trent, Controller of H.M. Household 1892–5.

183   The result at East Fife was—Liberal 4,332; Unionist 3,616 (1892 Liberal majority 294).

184   The result at Carlisle was—Liberal 3,167; Unionist 2,853 (1892 Liberal majority 143).

185   Matthews, Home Secretary 1886–92, was created Viscount Llandaff.

186   Of the nine seats which they had lost at bye-elections since 1892, the Liberals won back Huddersfield, Great Grimsby, Linlithgow, Forfar, Brigg, and Mid-Norfolk, and failed to win Hereford, Walworth, and Invernesshire.

187   Liberal M.P. for Hereford 1892–3; resigned in opposition to the second Home Rule Bill; later became Viscount Desborough.

188   M.P. for the Isle of Thanet; formerly Chief Secretary for Ireland 1878–80; he had advised Disraeli against making the Chair a matter of party patronage in 1874.

189   Nationalist M.P. for Mid-Cork; a notorious Parliamentary frondeur.

Index